Library of
Davidson College

The Collapse of Welfare Reform

The Collapse of Welfare Reform:
Political Institutions, Policy, and the Poor
in Canada and the United States

Christopher Leman

The MIT Press
Cambridge, Massachusetts, and London, England

© 1980 by
The Massachusetts Institute of Technology

All rights reserved. No part of this book may be reproduced in any form or by any means, electronic or mechanical, including photocopying, recording, or by any information storage and retrieval system, without permission in writing from the publisher.

This book was set in VIP Optima by Achorn Graphic Services, Inc. and printed and bound by The Alpine Press Inc. in the United States of America.

Written under the auspices of the Center for International Affairs, Harvard University, and the University Consortium for Research on North America, a partnership of Brandeis, Harvard, and Tufts Universities and The Fletcher School of Law and Diplomacy.

Library of Congress Cataloging in Publication Data

Leman, Christopher.
   The collapse of welfare reform.

   Bibliography: p.
   Includes index.
   1. Public welfare—United States.   II. Public welfare—Canada.   I. Title
HV91.L38   361.6'2'0973   79-24642
ISBN 0-262-12081-X

To My Parents

Contents

List of Tables, Charts, and Figure   x

Acknowledgments   xi

Introduction   xiii

1
The Welfare Crisis and Political Institutions   1
Common Problems   2
Common Concerns   6
Holding Socioeconomic Variables Constant   10
Rediscovering Politics   15

2
The Background of Poverty Policy in Canada and the United States   23
Beginnings   23
The Federal Role in the United States   26
The Federal Role in Canada   33
Definitions of Poverty   42
The Unevenness of Policy and the Powerlessness of the Poor   46

3
Welfare Reform and Guaranteed Income: The Emergence of Proposals   52
The Welfare Crisis and the Appeal of Broadening Welfare   52
Canada: Federalism and the Guaranteed Income   58
The United States: The "Welfare Mess" and the Negative Income Tax   70
Two Paths to the Political Agenda   76

4
Debates on the Nixon Family Assistance Plan and the Carter Program for Better Jobs and Income   78
Debacle: 1969–1970   78
Denouement: 1971–1972   82
Interlude: 1973–1976   90
Anticlimax: 1977–1978   94

5
The Canadian Social Security Review and Its Aftermath   113
Progress: 1973–1974   114
Crisis: 1975   122
Death and Transfiguration: 1976–1978   126

6
The Rules of the Game: Deductive and Inductive Styles of Policymaking   135
Inescapable Similarities   138
Intergovernmental Differences   141
Differences in Parties and the Legislative Process   145
Bureaucratic Differences   150
Differences in Nongovernmental Participation   158
Political Culture and Political Structure   162
Institutions and Policy Outcomes   165

7
The Terms of Debate: Impact of Policy Design   172
The Configuration of Policy: Whether Motherhood Is Good Politics   174
Unitary Negative Income Tax Proposals: Built to Self-Destruct?   178
The Political Appeal of Two-Tier Designs   184
Deciding How to Deliver the Benefits   189
Politics and Design   193

8
After the Collapse: Advance and Retreat   198
Triumph of Incrementalism?   199
Triumph of Reaction?   205
The Problem of Welfare Fraud   208
The Enforcement of Child Support   210
The Spread of Work Requirements and Work Relief   214
How Fast the Retreat?   219

Notes   228

Abbreviations Used in Text   277

Index   279

List of Tables, Charts, and Figure

Table 1.1
Welfare Spending by All Levels of Government as a Proportion of GNP   4

Table 1.2
Public Opinion on Welfare Spending   7

Table 1.3
Public Opinion on Reasons for Poverty   8

Table 1.4
Share of Aggregate Income Received by Families   11

Table 1.5
Income Assistance Usually Paid in States and Provinces to a Family of Four, July 1974 (per year)   13

Table 1.6
Government Spending for All Purposes: Proportion Spent by Each Level of Government, Selected Years   20

Table 2.1
Popular and Governmental Views of the Needs of a Family of Four   44

Table 2.2
Incidence of Income Below the Canadian Low-Income Cutoff, 1975   47

Table 2.3
Incidence of Income Below 150 Percent of U.S. Poverty Level, 1976   47

Chart 2.1
Summary of Provisions of Social Security Act and Important Amendments   28

Chart 2.2
Important Milestones in Canadian Income Maintenance Policy   34

Figure 7.1
Relationship of Reduction Rate and Break-Even Point for Proposed Federal Guarantee Levels (Family of Four)   179

Acknowledgments

In researching and writing this book, I have accumulated debts almost too lengthy to list and certainly too profound to acknowledge adequately. Most indispensable was the help of public officials and of interest group representatives. I regret that the requirements of confidentiality do not allow me to thank all these people individually. As a native of the United States, I was particularly dependent on the cooperation of thirty-eight present or former Canadian officials at the federal and provincial levels. Their help was crucial at every stage of the project, and knowing them has meant a great deal to me. Equally helpful were twenty-one present or former U.S. officials at the federal and state levels. I know that they would provide a Canadian the same good welcome that the Canadians provided me.

This book began while I was a graduate student in the Department of Government at Harvard University. Peter Gourevitch (now at the University of California at San Diego) impressed on me the value of the comparative method in studying government activities that made a difference in people's lives. Sidney Verba helped form my thinking in cross-cultural political studies; as my dissertation advisor, he was unfailingly patient while providing just the kind of guidance I needed. Others at Harvard who helped were Samuel Beer, Jorge Domínguez, Fen Hampson, Hugh Heclo, Samuel Huntington, Michael Mandelbaum, and Judith Shklar (all in the Department of Government), David Riesman (Department of Sociology), Laurence E. Lynn, Jr., and Edith Stokey (both at the Kennedy School of Government), and Timothy Matthews (now at the Law School). Others that I want to thank are Stefan Dupré (University of Toronto), Elliot Feldman (Brandeis University), Claude Forget (National Assembly, Quebec), Barry Friedman (Brandeis University), William Glaser (Columbia University), Marjorie Hartling (National Anti-Poverty Organization), Arnold Heidenheimer (Washington University), David Lindeman (Office of Income Security Policy, U.S. Department of Health, Education, and Welfare), Robert Katzmann (Yale University), Lawrence Leduc (University of Windsor), Stephan Leibfried (University of Bremen), Martin Levin (Brandeis University), Frank Levy (Urban Institute), John McAdams (Marquette University), Theodore Marmor (University of Chicago), Catherine Miller (Office of Family Assistance, U.S. Department of Health, Education, and Welfare), Richard Nathan (Princeton University), Richard Simeon (Queens University), Ralph Tabor (Ralph Tabor and Associates), Carole Uhlaner (Northwestern University), Richard Van Loon

(Carleton University), and Mark Worthington (Urban Systems Research and Engineering). Dupré, Lindeman, Worthington, and two Canadian officials (who cannot be named here) read the manuscript with special care, and I am particularly grateful for their patient help in correcting many errors. Of course, my consultants are not responsible for what I have written; some still disagree with my judgments.

My special debt to my parents, Craig and Nancy Leman, is inadequately repaid by this book's dedication. Unfailing support came from my brothers and sisters Valerie, Craig, Richard, Dorothy, and Hope, and a cousin Steven Farwell. My grandfather, Stanley P. Farwell, provided special inspiration by writing his own book at the age of ninety. Also important were my students at Harvard and Brandeis, who have taught me much.

While completing this book I have been an assistant professor in the Department of Politics at Brandeis University. Throughout the project I have been affiliated with the Center for International Affairs at Harvard University, most recently as an Associate. I also belong to the University Consortium for Research on North America. The project was supported in part by grant 10-P-90482/101 from the Social Security Administration, U.S. Department of Health, Education, and Welfare. Brandeis University paid for part of the typing.

Introduction

Canada and the United States in the last decade both went through major debates about proposals to expand cash welfare to new groups. Accounts of the unraveling of these efforts in each country could easily fill separate books about each country. This book has a somewhat different purpose; it tells the stories, but it also compares them. Ideally, this approach discovers more by studying the events together then they would yield separately. The lessons drawn here are based on the finding that despite ostensible similarities in the collapse of welfare reform in Canada and the United States, welfare politics actually differ dramatically. This difference is particularly intriguing because the two countries have so much in common, a fact that makes it possible to isolate the reasons for the difference in welfare politics. The spirit of the inquiry was summed up by the great historian Marc Bloch when he argued against the idea that comparison "has no other purpose than hunting out resemblances. . . . Correctly understood, the primary interest of the comparative method is, on the contrary, the observation of differences, whether they are original or the results of divergent developments from a common origin."[1]

Chapter 1 sets forth the basic framework of the study. In the past decade major expansions of cash welfare were proposed in Canada and in the United States. These proposals appeared while both countries were experiencing rapid growth in the size and cost of the welfare rolls and when the public was very upset about this growth. Yet only in the United States did debate on the proposals center on solving the welfare "mess." In Canada welfare reform was not sought primarily for this purpose. This difference in welfare politics is puzzling because the two countries have quite similar societies and economies. These socioeconomic similarities account for a convergence in the level of social spending in the two countries. But in order to explain the very real differences in how the money is spent and in how the programs are debated, we must look to differences in politics. A frequently cited difference between Canada and the United States is political culture. A major argument of this book is that political institutions are a more important reason for the two countries' differences in policy. Chapter 1 concludes by outlining how these institutions differ.

Chapter 2 provides historical and demographic background on poverty policies in Canada and the United States. The two countries underwent different developments, but the result was that benefits are distributed in roughly the same uneven proportions to various groups. Both countries help the aged a lot, mother-headed families somewhat, and most other groups much less. These amounts correspond to these different groups' relative political appeal, not to their political strength. Canada and the United States are similar in that the poor are left out of policymaking. The two countries differ, however, in the way that poverty policy is made. Later chapters argue that policymaking in Canada is more insulated than that in the United States from public antagonism toward the poor.

Chapter 3 describes the emergence during the 1960s of major proposals to extend the welfare system. Despite marked similarities in substance, these proposals had very different origins and rationales. In the United States the prime concern was problems in the existing welfare system. High-level planners obtained presidential support for their ideas only by linking them to this issue. As a result, President Nixon presented his plan to the country as welfare reform and denied its connection to the unpopular idea of the guaranteed income. No single actor on the Canadian scene had such an ability to shape the agenda and the terms of debate. However, the continuing crisis in Canadian intergovernmental relations gave a special boost to the effort to produce major proposals in poverty policy. Even aside from this added factor, the nature of the demand was quite different from that in the United States. The demand for a guaranteed income was stronger and more explicit in Canada, and leaders felt less compelled to portray their proposals simply as welfare reform.

Chapters 4 and 5 recount the U.S. and Canadian welfare debates, respectively. These chapters should be read as a unit with the following two chapters, which systematically compare the two stories, and with the final chapter, which brings the analysis to the present. A major argument of chapters 6 and 7 is that to focus on the players alone is to ignore the way that underlying factors shape the outcome by setting the rules of the game and the terms of debate. The effectiveness of political pressures depends on the political context in which they are exerted. Chapter 6 argues that political institutions had a key influence on the progress and outcome of debate in the two countries. Chapter 7 argues that the terms of political debate were also important barriers or openings for various political pressures and that these terms were set, for better and for worse, by the actual design of policy as inherited or proposed.

Chapter 6 shows that Canadian and U.S. political institutions created different channels for welfare debate that had profound implications for policy. In Canada federal-provincial negotiation, party discipline, and

xv
Introduction

ministerial prerogative in administration produce a "deductive" approach to policymaking that leaves little room for lobbying and change from outside. In the United States the president's ability to make proposals in a deductive manner is more than counteracted by the vast opportunities afforded Congress to block or change his proposals. This "inductive" way of shaping policy decisions produces a much more ambivalent attitude toward programs than is the case in Canada. Chapter 6 disputes the view that this difference in the tone of debates happens because Canadian political culture is more favorable to welfare programs. Rather, the Canadian public's very real welfare backlash simply has less institutional outlet than is the case in the United States. Chapter 6 concludes by examining strengths and weaknesses of the two countries' patterns of policymaking. Welfare reform collapsed in both countries, but for very different reasons. Canadian policymakers achieved basic agreement on the principles of an expanded welfare system but disagreed on questions of financing and jurisdiction. U.S. policymakers disagreed on the very principles of reform. The inductive pattern encouraged the deadlock that occurred in the United States. By closing out discordant elements, the Canadian deductive pattern helped promote consensus, but it also hampered outside pressure from assuring results when that internal consensus broke down.

Chapter 7 argues that the accumulation of past policies and the design of current proposals had a key impact on the political context within which welfare issues were debated in Canada and the United States. Welfare policy in the United States has historically singled out mother-headed families for a special program, while in Canada it has protected these recipients from public backlash by including in the program other more popular types of recipients. This difference in the visibility and stigma of welfare beneficiaries is reinforced by the greater presence of racial minorities on U.S. welfare rolls. However, race is a relatively minor reason for differences between welfare politics in the two countries.

The historic configuration of policy is not easily changed by today's policymakers, but they have more power over the design of new proposals. For example, the Nixon welfare reform package suffered politically because its outwardly unitary design gave identical federal benefits and work incentives to groups that the public thought should be treated differently. The 1973 Canadian welfare reform package had separate tiers: supplementation for employable people, support for the rest. These proposals escaped the built-in political problems that plagued Nixon's proposals. But the Canadian debate suffered politically from another aspect of design: the question of whether the two tiers should be administered separately or together. Whereas planners in the United States considered it axiomatic that administration should be unified, Canadian federal planners hoped to have the federal government administer supplementation, leaving support to the provinces. This division of administration ran afoul of technical objections and provincial political resistance. Federal officials gave their support to the unitary approach too late, and the three-year debate collapsed. (In the aftermath the federal government adopted a supplementation program within the federal tax system, but administering the program separately from provincial welfare programs inherently limited it.) Chapter 7 argues that experiences in both countries show that the designers of policy should consider not only technical questions but also political criteria that ultimately determine whether a proposal can pass.

Chapter 8 is not really the conclusion of the book, because all three final chapters constitute the conclusions. Chapters 6 and 7 show the importance of political institutions and of policy design in shaping the political context within which Canada and the United States debated proposals to extend the welfare system. The final chapter contrasts the patterns of policy development that emerged in the wake of the collapse of welfare reform. Because major policy debates occur continually in Canada and only rarely in the United States, we might expect the collapse of one set of proposals to stall the issue more in the latter country. Actually, Canada in recent years has been no more active than the United States in expanding its welfare system; in some ways it has been less so. Canada has not matched the U.S. ability to expand the welfare system incrementally and implicitly. Quiet growth in the United States has been so great that the "collapse" of comprehensive welfare reform did little damage to and may even have helped the effort to expand the welfare system.

But in another sense the collapse of welfare reform is very much upon us. Because of a profound shift in welfare politics, Canada and the United States have both become less active in explicitly expanding the welfare system. Chapter 8 shows that the welfare backlash is beginning to be translated into government policy in a big way. We may be entering a period in which welfare reform no longer means expansion but instead explicitly restricts welfare privileges. So far, the inductive pattern of

United States politics has encouraged this development most clearly. But once Canada's deductive system entertains public doubts about welfare programs, the reversal of these programs can be more direct and thorough than in the fragmented United States. Whether Canada overtakes the United States in the backlash sweepstakes depends on whether public outrage at welfare programs overcomes the special ability of Canada's leaders to convince the public that its outrage is sometimes misplaced.

Because this study is comparative, some cautionary notes are needed. The purpose of drawing distinctions between the two countries is not to identify one or the other as superior but to draw lessons from which both can learn. The effort to compare requires some trade-offs in choosing data. Sometimes the best data in one country were not available in comparable form in the other country. Specialists in each country may not find here all the data they are familiar with, but I hope they will agree that I exploited all available data that are comparable. The problem of comparison extends even to the choice of terminology. Whereas aid to the poor is called "social assistance" in Canada, it is called "public assistance" in the United States. Where possible, I have maintained each country's characteristic lexicon. I have tried to provide enough background so that discussions of these two countries can be understood by a reader who is familiar with only one or even neither of them. I have also attempted to explain in plain terms some of the difficult concepts of the negative income tax. I believe that the facts and issues in welfare reform can and should be made accessible to all.

The Collapse of Welfare Reform

I remember one day my little girl and I went into a supermarket, and when we got to the checkout counter, a lady behind me said, "These damn welfare people, they get all the breaks." My little girl, who was sitting in the shopping cart, said, "Mommy, why doesn't that lady like welfare people?"
U.S. divorcee

Quand le chèque entre au bureau de poste, vous allez là, les gens qui sont là, ils vous guettent avec des yeux comme pour vous manger. Quand vous sortez avec le chèque, il y en a qui disent: Tu as eu ton caritas. . . .
Canadian welfare recipient

My eldest who is in hi-school is the one that really suffers. . . . He can't buy the shoes and pants and the shirts that all the other kids wear and not a single girl has ever encouraged him to walk home. . . . The other night I heard him cry, so I sat beside his bed and stroked his hair. When he had calmed down he said, "Mama, I don't know what to do. I don't know what to do." I said, "Neither do I darling, but let's go on doing it." He laughed and fell asleep with a smile on his face; then I cried. . . . How does it feel to be on welfare. It's hard, buddy; if it weren't for the children I'd join my husband right now.
Canadian widow

. . . the present welfare system has to be judged a colossal failure. I propose that we abolish the present welfare system and that we adopt in its place a new family assistance system.
President Richard M. Nixon, 1969

The welfare system is too hopeless to be cured by minor modifications. We must make a complete and clean break with the past.
President Jimmy Carter, 1977

The truth is that Canada's system is one of the most advanced in the Western World and that it provides a solid foundation upon which to build in the context of today's needs.
Marc Lalonde, Minister of National Health and Welfare, 1973

1
The Welfare Crisis and Political Institutions

In the past decade the United States and Canada have each embarked on two unsuccessful ventures in welfare reform. Though basically similar in substance, the proposals differed dramatically in rhetoric. In 1969 President Richard M. Nixon declared that "the present welfare system has to be judged a colossal failure." Nixon recited a litany of failings: "It breaks up homes. It often penalizes work. It robs recipients of dignity. And it grows." He went on to propose "that we abolish the present welfare system and that we adopt in its place a new family assistance system. Initially, this new system will cost more than welfare. But unlike welfare, it is designed to correct the conditions it deals with and thus to lessen the long-range burden and cost."[1] Eight years later President Jimmy Carter asked Congress in almost identical terms to "abolish" the existing welfare system. "The welfare system is too hopeless to be cured by minor modifications. We must make a complete and clean break with the past."[2] In contrast, Canadian rhetoric was far more subdued. In 1970 Minister of National Health and Welfare John Munro pledged the federal government to "do all that it can to ensure that the existing social assistance systems will in future be undeserving of the criticisms now prevalent." He rejected "criticisms that Canada's income security system is needlessly complicated by the number of individual programs. . . ." Munro saved his own criticisms for programs that provide "universal payments which disregard the actual income of the recipient."[3] Cutting back on these universal programs could actually strengthen Canada's welfare programs. After these 1970 proposals had failed, Prime Minister Pierre Trudeau proposed in 1973 that "Canada's total social security system . . . must be reconsidered and reorganized. . . ."[4] But in presenting its proposals, his government did not suggest the need to reform a hopeless welfare system. Minister of National Health and Welfare Marc Lalonde presented the major proposals without attacking the system. Dutifully chronicling its deficiencies, he nevertheless denied that it was unsound: "The truth is that Canada's system is one of the most advanced in the Western World, and that it provides a solid foundation upon which to build in the context of today's needs."[5]

Despite a fundamental difference in tone, these Canadian and U.S. leaders were talking about programs subject to similar problems and about which the public in each country had similar reservations. Indeed by the late 1960s Canada seemed ripe for a backlash in welfare policymaking. The number of beneficiaries had grown dramatically, and welfare spending was increasing even more quickly. Broken families were increasingly dominating the welfare rolls. And the public was concerned about the increasing evidence that the welfare system discouraged work and rewarded fraud, especially among employable people. In the United States such trends produced an unrelieved sense of crisis about the "welfare mess" along with repeated efforts to reform it. But in Canada no such mood ever emerged at the national level. There *welfare reform* was not as common a term for the expansion of welfare being considered. When that term was used in Canada, it had a more positive meaning than it did in the United States. Why this difference, and why does it matter?

Common Problems

U.S. concern about a welfare crisis was fueled by extraordinary growth after 1967 of the program for Aid to Families with Dependent Children (AFDC). Between 1967 and 1969 the number of beneficiaries nationwide grew by 30 percent and spending went up by 51 percent. Adding to the sense of alarm was the accelerating trend revealed by each new month's figures. Expansion of AFDC between 1969 and 1971 was 55 percent for beneficiaries and 78 percent for spending. The increase was even steeper in some states; California experienced a 37 percent increase in AFDC families in 1970 alone.[6] Though this growth was politically explosive, the system was not out of control, nor was society disintegrating. In fact, the welfare rolls almost immediately began to level off. The earlier growth was the result not of demographic changes but of sharp increases in the rate at which potential welfare clients decided to seek benefits. Reasons for this shift included loosened state administration, court decisions, declining social stigma, and the efforts of welfare advocacy groups.[7]

The expansion of U.S. welfare programs was so dramatic that it has overshadowed the quiet but tremendous expansion in Canadian welfare programs that took place before the "welfare crisis" struck in the United States. For example, Canada's closest approximation to the AFDC program, Unemployment Assistance, expanded drastically after 1960, adding 132 percent more beneficiaries in three years, a period in which the AFDC program was growing by only 28 percent. And when this program was replaced by the more all-encompassing Canada Assistance Plan (CAP), the total number of welfare recipients in cost-shared programs jumped 91 percent between 1967 and 1969, a period when AFDC re-

3
Common Problems

cipients increased by only 32 percent.[8] It is difficult to compare welfare programs in the two countries because figures on the Canada Assistance Plan do not single out the costs of aiding families, a fast-growing section of the case load that the AFDC program concentrates on exclusively.[9] When AFDC is added to the U.S. programs aiding the aged and disabled, the "welfare crisis" in Canada becomes more serious than that in the United States. Between 1961 and 1971 total recipients increased by 119 percent in the United States, but they increased 129 percent in Canada![10]

Because Canadian welfare rolls had expanded so much during the 1960s, there was no room for rapid growth like the kind that hit the United States after 1967; most Canadian eligibles were already participating. No research exists that could establish conclusively why the Canadian welfare rolls opened up sooner than those in the United States. A fair hypothesis, however, is that social and administrative barriers were fewer in Canada. In 1969 the federal and provincial ministers of welfare commissioned a study on the expansion of welfare programs. The report called attention to factors such as more tolerant social attitudes toward welfare beneficiaries, the emergence of demand for assistance as a right, and the "demonstration effect" of provinces on one another and of other countries on Canada.[11] In the United States the barriers were more firmly rooted, and they gave way all at once. This difference in the precipitancy of change had profound implications for the politics of welfare in the two countries, for there was simply less notion of a welfare crisis in Canada. Indeed, after 1971 the Canadian case load leveled off and even decreased in some years. But the same thing began to happen by 1973 to the U.S. case load.[12]

In both countries costs increased even faster than beneficiaries. Direct comparison of AFDC with similar spending in Canada is again difficult because Canadian data do not identify the specific costs of aiding families that are not disabled or aged. However, even if the faster rising costs of aiding this group are not separated out, Canadian costs have clearly kept pace with those in the United States, particularly in the 1960s. Total spending in provincially administered social assistance programs increased 167 percent between 1959 and 1968, close to the 197 percent increase in total AFDC spending recorded in the United States.[13] Most Canadian data combine spending for social services with spending for income maintenance, and it is most useful to compare these data with U.S. data that include both functions. A comparison of such figures shows that, overall, Canadian welfare costs have increased even faster than U.S. costs. The federal share of cost-shared public assistance and social services in 1976 was eight times what it had been in 1960 in the United States, but it was eleven times what it had been in 1961 in Canada. Not only did U.S. spending grow less overall than Canadian spending, but its biggest growth came later. In Canada federal spending on these programs grew by 410 percent between 1961 and 1971, while U.S. spending grew by less, 376 percent between 1960 and 1971. Between 1971 and 1976 U.S. spending grew faster than Canadian spending, but not by much— 137 percent versus 118 percent.[14]

Canadian and U.S. growth in welfare case load and spending must be seen in context. During the ten-year period from 1959 to 1969 the general population increased 21 percent in Canada and 16 percent in the United States. Between 1960 and 1970 the gross national product grew by 123 percent in Canada and 93 percent in the United States. And the cost of living also increased dramatically. Spending by all levels of government increased as a proportion of GNP. In view of all these trends, it would be surprising if public assistance programs had not grown after 1960. But as table 1.1 suggests, programs for the poor grew fastest of all.

Table 1.1
Welfare Spending by All Levels of Government as a Proportion of GNP

Canada			United States	
Year	Public Aid	Old Age Pensions, Family Allowances	Public Aid	Year
1951	0.8%	1.8%	0.9%	1950
1961	0.8	3.0	0.8	1960
1970	1.8	2.6	1.7	1970
1976	2.4	2.9	3.0	1976

Sources: Statistics Canada, *Social Security: 1978*, pp. 28, 29, 31. Public Aid programs include Canada Assistance Plan and its precursors as well as Guaranteed Income Supplements. Figures in the source are for federal spending; provincial spending was estimated here by increasing these amounts on the basis of the 50 percent cost-sharing formula used in some programs.
Alfred M. Skolnik and Sophie Dales, "Social Welfare Expenditures, Fiscal Year 1976," *Social Security Bulletin* 40, no. 1 (January 1977), table 3. Includes Aid to Families with Dependent Children, Supplemental Security Income, Food Stamps, Social Services, and Medicaid.

5
Common Problems

Between 1960 and 1974 means-tested and needs-tested assistance in both countries as a proportion of GNP approximately tripled. Canada increased its spending faster than the United States until 1970, when the late-blooming U.S. growth occurred. The most significant U.S. growth was in Medicaid and Food Stamps, programs that Canada does not have. To keep the growth of conditional programs in perspective, it should be compared with the growth of other social programs. Throughout the 1960s the major Canadian income maintenance programs—the Old Age Security pension and Family Allowance programs—were not conditional but universal. While benefiting the poor, these programs also transfer many resources to the middle class. The same thing can be said of the massive U.S. veterans' programs, which consumed 1.2 percent of GNP in 1976. In addition, the United States has social insurance programs that dwarf its assistance programs, consuming 9.1 percent of GNP (1976). Canada's social insurance programs are more modest, representing 2.4 percent of GNP.[15]

The Canadian welfare rolls contain some of the same types of families that have made AFDC so controversial. Though people in the United States think of broken families as an American problem, the sociologists emphasize that the past three decades' gradual increase in divorce, separation, desertion, and illegitimacy has been worldwide.[16] Indeed the proportion of female-headed families among all Canadian and U.S. families actually increased very little during the 1960s. The United States began with a higher proportion (9.9 percent in 1961) than Canada (6.6 percent in 1961), and by the 1970s these levels had increased only slightly as a percentage of total families.[17] Widowhood in 1961 exceeded all other causes combined; by 1970 it was no longer the dominant cause of single-parent families in either country. A growing cause was divorce. The divorce rate in 1974 was twice as high in the United States as in Canada, but the gap was closing.[18] The two countries were converging in their rates of marital separations. The greatest growth has been in families headed by an unmarried female. Between 1961 and 1970 this group more than doubled in each country. The two countries' illegitimacy rates are nearly the same, and both are on the way up. Illegitimacy rates far higher than the Canadian average can be found in Alberta, British Columbia, and particularly Saskatchewan.[19]

Since Canada has the dubious honor of sharing with the United States similar trends in marital breakup, the country's poverty population and welfare rolls are nearly as filled with members of this group. Biennial surveys of the AFDC case load have shown with tiresome regularity an increase in the program's proportion of broken families. The proportion of AFDC families whose mother was divorced, separated, or deserted increased from 41 percent in 1961 to 45 percent in 1967 and to 52 percent in 1975. Families headed by an unmarried mother increased from 21 percent in 1961 to 31 percent in 1975.[20] Although this increase was widely seen as evidence of cascading deterioration in family life, t resulted largely from the delayed joining of AFDC rolls by many such families who had always been eligible. Thus during just the period between 1967 and 1970 the rate of participation by eligible mother-headed families on AFDC increased from 63 percent to 91 percent. In Canada such increases occurred gradually over a longer period of years. Even so, the proportion of low-income families headed by a woman nearly doubled in the five years from 1967 to 1972.[21] A 1970 survey of the Canadian welfare case load showed that in 72 percent of the absent-parent cases the parents were divorced, separated, or not married. More recent nationwide figures are not available, but single-parent families are prominent in provincial figures. Among absent-father cases in Ontario, 23 percent in 1970 involved unwed mothers, while this proportion had increased to 29 percent in 1976.[22] Similarly, female-headed families that were the product of divorce, separation, or desertion increased from 36 percent to 57 percent between 1970 and 1976. And in 1977 in Quebec 57 percent of female-headed families were the products of divorce, desertion, or separation, while another 27 percent had not married.[23]

Common Concerns

It is puzzling that Canadian policymakers made little effort to confront the growth in welfare programs. It is even more puzzling that they did so in the face of growing public concern about this growth. That public concern was growing is important because it is often assumed that the Canadian public is more favorable to big government programs than the U.S. public. But for social policy this observation is questionable. The evidence suggests that the difference in public thinking is relatively small. The publics in both countries express basic support for aid to the poor but qualify it with concern about costs and with suspicions about welfare beneficiaries. As shown in table 1.2, more than half of those willing to ex-

Common Concerns

Table 1.2
Public Opinion on Welfare Spending

	Canada, 1972	United States, 1973
Too Little	16%	21%
About Right	31	25
Too Much	53	54

Notes: In these polls, the undecided numbered 19 percent (1972) and 5 percent (1973). The figures reported in the table exclude the undecided.

Canadian poll: "Do you, or do you not think that the cost for welfare services in this country is . . . too high, too low, or about right?" Canadian Institute of Public Opinion, "Welfare Costs Too High: Tax Load Unfair, Say Most," *Gallup Report*, January 26, 1972.

U.S. poll: "Government spending in welfare is . . . too little/about right/too much?" James A. Davis, *National Data Program for the Social Sciences: Spring 1973 General Social Survey*, ICPR Study 7315 (Ann Arbor, Mich.: Inter-University Consortium for Political Research, July 1973).

press an opinion believe that welfare spending is too high. Less than a quarter feel that the spending is too low.[24] The softness of support for welfare spending is illustrated by a 1976 U.S. poll which showed that only 38 percent of the public felt it would be a "very serious loss" if welfare programs were cut back by a third. In a Canadian poll taken in 1973–1974, 82 percent agreed (most of them strongly) that "there is an atmosphere of welfare for anybody who wants it in this country." Many giving this reply probably disapproved of the situation.[25]

Despite this concern about costs, the Canadian and U.S. publics support welfare aid for some groups. Aid to the elderly is the most popular social program. In 1974, 69 percent of all Canadians polled felt that Old Age Security pensions were not high enough. Moreover young people felt much more strongly about this than people actually receiving the pensions.[26] Similarly in 1976 nearly half the U.S. public favored increasing Social Security benefits, "even if it means higher taxes."[27] Another group that the public theoretically wants the government to support is fatherless families. A Canadian poll showed that 62 percent approved of providing extra aid to mothers caring for children in the home. In Quebec and the Atlantic provinces more than 50 percent strongly agreed with this sentiment.[28] Similarly U.S. citizens claim to support such aid. A 1976 poll found that 74 percent agreed that "many women whose husbands have left them with several children have no choice but to go on welfare."[29]

A basic reason that the Canadian and U.S. publics can support aid to some groups while also feeling that welfare spending is too high is that they believe many people receiving welfare do not need it and should be working. The publics in both countries refuse to accept the idea that anyone who can work needs to be poor. In 1964 the Gallup organizations in each country asked "Which is more often to blame if a person is poor—lack of effort on his own part, or circumstances beyond his control?" In both countries nearly as many people cited lack of effort as circumstances, and many cited both (table 1.3). Canadians seem a little more willing to cite circumstances as a cause for poverty, but not much more. It is a shame that such a question has not been asked in Canada since 1964. A 1977 U.S. poll asked a question similar to the question in the 1964 poll. Fully 54 percent said they felt that "most people who receive money from welfare could get along without it if they tried."[30]

In view of the widespread reaction against welfare spending and suspicions about welfare recipients, it is not surprising that the Canadian and U.S. publics overwhelmingly agree that many recipients should be forced to work. In a 1964 poll 84 percent of the U.S. public favored a work requirement for able-bodied men. Indeed a similar proportion (82 percent) felt that recipients could be required to work on "streets, parks, and the like" if they could not find jobs.[31] In a 1969 poll 84 percent said that "there are too many people receiving welfare money who should be working."[32] A subsequent poll of eight states ranging from California to Georgia found that three-quarters felt all welfare recipients "who might benefit" should be required to accept training for employment.[33] Work requirements have long been common in programs of general assistance funded entirely by the states. After 1967 Congress also adopted such re-

Table 1.3
Public Opinion on Reasons for Poverty

	Canada	United States
Lack of Effort	30%	30%
Circumstances	34	31
Both	30	34
Undecided	6	5

Source: George Gallup, "Public's Views on Poverty Divide the Nation Politically," news release, American Institute of Public Opinion, December 16, 1964.

Note: The survey question was "Which is more often to blame if a person is poor—lack of effort on his own part, or circumstances beyond his control?"

quirements for some recipients in the federal-state AFDC program, with this requirement extended in 1971 not only to males but to mothers with no children under the age of six. Although Canada has no such national requirement, nationwide opinion just as strongly favors work requirements. In a 1976 poll 86 percent of the Canadians polled agreed that "an employable man who is receiving welfare assistance should be required to undertake any available work." This result was an increase over that reflected in a 1962 survey and was expressed as strongly in Quebec as in the rest of Canada.[34] And although they vary in intensity and coverage, work requirements can be found in every province. In 1978 Alberta began to apply a work test to mothers with children as young as four months—a more far-reaching regulation than in any U.S. state.[35] And while most provinces have milder work requirements than the United States, the idea is spreading in Canada.

Suspicion of welfare recipients extends to the imputation of outright fraud. The 1964 poll, in further inquiries unfortunately not duplicated in Canada, found that although only 7 percent in the United States felt that "most" were on relief for "dishonest reasons," another 61 percent felt that some were. These opinions were held nearly as strongly by those who sympathized with recipients as by those whose attitudes toward them were more negative.[36] In a 1969 poll 71 percent agreed that "many people getting welfare are not honest about their need."[37] And in a 1976 poll 85 percent of the U.S. public agreed that "too many people on welfare cheat by getting money they are not entitled to."[38] Even in Boston, one of the most prowelfare areas in the country, the average estimate by the public of the percentage of recipients who lied about their finances was 41 percent.[39] While fewer polls exist that measure this suspicion in Canada, indirect evidence suggests its strength. For example, Canadians are very critical of fraud in Unemployment Insurance, a program that is often linked with welfare in the public mind. In a 1973 survey the most frequent change in Unemployment Insurance suggested nationwide was the need to institute better control. Nearly half of those surveyed in Ontario and the provinces west of it took this position, while the proportion was considerably less in Quebec and the Atlantic provinces.[40] In an Alberta survey nearly half of those answering felt that 30 percent or more of all welfare recipients were abusing the system.[41] That the provinces are doing less than most states to combat fraud should not obscure the Canadian public's outrage. In 1972 the socialist premier of Manitoba initiated a study of fraud and warned of a "profound, seething resentment against the whole welfare system."[42]

Holding Socioeconomic Variables Constant

Why were Canadian income supplementation proposals presented as an extension of rather than an answer to existing welfare programs? When these proposals failed, why was this failure not the result of public backlash? Why, indeed, did Canada not undergo a nationwide welfare backlash like that which felled the proposals of two U.S. presidents and motivated continuing national efforts to tighten existing welfare programs? These queries frame a classic problem of comparative analysis. By major economic and social indicators, the two countries are strikingly similar; why then did their policy debates differ? Existing comparative studies of social policy worldwide have emphasized the singular importance of economic and social development. For example, Phillips Cutright and Frederick Pryor argue that social spending as a percentage of GNP is more closely related to a country's level of economic development and the age of its social security system than to political variables as basic as whether it has a communist or capitalist system.[43] Harold Wilensky has deepened this argument by pointing out that despite the striking relation of social spending to industrialization, some differences remain to be explained. He argues that a welfare backlash is promoted by political decentralization, social heterogeneity, widespread private pensions and insurance, a tax system that makes the costs of welfare explicit, a weakly organized working class, and a large middle class containing many self-employed people.[44] In comparison with Europe, Wilensky finds, both Canada and the United States exhibit many of these features and are therefore subject to welfare backlash. Thus we still lack a theory that can explain why public assistance programs are such bigger issues in the United States than in Canada.

Although Wilensky and the others do not capture certain crucial differences between Canada and the United States, they are justified in pointing to similarities in economic and social structure that promote convergence in public policy. Set beside other industrialized societies, the two look very much alike. For example, between 1960 and 1969 they were nearly identical in having higher unemployment and lower inflation than the European countries.[45] Economic growth has followed similar paths, with gross national product per capita reaching a 1976 level of $8096 in Canada and $7864 in the United States.[46] The proportions of their work forces organized into labor unions are similar, and low by European standards. The distribution of income in the two countries is quite similar. As suggested by table 1.4, the richest fifth in both Canada and the United States receives roughly two-fifths of family income, while the poorest fifth receives about 6 percent. This situation has changed only marginally since 1951. Despite these similarities, the Canadian distribution of income is slightly less skewed than the U.S. distribution. Not only does the lowest fifth in Canada receive a little more of total income, but some in this group receive a higher absolute income than any in the corresponding U.S. quintile. The level and direction of government spending in Canada and in the United States are also similar. By the mid 1970s spending by all levels of government was just under two-fifths of gross national product in Canada, slightly less than that in the United States. Both levels are less than European levels. Spending for income maintenance as a proportion of gross national product in 1974 was 7.3 percent in Canada and 8.0 percent in the United States, again significantly below most European nations. A particularly notable kinship is that Canada and the United States devote a much larger proportion of income maintenance expenditures to means-tested or needs-tested aid than does any

Table 1.4
Share of Aggregate Income Received by Families

	Canada		U.S.	
	1951	1975	1950	1975
Lowest Fifth	6.1%	6.2%	4.5%	5.4%
Second Fifth	12.9	13.0	12.0	11.8
Middle Fifth	17.4	18.2	17.4	17.6
Fourth Fifth	22.4	23.9	23.4	24.1
Highest Fifth	41.4	38.8	42.7	41.1
Upper Limit of Lowest Fifth	$1820	$8214	$1661	$6914
Lower Limit of Highest Fifth	$4640	$22,823	$5283	$22,037

Sources: Canada: 1951: Cited from Statistics Canada by David Ross, *Canadian Fact Book on Poverty* (Ottawa: Canadian Council on Social Development, 1975), table 10; 1975: Statistics Canada, *Income Distributions by Size in Canada*, 1975, table 67.
  U.S.: Bureau of the Census, *Statistical Abstract of the United States: 1977*, table 713.

other major industrialized nation. And although it is true that Canada had Family Allowances while the United States did not have a similar program, Canada's program has consistently ranked as one of the smallest among countries that have such programs.[47]

These underlying similarities in social spending reflect the common action of fundamental economic and social forces in Canada and the United States. But if the socioeconomic kinship is so real, then how can one explain policy differences not reflected in those aggregate spending figures? This is not just an academic question, because spending levels, especially aggregate measures such as those used by Cutright, Pryor, and Wilensky, do not tell the whole story of policy. Lumping together all social spending obscures cross-national differences in the distribution of the funds and makes no distinctions in the way that programs are financed. Canada's universal Family Allowance program aids many families who would receive no government benefits in the United States; its Old Age Security pension program is financed by income taxes rather than the less progressive payroll tax used by the Old Age Insurance system in the United States. Even when spending and financing of a specific program are similar in the two countries, as is the case with public assistance programs, the programs may well differ in important ways not captured by the aggregate figures.

The similarity in Canadian and U.S. spending for low-income assistance is deceptive. Benefits in Canada do not vary as much from place to place as they do in the United States. Thus when Marc Lalonde warned in 1973 of variation among provinces, monthly benefits ranged only from a high of $50 per child (British Columbia, Saskatchewan, and Manitoba) to a low of $32 per child (Newfoundland). In contrast, the spread in the average U.S. welfare payment that Richard Nixon attacked in 1969 ranged from $65 for each child (New Jersey) to $10 (Mississippi).[48] Table 1.5 contains more recent comparisons. The Canadian figures are budget standards for basic needs observed by each province. Budget standards are also available in the United States, but they are a misleading guide to the benefits actually paid, because it is common for a state to reduce benefits across the board below the "standard of need." Only twenty-two states pay according to the full standard, whereas only in exceptional and temporary cases do the provinces pay below the standard of need. The U.S. figures presented in table 1.5 are benefits actually paid in each state. In addition to Aid to Families with Dependent Children, they include food

Table 1.5
Income Assistance Usually Paid in States and Provinces to a Family of Four, July 1974 (per year)

	Canada (Social Assistance)	United States (AFDC and Food Stamps)
Low	$3,780 (New Brunswick)	$2,364 (Mississippi)
High	4,320 (British Columbia)	5,664 (Hawaii)
Unweighted Average	4,041	4,054
Largest Jurisdiction	4,224 (Quebec)	4,464 (California)

Sources: Canada: Federal-Provincial Conference of Ministers of Welfare, *Background Paper on Income Support and Supplementation* (February 1975), table 5. A family is two parents and two children. Figures are budget standards and include rent, fuel, and utilities. Family Allowances are counted as income, reducing the other benefits payable. Quebec had the largest social assistance case load. These figures exclude the territories.

United States: HEW, *Income Supplement Program (1974 HEW Welfare Replacement Proposal)*, Technical Analysis Paper No. 11, Office of Income Security Policy, Office of the Assistant Secretary for Planning and Evaluation (October 1976), table C-2. Family type is unspecified. The figures combine AFDC and food stamp benefits. These figures are not budget standards, but rather the largest amount normally paid for basic needs in each state. As explained in the text, budget standards in the United States are not a reliable indication of benefits actually paid. California had the largest AFDC case load, although New York had more food stamp beneficiaries. Figures exclude Guam, Puerto Rico, and the Virgin Islands.

stamps, another major program. Table 1.5 shows more variation in the United States than in Canada. For a family of four, benefits in the states range from $2364 to $5664 while in the provinces they range from $3780 to $4320.[49]

Aggregate spending figures disguise not only regional variation in benefits but also a number of other important questions about the administration of the funds. As Kirsten Gronbjerg has pointed out, how much should be spent on welfare may be a less important question than who gets the benefits. Gronbjerg found considerable variation by region and over time in who was eligible as determined by the states.[50] If such policies vary with the state, they vary with the country even more. Throughout the 1960s Canadian welfare programs were more open to poor families, perhaps especially to the single-parent families which in the United States began to join the AFDC program only late in the decade. Efforts to discourage such families and to impose work requirements on them seem to have been more widespread in the United States than in Canada. Even if U.S. administrative and social barriers did not always prevent a poor person from taking advantage of welfare benefits, they could still increase his feelings of fear, guilt, or shame. Though such measures are not at all reflected in spending figures, they make a tremendous difference in people's happiness as well as in the further development of policy. Alexis de Tocqueville argued long ago that while equality was inexorable, politics would decide whether it would lead "to servitude or freedom, knowledge or barbarism, prosperity or wretchedness."[51]

In citing these important differences in policy and in policymaking, I do not deny that aggregate spending for the poor is similar in Canada and the United States and that the two countries' similar economic and social development is most responsible for this convergence. Indeed the attractiveness of the Canada–United States comparison is precisely that it allows us to "control for" the usually dominant socioeconomic variable; if there are important policy differences between Canada and the United States, then we will have to look to explanations other than economics. The comparison allows us to isolate important political variables that comparative welfare studies often overlook. In this sense it is a "most similar systems" design as expounded by Przeworski and Teune.[52] When countries with much in common are compared, the remaining differences should be easier to explain. Typically this approach has been used in "area studies" such as those of Scandinavian countries.[53] Canada and the United States seem ideally suited for such comparative work, but curiously, there is no wealth of such studies.[54] Though Canadians have made such comparisons more often than U.S. scholars, S. A. Longstaff looks at his fellow Canadian social scientists and finds it "puzzling that studies comparing Canada and the United States have been so little in vogue."[55] Although some important work has compared health policies in the two countries, few other policies have been the subject of comparative study.[56]

My comparison of two countries cannot claim to complete a theory for all societies, but it is not atheoretical. Aggregate studies comparing many nations have failed to capture the complex differences or to produce the discriminating theory needed to explain these differences. Most needed at this point is the "disciplined-configurative" analysis called for by Sidney Verba and elaborated by Alexander George, among others.[57] This approach combines a sensitivity to the special features of each case with an insistence that explanations, however configurative, refer to general rules whose validity can be tested elsewhere. "Explanations may be tailored to the specific case, but they must be made of the same material and follow the same rules of tailoring."[58] This approach ideally uncovers the rich reality of social causation while also making social science a truly cumulative enterprise.

One complication in constructing a comparison of Canada and the United States is the great difference in their sizes. The United States has nearly ten times the population and gross national product of Canada. Thus even if Canada and the United States were identical in most ways, the difference in scale would itself produce some differences in policymaking. Aside from these theoretical questions, Canada suffers the very real effects of "sleeping with an elephant." As neighbors, the two countries have a most unequal relationship. American news, products, businesses, and ideas are omnipresent in Canada, while Canada remains invisible to most Americans. The impact of the United States is increased by the fact that half of all Canadians live within fifty miles of the border. Thus U.S. influence is a leading issue in Canada, and it creates special questions in comparative analysis. It would be wise, however, to recognize that internal factors are still central to Canadian development, particularly in social policy. Stein Rokkan has splendidly challenged the view that smaller countries are too dependent to be compared with larger ones. He points out that "Greece and Israel provided the greatest innovations of the ancient world and Sweden, the Netherlands and Switzerland can hardly be fruitfully studied as passive victims of exogenous pressures."[59]

Rediscovering Politics

If the economic and social structures of Canada and the United States do not differ enough to explain the greater degree of welfare backlash exhibited in U.S. policymaking, then what differences are responsible? Central are political structure and political values. The most exciting comparative studies of Canadian and U.S. politics have focused on differences in political culture. A basic argument of this book is that greater weight should be given to political institutions. But there is no question that a difference in political culture exists. It can be traced to Canada's origins as a haven for loyalists fleeing the American Revolution and as a holdout against U.S. expansionism. S. D. Clark observed that "Canadian national life can almost be said to take its rise in the negative will to resist absorption in the American Republic."[60] Whereas the United States represented a new individualism hostile to government, Canada held to a corporate view of society more friendly to strong government.[61] Such differences between Canadian and U.S. politics are not difficult to sense. For example, Canada has long had a stronger government role in transportation, mining, broadcasting, and health care.[62] However, it is not clear that these differences stem specifically from the public's preferences on the substance of policy. The polls cited before reveal Canadians to be nearly as critical of welfare programs as the U.S. public. And even when substantive preferences differ in the two countries, the most important influence of political culture may be more diffuse, in fostering institutions and political alignments that in turn favor particular policies. In the United States the major parties are relatively homogenized and leave little room for parties that do not fit the liberal mold. In Canada the Liberal party has ruled for thirty-eight of the last forty-three years, whether as a minority government or with an outright majority. But the opposition is varied, comprising both tories and socialists—heresies in the United States. Of course there are limits to this distinction between Canadian polarity and U.S. consensus. "Just as the Progressive Conservative Party cannot wean itself from a heavy reliance on liberal ideas if it is to be electorally successful, so the NDP is equally reliant on a heady dose of liberalism in addition to that party's socialism."[63] Moreover the NDP is condemned to permanent minority status. Even Seymour Martin Lipset, who once argued that socialism was stronger in Canada, now feels that it is subject to the same limitations faced by socialists in the United States.[64]

Even if political culture has a limited direct effect on the substance of policy and on the platforms of the political parties, it has a subtler but possibly more important indirect effect on policy through the establishment of authority patterns. The U.S. public is irreverent and ubiquitous in its attempts to influence policy, especially in Congress, where a legislator is constantly asked to justify his votes. In contrast, Canadian deference to authority insulates elites from everyday pressures and frees them to pursue long-term policy objectives. Thus elite culture is a more independent force in Canada than in the United States, and elites have often favored major policies in advance of the public. Of course, this difference is not entirely a matter of political culture. Canadian and U.S. institutions reinforce the difference.

Canada and the United States are both "federal societies." The very breadth of each country separates the population into regions of differing economies, habits, political cultures, and policy preferences. However, political structure has accommodated this diversity in quite different ways in the two countries. In Canada the provincial governments have great authority in social policy. They not only administer many policies, but also collaborate directly with national officials in the formulation of federal guidelines and legislative proposals. Moreover the provinces have authority even in areas that in the United States would be the responsibility of local governments. The most important decisions on social policy are made not within the national government but between it and the provincial governments in conferences between top political leaders. Thus in Canadian federalism, policy debates resemble the process of diplomacy between governments more than a process of decision making within a single government. In contrast, federalism in the United States operates in a way that can best be described as intragovernmental. Far more than the Canadian parliament, the U.S. Congress is chosen by local methods and is organized into regional caucuses of western, southern, northern, urban, big-state, and agricultural legislators.[65] States and localities participate not as sovereign entities but as an outside lobby. This "intergovernmental lobby" works only if it can affect the *intra*governmental balance within Congress. Regional interests are expressed very effectively in this way, but it is federalism with a difference.

Thus power is not decentralized to regional governments in the United States, and the price is that the national government is itself decentralized. In Richard Neustadt's phrase, U.S. government is "separated institutions sharing powers." The central division is between president and Congress, each with its own electoral base. Whereas the appointive Senate in Canada presents no challenge to the House of Commons, the U.S. Congress is divided into two strong, often dissonant branches. The U.S. Senate and House are in turn divided against themselves in an endless array of powerful committees and subcommittees. Parties and elections rarely succeed in pulling together this patchwork. American parties have long been an expression of localism rather than an antidote to it, and today Congress is increasingly peopled by unbeatable incumbents who are free even of that constraint. A U.S. congressman votes with his party in choosing leaders and rules because his own interest commands it. But his interests are not so closely linked to party cohesion on substantive issues.[66] This division and dispersion of power within U.S. national government have given legislation a "strong tendency to go to pieces."[67] Congress responds to presidential proposals by delay and bargaining. The coalitions that pass different pieces of legislation are temporary and shifting, and the result is often uncoordinated and incomplete. Full agreement between Congress and the president on sweeping new legislation usually awaits conditions of national crisis and social outcry.

In contrast to the U.S. dispersion of authority at the center, Canadian national government—what there is of it—is more centralized. The majority party and the bureaucracy obey the prime minister and his cabinet. Unlike a U.S. congressional election, the choice of a Canadian federal legislator involves a judgment not just of that individual's personal worth and philosophy but also of which party and prime minister should rule. The Opposition in Canada has much less chance than in the United States to persuade or to bargain, and it adopts an adversary role, looking to the next election.[68] In view of this uniformity in the lives of the majority and the opposition parties, it is not surprising that Canada's regional diversity has sometimes manifested itself outside the two major parties. In provincial politics parties have a life quite independent of the federal party system, and this provincial dynamism even spills over into federal politics, supporting regionally based third parties in Parliament. The best example is the New Democratic Party. With little realistic chance of gaining power, it nevertheless picks up parliamentary seats in Ontario, British Columbia, and elsewhere. The same is true for the ralliement des Créditistes, with its base in Quebec. These third parties gain despite winner-take-all electoral rules that discourage such parties in the United States. In the United States, regional movements are more likely to find expression through caucus or insurgency within the major parties—a strategy not possible in Canada where the parties are not as open to such improvisation.

In view of Parliament's inability to give expression within the national government to the regionalism manifested in intergovernmental negotiations, Seymour Martin Lipset has argued that Canadian politics represents the "failure of the British parliamentary system to work in a society with complex internal divisions."[69] Although it has a parliamentary majority standing ready to pass its program, the federal government finds itself unable to reconcile regional interests within the federal framework. In attempting to accommodate diverse interests, a prime minister may actually be handicapped by the need to maintain his majority on every parliamentary vote. Leon Epstein has emphasized the comparative appeal of the U.S. practice of allowing the president to "have his policies enacted by majorities that are differently composed for different occasions."[70]

Even so, such splintering at the national level could be fatal in Canada, where the success of the federal government in coordinating policy with the provinces depends on its ability to speak to them with a single voice. The provinces, too, have political systems that allow them to take strong stands in negotiations. Few state leaders in the United States can commit their government to a position without fear of being overruled by the legislature.[71]

A combination of factors has contributed to the hegemony of the provinces. A continuous source of provincial strength vis-à-vis the federal government has been the small number of provinces (only four in 1867, seven in 1900, and ten today—plus two territories—in a country whose area exceeds that of the United States). Moreover two of the provinces, Quebec and Ontario, together contain three-fifths of the population, giving them great leverage on the federal government and the other provinces. Most important, political boundaries coincide with a profound cultural division that has determined the country's constitutional development from the beginning. Quebec has more than a quarter of Canada's population and is 80 percent French speaking; of the other provinces, only New Brunswick has a population that is as much as 35 percent French speaking.[72]

The provincial foothold was secured by interpretations of the country's 1867 constitution, the British North America (BNA) Act. Under the BNA Act the federal government was given what were then considered the major functions of government and actually had greater powers than allowed by the Constitution of 1787 to the federal government of the United States. But while the U.S. government expanded irresistibly into social policy and other fields not explicitly granted to it, the provinces, aided by the courts, have frustrated most efforts of the Canadian federal government to expand into fields not covered by the BNA Act. In some cases, however, the federal government has been able to use the lure of its revenues to convince the provinces to amend the BNA Act, giving it a share of social policy, or to shape provincial policy indirectly by means of conditional cost-sharing programs similar to those so common in the United States. Unlike the states, however, the provinces have been unwilling to concede that federal taxes "belong" to Ottawa. Indeed during World War II the provinces gave the federal government their powers to tax personal income, corporate income, and inheritance. Canadian politics since then has been the story of provinces gradually winning back these tax powers. Because of this ambiguous status of federal revenues, cost-sharing programs have been a special object of contention in Canada, with provinces objecting to the conditions and demanding unconditional return of the funds either through transfer payments or by outright transfer of taxing powers and tax "room."[73]

The stark facts of provincial assertiveness are reflected in table 1.6, which follows the distribution over time of expenditures among the three levels of government in Canada and the United States. Whereas U.S. localities have always outspent the states, the provinces historically have either equaled or exceeded municipal spending, and since the 1960s they have pulled ahead permanently. While local government has been the fastest growing sector in the United States, it grows more slowly in

Table 1.6
Government Spending for All Purposes: Proportion Spent by Each Level of Government, Selected Years

	Federal	State/Provincial	Local
1938			
Canada	34	36	30
United States	44	16	40
1948			
Canada	55	25	22
United States	62	13	25
1962			
Canada	47	25	27
United States	58	14	28
1971			
Canada	41	34	25
United States	54	18	28
1974			
Canada	45	33	22
United States	53	18	28

Sources: Canada: 1938, 1948, and 1962: Richard Bird, *The Growth of Government Spending in Canada* (Toronto: Canadian Tax Foundation, 1970), table 1; 1971 and 1974: Canadian Federation of Mayors and Municipalities, *Puppets on a Shoestring* (Ottawa, 1976), table 3. Federal and provincial transfers are credited to the receiving government. Excludes Canada Pension Plan/Quebec Pension Plan.

United States: 1938, 1948, and 1962: Frederick Mosher and Orville Poland, *The Costs of American Governments* (New York: Dodd, Mead, 1964), table 3–2; 1971 and 1974: U.S., Bureau of the Census, *Statistical Abstract of the United States: 1977*, table 455. Figures include social insurance. General revenue-sharing expenditures are credited to the level of government that actually uses the money.

Canada. The hegemony of the provinces is at the expense not only of local but of federal government. The U.S. federal government expanded its role in World War II, and since then it has kept responsibility for more than half of expenditures by all levels of government. The Canadian federal government also expanded during the war, but by the 1960s its share of total spending had dropped below half. The ascendancy of the provinces is well illustrated in the sharing of federal revenues. In the United States the demands of the localities and states resulted in the 1972 enactment of general revenue sharing by the federal government, whereas Canada has had such sharing since World War II, and on a smaller scale ever since Confederation. Moreover much more revenue is shared in Canada than in the United States—6 percent of the Canadian federal budget and 2 percent of the U.S. budget (1978). The U.S. federal government shares as much as two-thirds of these funds with local governments, whereas local governments in Canada receive only negligible amounts from the Canadian federal government. Canadian local officials discuss the consequences of this balance in a 1976 report aptly titled *Puppets on a Shoestring*.[74] Another significant difference between Canadian and U.S. federal revenue sharing is that Canadian "equalization payments" are far more redistributive. U.S. sharing guarantees funds to every state, no matter how prosperous and assures that no locality will get less than 20 percent of the per capita state average. Thus even Beverly Hills and other rich communities receive federal funds. In contrast, Ontario, Alberta, and British Columbia are considered "have" provinces and receive no payments at all.[75]

In a federal system the degree of diversity shapes the very issues in social policy debates. Efforts to enforce nationwide standards are greater in the United States partly because the states vary more in their goals than do the provinces. The greater similarity among the provinces in the level of welfare benefits was not imposed by the federal government; instead it was the voluntary product of similar outlooks by each government. Yet if provincial philosophies have converged to some extent, economic conditions in Canada are probably even more varied than they are in the United States. Whereas large states like California and New York share poverty problems of similar magnitude, Canada's biggest provinces are not as alike in this respect. In proportion to their populations, Quebec has more welfare recipients than the national average, while Ontario has fewer.⁷⁶ This cleavage helped produce different provincial stances toward major expansions in federal aid to the poor.

The concrete problems of welfare policy do not alone shape Canadian and U.S. debates. Even if policymakers agreed on the substance of needed policies, they could disagree on which level of government should be responsible for the solution. In Canada's deadly serious intergovernmental relations, federal and provincial conflicts over jurisdiction are far stronger than in the United States. While the states have often called for outright federal takeover of welfare functions, the provinces have long sought to weaken the already weak restrictions on how they spend federal aid. Passage and even discussion of national welfare policies are much more difficult in Canada. And even if Canada's brand of federalism did not erect special barriers to the emergence of a nationwide welfare backlash, the internal structure of government would discourage that. At both the provincial and the federal levels responsibility for social policymaking is more centralized than in the United States, allowing elites to chart a long-range course in expanding welfare programs. In contrast, the U.S. political system fosters a more disjointed "inductive" environment in which elites are divided and are more responsive to public attacks on the welfare system. The difference in policymaking, I argue, is rooted not in fundamentally different public values but in structural differences. Issues must be filtered through institutions.

2
The Background of Poverty Policy in Canada and the United States

During most of Canadian and U.S. history care of the poor was not a federal responsibility. Decades after European countries had national policies for public assistance, social insurance, and universal services, the federal governments of Canada and the United States in the second quarter of this century began to move into this sphere. Although social policy in the two countries by the mid 1960s bore some striking similarities, the patterns of its development differed markedly. The U.S. welfare universe began with a "big bang," while the Canadian universe developed by a "steady state" of continual growth. In one year, 1935, the United States adopted a wide range of federal assistance and insurance programs, and then it rested. Canada never had such a comprehensive period of change, but over the years the federal role has expanded into a wide range of income maintenance policies.[1] Whereas U.S. cash welfare policy never outgrew the "categorical" cost-sharing framework impressed on it in 1935, Canadian policy steadily allowed for federal sharing of aid to ever broader ranges of recipients.

Beginnings

In the nineteenth century and before, care of the poor was not the responsibility of the national government or even of the state, provincial, or colonial governments; it was a function reserved for local government, private charity, and, in Quebec, for the Roman Catholic church.[2] The legal claims of the poor for assistance were considerably weaker in North America than they were in Europe. At the 1792 founding of Upper Canada (later to become Ontario), English laws were copied freely, but the English Poor Law's insistence on government responsibility to the poor was specifically rejected. Only the Atlantic provinces accepted this tradition. States in the United States rejected it out of hand. Thus the poor in North America have had "no enforceable recourse to government to have their needs met, even for the most basic necessities of life."[3] Those receiving benefits were often required to have lived in an area for some time or even to have owned property there. Only when an individual fell between jurisdictions would a state legislature or provincial government appropriate relief funds. Local aid was usually ad hoc, being reserved for emergencies such as a depression, a hard winter, a flood, an illness. Worrying that the poor would spend cash unwisely, local officials often gave in-kind aid such as fuel, food, clothing, or medicine.

Background of Poverty Policy

Aid to the poor remained a local responsibility in Canada and the United States until well into the twentieth century. Whereas the United Kingdom in 1834 passed the nationwide Poor Law Act consolidating thousands of parishes into districts, not for a century did Canada or the United States pass national legislation on aid to the poor, and the states and provinces themselves made few steps toward consolidation and centralization of such aid. State and provincial legislators attempted to emulate the English concept of "indoor relief," although poorhouses were never as widespread in North America as they were across the Atlantic. At first such aid was based on the inability of some people to care for themselves, even with the help of local cash or in-kind "outdoor relief." Handicaps and misfortunes such as retardation, insanity, illness, disability, unemployment, widowhood, and orphanhood, which today receive differential status and treatment, were in those days significant mainly because they reduced the victim to helpless poverty. These victims were housed together in a "general, mixed" poorhouse. The campaign to provide special state or provincial institutions for the deaf, blind, retarded, mentally ill, for abandoned and orphaned children, and for others brought about the first large-scale aid from this level of government to those considered poor.[4]

State and provincial cash assistance programs began to develop after 1910. In the United States the progressive era produced much state legislation for social policy. Many states adopted programs for the aged and blind. The mother's aid movement swept the United States and spread to Canada. In 1911 Missouri and Illinois adopted the first state programs for mothers' aid. By 1912 twenty states had followed suit, and the Children's Bureau was established in the federal Department of Labor to spread the gospel further. By 1919 thirty-nine states had such legislation. In Canada, Manitoba was the first province to establish mothers' allowances, in 1916. Three years later the Department of National Health was founded at the federal level, with the Division of Child Welfare that spread the word about such legislation to the other provinces. By 1923 five of the nine provinces had mothers' allowances. In both countries provision was made mainly for widows and the disabled and in some cases excluded those who had been deserted or were not married. Many of these programs were optional for the municipalities that administered them and were not always in force. It was also during this period that the states and provinces began to adopt minimum wage laws, at first applying only to women and children. The first such laws were adopted in 1913 in the United States and in 1917 in Canada. A federal minimum wage was established with the U.S. Fair Labor Standards Act (1938) and the Canada Labour (Standards) Code (1965).[5]

Long before the states or the U.S. federal government got involved in cash welfare for the poor, they were giving means-tested pensions to war veterans. This movement began after the Civil War. Pensions were not as widespread after the Revolutionary War, the War of 1812, or the Mexican-American War. By 1910 all but six states had pension programs for Civil War veterans, and the federal government provided pensions for disabled veterans. Well into the twentieth century, veterans' benefits were the leading form of U.S. federal income maintenance. Still standing in Washington, D.C., is the huge Pension Building constructed in that era. After World War I, U.S. federal veterans' pensions were extended even to those poor who had been disabled after their wartime service. Benefits were also made available on a means-tested basis to the survivors and dependents of veterans, and the system has evolved into a major welfare program in its own right. Veterans' hospitals were founded in the 1920s, eventually expanding to include 7 percent of the current U.S. inpatient capacity. Veterans also receive many other benefits at the federal and state levels, including housing and educational assistance, social services, and preference in civil service hiring.

Canadian veterans' benefits began later, are not as extensive, and are retreating, unlike their counterparts in the United States. Canada has been in fewer wars and thus has fewer veterans. Moreover the Canadian political system is not as open to pressure like that exerted by the veterans' lobby. The first Canadian federal benefits came in the 1880s and after World War I, providing land to returning servicemen (a benefit that was terminated in 1975) and pensions to veterans or their survivors because of wartime disability or death (not because of disability unconnected to war). In 1930 means-tested allowances for these groups began, but it was not until 1975 that the allowances were finally extended to children of veterans. Education, health, social services, and other benefits have not been as generous for veterans in Canada as in the United States. The health benefits in particular have declined since 1957, when national health insurance began. Whereas the U.S. veterans' hospital system is strong and even expanding, the Canadian health system for veterans is being dismantled, and control of the hospitals is being transferred to local hands. Compared with the United States, Canada offers few services specifically to veterans. Thus in 1972 the United States spent 2.7 percent of its federal budget on veterans' compensation and pensions alone (aside from services and health care), while Canada spent only 2.3 percent of its federal budget on veterans' aid of any kind.[6]

The original, now displaced inhabitants of North America are special targets of social policy in Canada and the United States. Although Indians represent less than 1 percent of the population of either country, they have a high incidence of poverty, especially the seven of ten that live on lands reserved for them. Relative to the countries' populations, Canada had more Indians living on reserves in 1976 (210,000) than did the United States (543,000). In both countries the federal government provides a range of services as well as cash assistance. In Canada Indians are covered under the system of provincially administered national health insurance, while in the United States Indians on reservations receive free care in hospitals staffed and administered by the Department of Health, Education and Welfare. The Department of the Interior administers cash assistance, which in combination with state assistance reaches 28 percent of those on reservations. In Canada more than half of Indians residing on reserves receive social assistance administered by the Department of Indian and Northern Affairs.[7] Indians are also eligible for nationwide programs like Family Allowances, Old Age Security pensions, and Guaranteed Income Supplements.

The Federal Role in the United States

Much of current American welfare policy has roots in a single piece of legislation, the Social Security Act of 1935. This sweeping legislation was a product of upheaval, and it established precedents that strongly influenced future debates. Prior to the depression that began in 1930 the federal government had provided no funds for public assistance. Even when the depression hit, federal funds were not immediately made available. Municipalities attempted to accommodate their existing assistance programs to the new unemployed. After 1931 many states moved for the first time to help the localities with emergency relief spending. Three depression winters passed before the federal government became involved, and it did not do so until May 1933, when the New Deal Congress elected along with President Franklin D. Roosevelt created the Federal

Emergency Relief Administration (FERA). In two and a half years FERA distributed more than $3 billion, first in matching grants to the states and then free to states whose funds were exhausted. At the program's height in January 1935, 20.7 million citizens, or 16.3 percent of the population, were receiving emergency relief. In some states the proportion exceeded one-fifth. The relief rolls experienced frequent turnover, meaning that an even larger proportion of the population was on relief at one time or another. FERA technically funded only employable people; unemployables remained the responsibility of localities or states. Administration of the program varied widely, because localities usually disbursed the benefits. Federal regulations required eligibility to be determined by a home visit and monthly follow-up investigations. The problem of compliance was serious enough that FERA took over full control of distribution in six states.[8]

Federal emergency relief ended as abruptly as it had begun, replaced in the short term by public employment offered by the Works Progress Administration and related agencies. Founded in 1935, the WPA produced an average of about 2 million jobs in the years between 1935 and 1940.[9] For the longer term Roosevelt proposed that the federal government's role be limited to insuring people against the risks of old age and unemployment and providing grants to the states for public assistance. Roosevelt established the Committee on Economic Security to recommend a bill. The legislation that resulted is summarized in chart 2.1. It established the following programs: old age insurance, unemployment insurance, and cost-shared public assistance and social services for the aged and blind (the "adult categories") and for dependent children. The federal government would pay half the cost of the adult categories and one-third the cost of Aid to Dependent Children (ADC). The maximum shareable ADC payment was $18 per month for each child. In 1939 important amendments extended retirement insurance to survivors and dependents and improved the rate of federal matching for ADC. Future decades were to see the expansion of retirement insurance into a virtually universal system, but the delineation of federal responsibility for public assistance remained substantially unchanged for a quarter century. The only major changes were laws extending federal cost-sharing in 1950 for Aid to the Permanently and Totally Disabled (APTD), and in 1960 for aid to the medically indigent elderly (Kerr-Mills). Poor people not falling into the accepted categories were left to be aided through general assistance

Chart 2.1
Summary of Provisions of Social Security Act and Important Amendments

Title I
Grants to States for Old Age Assistance (1935)
Medical Assistance for the Aged (1956, 1960), superseded by Titles XVI, XVIII, and XIX

Title II
Federal Old Age, Survivors, and Disability Insurance Benefits (1935, 1939, 1956)

Title III
Grants to States for Unemployment Compensation Administration (1935)

Title IV
Grants to States for Aid to Dependent Children (1935)

Title X
Grants to States for Aid to the Blind (1935), superseded by Title XVI

Title XIV
Grants to States for Aid to the Permanently and Totally Disabled (1950), superseded by Title XVI

Title XVI
Supplemental Security Income for the Aged, Blind, and Disabled (1972)

Title XVIII
Health Insurance for the Aged (1965) and Disabled (1972) (Medicare)

Title XIX
Grants to States for Medical Assistance Programs (1965) (Medicaid)

Title XX
Grants to States for Social Services (1975)

programs funded by states and localities alone. Title IV of the Social Security Act provided aid to children "deprived of parental support or care by reason of the death, continued absence from the home, or physical or mental incapacity of a parent." Thus the program did not allow federal funds to be spent to help poor families with two able-bodied parents in the home, even if the father was unable to find a job or if he was employed but receiving wages too low to support his family. In the early years of the program, this exclusion did not hurt those families who received aid through the massive job-creation programs of the New Deal era. However, as these job programs were phased out, ADC was not correspondingly changed to make room for many families that had benefited from them.

Aid to Dependent Children was adopted at a time when most believed that a mother's place was in the home. Working mothers were not as common as they are today. An explicit rationale for the program was to allow mothers to remain home to care for their children. President Roosevelt had repeatedly argued that it was cheaper to maintain a mother in the home than to provide institutional care for her children. In general the issue was an invisible one. Aid to Dependent Children was the brainchild of officials working within the Committee on Economic Security (CES), which Roosevelt had appointed in 1934 to prepare proposals for an economic security act. A few participants advocated a broad definition of eligibility to include children of the working poor.[10] However, those drafting the bill avoided any controversial proposals for fear of drawing attention to this section of the social security bill. Congress was so absorbed by the provisions for old age assistance and retirement insurance that Title IV, Grants to States for Aid to Dependent Children, was hardly discussed. The executive director of the CES wrote later that "nothing would have been done on this subject if it had not been included in the report of the Committee on Economic Security."[11] Few in Congress saw the program as more than a way of aiding widows not covered under retirement insurance. Indeed, when old age insurance was extended to cover the survivors and dependents of participating workers in 1939, federal officials began predicting a decline in the AFDC rolls.[12]

The Social Security Act of the 1930s established the framework for the succeeding three decades of debate on income maintenance policy. Within this framework far greater progress was achieved in extending social insurance than in extending public assistance. The expansion of U.S. retirement insurance to cover new groups, new risks, and higher benefits is a classic example of the large impact that a series of incremental changes can have. Between 1950 and 1960 a series of steps brought participation in the program from only a fraction of the working population to virtually all of it. Also during this time benefits were continually increased, and coverage was extended to the permanently and totally disabled. In many other small ways the program was liberalized. However, none of these changes altered the dependence of the program for financing on the payroll tax. Indeed adoption of this mode of "self-financing" had been embraced in 1950 by supporters of the program as a means of protecting it from attack. During the 1940s the Old Age, Survivors, and Dependents Insurance system had not been fully accepted by the Congress.[13]

While in succeeding decades Congress vastly expanded on the 1935 old age insurance legislation, it did not similarly extend the law's provisions for public assistance. After 1935 the only major extensions of cash assistance were the 1950 addition of the permanently and totally disabled (APTD) as a new category and the 1961 extension of AFDC to families with an unemployed parent (AFDC-U), an optional reform that half of the states never implemented. The Truman administration failed in its 1950 attempt to persuade Congress to share in state costs for General Assistance and thus extend federal assistance to some families with two able-bodied parents.[14] Although Congress was unwilling to abandon the categorical approach, it made some incremental improvements within the AFDC program. In 1950 it readily approved administration proposals to give AFDC benefits to one parent in a family where the children were already receiving benefits. Congress also authorized "vendor payments" for the health bills of public assistance recipients. Along with the adult categories, it increased AFDC benefits in 1948, 1954, 1958, 1961, 1962, and so on, often over presidential objection.[15] In 1958 the federal share of AFDC spending was made to vary slightly according to a state's relative per capita income. Monthly benefits between $17 and $30 would be matched at a rate ranging from 50 percent for the most prosperous states to 65 percent for the poorest states. Federal matching for benefits above and below that range was not related to the wealth of a state. This minimally redistributive feature of AFDC has not basically changed in twenty years.

Gilbert Steiner points out that during the 1950s congressional policy toward AFDC had two faces. In addition to its permissive attitude, it exhibited a critical one aimed at cutting back on benefits to the undeserving poor. One unsuccessful crusade was that of Representative Winfield K. Denton (Democrat, Indiana) for a "runaway pappy" law that would make desertion a federal crime.[16] (As Chapter 8 shows, Denton was vindicated two decades later, beyond his wildest dreams.) Although Congress did not pass Denton's proposal, it did in 1950 require that AFDC officials notify law enforcement authorities when desertion cases appeared on the welfare rolls. In 1951 the Jenner amendment allowed states to adopt laws opening their welfare rolls to public inspection. As of 1978 about thirty-two states had adopted such laws. However, HEW officials have interpreted the Jenner amendment to allow public access only to name, address, and the amount of assistance, not to confidential files. Moreover publication of the names and addresses of recipients is prohibited. Except for occasional flurries of interest, this access to the welfare rolls has rarely been exploited. One use has been by businesses unwilling to grant credit until shown that a poor person has access to government benefits. Significantly, however, most states that have taken advantage of the Jenner amendment have prohibited the release of any information on vendors (doctors, merchants, landlords, and so on) who receive payment for services to the poor.

Despite frequent expressions of concern over the growth in the AFDC program, Congress in the 1950s made few efforts to curtail its growth. Not until 1967 did it take strong measures. Prior to that time the major experiment in welfare reform was the Public Welfare Amendments of 1962. Major new grants became available for a broad range of family services aimed at motivating recipients to seek jobs. To emphasize the new family approach, the old name of Aid to Dependent Children was changed to Aid to Families with Dependent Children (AFDC). In addition to initiating a services strategy to help welfare recipients back to work, the 1962 legislation also made a start toward a benefit structure that did not discourage work. Until then, an AFDC recipient had real disincentives to seek work. Earnings usually resulted in a dollar-for-dollar reduction in benefits. The 1962 legislation provided that work-related expenses would be disregarded in calculating need. This provision later became controversial, as it allowed some families to disregard unreasonably high "work expenses" such as a luxury car.[17] In general, however, the 1962 AFDC legislation left many of the program's work disincentives intact. For example, even though states were now allowed under the Community Work and Training program to provide employable AFDC volunteers with work experience, the earnings under this program still resulted in a dollar-for-dollar reduction in welfare benefits. The same problem plagued the 1964 Work Experience and Training program. The absence of work incentives was especially poignant in the federal decision in 1961–1962 to allow states at their option to extend AFDC to unemployed parents (AFDC-U). Even though it was designed for people with a demonstrated ability to hold a job, AFDC-U reduced benefits in direct accordance with most earnings, and it disqualified anyone who worked more than one hundred hours a month.

The civil rights movement in its early years focused not simply on the destitute conditions of many minorities but on ending the discrimination that kept them from joining the economic and political system.[18] The methods refined in this movement helped produce the landmark Civil

Rights Act of 1964 and the Voting Rights Act of 1965; they also revolutionized social policymaking in the 1960s. Presidents John F. Kennedy and Lyndon B. Johnson helped focus the nation's attention on the poor, and Congress enacted a fusillade of ideas that had been only at the discussion stage for many years. Most important in this period was the Economic Opportunity Act (1964), which established the Job Corps, VISTA, and Community Action programs, to be administered by the new Office of Economic Opportunity (OEO) located in the Executive Office of the President. Programs passed in 1965 and 1966 that solely or partly aided the poor included regional development, especially Appalachian aid; expanded housing assistance, including Model Cities; Medicaid; and various education programs.

Although the new concern for poverty policy in the 1960s did not focus on income maintenance policy, the Food Stamp program became firmly established in this period. It became a major source of income for families and others who did not qualify for cash welfare but whose earnings left them in poverty. Food stamps are a form of aid peculiar to the United States. The recipient may spend them only on specified items; coupons must be used instead of cash, forcing the user to identify himself to others. Many recipients would prefer cash, but millions choose to participate anyway. Canadians are entitled to question the intrusive aspects of the program; many critics in the United States feel the same way. But an income supplementation program for this clientele might never have developed if cash rather than stamps were the benefit. Moreover, Canada has no program that comes anywhere near giving the benefits to some groups that food stamps provide.

The first major impact of food stamps on poverty came in the wake of 1964 legislation. Prior to that time a temporary program had existed from 1939 to 1943, under the authority of the Agricultural Adjustment Act of 1933. At its peak 4 million persons were able to use the stamps to buy foods designated as surplus. Particularly notable about this early program was that food stamps were available to all the poor, whether or not they were employable or had children. Food stamps were not limited to specific categories as was Aid to Families with Dependent Children. This universality has been a hallmark of food stamp programs ever since. In 1961 President Kennedy revived food stamps on a pilot basis, with no stipulation that surplus foods had to be purchased. In 1964, at the behest of President Johnson, Congress passed the major new Food Stamp Act.

Food stamps were sold to the poor at a generous discount based on their ability to pay, although even the poorest were subject to a purchase requirement until the 1970s. Communities administered the program at their own expense but bore no expense for the stamps themselves. Each community was able to choose between the Food Stamp program and the commodity distribution program, which provided specified surplus items and had no purchase requirement. As the Food Stamp program grew, its emphasis shifted from reduction of farm surpluses to aiding the poor—"the famished rather than the farmer."[19]

In view of the historic shift of food stamps from serving agricultural to social goals, it may seem surprising that the program continues to be administered by the Department of Agriculture. This arrangement reflects the logrolling that has sustained the program for more than a decade. For example, Representative Leonor Sullivan (Democrat, Missouri) masterminded a 1967 effort by food stamp supporters to overcome the opposition of the House Agriculture Committee to a two-year extension of the program. She organized a coalition that threatened to defeat a farm bill unless its supporters befriended food stamps.[20] In later years Agriculture Committees showed that two could play that game and consciously began to hold the Food Stamp program hostage to obtain support for farm programs from its urban supporters.[21]

Though the distribution of food stamps increased rapidly in communities that had the program, many communities were slow to adopt it. It was not until 1969 that the federal government began to share even half of the cost of administration. As late as 1968 only a third of the nation's counties were in the Food Stamp program. Some preferred to participate in the commodity distribution program, which because it had no purchase requirement was generally more accessible to the desperately poor. Between 1961 and 1968 communities switching from commodity distribution to food stamps experienced an average drop of 40 percent in the number of beneficiaries.[22] Some communities participated in neither program.

The Federal Role in Canada

Whereas the U.S. federal role in income maintenance arose in the 1930s within a relatively short time, the Canadian federal role developed gradually over forty years. The major steps are shown in chart 2.2. The first

Chart 2.2
Important Milestones in Canadian Income Maintenance Policy

1927
Old Age Pensions Act (means test)

1940
Unemployment Insurance Act (social insurance)

1944
Family Allowances Act (demogrant)

1951
Old Age Security Act (demogrant)
Old Age Assistance Act (means test)
Blind Persons Act (means test)

1954
Disabled Persons Act (means test)

1956
Unemployment Assistance Act (means test)

1957
Hospital Insurance and Diagnostic Services Act (universal)

1964
Youth Allowances Act (demogrant)

1965
Canada Pension Plan (social insurance)

1966
Guaranteed Income Supplements (income test)
Canada Assistance Plan (needs test with asset limitations)
Medical Care Act (universal)

1971
Unemployment Insurance expanded (social insurance)

1973
Family Allowances modified and made taxable

1975
Spouse Allowance added to Guaranteed Income Supplement (income test)

1978
Child Tax Credit (income test)

major federal step in Canada actually preceded the U.S. initiative by nearly eight years. A 1927 federal program shared costs with the provinces for means-tested assistance ("pensions") for those over age seventy (extended in 1957 to persons over forty). Liberal prime minister W. L. MacKenzie King supported the measure in exchange for needed parliamentary support from Progressive legislators.[23] Canada adopted this program in a time of relative prosperity, whereas the U.S. federal role in old age security did not begin until the country was hit by depression. Yet when the Great Depression hit both countries, federal social policy expanded dramatically in the United States, while in Canada it did not expand as much. Whereas U.S. emergency grants to the states eventually gave way to a permanent set of social programs, Canada relied on annual relief acts between 1930 and 1940. These grants varied according to the degree of emergency in each province.[24]

In 1935 Conservative prime minister R. B. Bennett attempted to replace the yearly relief acts with a permanent program of social policies emulating Roosevelt's New Deal. On the eve of the parliamentary elections Bennett's parliamentary majority actually enacted an impressive program of unemployment, old age, and health insurance, cost-shared social assistance and public works, and measures to help people with mortgages and to help farmers obtain higher prices. This "deathbed conversion" of the government did not help at the polls, where it lost power a few months later to King's Liberals.[25] In 1937 all three of Bennett's landmark measures were invalidated by the Judicial Committee of the Privy Council, an imperial body located in London England, that for decades had interpreted the Canadian constitution to prohibit the federal government from infringing on many areas traditionally reserved for the provinces. Ontario, Quebec, and New Brunswick had brought suit objecting to the federal government's role in compelling contributions from individuals. Whereas a storm of criticism eventually helped convince the U.S. Supreme Court to reverse its decisions blocking social legislation, the Judicial Committee's veto was allowed to stand in Canada, with comparatively little public outcry.[26]

The 1940s and 1950s saw a wide range of income maintenance policies adopted in Canada. In the face of the unconstitutionality of the Bennett "New Deal," Prime Minister King successfully sought agreement from the provinces to a constitutional amendment authorizing a nationwide system of unemployment insurance. Unlike the state-federal U.S. program, the Canadian system was administered and funded entirely by the federal government. The first benefits were paid in 1942. At this time the federal government did not expand its role in old age security, nor did it begin to share in provincial social assistance costs. It did propose such changes, along with national health insurance, in the 1945 Green Books, but the provinces were put off by the accompanying proposal that the federal government receive exclusive jurisdiction over income and inheritance taxes. Activity in Canadian social policy shifted to "demogrant" programs, where there were fewer political objections that could be expressed in constitutional terms. In 1944 Canada took a step toward helping poor families by adopting the European innovation of universal family allowances, providing after 1949 at least $60 a year tax free for every child under sixteen attending school. The demogrant approach was extended in 1951, when an amendment to the BNA Act authorized federal pensions to people over seventy. The blind and those sixty-five to seventy years old were made eligible for means-tested public assistance administered by the provinces, with the cost shared by the federal government. In 1954 an additional "categorical" means-tested program aided the disabled.

Not until 1956 did Canada adopt a federal program specifically to share the cost of means-tested assistance to able-bodied people. Before that time, only Family Allowances and Unemployment Insurance provided any federal help to such people. The absence of federal sharing for many social assistance cases increased the pressure on Unemployment Insurance, and in 1950 this program was changed specifically to help some workers whose employment ran out during the winter and who under the previous rules would have exhausted their benefits.[27] Finally in 1956 the federal government adopted the Unemployment Assistance Act, under which it would share half of the cost of social assistance to a wide range of recipients. The federal government formally agreed to assist only those people who could work, and the provinces agreed to pay the full bill for unemployables—a number set arbitrarily at 0.45 percent of each province's population (this being the percentage estimated to be unemployable). Then 1957 legislation removed this limitation, expanding the potential reservoir of recipients eligible for federal cost sharing. Though aid to mother-headed families was still not shareable, beneficiaries included "persons and their dependents who cannot qualify for any other forms of aid" and "persons whose benefits under other programs are not considered adequate." Thus the federal government was sharing the cost of general assistance to groups that in the United States have been aided entirely at state expense.[28]

During the late 1950s and early 1960s it was health policy that experienced the greatest growth in Canada. Compulsory provincial hospital insurance programs had been spreading since the 1940s, and in 1957 the federal government began to pay half of the cost of universal hospital coverage. In 1964 a royal commission appointed in 1960 by Prime Minister John Diefenbaker proposed a comprehensive tax-financed program of coverage for most other health needs. Despite some resistance from doctors, Canadian Medicare passed easily in 1966. Although some provinces charge premiums for this coverage, in no case do these charges cover the total cost of health services provided. Canadian health "insurance" is really not insurance, but a massive in-kind demogrant program. The poor in Canada, unlike those in the United States, are guaranteed basic medical care on the same basis as most others in society. The hospital insurance and Medicare schemes do not cover some health needs such as dental care, drugs, and eyeglasses, where welfare beneficiaries still depend on means-tested benefits.

During the 1960s Canadian social policy was transformed by the conjunction of two major forces: a provincial drive to gain from the federal government more control over social policy and a crusade against poverty at both levels. The more vital force was the attack by Quebec and the other large provinces on the federal system of conditional grants. Under Union Nationale premier Maurice Duplessis, Quebec had refused even to participate in the hospital insurance program; and beginning in 1960 under Liberal premier Jean Lesage, it fought to force the federal government to replace the conditional grant programs with block grants and a transfer of taxing powers. In the 1963 campaign the federal liberals promised Quebec voters to allow the province to "opt out" of existing shared-cost programs, and in 1965 this alternative was made possible by the Established Programs (Interim Arrangements) Act. Provinces specifically could opt out of social assistance, hospital insurance, and several other programs. Only Quebec took advantage of this opportunity. While other provinces were slow to share Quebec's desire for formal detachment from federal social programs, many agreed that their flexibility was constrained by the existing system of categorical social assistance grants for the aged, disabled, blind, and the "unemployed." This pressure led in 1966 to the consolidation of federal aid for social assistance into a single program, the Canada Assistance Plan (CAP), with Quebec opting out of the fiscal arrangements. This legislation established for the first time a major federal role in sharing the cost of conditional aid to mother-headed families as well as in sharing the cost of social services and of health care not covered by national health insurance.

Under the CAP legislation the provinces were to administer funds to "persons in need," defined as "a person who, by reason of inability to obtain employment, loss of the principal family provider, illness, disability, age or other cause of any kind acceptable to the provincial authority, is found to be unable . . . to provide for himself, or for himself and his dependents. . . ."[29] It was understood that mother-headed families were included among the program's beneficiaries, allowing the addition of two hundred thousand such families who had previously been excluded from the Unemployment Assistance program.[30] CAP, like the Unemployment Assistance program it replaced, technically made aid available to able-bodied people unable to obtain enough employment income; the potential beneficiaries included both families and people without children. Despite this potential, it was not until the 1970s that the provinces made much effort to help such groups, and even then they were such a small fraction of the case load that federal policymakers sought new ways to channel aid to more of them. One reason that CAP did not dramatically transform the social assistance case load was that municipalities administered such aid in several provinces. Only in New Brunswick, Newfoundland, Prince Edward Island, and the two territories was social assistance fully centralized provincially. Provincial authorities controlled administration in Saskatchewan and Quebec with certain exceptions, the most notable being Montreal. The other provinces administered social assistance only to certain beneficiaries, usually including the aged and some mother-headed families; the municipalities were in charge of short-term or residual recipients. Municipalities received federal funds passed through the province as well as some provincial assistance but raised the rest themselves. That the municipalities were picking up some of the tab subtly discouraged some provincial governments from proposing national policies that would lodge more social assistance responsibility at the provincial level.

The federal government promised in CAP to match, dollar for dollar, provincial spending benefits and administrative expenses. Before the bill was introduced in Parliament, the poorer Atlantic provinces attempted to raise the issue that an across-the-board percentage in cost sharing would hurt them, because they had proportionately fewer revenues and more poor people. Though officials of the Department of National Health and Welfare were sympathetic to this plea, it was successfully resisted by the richer provinces and the federal Department of Finance.[31] While AFDC only slightly tailors federal matching to fiscal capacity, CAP does not do so at all. As a result, a poor province like Newfoundland, with the fourth largest case load of any province, spent in an early year of CAP (1968) more than 10 percent of its revenues on social assistance, while Ontario spent only 4 percent. Quebec, with a smaller population than Ontario but a larger case load, had to spend 7 percent.[32] These disparities are of course corrected somewhat by federal revenue sharing that far more than in the United States redistributes revenues based on fiscal capacity.

The CAP legislation laid down conditions on federal cost sharing, and these conditions were formalized in individual memorandums of agreement signed jointly by the federal minister of national health and welfare and each provincial minister of welfare. Among the federal conditions were that no residence requirement be imposed; appeals procedures be adopted and publicized; and each person's "budgetary requirements" be considered in determining his grant.[33] The last provision, called a needs test, was strongly emphasized by the government in Parliament as replacing the demeaning means test. However, a government minister confessed in debate that CAP "does contain an element of the means test."[34] Federal CAP administrators have understood the law to require each province to consider at least one variable measure of need in determining benefits, a contrast to the U.S. trend toward standard intrastate benefits under AFDC. While this question has been a matter for federal-provincial consultation, the greatest degree of such contact has been not in cash assistance but in CAP's provisions for social services intended for the poor. The federal-provincial agreements list the homes for special care and other agencies that are shareable. This listing process is an occasion for negotiation and has prompted some provinces to suspect that others are receiving federal aid for institutions that are not eligible elsewhere.

Quebec removed itself somewhat from the CAP cost-sharing process by contracting out. Instead of a check from federal welfare officials, the province would receive additional taxing powers and a balancing check from (or would pay a balancing amount to) the federal finance department. Claude Morin is basically correct in arguing that in contracting out of CAP, the province did not win much greater control over the program than was available within it.[35] The 50 percent matching, the federal conditions, and the process of listing all apply to Quebec just as they do to the other provinces. Morin did not mention, however, that the change in the way Ottawa shared the cost was profitable for Quebec. The other provinces receive full reimbursement only after federal authorities have ascertained which of their payments were not in compliance with CAP regulations. In contrast, Quebec by receiving part of its share of federal aid in the form of taxes has the money before it is spent. Thus when the auditors eventually determine which of Quebec's claims are not shareable, the money is withheld from current payments, but the province has had the unique advantage of drawing interest on it all that time. This profit is increased by the length of the audit process. In June 1978 federal and provincial authorities had just completed reconciliation of the budget for 1974!

At the same time that the Canada Assistance Plan emerged, Canada was debating a wide range of other policies. The most important was a contributory old age pension plan to supplement the Old Age Security demogrants. Quebec had objected to 1963 federal proposals that would not have allowed the rapid accumulation of reserves. The province insisted that the contributions of Quebec citizens should produce a Deposit and Investment Fund for economic development. For different reasons, Ontario also opposed the pay-as-you-go approach. Because provinces could withhold approval from the essential constitutional amendment, the federal government yielded.[36] Pressure from Quebec also encouraged Ottawa to expand the plans to include benefits for survivors and the disabled. As a result, Canadians in Quebec are covered by the Quebec Pension Plan, run entirely by the province, and Canadians in the rest of Canada are covered by the federally administered Canada Pension Plan, whose funds are available for investment by the other provinces.

The need for rapid accumulation of reserves prevented these plans from extending coverage to those already past retirement age or from offering adequate benefits to those who had contributed for only a few years. To care for these groups, the federal government enacted in 1966 the Guaranteed Income Supplement program, which provided the aged an income 40 percent higher than the amount provided by the existing Old Age Security pensions. In order to encourage saving, the program allowed recipients to keep 50 cents of each dollar in pensions, unearned income, or earnings. Although the work incentives afforded by this provision were not a major reason for its adoption, it was the country's first nationwide adoption of such incentives in a conditional program. No such nationwide benefit structure was adopted under CAP, but under that program the federal government was always willing to share the additional cost of benefits if a province wished to allow recipients to keep a portion of their earnings. Unfortunately, the provinces were slow to take advantage of this opportunity. Whereas 1967 U.S. legislation allowed AFDC recipients to keep the first $30 in earnings and a third of the rest, only a few provinces at this time exempted much in initial earnings, and beyond this exemption they all reduced benefits by an amount equal to earnings. Only in the 1970s did the provinces begin to adopt policies that as a matter of principle allowed recipients to keep a portion of what they could earn from employment.

The major Canadian initiatives in social policy were not all embroiled in federal provincial politics as were CAP and the pension programs. By 1964 the Pearson Liberal government was putting together Canada's own war on poverty, and a number of other programs were considered that would also help fight poverty, even if they were not seen primarily as poverty programs.[37] Measures that passed included area redevelopment (1963 and later years), Youth Allowances (1964, except in Quebec, which already had them), urban renewal and public housing (1964–1965), the Company of Young Canadians (1966, community action program), Medicare (1966), Adult Occupational Training (1967), the Local Initiatives Program (1971), and Opportunities for Youth (1971). A new federal manpower department was established in 1967. Canada's war on poverty did not produce as many programs as did its U.S. counterpart, but it continued to attract attention and produce legislation while the United States shifted from the war on poverty to the war in Vietnam. Moreover Canada did not limit itself to a services strategy but also expanded its income maintenance system. CAP in the United States was the Community Action Program; in Canada it was the Canada Assistance Plan. Both the United States and Canada eventually debated proposals for expansion of welfare into a guaranteed income, but the preludes to these proposals differed greatly. In the late 1960s the United States was preoccupied with trying to stem growth and abuse of public assistance. President Nixon presented his guaranteed income proposals as "welfare reform." In contrast, the idea of a guaranteed income was widely discussed in Canada between 1966 and 1970. The government proposals made there in 1970 and in 1973 reflected a basic continuity in Canadian efforts to relieve poverty.

Definitions of Poverty

After decades of new programs and after some years of explicit efforts to eliminate poverty, what has changed? The relative distribution of income has scarcely changed in either country, but the absolute level of poverty has fallen. In both countries unequal distribution of income has persisted (recall table 1.4). Yet the poverty gap—the value of resources that would be needed to bring everyone above the poverty line—has narrowed. Between 1968 and 1972 Canada's poverty gap dropped by as much as 25 percent, while the U.S. poverty gap dropped by either 7 percent or 36 percent depending on which figures one chooses.[38]

Because the relative figures on change in poverty are so much more discouraging than the absolute figures, it is not surprising that both Canada and the United States have tended to define poverty by absolute measures. In contrast, European concepts of inequality tend to be more relative, based on the difference between a person's income and the prevalent standard of living. Most European countries do not even define the poverty line.[39] North American governments, on the other hand, have adopted lines based on the cost of certain basic necessities. This idea says a family is poor if it must spend more than a certain proportion of its income on such necessities.

In 1963 a specialist in the U.S. Social Security Administration developed a "market basket" approach: a poor family is one that must spend more than one-third of its income on the price of food comprising a "minimum adequacy" diet. The Council of Economic Advisors adopted this standard in its 1964 *Economic Report of the President*. The Social Security Administration and the Office of Economic Opportunity together regularly updated this poverty guideline, and in 1969 the Office of Management and Budget made it the official basis for reports by the Bureau of the Census.[40] In 1965 a specialist in Statistics Canada developed a low-income measure based on expenditures not only for food, but for clothing, and shelter. This line was drawn at the point where a family's income is low enough that it spends 70 percent or more on these necessities.[41] From the beginning, the Canadian low-income cutoff was somewhat higher than the U.S. poverty guideline; projected back to 1961 for a family of four, the levels were $3500 for Canada and $3054 for the United States. To some extent, the cross-national difference is attributable to the greater need for protection against the Canadian winter. But the difference goes deeper than that, and it was widened considerably in 1974 with a major revision of the Canadian cutoffs. Taking note of evidence that necessities were taking a smaller proportion of all families' incomes, Statistics Canada decided to label a family as low income if it spent more than 62 percent of its income on the major necessities. Thus in 1976 the low-income cutoff of an urban family of four was $8478 in Canada, while in the United States it was only $5674.[42] Because of this great disparity, comparisons that follow use a U.S. level that is 150 percent of the official standard. This practice has become increasingly common because the U.S. poverty line has not been keeping up with increases in consumption by nonpoor families.[43]

The absolute character of low-income lines in the United States and Canada has tended to keep these lines behind general trends of rising income as well as below popular conceptions of the resources needed to live comfortably. For many years pollsters have asked the public how much a family needs to "get along in this community." The answers are strikingly similar in the two countries. At the same time Lee Rainwater has pointed out that these levels have consistently exceeded most popular and government definitions of poverty.[44] Thus, as table 2.1 shows, the poverty line identified by the U.S. government has consistently stayed at about three-fifths of the amount the public feels necessary to "get along." In Canada the proportion is four-fifths—still lower than the public's standard, but closer to it.

Not only do government poverty lines fall short of public estimates of need, but actual welfare benefits in turn fall below the poverty lines. Table 1.5 showed that the unweighted average of welfare assistance to a family of four in 1974 was $4041 in the provinces and $4054 in the states. Though similar in absolute terms, these amounts differ in their relation to each country's poverty line. The U.S. benefits are four-fifths of the poverty line, while the Canadian benefits are less than three-fifths of the higher Canadian low-income cutoff. (When a U.S. line that is 150 percent of the standard line is used, benefits in the U.S. also amount to less than three-fifths of that poverty line.) In 1974 all provinces normally paid benefits that were less than the low-income cutoff, and only four states paid benefits that exceeded the lower U.S. poverty line.

Just as welfare payments do not bring a person above the poverty level, neither, depending on the size of his family, does the minimum wage. In 1974 the U.S. minimum wage was $2.00; in Canada the unweighted

Background of Poverty Policy

Table 2.1
Popular and Governmental Views of the Needs of a Family of Four

Year	Public's View of Amount Needed to "Get Along" (1)		Poverty Line (2)		Ratio of Columns 1 and 2	
	Canada	United States	Canada	United States	Canada	United States
1967	$5,200	$5,252	$4,060	$3,410	0.78	0.65
1969	6,500	6,250	4,420	3,743	0.68	0.60
1973	7,600	7,750	5,295	4,540	0.78	0.57
1976	10,400	9,200	8,478	5,659	0.82	0.62
1978	10,400	10,452	9,976	6,367	0.96	0.61

Sources: Column 1: Canadian Institute of Public Opinion, "Family of Four Needs Minimum Two Hundred Dollars per Week," *Gallup Report* (April 12, 1978). Question: "What is the smallest amount of money a family of four needs to get along in this community?" Canadian figures include both nonfarm and farm families, while U.S. figures include only nonfarm families.
Column 2: Statistics Canada, *Revised Low Income Series and Updated Low Income Series* (January 20, 1978); low-income cutoff is for a family of four residing in a city of population 100,000–500,000; Bureau of Census Official Poverty Threshold: 1967–1973, reported in "The Low Income Population: What We Know about It," in HEW, *1977 Welfare Reform Study*, paper no. 3 (April 6, 1977), table 3; 1976–1978, reported in Congressional Budget Office, *Welfare Reform: Issues, Objectives, and Approaches* (July 1977), table C-2. Figure is for nonfarm family, average of levels for male-headed and female-headed.

average of provincial minimums was $2.05.[45] A full year of work at the U.S. wage would yield $4160, $390 below the poverty line. Similar labor in Canada would yield $4264; even when this amount was supplemented by the average payment under Universal Family Allowances, it would yield $4880, more than $2000 below the low-income line.[46] Even with the highest minimum wage in the Western hemisphere, a full year's work in Quebec would not bring a family over the poverty cutoff.

The U.S. poverty line is more institutionalized than the Canadian low-income cutoffs. Even in the United States, however, the poverty line shares the field with the "standard budgets" published by the Department of Labor. In response to congressional request, the Bureau of Labor Statistics (BLS) began in 1946 to prepare estimates of living costs in large cities. By 1967 this practice had expanded to the publication of three different standards in the purchase of food, housing, transportation, medical care, and other items.[47] In 1977 the BLS "lower standard budget" was about

$9700 for a family of four, a little less than the amount the U.S. public felt was necessary to "get along." No Canadian agency has tried to compile standard budgets such as those by the U.S. Department of Labor, but Canada has no lack of alternatives to the Statistics Canada low-income cutoff. The most widely discussed was that proposed by the Special Senate Committee on Poverty. In its 1971 report the committee proposed a quite high 1969 level of $5000 for a family of four. In 1973 this figure was the equivalent of $7231, just the size of the revised Statistics Canada income cutoff. Dissenting staff members who resigned from service with the committee proposed their own relative poverty line, which was $6601 in 1973, ironically less than the Senate committee line. In 1973 the poverty line proposed by the Canadian Council on Social Development was $6358. For comparison, the revised Statistics Canada low-income cutoff was the equivalent of $6417 in 1973.[48]

If Canada has experienced more debate on the proper level for a poverty line, it has also produced more criticism of that line as a measure of poverty. Critics in both countries have pointed out that the notion ignores wealth, the presence or absence of which can make a great difference in the impact of low income. Moreover it makes no distinctions between those barely poor and those deepest in poverty and ignores families just above the line.[49] These fundamental criticisms have been more successful in Canada than in the United States. Experts and officials in Canada have tended more than their U.S. counterparts to focus on European-style relative measures of the distribution of income and wealth such as the Gini index, Lorenz curves, quintiles and deciles, and other dismal indicators.[50] Indeed, for this very legitimate reason, data specifically on changes in the population below the "poverty line" are less complete than in the United States.

The most successful criticisms of the U.S. poverty line have aimed not to abolish but to improve it. In particular, the Census Bureau's data have been criticized for ignoring in-kind transfers in calculating the number of people under the poverty line. Since the poverty line was first established, the United States has experienced an unprecedented expansion of such transfers, particularly food stamps, housing aid, and the biggest program of all, Medicaid. These programs add materially to the resources of the poor.[51] A fundamental difference between the United States and Canada lies in the distribution of health care. Canada's lack of in-kind welfare programs extends even to this major area, because poor people receive health benefits on the same basis as everyone else: national health insurance provides in-kind care to all, poor or not. In the United States, only the aged and the poor (along with veterans, the military, and Indians) receive government health coverage. Thus it would be misleading to count Medicaid as a benefit for the poor in the United States, because similar benefits are available in Canada without even being considered a poverty policy. There is no best way to deal with this problem. If medical benefits are omitted, then the figures show the United States to have artificially high poverty after transfers; but if medical benefits are included in the U.S. transfers, then the country seems to help out its poor far more than does Canada.

The Unevenness of Policy and the Powerlessness of the Poor

It is difficult to assemble comparative data on the effects of poverty spending in Canada and the United States. Reliable data on the poverty population before and after government help is taken into account have only recently become available in the United States. Official data of this before-and-after sort have never been compiled in Canada, although Health and Welfare Canada has begun an effort to do so. A major problem in Canada is that the Consumer Finance Survey by Statistics Canada, on which most data is based, does not adequately measure income received from government benefits. As a result, the survey overstates the actual poverty of some groups (a problem also present in U.S. census surveys). Yet because the survey counts some government benefits, it does not fully measure the extent of poverty that would exist without government transfers. This problem explains why table 2.2 does not provide before-and-after data for Canada, whereas table 2.3 does so for the United States. Purists may object that the U.S. data are also not ideal and that better are available. For example, a number of important revisions have been proposed in how to measure poverty in the United States.[52] However, when one is comparing countries, the best data are not always compatible. Statistical agencies and scholars in the two countries have their own ways of reporting data, and the comparison in these tables is the best that can be pieced together.

It is clear from tables 2.2 and 2.3 that the people most often poor are the aged, the mother-headed families, and unattached individuals. In both countries, more than half of the aged are poor before government

Table 2.2
Incidence of Income below the Canadian Low-Income Cutoff, 1975

	Proportion with an Income beneath the Cutoff
Mother-Headed Families	40%
Intact Families	9
Unattached Individuals	38
Individuals over 65	57

Source: Statistics Canada, *Income Distributions by Size in Canada, 1975* (July 1977), table 78.
Note: The 1975 low-income cutoff amounted to $7886 for a family of four living in a city with population 100,000–500,000. In-kind income is not counted in this survey. The survey attempts to count government benefits received, but does so very incompletely.

Table 2.3
Incidence of Income below 150 Percent of U.S. Poverty Level, 1976

	Before Transfers	After Transfers, before Medical Benefits	After Both Transfers and Medical Benefits
Mother-Headed Families	57%	41%	35%
Intact Families	20	11	10
Unattached Individuals	56	42	32
Individuals over 65	68	35	20

Source: Calculated from Congressional Budget Office, *Welfare Reform: Issues, Objectives, and Approaches* (July 1977) p. 121.
Note: Transfers include social insurance and cash and in-kind welfare benefits. Income is before taxes. One hundred and fifty percent of the poverty level amounted to $8511 for an urban family of four in 1976.

help is taken into account. The U.S. data show that transfers dramatically help this group, better than halving its poverty rate—a greater improvement than that for any other group. If accurate figures were available on the impact of public spending on the Canadian aged, they would probably be similar. Virtually all the aged poor in both societies receive some government benefits. This result is achieved mainly not through means-tested programs but through social insurance and universal programs. Government transfers help fewer mother-headed families than aged people escape from poverty. Somewhat fewer mother-headed families than aged people are poor in the first place, but more remain poor after benefits are taken into account. Even if the Canadian figures were corrected for the underreporting of benefits on the survey, probably one-third of all mother-headed families would be classified as poor after transfers are taken into account, a proportion similar to that in the United States. Benefits to this group are widespread, though not as universal as for the aged. In the United States about 83 percent of all poor female-headed families receive some government benefits. In Canada every family with children receives Family Allowances, and 60 percent of all mother-headed families receive needs-tested aid.[53]

Some other poor families receive little aid and are forced to depend on their inadequate earnings. Though sometimes called the working poor, this group is probably best termed the nonwelfare poor (because many welfare recipients work). Except for food stamps in the United States and the 1978 Canadian child tax credits, neither country has a national program offering aid to this group simply because they have no income. Of course, some aid is available to individuals who qualify for unemployment insurance or veterans' benefits, and some states and provinces routinely give welfare benefits to selected members of this group. But many poor people receive no government benefits at all. Especially neglected are childless couples and unattached individuals. In the United States fully 57 percent of this group received no benefits whatsoever in 1971.[54] But poor intact working families are nearly as unlucky, with 51 percent receiving no benefits. Although virtually all such families receive Family Allowances in Canada, the proportion receiving no other benefits seems to be about as high as it is in the United States.[55]

Data on poverty are usually expressed as the number of people who have low income on an annual basis. But an increasing body of evidence suggests that this period is too brief to measure some kinds of poverty and too long to measure other kinds.[56] Within any given year many people whose annual income exceeds the poverty line nevertheless experience a temporary lapse into poverty. From year to year the poor population shifts even more. A major U.S. survey has produced results of relevance to both U.S. and Canadian policy. In any single year one-fifth of the entire population falls below 150 percent of the U.S. poverty line. During a six-year period over one-third of the population falls below that line in at least one year.[57] Such results challenge the view that the poor constitute a permanent or welfare class and recall Joseph Schumpeter's definition of social class not as a stable grouping but as "a hotel or an omnibus, always full, but always of different people."[58] Only about one-fifth of U.S. welfare recipients in 1976 had received benefits constantly during the preceding nine years.[59] Similarly a 1970 survey of Canadian welfare recipients showed that less than half had received benefits for five years or more, while 11 percent had received benefits for the first time in 1970.[60] Such results will change the strategy of government in dealing with poverty. For example, the "transitory" poor have better education and work experience, and policy might better be aimed at helping them back to work rather than simply at giving them income support. At the same time, however, the new data emphasize the peculiar problems of the persistently poor. Data in both countries indicate that this group includes an even greater proportion of undereducated and inexperienced "multiproblem" families than the general poverty population. Female-headed families and blacks are disproportionately represented in the persistently poor population.[61]

By the late 1960s leaders in both Canada and the United States proposed to extend cash assistance to vast new groups of poverty-stricken people. Yet the prospective beneficiaries had little hand in bringing this measure to the agenda, nor were they very active in the ensuing (and unsuccessful) debates. The study of poverty politics must begin by recognizing the basic powerlessness of the poor. This observation seems challenged by the discovery that poverty is often transitory. Why the poor are weak was best argued by John Kenneth Galbraith, who eloquently showed how the historic spread of affluence had destroyed the political power of the dispossessed. Past advocates of the poor could count on support from the large majority of society that was actually poor; today their electoral rewards are small.[62] For example, in 1976 beneficiaries under CAP represented only 6.5 percent of the population in Canada, and AFDC beneficiaries only 4.6 percent in the U.S. Although this proportion was higher in some areas, recipients were still distinctly in the minority.[63] But given the newly discovered fluidity of the poverty population, perhaps poverty is a more pervasive political question than had been thought.

In unpublished research Alexander Keyssar has shown that spells of joblessness are much more widely experienced than the annual unemployment rate reveals. Keyssar argues that the risks of unemployment are so widely shared that they can foster a kind of working-class consciousness. But he also shows that the translation of this kinship into political power is discouraged by the special organizational disabilities and barriers that face the unemployed. A similar argument can be made about the poor. Since more than a third of the entire population has experienced poverty in the last six years, this group in theory constitutes a massive political base. Unfortunately, the problems of organizing the poor are nearly prohibitive. Moreover poverty imparts less sense of fellowship than does unemployment. The temptation of upward mobility and the cleavages between the persistent and the transitory poor encourage escapees to abandon their former peers. Despite the turnover, experience with poverty is not randomly distributed in society. If one-third of the population has experienced poverty, two-thirds has not. Of course, many within this secure majority might experience or have to plan against poverty were it not for social insurance, pension, and other programs that cover needs of retirement, sickness, disability, and unemployment. The beneficiaries of these programs do not imagine themselves to face the plight of the poor because programs aiding that minority are separated from the others. The removal from the public assistance rolls of the aged and other "respectable" groups politically isolates those left over. The social stigma of being poor is intensified by the disproportion of unpopular social pathologies that concentrate (or seem to) among welfare recipients: crime and juvenile delinquency, alcohol and drug abuse, illegitimacy, and family instability. This stigma is intensified by the greater likelihood of U.S. racial minorities to be poor, although chapter 7 shows that this fact probably does not cause much of a divergence in Canadian and U.S. attitudes toward the poor.

If poor people receive little sympathy from the rest of society, perhaps organization could change this situation. Two different functions of protest are to attract voluntary support by dramatizing the plight of the poor and to coerce society into granting demands by the threat of disruption.[64] Special barriers prevent other political alternatives. Every study ever done on this subject has shown that the poor do not campaign, petition officials, or engage in cooperative activity as much as other groups.[65] Alienation and defeatism, often rational, discourage collective action. Many poor people lack the experience and the resources to organize. They have been most responsive to activity that promises an immediate material benefit. While frequently successful, such protest is not self-sustaining, especially because organizations cannot restrict rewards to those willing to join the protest. Moreover protest activity is difficult to channel into larger political objectives. And while some organizations have succeeded in appealing to people on political and personal rather than material grounds, these successes have depended on extraordinary leadership that is all too scarce.[66]

Emblematic of the many barriers to effective organization by the poor is the unhappy history of efforts to organize at the national level. In both countries the strongest organizations lobbying for the poor have had virtually no poor members; rather they have been composed of social workers and others with a professional or political stake in poverty policy. In Canada the most ubiquitous lobby, the National Council of Welfare (NCW), is not an outside organization but an official federal advisory body (with some poor members). The first nationwide poverty organizations since the Great Depression were founded in 1966 in the United States and 1971 in Canada, and only the Canadian group survives. The National Welfare Rights Organization (NWRO) was based on local chapters, focusing on welfare recipients in large U.S. cities. The NWRO founder and executive director, George Wiley, was a savvy academic. Though Wiley played a highly visible role in the 1970–1972 debates on welfare reform, his organization was already disintegrating.[67] Today the United States has no true national poor people's organization. In Canada the National Anti-Poverty Organization (NAPO) is still very much alive. This confederation of eighteen hundred advocacy groups and cooperatives is held together by its tireless executive director, Marjorie Hartling, a former member of the NCW. Despite her efforts, NAPO might have gone the way of NWRO were it not for an annual sustaining grant from Health and Welfare Canada. Federal money also maintains the Canadian Council on Social Development, an umbrella group that lobbies and conducts research. In the United States federal grants support similar centers at the Institute for Research on Poverty (Madison, Wisconsin), the Urban Institute, the Brookings Institution, and the American Enterprise Institute (all in Washington, D.C.).

3
Welfare Reform and Guaranteed Income: The Emergence of Proposals

By 1970 both Canada and the United States had begun a series of major debates on extending cash welfare to intact working families. But the processes by which guaranteed income proposals reached the agenda differed markedly. In Canada the government initiative was preceded by several years of public discussion. In the United States, the proposals were surfaced by President Nixon, surprising nearly everyone outside his administration. The United States in the 1960s was a particularly unlikely place for the emergence of such proposals. In five different polls taken between 1965 and 1968, the U.S. public opposed guaranteed income proposals by amounts ranging from 53 percent to 67 percent.[1] Unfortunately no polls on this subject were taken in Canada during this period. However, there is little evidence of widespread public support for guaranteed income until political leaders themselves began to advance the idea. The idea simply did not arise in debates on the 1966 Canada Assistance Plan. But once guaranteed income had reached the Canadian agenda, public support for it exceeded that in the United States. After Nixon's proposals had died in Congress, the idea did not return to the U.S. political agenda for another five years. In Canada, on the other hand, the failure of guaranteed income proposals in 1972 almost immediately gave way to a flurry of new government activity. This difference was partly attributable to public opinion, but even more important was a constitutional dialogue between federal and provincial governments over social policy jurisdiction that gave a special boost to the guaranteed income.

The Welfare Crisis and the Appeal of Broadening Welfare

Canada and the United States differed in the ease and permanence with which guaranteed income proposals moved onto the agenda. The two countries also differed in the presentation and perception of these proposals, even though the substance of the proposals was basically similar. The case for broadening welfare can be made either on philosophical grounds of equity between the working poor and welfare recipients or on grounds of practicality that the working poor may otherwise be tempted to quit their jobs and go on welfare. While both arguments were used in each country, Canada favored the philosophical approach and the United States favored the practical approach. The U.S. proposals were pressed not as a way to extend needed welfare to new groups (though they were) but as a cure for the ills of the existing welfare system. In contrast, Canadian leaders presented the issue directly as one of extending welfare to new groups, and they underplayed the connection with reforming the welfare "mess." Welfare reform and guaranteed income are both such vague and subjective notions that it was possible for each country to choose one question and ignore the other, even though they were talking about similar concrete proposals.

U.S. politicians have desperately avoided identification with the issue of guaranteed income. Indeed in presenting his Family Assistance Plan to the country, President Nixon explicitly denied that the proposal's national income floor was an income guarantee, citing his plan's work requirement and arguing that a guaranteed income "would undermine the incentive to work."[2] In making this argument, Nixon chose to define the term extremely narrowly. By most standards his proposal *was* a guaranteed income. Of course, the idea of a guarantee can be construed narrowly enough to disqualify almost any proposal. One meaning might be that benefits go to everyone in a certain group regardless of need; examples are Canadian demogrants such as Family Allowances and Old Age Security pensions. Another sense of guarantee is to promise help to all poor people to reach a certain income floor. In this sense a guaranteed income plan is incomplete if it covers only a segment of the poor, such as the aged or families with children. But for those covered by such a plan, it is a real guarantee indeed. The principle is that anybody in that category will receive similar benefits. Even Aid to Families with Dependent Children, food stamps, and benefits that are cost-shared under the Canada Assistance Plan provide a kind of guaranteed income. While benefits vary from province to province and state to state, they usually do not vary within these jurisdictions. Efforts in the United States to reduce the interjurisdictional variation have wisely avoided terming the desired result a guaranteed income because public opinion would object to that term. But where U.S. proposals have characteristics of a guaranteed income, our analysis should use that term unashamedly.

Guaranteed income is not simply a way to extend welfare to people currently excluded; it is also a way to combat the current ills of the welfare system. Concern about the "welfare mess" was a leading political issue in the United States, and guaranteed income was a viable political issue only because it could serve as a vehicle for welfare reform. Canadian experts and officials did not have to sell the program solely on this basis. Indeed, although Canadian officials were aware that guaranteed income proposals would correct some of the defects of welfare, they were not as strongly motivated by this need as were their U.S. counterparts. This difference is intriguing given that Canada's welfare system faced problems nearly as serious as those in the U.S. system. Central features of the welfare mess are that it rewards families for breaking up and discourages recipients from working for a living.

A major problem of the welfare system in both Canada and the United States has been that it discourages recipients from working their way back to self-sufficiency. Important here is the marginal tax rate, which describes the severity with which welfare benefits are reduced in response to the next dollar of earned income. Without a favorable rate, earnings have less appeal. Moreover welfare dollars are worth more than earned dollars. For one thing, they are not taxable. Also, a person who chooses employment over welfare incurs opportunity costs of holding a job: leisure time lost and job-related expenses, risks, and worries gained. In calculating welfare benefits, each state and province disregards the first few dollars of earnings and allows for some work expenses. In the United States the work expenses exempted can be quite generous and can help improve work incentives. Calculation of marginal tax rates is complex and is not pursued here.[3] For illustrative purposes, discussions in this book focus on the initial earnings disregarded before benefits begin to drop and on the reduction rate—the formal rate at which earnings produce a drop in benefits.

The essence of a negative income tax is to reduce benefits at a rate of less than 100 percent of income earned. In both countries the first use of this concept was not to tempt employable people off the welfare rolls but to allow blind or aged people to supplement their government benefits with outside income. The first application in the United States was in 1960, when states were allowed (and after 1962 required) to disregard the first $85 and half of the additional earnings in figuring benefits under the Aid to the Blind program. A similar arrangement is now a part of Supplemental Security Income, which also includes the aged and disabled. In Canada the 1966 Guaranteed Income Supplement program reduced benefits to the aged by half of any increases in outside income; however, work incentives were not an explicit basis for this policy. Only later did either country extend negative income tax rates to many employable welfare recipients. The United States established a nationwide AFDC reduction rate of 67 percent (after $30 in monthly earnings were disre-

Appeal of Broadening Welfare

garded) in the 1967 Work Incentive (WIN) amendments. A number of states have been able to achieve significantly lower reduction rates by capitalizing on the payment of benefits considerably below their standard of need. Since benefits were so low to start with, these states could allow recipients to keep a large share of earnings before they reached the standard. As of 1976 Mississippi had an effective reduction rate of about 30 percent, and five states were under 50 percent.[4]

In Canada the provinces have been slower to adopt negative income tax rates, even though such rates were always allowed under CAP and did not require special legislation such as that passed in the United States in 1967. In the early 1970s Nova Scotia and Saskatchewan adopted reduction rates of 50 percent, and Ontario a rate of 75 percent. Unfortunately the improvement of work incentives for current beneficiaries has clearly in the United States, and apparently in Canada, created a new inequity between welfare beneficiaries and welfare applicants. Since the negative income tax rate is available only to recipients and not to applicants, the earned income above which an applicant is refused aid is actually lower than the combined benefits and earnings of some beneficiaries.[5]

A major boost for proponents of a pure negative income tax stems from its ability to "cash out" some of the in-kind benefits that reduce work incentives. These in-kind programs mean that the incentive to work away from welfare is actually worse than reflected in the reduction rate for the cash program alone.[6] In Canada recipients have access to legal aid, health benefits not covered by public insurance (for example, dental care and drugs), housing assistance, and a wide range of social services. Some provinces provide transportation, home repair, and other subsidies. In the United States cash welfare is supplemented by an even richer selection of in-kind benefits, including food stamps, Medicaid, housing assistance, legal aid, and social services. Even if these programs individually have favorable reduction rates, these rates pile onto one another until the cumulative marginal rate is rather high and in some cases above 100 percent. When the cumulative rate exceeds 100 percent, a welfare recipient actually experiences a net loss in real income as a result of increasing his earned income.

The point in a graph at which the marginal tax rate suddenly exceeds 100 percent is called a notch. The worst cause of notches in the United States is Medicaid. AFDC recipients are automatically eligible for the program, while many others are categorically excluded. Once a person leaves the welfare rolls, he completely loses access to this windfall. A milder notch occurs in the Food Stamp program. While food stamps are available to nonwelfare recipients on the basis of income, welfare recipients are automatically eligible, with no income limits. Canada has fewer notches because most health benefits are not income conditioned. But because Canada's cash programs themselves have high reduction rates, the problem of cumulated marginal rates is still a real one. In both countries a welfare recipient would be foolish to jeopardize his good fortune by working enough to be excluded from welfare entirely. Even if a good job is preferable to benefits, the recipient may wish not to leave the rolls because it would be difficult to get back on if the job did not work out. The welfare trap is perpetuated because a person in this position need not learn how to manage on his own.

The *principle* of the negative income tax is recommended by concern for work effort and by the problem of cumulative marginal tax rates of overlapping programs. A strong argument for extending *coverage* of such a system to people not already covered by welfare is that the current system is unfair to intact families and tempts them to break up. Cash welfare programs in both Canada and the United States often deny aid to a family if the father is present and able-bodied. The inequity between welfare beneficiaries and the nonwelfare poor is exacerbated by the fact that the welfare beneficiary pays no taxes on his government benefits. The result, as a 1972 U.S. study showed, was that AFDC and food stamps made it possible for a father to increase his family's income by an average of one-third to one-half by deserting. The average welfare family in New York City received a total income of $6088 in 1974, with considerably higher levels for large families.[7] Considering that U.S. federal income taxes started at an income of $6000 and Social Security taxes much earlier, many nonwelfare families were obviously worse off than the welfare poor. On the bases of fairness and of avoiding incentives for family breakup, these disparities make a strong case for extension of some welfare benefits to the nonwelfare poor.

However fair and profamily the extension of welfare to the nonwelfare poor is, inevitable questions arise about possible decline in work effort by these families. Adoption of negative income tax rates for people already on welfare can only encourage them to increase their work effort. But giving such benefits to new groups cannot conceivably increase their work effort and is almost certain to decrease it at least somewhat. The

Appeal of Broadening Welfare

major controversy over the issue has been whether this reduction in work effort is likely to be large or small. In four separate income maintenance experiments conducted throughout the United States, the average decline in work hours never exceeded 13 percent. And because many wives used the benefits to cut back on their part-time jobs, the average decline for husbands was not higher than 7 percent.[8] Of course the seriousness of this decline in work effort is in the eye of the beholder; for some observers even 13 percent is too much. These experiments have been criticized on a number of grounds; one criticism is that they do not test for the possible effects of a permanent program that is prevalent everywhere, possibly degrading the work ethic in the long run.[9] While this objection is difficult to counter, efforts have been made to saturate three towns: Dauphin, Manitoba, was treated this way in the Manitoba Basic Income Experiment, and Gary, Indiana, and Green Bay, Wisconsin, were saturated with housing allowances in other experiments.

In view of the difficulty of reconciling positive work incentives with the adequacy and cost of a negative income tax plan, policymakers and the public are often attracted to a more direct approach, the work requirement. Unfortunately, designing a workable work requirement is difficult. To require the able-bodied to work, jobs must be available. But there are not enough jobs, and many welfare recipients do not live near jobs or they lack the training for the available ones. The problem of training is serious. In the United States, 58 percent of all AFDC mothers have not completed high school, and 13 percent never got beyond the seventh grade. In Canada 87 percent of all heads of welfare households under the age of forty-five have not completed high school.[10] Any attempt to require work by many welfare recipients involves large government efforts at training and job creation, to say nothing of providing job-related necessities such as day care. These are expensive tasks—often more expensive than maintaining the client on welfare—and the resources allocated have always lagged far behind need. As a result of the limitations on the supply of jobs and training slots, work requirements have realistically been limited to the requirement that welfare recipients register for such opportunities and that they not refuse them if offered.[11]

The problems of the existing welfare system were prime reasons for the proposal of the U.S. Family Assistance Plan, and the Nixon administration emphasized this connection even more strongly in trying to sell the plan to the country. President Carter's Program for Better Jobs and Income was also conceived and presented in this spirit. In Canada the welfare crisis contributed to the federal proposals of 1970 and 1973 and was cited in their defense, but that issue played a secondary role. Rather, the substance of guaranteed income proposals was discussed more directly than ever occurred in the United States. Yet Canadian policymaking was ultimately shaped by a factor even stronger than concern about the welfare mess or the substance of the guaranteed income. The pressures of federal-provincial politics set major directions and limits for social policy debates.

Canada: Federalism and the Guaranteed Income

Implementation of the Canada Assistance Plan had hardly begun before political debate considered restructuring and expanding Canada's income maintenance system. Proposals for a guaranteed income sprang quickly to the agenda because they became the answer to independent and relentless trains of events: commitment by elites to the proposal and deadly serious constitutional debate. After 1974 these separate processes began to work at cross purposes, but between 1968 and 1973 they acted in conjunction to place guaranteed income squarely at the center of debate.

The dominating question in Canadian politics after 1968, as in the preceding five years, was federal-provincial relations and especially the division of power between Ottawa and Quebec City. The increasing focus of federal-provincial debate on social policy owed much to the growing feeling among the elites that CAP was not the final answer to poverty. The most prominent early expression of this view was in September 1968 with the *Fifth Annual Review* of the Economic Council of Canada. A powerful chapter analyzed Canadian poverty and suggested the need for new government policies. Surveying the U.S. War on Poverty, the report concluded that a balanced attack on poverty should include advances in income maintenance as well as in social services and manpower. It also warned that antipoverty efforts should not focus just on groups suffering an unusually high incidence of poverty; such an effort would "neglect unduly the very considerable group whose poverty problems are associated not with an absence of earnings, but with an insufficiency of earnings." Among the report's revelations was that fully two-thirds of poor families were employed at least part of the year. Such people were not receiving enough help from provincial assistance programs cost-shared under the Canada Assistance Plan, even though the legislation would allow such aid. The Economic Council suggested that the Canadian Senate establish a committee to study poverty and make recommendations.[12]

Barely two months after publication of the *Fifth Annual Review,* the Senate established the Special Committee on Poverty, chaired by David A. Croll, an Ontario Liberal. Croll had chaired the earlier Special Committee on Aging, whose 1966 report calling for a "guaranteed income program" for the aged had helped pave the way for the Guaranteed Income Supplements passed in that year.[13] Between 1968 and 1971 the new poverty committee began to publicize proposals for a guaranteed income for all. Eventually it held public hearings in every province, taking testimony from 810 witnesses and receiving 109 briefs. Senators also met with the poor in their homes and at evening gatherings. The committee's 1971 report decried government neglect and popular mythmaking, arguing that the poor were "neither morally flawed nor physically idle by nature." The committee proposed a massive guaranteed income system as "the major weapon in solving the poverty problem."[14] A negative income tax would completely replace demogrant programs such as Old Age Security pensions and Family Allowances. A critique of the demogrant programs was becoming widespread and had been foreshadowed in 1960 by an influential paper by Tom Kent, who argued for "more precisely effective measures" to aid the poor.[15] Pierre Trudeau put the point more directly with his 1968 remark, "No more of this free stuff."

Proposals for guaranteeing the poor an income gathered support from groups like the Canadian Association of Social Workers, the National Council of Welfare, the Canadian Council for Social Development (CCSD), and (by 1971) the new National Anti-Poverty Organization. At the urging of Reuben Baetz, executive director of the CCSD, the Progressive Conservative party flirted with the concept. In the 1968 election campaign, party leader Robert Stanfield promised to "establish a guaranteed annual income for all Canadians who cannot earn for themselves and who live below the poverty line."[16] Even businessmen listened patiently to talk of a guaranteed income. Baetz took his case to the 1969 convention of the Chamber of Commerce, where one business leader remarked: "My, how times have changed; you would never have heard this kind of talk even a few years ago."[17]

It was in this atmosphere of concern about poverty and the wastefulness of demogrants that the Liberal government (under the name of John Munro, minister of health and welfare) presented proposals for increased aid to the poor in its 1970 white paper, *Income Security for Canadians.* That the measure did not have top priority was suggested by the government's commitment of only $150 million in new money for the whole package. The white paper did not propose the consolidation of all existing income maintenance programs into a single guaranteed income scheme, but it did propose that the universal Family and Youth Allowances be converted into a selective guaranteed income program, the Family Income Security Plan (FISP). A bill was not actually introduced until September 1971, and it never passed. Another part of the white paper quickly passed, however: major changes in Old Age Security (OAS) pensions and Guaranteed Income Supplements (GIS). GIS was made permanent and increased to guarantee $3060 for a couple, in addition to the earnings allowed them under the program's work incentive provisions. To redirect funds currently being spent on OAS pensions, the white paper proposed to freeze them at $80 a month, no longer adjusting them for the cost of living and therefore making poor recipients more dependent on GIS, which was more inflation-proof. This legislation passed in December 1970.

While in 1970 white paper whittled away at Old Age Security pensions, it attempted a frontal assault on another demogrant program, Family Allowances. Existing benefits were inadequate and necessarily went to more well-to-do families than to poor ones. The government proposed that the allowances be doubled to $16 monthly per child but also for the first time be related to income and be made taxable. This "major antipoverty initiative" would finance itself entirely by terminating the benefits of well-to-do families and reclaiming some other benefits through the tax system.[18] There was a peculiar symmetry in Canada's proposal of a Family Income Security Plan at the very time that the United States was debating a Family Assistance Plan. Comparison reveals some important differences between the two proposals, however. While the U.S. FAP provided an annual federal payment of $1600 to a family of four, Canada's FISP provided only $384. Moreover, while FAP gave benefits on the basis of up to $3920 income for a family of four, FISP gave benefits to families with incomes up to $10,000. While only families with an income below $4500 a year (20 percent of the population) would get the full FISP amount, a family with income of $10,000 would still receive $5 a month for each child. Under FISP 70 percent of all families would continue to receive an allowance of some amount, while more than half would receive a higher benefit than before. Despite the breadth of the program, its constituency could not compare with that for the existing universal system, as later events proved.

While the FISP proposals languished, Parliament in 1971 passed a major new Unemployment Insurance Act, appreciably liberalizing benefits and eligibility. The Liberal minister of labor defended the proposal as having some features of the guaranteed income. The opposition attacked the measure as "welfare in disguise."[19] The vast growth of Unemployment Insurance after 1971 became a bitter political issue, affecting policy debates on other income maintenance programs.

In view of the ongoing crisis in federal-provincial relations, the federal FISP proposals were unrealistic. Here was a federal program that would avowedly make provincially administered social assistance "increasingly less important."[20] Moreover the 1970 proposals not only expected Quebec to alter its Schooling Allowances but also provided no satisfaction to the province in its desire for more control over federal Family Allowances. Passage of the Canada Assistance Plan in 1966 had maintained the conditional paradigm of past social programs and had not given the provinces any more control over federally administered programs. A wide range of different organizations and spokesmen in Quebec saw social policy as a special test of Canada's abilities to respect the province's need for autonomy. With the status quo considered unsatisfactory, the alternatives ranged from complete separation to Lesage's special status, where the province would be freed of federal conditions and could design its own policies with a combination of tax powers and equalization payments. At Quebec's insistence, preparations for a constitutional review began in 1967.

Fast-breaking events of the late 1960s lent special urgency to social policy discussions in the Constitutional Review of 1967–1972.[21] In 1966 the Lesage government was ousted by a Union Nationale government unafraid of hinting at separation. Unrest and violence that had waned since 1964 began to return. An effective separatist party was coalescing around René Lévesque, a charismatic former minister in the Lesage government who left the provincial Liberals in 1967 and helped found the Parti Québecois in 1968. The growing crisis helped catapult Pierre

Trudeau, justice minister in the Pearson government, into the leadership of the National Liberal party when Pearson retired, and Trudeau shortly led the party in June 1968 elections to the first majority government since 1962. Trudeau opposed special status for Quebec, arguing that the federal government should stop divesting itself of responsibilities. Members of Parliament from Quebec (on which the Liberal party depended for half or more of its majority) needed federal programs to retain a link to their constituents. Trudeau argued that changes in federal jurisdiction should apply equally to all provinces, not just to Quebec. He supported the entrenchment of language and civil rights in a repatriated constitution. The chances of reaching some Ottawa–Quebec City accommodation seemed enhanced by the return of the provincial Liberals under Robert Bourassa in April 1970. In general, the province continued its traditional opposition to shared-cost programs. Moreover the Quebec Working Paper on the Constitution formally demanded that federally administered programs such as Old Age pensions and Family Allowances be turned over completely to the provinces. The federal government's 1969 response was to reject this position, proposing even to reverse provincial gains achieved in the 1965 passage of the Canada Pension Plan/Quebec Pension Plan.[22] An impasse on social policy jurisdiction continued throughout 1970. The terror and response constituting the October Crisis underlined the seriousness of the Quebec question.

During the years of constitutional haggling Quebec was being armed at last with technical backing for its past theoretical arguments on behalf of devolution in social policy. Detailed proposals for a global integration of all social policies at the provincial level were contained in early releases from the Quebec Commission of Inquiry on Health and Social Welfare (1966–1970). Years in the making, this Castonguay-Nepveu report eventually totaled seven volumes with twenty-eight appendix volumes. It proposed to restructure and coordinate a wide range of health, social service, manpower training, and income security programs. The income security proposals envisioned a three-layer integrated structure consisting of social insurance, general social allowances, and family allowances.[23] The social allowances would replace social assistance and would have separate benefit schedules for the employable and the unemployable. Family allowances would serve as the hinge between insurance and social allowance and, although still universal, would vary according to the age and number of children. There was no place in these proposals for existing federal programs of OAS, GIS, Family Allowances, or even CAP as it then existed.

In January 1971 the Quebec cabinet insisted that the division of social powers be placed on the constitutional agenda. A resolution of this question was the province's price for agreement to an amending formula. The stage was set for a climactic constitutional conference held in Victoria, British Columbia, in June. Claude Morin recalls that Quebec had rushed into print with the Castonguay-Nepveu volume on income security, translating it into English to ensure that the seriousness of its case for integration was understood.[24] Claude Castonguay, now Quebec's minister of social affairs, was brought to the conference to expound the new plan. Now Quebec proposed that the provinces have paramount power, with compensation from the federal government, in the following areas: Family and Youth Allowances, Unemployment Insurance, and Guaranteed Income Supplements.[25] Castonguay said that the federal government could still administer the program as long as Quebec could decide how they would be distributed. In the ensuing discussions the federal side offered to cede to the provinces a veto power over its enactments in Family and Youth Allowances and occupational grants. But it refused to give the provinces a say over the Old Age Security and Guaranteed Income Supplement programs. Nor did it agree to provide compensation to allow a province to take over any of these programs. The federal authorities argued that Castonguay's proposals could be accommodated without constitutional change.[26] A full-scale constitutional charter was drawn up in June 1971, with most provinces expressing tentative and then formal approval. When Bourassa took the charter to his cabinet, however, it was rejected. The years of constitutional wrangling had come to nothing.

Quebec's desire to achieve a new division of power over social policy did not abate with the failure of the Constitutional Review. The province focused specifically on the question of Family Allowances. Quebec representatives pressed this point with federal authorities in bilateral meetings and in multilateral federal-provincial conferences. As a result, some changes were made in the FISP bill finally introduced in Parliament in September 1971. Benefits would not be taxable and would vary according to the age of the child. This bill died with the legislative session, partly because of ongoing negotiations over Family Allowances between Ottawa and Quebec City; however, the measure also faced opposition in Parliament, as the following year proved. Negotiations with Quebec continued into 1972 but did not produce the results provincial leaders desired. In March the federal government reintroduced its 1971 measure in Parliament, where the bill was welcomed by members of no party, including the Liberals; an election was in prospect.

Parliament had been delighted to pass the government's May 1972 proposals to increase Old Age Security pensions and Guaranteed Income Supplements, a step that infuriated Quebec provincial officials.[27] In contrast, dismantling Family Allowances was a dubious vote getter. Although more than half of all families would receive an increase, 17 percent faced a reduction and 30 percent were to lose their allowances entirely.[28] And of course these middle- and upper-income people were best situated to let their objections be heard. Debate dragged on, but Liberal party leaders insisted that the bill should pass. It came up for final reading on a July day that was the last before the summer recess. Because the sitting extended beyond four o'clock, unanimous consent was required to continue. Each of the parties had agreed to continue, but one member of Parliament, Paul Hellyer, alone refused to give his consent, killing the bill for that session. Hellyer had in 1968 been defeated for leadership of the Liberal party by Trudeau, and after an unhappy experience in the Trudeau cabinet had left the party. He eventually joined the Progressive Conservatives, but in July 1971 he was connected with no party. Hellyer's temporary independence allowed him to block a vote on FISP. Many legislators received his action with relief and gratitude.[29]

By 1972 events in the provinces reflected an emerging welfare backlash. A 1971 meeting of the Association of Ontario Mayors and Reeves endorsed a proposal that able-bodied welfare recipients be forced to work for their benefits. In December 1972 New Brunswick cut employable male recipients (but not their families) completely off the rolls; this step was reversed only later.[30] Also during this period a convention of western municipal officials meeting in Alberta actually endorsed a resolution urging that welfare recipients be denied the right to vote; this stand was reversed under pressure from provincial authorities. The welfare backlash even found its way to socialist Manitoba. In 1972 the Union of Manitoba Municipalities voted to ask the provincial government for a list of able-bodied people then in receipt of social assistance from the province, in order to assure that these people were not also drawing benefits from the municipalities. In November the New Democratic Party government agreed to share this information, and as mentioned earlier, the

NDP premier also initiated a review of welfare abuse, warning of a "profound, seething resentment against the whole welfare system."[31]

Welfare issues loomed large in the October 1972 federal elections, although the influences were contradictory.[32] While polls showed the economy to be the biggest issue, welfare abuse was also frequently mentioned. Most attention focused on the unemployment insurance system, which after the 1971 liberalizations was experiencing vast cost overruns and provoking fears of a decline in work effort. Progressive Conservative leader Robert Stanfield cited figures showing a rising share of national income going to those not working, and he urged voters to repudiate the Liberals "so a Stanfield Government can get Canadians back to work." The prime minister himself deplored "welfare freeloading." New Democratic Party leader David Lewis attacked Trudeau for "fueling backlash and prejudice" against welfare recipients, and he waged his own campaign against "corporate welfare bums"—businesses favored by subsidies and tax privileges.[33] Polls indicated some voter interest in the concept of a guaranteed income, and a party long identified with the idea, the ralliement des Créditistes under leader Réal Caouette, gained support from one-quarter of the Quebec electorate. Caouette proposed a universal scheme providing an annual income of $1200 for each adult and $250 for each child. The Stanfield challenge fell far short of expectations, and although the Trudeau government lost forty-six seats in the House, it was able to stay in power with support from the New Democrats. Thus the alignment in Parliament subjected the Liberal government to cross currents: encourage work but expand welfare. The government began to put together welfare proposals that would fit these seemingly contradictory demands.

With the conclusion of the 1972 elections Quebec and Castonguay continued to press the federal government for more social policy jurisdiction. At Castonguay's urging, a November interprovincial meeting of ministers of welfare agreed that "provinces should have the option, without financial loss, to administer the family allowance programme within a provincial social security system." The group also challenged the federal government to convene a federal-provincial meeting for the purpose of "far-reaching reform." Included in the comprehensive review would be all major income security and manpower programs, with explicit attention given to the "re-allocation" of funds among programs.[34] The federal government soon took up the challenge. In January 1973 Trudeau's

Welfare Reform and Guaranteed Income

Speech from the Throne proposed to reconsider and reorganize Canada's "total security system—including both federal and provincial elements. . . ." Among the major propositions were that those who cannot work should receive a "compassionate and equitable guaranteed annual income" but that for the rest the system must have a "greater emphasis on the need to get people who are on social aid back to work." The government now agreed that the provinces could "have the structures of social security vary in accordance with the social needs, income standards and the cost of living in different communities." Moreover Trudeau proposed that the reconsideration be conducted jointly between the federal and provincial levels.[35] To lead this proposed new experiment in federal-provincial cooperation, Trudeau appointed as minister of national health and welfare a close associate, Marc Lalonde. Lalonde had been the prime minister's primary policy secretary during the years of the Constitutional Review. Lalonde in turn brought as his deputy minister A. W. (Al) Johnson. Johnson, a former deputy treasurer in the Saskatchewan New Democratic Party government and at that time the federal secretary to the Treasury Board, had served as the federal strategist on social policy in the Constitutional Review.

In April 1973 Lalonde published a coordinated set of proposals in his *Working Paper on Social Security in Canada*. By its color the report became known as the "Orange Book" ("Halloween book" to its detractors). The federal government conceded for the first time that the provinces should be "given the power to vary the levels of universal and other allowances paid under federally administered programmes" and that a provincial reduction of benefits under one federal program would be compensated by transferring the funds to another program aiding the provincial population.[36] In accordance with this principle, the Orange Book proposed to allow each province to apportion them in its own way (deciding whether to vary them by age of children, size of family, and so on). The federal proposals were close to what Quebec had been holding out for since 1971. Notably, however, the federal government would still disburse the benefits, retaining this important link to the public. In addition, the Family Allowance was to be nearly tripled and indexed to inflation. This decision was interpreted by many observers as a gesture by the federal Liberals to Quebec voters, who are very fond of the Family Allowance. The Orange Book proposed to keep at least one thing about the Family Allowance the same: its universality. The government had learned from the FISP debacle. However, it proposed to make the allowances taxable, allowing recovery of some funds from higher-income people.

In addition to the Family Allowance proposals, the other major change envisioned in the Orange Book was expanding the current system of social assistance into two separate tiers. Those unable to work would continue receiving social assistance ("support") as under the Canada Assistance Plan, while others would be eligible for income supplementation, providing them "an incentive to keep on working rather than giving up and living on social aid."[37] These proposals were strikingly similar to the two-tier plan advanced in the Castonguay-Nepveu report in 1971. That report had emphasized the need to have separate plans for employable and unemployable people. According to the Quebec plan, a four-person family with an employable head would receive $2500, while a family with an unemployable head would receive $4050 (1971). The earnings of unemployable families would result in loss of benefits at a greater rate than would be the case for the employable people receiving smaller benefits.[38] An employable person who could not find a job would be moved to the other tier after a three-month waiting period. The Orange Book followed this pattern. The federal government envisioned a "support" tier similar to provincial programs cost-shared under the Canada Assistance Plan. It would include single-parent families and would provide generous benefits but few work incentives. Those expected to work would receive "supplementation"—low benefits but high work incentives.[39]

The similarity in scope and substance of the Castonguay-Nepveu report and the Orange Book was not accidental. Richard Van Loon has pointed out that from the federal perspective the publication left social policy initiative in Canada squarely with the government of Quebec, a situation that was difficult to countenance for "the feds" who had traditionally viewed themselves as playing the leadership role in social policy in Canada.[40] The comprehensiveness of the Quebec proposals almost dictated that the federal proposals would also have to be as ambitious. Despite its proposal of the Family Income Security Plan, Ottawa had refused to commit itself to a full-scale guaranteed income. With the appearance of the Castonguay-Nepveu report this attitude became less prevalent at the federal level. Some signs of this change were evident even before 1971. The 1970 white paper had suggested federal-provincial experimentation with the guaranteed income approach, and this idea was discussed at the same January 1971 conference at which the

Castonguay-Nepveu report was presented. The federal government reached an agreement in November 1971 with Manitoba for such an experiment.[41] In the aftermath of the 1972 election, of course, the Liberals came under increasing pressure from the strategically placed NDP to make a major initiative in this area, even while the Progressive Conservatives were taxing them for Liberal contributions to the welfare crisis. Guaranteed income proposals became heir to these contradictory pressures. The situation was anticipated by one reporter, who wrote in 1970, "For the first time, the archetypal conservative waging the never-ending fight against sloth and his liberal counterpart squeezing the social conscience dry, stand blinking at each other on the same platform."[42] When in November 1972 the provinces added to this rising outcry their own expectation of a federal initiative, Ottawa had little choice but to produce.

Though Quebec's guaranteed income plan helped press the federal side to come up with its own income security proposals, it also influenced their substance. Ottawa was not unaware that proposing a scheme similar to Quebec's undercut the province's argument that the federal system cramped its style.[43] Moreover, whereas a unitary system would surely be administered by the provinces, a two-tier scheme would be more likely to give the federal government a direct role in administration. Later Lalonde fought to have the supplementation tier run by the federal government, and the two-tier approach's opening for such a federal role probably enhanced its original attractiveness for federal authorities. Ideally many federal designers preferred that the supplementation tier be removed entirely from the welfare approach then common in the provinces, preferring instead that supplementation be administered through the federal tax system. This alternative was not extensively discussed during the ensuing Social Security Review, partly because serious examination of it would require consulting with experts in the finance ministry, producing delay and possible opposition. Not until 1977 was there a full-scale feasibility study of whether income transfers could be administered through the tax system. As it turned out, the Trudeau government in 1978 proposed and obtained parliamentary agreement to a limited initiative that took precisely this approach.

Aside from these considerations of federal-provincial strategy, the federal authorities were attracted to the two-tier proposals of the Castonguay-Nepveu report because these represented a real breakthrough in the design of income programs. The Quebec report reflected close study of the ongoing U.S. debate on the Family Assistance Plan, devoting an appendix to describing this and other existing proposals. The Castonguay-Nepveu report advanced the two-tier scheme expressly to eliminate "conflict between a decent income level for persons or families without any income and a reasonable rate of taxation or earned income from those who already have a certain income." Federal officials were aware of the technical dilemmas inherent in unitary plans. Moreover the federal designers were aware of the political attractions of two-tier proposals. They "had read and been strongly influenced by Daniel Moynihan's recently published *The Politics of a Guaranteed Income*."[44]

A major difference between the Quebec City and Ottawa proposals was that whereas the Castonguay-Nepveu report had both benefit schedules administered within the same program, the federal report held open the possibility that the two sets of beneficiaries should be separated into different programs. This difference later became a source of friction between the two capitals, as well as within the Department of National Health and Welfare. When Deputy Minister Johnson came to the department in February 1973, he undertook a far-reaching reorganization of the department's Research, Planning, and Evaluation Branch (Welfare), then headed by Assistant Deputy Minister John E. Osborne. Two branches were established with quite different personnel. Johnson brought T. Russell Robinson, an economist from the Treasury Board, to be assistant deputy minister of the new Policy Research and Long-Range Planning Branch (Welfare).[45] Robinson's branch began with several economists and other planners transferred as a result of Johnson's reorganization. In addition, Robinson brought from the Treasury Board's planning staff and from other agencies and academe a group of bright young economists, computer specialists, and others.[46] Analysts from Osborne's old branch who did not fit this pattern were transferred to a new Policy and Program Development and Coordination Branch (Welfare), with Osborne again as assistant deputy minister. Osborne's new branch added a number of other personnel trained in sociology or social work. Robinson and Osborne, along with Johnson, served as the steering committee for federal involvement in the Social Security Review.

Johnson explained the existence of two separate policy branches by distinguishing between their inductive and deductive approaches. Osborne's branch would seek to evaluate policy alternatives based on familiarity with policies as they had been practiced and studied in the past; in addition, the branch would seek to predict the public reception for different proposals and to build public support. Robinson's branch would apply high-powered economic analysis and other new techniques. As it turned out, these two contrasting approaches to policy analysis were not drawn on equally in the Social Security Review. The design of proposals and of negotiating strategy became increasingly centralized in the Policy Research and Long-Range Planning Branch (Welfare). The deductive approach took precedence over the inductive approach.

As later chapters will show, the evolution of federal strategy in the Social Security Review was not always based on lessons drawn from the workings of existing programs. Many provincial administrators believed that it would not be practical to divide clients into two separately administered programs because beneficiaries would constantly be shifting between the two programs and because the distinction would not always be clear-cut. Even Saskatchewan, which on its own adopted in 1974 a two-tier program that separated the tiers administratively in some ways, felt that some integration was necessary and that this could be achieved only if the two tiers were located at the provincial level. Federal administrators who were closest to the provincial programs felt that separation of the two tiers between different programs and different levels of government could be a mistake. Yet for more than two years federal planners preferred that the two tiers be administered separately, with the federal government in charge of the supplementation tier. This preference caused the federal side to insist on keeping open the question of who should administer the supplementation tier, even when this insistence went against federal-provincial political realities as well as the lessons of provincial experience. Al Johnson's efforts to revolutionize policy planning at Health and Welfare Canada seem to have produced a curious mix of triumphs and troubles. Certainly his influence made the Orange Book a more comprehensive set of proposals than had ever before come from the department. But the reorganization also contributed to some practical defects in the federal proposals and discouraged efforts to correct them.

The United States: The "Welfare Mess" and the Negative Income Tax

While proposals to extend welfare to new groups emerged gradually in Canada, they exploded onto the U.S. agenda later and all at once. President Nixon proposed his Family Assistance Plan in August 1969, and

Congress soon began serious debate on the measure. But only two years before, a survey of the Senate Labor and Public Welfare Committee and the House Education and Labor Committee had showed that no member felt that Congress would seriously consider guaranteed income within five years, and "many put it twenty-five years off." March 1969 interviews with fifty congressmen found most to be opposed to "income by right."[47] There was obviously no long period in which U.S. elites prepared the ground for such proposals. Rather Nixon sprang his proposals on a surprised country, and he was able to do so convincingly because he sold the proposals as the answer to the "welfare mess." Though the United States by the late 1960s did not experience a gradual emergence of interest in guaranteed income proposals, the welfare crisis had grown as a political issue. Nixon's ability to catapult his Family Assistance Plan onto the political agenda depended on his ability to portray it as the answer.

While Congress was preoccupied with debate on the many antipoverty programs proposed by President Johnson, the growth of the AFDC rolls accelerated. The 1962 social services answer to the problems of AFDC approached its 1968 expiration date with no discernible effect in slowing the program's growth. Embarassed by the failure of this approach to live up to its promise, HEW authorities proposed to Congress a change in the benefit structure to pull recipients back into the working world and a work requirement to push them off welfare. The resulting 1967 WIN (work incentive) legislation allowed (and after 1969 required) states to provide the working recipient a "work bonus" of $30 a month. Further earnings above that would reduce the benefits, not dollar for dollar, but at a 67 percent reduction rate—for every three dollars earned, the recipient could effectively keep one of them. In addition to these positive work incentives, officials within HEW were becoming increasingly sympathetic to requiring recipients to undertake work and training. They worked closely with staff of the House Ways and Means Committee under Chairman Wilbur Mills in establishing the nationwide requirement that certain employable recipients participate in the WIN program.[48] WIN involved an unpromising partnership between the Labor Department and HEW Department and state welfare and employment offices. Under the 1967 WIN legislation the states were required to refer to the program all "appropriate persons." The Ways and Means Committee made it clear that this category included children over sixteen not in school and AFDC-U fathers, as well as welfare mothers if the state chose to apply the work requirement to them. Despite these efforts the 1967 legislation made little provision to enforce the "mandatory" procedures on the states. Moreover the law was watered down by outgoing HEW Secretary Wilbur Cohen, who issued regulations allowing the states to apply the work requirement to mothers only after applying it to all AFDC-U fathers and teenagers and after accommodating all volunteer mothers.[49]

In addition to the earnings exemption and work requirement, the 1967 AFDC legislation threatened a freeze in the federal funding of families headed by an unmarried or deserted mother. Federal sharing would continue in cases where the father was dead or unemployed and under AFDC-U. But for the other families the state could receive federal sharing only for the number that it was aiding before the law passed. This AFDC freeze never went into effect. Its effective date was postponed by Johnson and Nixon, and Congress repealed it in 1969. But it was a remarkable indication of the growing congressional concern with broken families and the welfare syndrome. Also indicative of this mood was other 1967 legislation that did go into effect, changing the AFDC–Unemployed Parent program to the AFDC–Unemployed *Father* program. The Senate Finance Committee, led by Senator Russell Long (Democrat, Louisiana) was concerned that some mothers were receiving benefits even though their husbands were present and working, turning AFDC-U into a de facto program of aid to the employed. The 1967 legislation stopped this practice.

While Congress was exhibiting its concern about the welfare mess by tightening up the AFDC program, the new Food Stamp program came under very different pressures to expand. Hunger was surfacing as a political issue in 1967. Senators Robert F. Kennedy (Democrat, New York) and Joseph Clark (Democrat, Pennsylvania) publicized the problem of malnutrition in the Mississippi delta and elsewhere, and in 1968 the Senate established the temporary Select Committee on Nutrition and Human Needs (abolished in 1977), chaired by Senator George McGovern (Democrat, South Dakota). Under pressure from Congress and the media, the Agriculture Department began to lower the purchase requirements. Yet reformers failed to obtain support for legislation requiring every community to have a food stamp program; as late as 1973 one-quarter of the nation's communities did not. In 1968 in the aftermath of the assassination of civil rights leader Martin Luther King, the Poor People's Campaign encamped in Washington, making food its top issue.

Congress was sympathetic to legislation expanding the program; but because of budgetary constraints brought on especially by the Vietnam war, no action was forthcoming. With the election of Richard Nixon the Republicans controlled the White House, and congressional Democrats felt less constrained in criticizing presidential foot-dragging on food stamps. It was such pressure that encouraged Nixon to make the initiative that Johnson had refused to make.

Under Democratic pressure the Nixon administration early began considering major Food Stamp reform of its own. Long before a consensus was reached on welfare reform and the Family Assistance Plan, the president had expressed a tentative preference for Food Stamp reform making free benefits available to the most needy and increasing and equalizing benefits. This expanded program would continue to extend eligibility to all the poor, whether or not employed and with or without children. It covered many people untouched by the AFDC program. Nixon's decision to expand the Food Stamp program was cheered by Secretary of Agriculture Clifford Hardin and Secretary of HEW Robert Finch, and opposed by Arthur Burns, counsellor to the president for domestic policy. Before the decision could be formalized, a strong internal debate over welfare reform sidetracked the food stamp issue. Leaks to the press made this delay public, and Senator McGovern intensified the administration's discomfiture by introducing his own food stamp bill and inviting Hardin and Finch to testify at hearings of his committee. These hearings ultimately provided the impetus for the administration to commit itself to major reform.[50] Efforts by Agriculture and HEW officials to put together a defensive strategy against McGovern's expected onslaught only convinced them that the administration had to propose a major reform. Only two days before the scheduled hearings, Nixon formally decided to propose his own major Food Stamp reform. Vincent and Vee Burke justly describe this proposal as Nixon's "other" national income guarantee proposal.[51]

When Nixon entered office, something "had to be done" about AFDC. Congress was rebelling at the increasing costs of the burgeoning welfare rolls. State and local governments were clamoring for fiscal relief—a special imperative for Nixon because the governors of major states like California, New York, Illinois, and Pennsylvania (these four alone with more than a quarter of the AFDC case load) were all Republicans. Rarely can an administration withstand such a confluence of pressures without making some legislative proposals. The substance of these proposals remained very much a matter of discretion, however, as long as a minimum amount of fiscal relief was guaranteed. It was in this vacuum that the new Nixon administration and HEW technocrats combined to propose a negative income tax. The latter had been advocating the idea since 1965 but had found no sympathizers within the Johnson administration. The idea of a negative income tax was conceived in 1943 by Milton Friedman, and it was advocated by James Tobin, Robert Lampman, and other economists. The first government attention to the idea was not in Congress or HEW but in the Office of Economic Opportunity, which existed in 1964–1973 in the Executive Office of the President and had no stake in the existing welfare system. In February 1965 Lampman suggested that OEO economists study the idea, and within seven months OEO director Sargent Shriver had proposed it to the president, as he was to do repeatedly for the next four years. Meanwhile analysis continued in both OEO and the Council of Economic Advisors. A negative income tax bill written anonymously by OEO economist James Lyday was introduced in Congress in 1968 by Representative William Fitts Ryan (Democrat, New York), but it attracted little attention. Proponents in OEO in 1967 had initiated a major social experiment to supplement the earnings of male breadwinners in families not eligible for AFDC. The purpose was to test for possible decline in work effort, with the hope that the findings would strengthen the case for the negative income tax. Shriver approved the experiment only on the condition that the term negative income tax not be used. The name chosen was the New Jersey Graduated Work Incentive Experiment.[52]

The analysts pushing the negative income tax proposal found the Nixon administration considerably more receptive to their ideas than the Johnson administration. In his successful presidential campaign Nixon had made an issue of welfare, saying in his convention acceptance speech that "what we need are not more millions on welfare rolls, but more millions on payrolls." Upon election, Nixon appointed the Transitional Task Force on Public Welfare, chaired by Richard P. Nathan. Nathan set a limit of $2 billion on the cost of the eventual recommendations. The task force proposed a federally funded nationwide income floor for AFDC families, raising benefits in poor states and relieving state budgets everywhere. Arthur Burns opposed this proposal as expensive and urged that measures be taken to reduce the welfare rolls. But barely a month after the inauguration, HEW Secretary Robert Finch and

Urban Affairs Assistant Daniel P. Moynihan were able to persuade the president to support nationwide AFDC guarantees.[53] Even though this decision alone would have been a dramatic reform of the fragmented AFDC program, internal White House debates increasingly centered on proposals that went even further—to fund national benefits not only to AFDC recipients but also to intact families with a working breadwinner. This transition occurred in two stages, one at the subcabinet level, the other within the White House itself.

The first step in the Nixon administration's endorsement of a negative income tax was the replacement of the Nathan plan by a more comprehensive plan as the main proposal emanating from the bureaucracy. A task force of HEW and Budget Bureau officials had been assigned to refine the Nathan plan. Among its members were Nathan himself and John Veneman, the new HEW undersecretary. This group in turn established an expert work group. The working group fortuitously included two proponents of the negative income tax; one was Worth Bateman, outgoing HEW deputy assistant secretary for program analysis. Bateman brought in Lyday from OEO. Supported by Veneman and Finch, these three secretly prepared a comprehensive proposal to compete with the Nathan plan and then manipulated the members of their parent task force into adopting it.[54]

The next and more difficult step for the negative income tax idea was to obtain consent from the new Republican president and his cabinet. A three-month internal debate ensued. Moynihan, a former official in the Kennedy and Johnson administrations, was the plan's most vigorous defender; Burns, Moynihan's nominal superior, was its most unrelenting critic. Burns proposed an alternative similar to the Nathan plan, providing fiscal relief to high-benefit states and strong financial incentives for states with low benefits to improve them. AFDC-U would be made mandatory on all states. At one time or another virtually every member of the cabinet took a position for or against the negative income tax proposal. Nixon's budget director, the secretary of the Treasury, and the chairman of the Council of Economic Advisors all came to favor Burns' position. Such opposition, as well as reports of possible Republican opposition on Capitol Hill, nearly blocked the plan, and these forces persuaded the president that any such proposal should at least have a strong penalty to enforce work, in addition to better positive incentives. George Schulz, secretary of labor, redesigned the proposal to these specifications. In favor of the negative income tax proposal were not only Moynihan and Finch but also Nixon's rising aide John Ehrlichman, who used the issue to cement control over domestic policymaking in the White House. In June 1969 Nixon authorized Ehrlichman to begin supervising the drafting of legislation. Despite some last-minute heroics by Burns and the opposition of a majority of the cabinet, the plan received final presidential approval in August.[55] The president went on nationwide television to present his Family Assistance Plan as a cure for the ills of the welfare system.

Two Paths to the Political Agenda

Whereas guaranteed income proposals in Canada gradually gained general currency, in the United States they never did. Rather President Nixon sprang his Family Assistance Plan on an unprepared country and Congress, and he continued to deny that his proposal was a guaranteed income. Nixon's announcement represented the culmination of two very different trends—the growing welfare backlash in society and the internal efforts by bureaucrats to sell their negative income tax proposals as an answer to the welfare crisis. In Canada the 1973 proposals responded to public outcry about the welfare system, but they were more strongly influenced by long-standing demand for a program that would extend aid to people not already covered.

It is surprising that a president in 1969 proposed what was in effect a guaranteed income. It is incredible that this president was a Republican whose preference was opposed by a majority of his cabinet and of his party in Congress. The U.S. political system puts unusual powers of initiative in the president. To interpret why Richard Nixon used this power as he did requires as much psychology as political science. By some accounts the neophyte administration was hoodwinked by holdovers from the Johnson administration. While there was an element of this, the analysts were in on the first stage of the drama; the second debate took place within the White House, and they were excluded even from drafting the bill. Within the White House the proposal had influential and effective friends, particularly Finch and Ehrlichman. Moynihan was a skilled rhetorician who held the plan's critics at bay while flattering the president shamelessly. In a key memo Moynihan warned Nixon that he might not have a "single distinctive Nixon program" at the end of his term and should "go up now with a genuinely new, unmistakably Nixon, unmistakably needed program, which would attract the attention of the world, far less the United States."[56] Nixon came to see his bill as more than just a way to reward work and combat AFDC's baleful impact on intact families. "Income by right" was also a way to streamline and restrain a wasteful and intrusive welfare bureaucracy. By making the United States the first country to supplement the wages of the working poor, he hoped for a place in history. And he also could steal a march on the Democrats, threatening their claim to leadership in social policy.[57]

No single person in the Canadian political system had such power to surface a major proposal. Indeed the federal government as a whole was unable to act without extensively consulting provincial governments. But the federal-provincial relationship helped keep guaranteed income proposals on the agenda. Whereas public discussions had made the guaranteed income desirable, federal-provincial politics made it necessary. In the aftermath of the failed Victoria conference, progress in the resolution of social policy questions was a decisive condition for Quebec leaders' continued faith in confederation. The massive sweep of the Castonguay-Nepveu proposals put federal authorities on the defensive. When the provinces challenged the federal government to undertake the Social Security Review, Ottawa had little choice but to respond with proposals to extend welfare to new groups.

4
Debates on the Nixon Family Assistance Plan and the Carter Program for Better Jobs and Income

The U.S. debates over welfare reform took place mainly in Congress. President Nixon's 1969 Family Assistance Plan easily cleared the House of Representatives in 1970, but the Senate Finance Committee rejected it. The proposal was also rejected on the Senate floor, and it died with the conclusion of the Ninety-first Congress. With the new Congress the administration proposals were revamped under the leadership of the House Ways and Means Committee. They passed the House in 1971, but the Senate again rejected them in 1972. Between 1973 and 1976 presidents Nixon and Ford did not advocate comprehensive welfare reform measures. In 1977, however, President Carter proposed the major new Program for Better Jobs and Income. While the bill was approved by a special Welfare Reform subcommittee in early 1978, it encountered fatal House opposition and never reached the House floor. Efforts to achieve a compromise in May and June of 1978 fell through.

Debacle: 1969–1970

Under the Nixon Family Assistance Plan all families with children would become eligible for a federally financed floor of $1600 a year for a family of four, with this amount to be supplemented by food stamps and by additional state benefits in the forty-two states where the federal payment was less than current AFDC benefits. The work incentives allowed the first $60 in monthly earnings to be disregarded, and then the federal benefit would be reduced at a rate of 50 percent, providing a break-even point of $3960. In addition to these positive incentives, the plan also contained a work requirement: if a family head considered employable did not accept suitable work or training, he would suffer the loss of $300 from the basic grant. Those considered unemployable were not subject to this penalty.

Fiscal relief for the states and counties had been a prime Nixon concern in the internal deliberations on welfare reform.[1] This concern was most responsible for initial proposals for a federal takeover of state AFDC costs up to a nationwide standard. FAP extended such a federal floor not only to AFDC families but also to new families never before covered by federal cash assistance. However generous and revolutionary this step, it lessened the level of federal relief for existing state and local AFDC spending. For the states and localities the most attractive feature of FAP was its promise that they would have to pay no more than 90 percent of what

79
Debacle

they had been spending under AFDC. But many were unhappy with FAP's proposed requirement that they supplement the federal payments up to existing AFDC levels. This feeling, along with general disappointment at the magnitude of the fiscal relief promised, lessened the enthusiasm for FAP of the intergovernmental groups, its most powerful potential allies. Throughout 1970 the administration was frustrated in its efforts to marshall the National Governors Conference, or even a majority of governors, behind the plan. The National Council of State Public Welfare Administrators never took a formal position on the measure. Among the intergovernmental associations only the National Association of Counties strongly supported FAP in 1970, and this only after changes were obtained to assure that more relief flowed directly to counties instead of through the states.[2] The full support of such groups was obtained only in the second round of debate in 1971–1972, when the administration supported a bill materially more generous to them.

The Family Assistance Plan was treated gently in 1969–1970 by the House Ways and Means Committee under the leadership of Chairman Wilbur Mills (Democrat, Arkansas). Mills favored the bill as an answer to general revenue sharing, which he opposed. John Byrnes (Republican, Wisconsin), the ranking Republican member of the committee, shared this view. He led the Republican members of the committee in unanimous support of the bill, helping it pass by the overwhelming vote of 21 to 3. The House traditionally accepted without question bills recommended by the Ways and Means Committee, and this bill was no exception. It was considered under a closed rule—no amendments allowed. The House quietly passed it, 243 to 155, in April 1970. The prospects for Senate enactment of FAP in 1970 seemed good. Even the National Welfare Rights Organization was not opposed, stressing only the need for higher benefits.[3] As 1970 wore on, however, the NWRO turned against the bill and the Senate Finance Committee began a coordinated attack.

Even as the House passed FAP, the Senate Finance Committee was preparing a wintry reception. At hearings in April 1970 Senator John J. Williams (Republican, Delaware), Byrnes' senate counterpart as the senior minority member of the committee, dramatically revealed that FAP, when considered along with in-kind programs such as Medicaid and Food Stamps, had troublesome notches that would punish recipients for working their way off welfare. Williams had asked HEW to prepare the very charts that he used to ridicule the administration bill. But Secretary

Finch and other administration witnesses were caught unaware, and the committee chastised them for it. Notches were not unique to the 1969 Family Assistance Plan; they were a central feature of the existing welfare system. But FAP could be accused of increasing the welfare mess by ensnaring working people not already receiving benefits. In failing to anticipate these objections, the administration showed a shocking lack of preparation. Arthur Burns's deputy Martin Anderson had alerted the White House to these objections, but few had listened.[4]

It was not until June 1970 that the administration produced a bill free of notches. In the new bill Medicaid was to be replaced by a Family Health Insurance Plan, with premiums tailored to income and therefore not subject to "sudden death." Food stamp benefits would also taper off more gradually. Because the administration did not want to increase the cost of the program, this tapering of benefits at incomes near the break-even point was achieved by worsening the reduction rate at lower levels of income, raising the specter that some recipients might prefer not to work at all. The penalty for refusing to work was raised from $300 to $500. The new bill also retreated from Nixon's earlier pledge that no current AFDC beneficiary would suffer lower benefits under FAP; former AFDC-U recipients were now to be denied this protection. This change antagonized the National Welfare Rights Organization (NWRO), whose members were concentrated in states where benefits already exceeded the FAP guarantee.

Although the administration's revised bill was ready on June 10, the Senate Finance Committee did not hold hearings until July, or hear public witnesses until late August. It was clear that conservatives of both parties were not sympathetic to it. Not one of the committee's six Republicans was willing to sponsor the Republican administration's bill, and only two gave even qualified support. Several Democrats, including Chairman Russell Long (Louisiana) and Herman Talmadge (Georgia), were unalterably opposed. Conservative critics of FAP shifted their attack from the notches at the higher levels of income to work incentives at the lower levels. This switch was ironic because the weakening of incentives at the lower levels of income was done in order to meet the committee's demand that the notches be eliminated. The new secretary of HEW, Elliot Richardson, patiently explained that difficult trade-offs were required. However, conservative members of the committee were unwilling to extend such a system to new groups, for fear of an increase in dependency and a decline in work effort. The committee staff prepared dramatic charts illustrating the inadequacies of the bill's work incentives and showing that vast numbers of people would be added to the welfare rolls—35 percent of the population of Mississippi alone.[5]

The Nixon administration was estimating during the summer and fall of 1970 that it had sixty votes for FAP, if the Senate could only be brought to vote on it.[6] Conservatives on the Finance Committee were attempting to stave off that vote. Ultimately this strategy paid off. Congressional elections were scheduled for later that year, and Vice-President Spiro T. Agnew was polarizing the country by emotional attacks on "radical liberals," by which he meant liberal Democrats and even some members of his own party. One of Agnew's successful kills in the election was Senator Albert Gore (Democrat, Tennessee), a member of the Finance Committee considered to be leaning toward FAP. Because the president had been unable to convince even a majority of his own party's Senators to support FAP, its passage depended on Nixon's ability to woo Democratic support.[7] But through the administration's own doing, the atmosphere following the election was partisan and highly charged, making Democrats unwilling to give the president a victory.

The bitterness of the 1970 congressional elections gave legitimacy to attacks on FAP by the NWRO. Senator Eugene McCarthy (Democrat, Minnesota), a member of the Finance Committee, sponsored an emotional informal hearing at which NWRO representatives deplored the work requirement and demanded a higher guarantee. The NWRO also sabotaged an effort led by Common Cause, a citizens lobby, to marshall a coalition behind a compromise. Such compromise efforts would in any case probably have come too late to affect the committee vote.[8] The vote came on November 20, and the bill failed 6 to 10. Four Republicans voted against the bill and three voted for it, as expected. The surprise was that joining conservative Democrats in killing the bill were four liberal Democrats: McCarthy, Gore, Clinton Anderson (Democrat, New Mexico), and Fred Harris (Democrat, Oklahoma). Harris in particular was strongly influenced by pressure from NWRO and helped draw the others to his side.[9] In view of this striking committee defeat, attempts to bring the measure to a vote on the senate floor were almost anticlimactic. Yet Senator Abraham Ribicoff (Democrat, Connecticut) worked closely with Richardson in working out a compromise offering special concessions to the liberals. With time running out, however, the effort failed, 21 to 49.[10]

In view of the bitter controversy over the Family Assistance Plan in 1970, it is remarkable that the Nixon administration's major Food Stamp reform proposals cleared Congress at virtually the same time. During 1969 and 1970 the Department of Agriculture had been expanding the program administratively, doubling the benefits of more households and guaranteeing that recipients would not have to pay more than a quarter of their income for the stamps. By the end of 1970 either commodities or food stamps were distributed by 3072 of the nation's 3129 communities.[11] The number of Food Stamp beneficiaries tripled in one year, and spending quintupled. The administration bill established national standards, to complete the program's development into a major income guarantee paralleling the proposed Family Assistance Plan. Indeed the Food Stamp program went beyond FAP in benefiting even unattached individuals and couples without children. Instead of resistance, Nixon found Congress wanting to vote more money for food stamps than he did. And, ironically, it was the Senate that wanted the most—at the very time when it was rejecting FAP. Moreover the House, which had been so cooperative on FAP, wrote into the food stamp bill a work requirement that the administration felt was too harsh. This requirement allowed an entire family's benefits to be cut off if the head refused to work. With this provision, both houses easily passed the food stamp bill in the final weeks of the Ninety-first Congress.

Denouement: 1971–1972

When FAP died in the Ninety-first Congress, President Nixon vowed to make it his "major legislative goal" for 1971. Mills, too, redoubled his efforts.[12] He demanded that HEW prepare a detailed analysis of every objection brought up in the thousands of pages of congressional debate. Mills also insisted that the administration submit revised proposals to meet "legitimate criticism" raised by the Senate Finance Committee, and he gave a number of guidelines for what he wanted. Among other changes, the administration was thus persuaded to make families ineligible for food stamps and to increase the FAP basic payment accordingly to $2200, with a new reduction rate of 67 percent. Between February and April 1971 Mills led his committee, in consultation with HEW, through a major reworking of FAP legislation. The new bill, designated HR 1 to indicate its top priority, treated food stamps as the administration proposed and raised the FAP floor to $2400. The bill would fully federalize programs for aged, blind, and disabled, placing these categories in a program separate from families. The national floor, $2400 for a couple in this program, was to be the same as for a family of four of the other type. The new bill dropped the previous requirement that states provide supplemental payments to maintain existing public assistance levels. Thus states could reduce benefits but would receive federal incentives not to do so.

In addition to the changes in benefits and structure that HR 1 made in the original FAP concept, the bill tightened work requirements and weakened procedural rights. As for work requirements, the Ways and Means Committee made several decisions that displeased HEW but were probably applauded by the president.[13] One step was to separate employable and unemployable families into different programs, though benefit structures would remain the same. Those with no members subject to the work requirement would receive their benefits under a Family Assistance Program administered by HEW. Families with an employable head would be placed in a program called Opportunities for Families administered by the Department of Labor. In addition, the proposed requirement itself was made more severe. Contrary to the HEW recommendations, it was expanded to include mothers of children as young as three. HR 1 also omitted the earlier proviso that recipient's could refuse anything but "suitable work." And it raised from $500 to $800 the penalty for refusing work. HR 1 was more conservative than the original FAP in its work requirement and in its treatment of procedural welfare rights. In particular, the right to appeal was curtailed by eliminating the right to free legal counsel and by foreclosing judicial review of administrative appeal boards. These and other restrictive measures were strongly opposed by the NWRO and other poverty advocacy groups. In some ways these groups were more concerned about this issue than about the level of the FAP floor.[14]

Because of the loss of food stamp benefits, families would receive no higher floor under HR 1 than under the original FAP. Clearly the states were to reap the difference, relieved by federal aid of that much more of the burden of supplementing the FAP payment so that it met the existing level of AFDC plus food stamps. Rather than requiring the states to supplement, this bill made the matter voluntary but offered generous financial incentives for them to do so. The increased FAP floor would relieve twenty-two states, of all family welfare costs, as opposed to only eight under the 1969 bill.[15] Aware that state and local ambivalence had damaged FAP's chances in 1970, the administration made HR 1 more attractive to these interests. Mills supported these changes as an alternative to general revenue sharing, which he opposed. Revenue sharing had been proposed by the president in 1969, but the opposition of Mills and other congressional leaders had stalled the proposal. HR 1 would cost $6.1 billion more than the original FAP proposal, and as much as 30 percent of this extra cost would go directly for state and local relief.[16] These changes successfully rallied state and local governments to the support of HR 1, but a combination of circumstances produced a repeat of the 1970 debacle.

In 1970 an HEW official troubled by the carnage in Congress suggested that nongovernmental groups favorable to FAP coordinate their efforts. By 1971 a coalition of groups was meeting weekly; it included representatives of as many as twenty-five organizations—among them churches, unions, social worker representatives, and intergovernmental lobbies. It was a marriage of convenience among groups with important differences in interest and outlook. The intergovernmental groups were most concerned with fiscal relief, while others were more fixed on the desirability of extending welfare to new groups. Although the National Association of Counties became the convenor of these meetings, it and the other groups avoided affiliating with each other formally; for some, a public alliance would have been politically impossible.

The National Welfare Rights Organization continued to take an irreconcilable stance on many of these efforts to reach a compromise. Its own bill was introduced in the House in April 1971 by the entire House black caucus and by a dozen white congressmen. George McGovern and others introduced the bill in the Senate in July. The NWRO bill called for a guarantee of $6500 and a reduction rate of 67 percent.[17] Despite his organization's public stance, George Wiley secretly encouraged the introduction of several more moderate bills. He also engaged in discreet talks with Senator Ribicoff's staff and with others seeking to promote a compromise. However, though Wiley was at times willing to compromise, the NWRO board of directors had become irrevocably committed to the "$6500-or-fight" principle, a constraint that ultimately prohibited such a move.[18]

HR 1 passed the Ways and Means Committee 22 to 3 in May 1971, although not before urban congressmen insisted on extra federal help for states to supplement the FAP floor up to existing AFDC levels. Under Mills's strong leadership, the full House in June passed the measure 234 to 187, under a closed rule.[19] The Senate Finance Committee, of course, remained the big stumbling block, but efforts by Ribicoff and others to marshall support in the full Senate looked promising.[20] A combination of circumstances conspired, however, to reduce the urgency of welfare reform and to delay Senate consideration long enough that the bill ran afoul of election year politics, as had happened in 1970. The urgency of the reform was reduced both by events and by choice. One change was evidence that the national AFDC case load was no longer growing. In April 1971 monthly figures showed that the number of beneficiaries had actually dropped slightly, for the first time in three years.[21] Some states were beginning successful campaigns to reduce welfare rolls. Aides to Governor Nelson A. Rockefeller concluded that not enough states were really hurting from the welfare burden for FAP's fiscal relief arguments alone to help it pass the Senate.

Other blows to HR 1 occurred when Congress began to adopt its most attractive features piecemeal, without the family assistance provisions. The best example of this process was the successful effort of Senator Talmadge to obtain passage of FAP's work requirement in late 1971. He proposed to amend an obscure Social Security bill to include provisions for a nationwide AFDC work registration requirement. At the time, states decided for themselves who was "appropriate" for referral to the WIN program. The Talmadge amendment reversed the 1967 WIN provision allowing states to apply the work requirement even to mothers with infants. But now all adult AFDC recipients were compelled to register for WIN unless they received an exemption. Automatic exemptions were provided in cases of ill health; incapacity; old age; student status; lack of access to day care, transportation, or employment; or the need to care for a preschool child. Under the 1971 legislation a child of six years or younger would exempt a mother. This provision was actually more liberal than the work requirement in HR 1, where only a child of three years or younger would exempt a mother. But the Talmadge amendment clearly had a more far-reaching work requirement than existing law. Despite its severity, the legislation encountered little debate or even discussion in Congress and it passed easily, with not a single senator objecting. Some supporters of the move feared only that the chances for senate passage of HR 1 would be hurt because the FAP work requirement was, in Congressman Byrnes's words, "what some consider the sweetener." Talmadge and others were well aware that his amendment would have this negative effect on HR 1.[22]

The Nixon administration could do little about the Talmadge amendments. It could and did do other things that hurt the cause of HR 1 in the Senate. By 1971 the White House attitude toward liberal measures had hardened.[23] Ehrlichman and H. R. Haldeman, the president's closest advisors, had helped drive Moynihan from the White House by the end of 1970, and when Ehrlichman began to lose interest in the welfare reform package that he had helped write, no Nixon intimate would fight to keep the president dedicated to FAP. This lack of interest became a problem when the lobbying for FAP was left increasingly to Richardson and his people at HEW, and the White House staff did not show the Senate that Nixon still cared about the bill. For weeks and even months on end the president refused even to meet with Richardson. In this atmosphere the president was willing to subordinate his proposal to the new economic policy announced in August 1971. As a measure of austerity, Nixon proposed to delay for a year the effective date for the reform. Though the Finance Committee had begun hearings, Chairman Long was delighted to shelve it. One consequence of the delay was to throw the attention of the intergovernmental lobby, HR 1's most faithful supporters, away from welfare reform to general revenue sharing. The administration had produced a new revenue-sharing bill in February 1971, and Mills converted, producing his own proposal in June.

The Senate Finance Committee retained the franchise on the HR 1 title, though there was no chance that its version would resemble the House version. The committee resumed public hearings in February 1972, and in April for the second time in two years it rejected the administration's proposals. But that was expected; perhaps more damaging to the cause of welfare reform was that the committee delayed this decision so long and then further delayed its decision on the legislation to recommend to the full Senate. The committee had the issue on its agenda for more than fourteen months before it finally reported a bill. This senate version of HR 1 actually cut back on AFDC, totally excluding the 40 percent of beneficiary families with an able-bodied father or mother and no child over six. The only way those groups could get assistance was through a government-sponsored job or through wage subsidies and a "work bonus." Senator Long had done his work well; a majority of the committee's Democrats and all but one of its Republicans supported the bill.[24]

The Senate Finance Committee's "guaranteed jobs" bill had little chance of passing either house of Congress. With the committee so hostile to alternatives, the major reform efforts shifted to negotiations between the administration and Ribicoff, a member of the Senate Finance Committee. Introduced in October 1971, Ribicoff's new bill covered individuals and childless couples as well as families. It provided a federal floor of $3000 for a family of four, with state supplementation up to existing AFDC levels. By January 1972 the proposal was supported by twenty-two senators of both parties, fifteen governors, and most of the nongovernmental coalition.[25] During this period the administration was showing unmistakable signs of ambivalence about its proposals, and Ribicoff publicly questioned the president's commitment. This episode at least temporarily kept the administration on track, and negotiations between Ribicoff, HEW Secretary Richardson, and Secretary of Labor James Hodgson produced in June 1972 a compromise giving $2600 to a family of four, to be raised five years later to $3000. Ribicoff yielded on his desire for coverage of those without children, and the administration acceded to requiring the states to supplement up to existing AFDC levels.[26]

The negotiations between Ribicoff and the administration were breathtakingly close to a settlement, but as in 1970 the measure became snarled in election-year politics. Early in his presidential primary campaign, Senator McGovern had proposed that every man, woman, and child receive a $1000 grant. A poor family of four would thus be guaranteed $4000. Families with significant income would have part of their grant taxed back, but only one-fifth of families would fail to retain at least part of the grant. The proposal was not much different from demogrant proposals popular in Canada and Europe, but Americans were suspicious of it and McGovern was unable to defend it adequately. He was plagued by questions and criticisms about the plan, particularly in two nationally televised debates with an opponent in the primaries, Senator Hubert Humphrey (Democrat, Minnesota). Even before these events, Nixon was increasingly sympathetic to attacks by Ehrlichman and especially Haldeman on the welfare reform package and the continuing HEW efforts to obtain its passage. This shift was completed when Ehrlichman and the president in June 1972 rejected the compromise on HR 1 negotiated by

Richardson and Hodgson. An HEW "option paper" assured the president that the eventual legislation would be similar in many ways to the original 1969 FAP proposal, but without compromise no bill could pass.[27] Despite a signed plea from nineteen Republican senators, including one who was the Republican party's national chairman, Nixon stood pat. Antiwelfare sentiments that he had once used to push FAP were now used to attack anyone who followed that road. In August the Republican party platform declared:

We flatly oppose programs or politics which embrace the principle of a government-guaranteed income. We reject as unconscionable the idea that all citizens have the right to be supported by the government, regardless of their ability or desire to support themselves and their families.[28]

Although McGovern after his nomination had disavowed his $1000-per-person plan, Nixon and his cabinet hammered away at the Democrats as representing the "welfare ethic."

The president was not the only one to abandon the administration's welfare reform package. The intergovernmental lobby, which had been the staunchest and strongest supporter of the House bill in 1971, began to lose heart as the measure languished in the Finance Committee. General revenue sharing, in contrast, seemed increasingly likely to pass. With Mills now behind the measure, the biggest barrier was removed. A bill passed the Ways and Means Committee in April 1972 and passed the House, dramatically, in June. General revenue sharing undermined the fiscal relief arguments for welfare reform. Though the states and localities had extra reason to desire the freedom afforded by unrestricted federal grants, general revenue sharing actually promised to meet rising welfare costs more quickly than the welfare reform package: a new welfare system would take years to implement, whereas revenue sharing would begin within months. For this reason and because revenue sharing seemed more likely to pass, the intergovernmental lobby shifted its resources away from welfare reform. Senator Long seems to have been aware that his committee's delay in welfare reform was fueling the movement for general revenue sharing and that in a head-to-head encounter the intergovernmental groups would opt for the latter. In June Senate leaders finally asked Long to report the revenue-sharing bill, implicitly recommending that his committee lay aside welfare reform.[29]

Despite the abandonment of the Family Assistance Plan by the president and the intergovernmental groups, some supporters still sought a Senate compromise. Suspicion of HR 1 had been registered at the Democratic convention where the platform declared:

H.R. 1 and its various amendments, is not humane and does not meet the social and economic objectives that we believe in, and it should be defeated. It perpetuates the coercion of forced work requirements.[30]

The softness of support for the measure was ultimately confirmed when the Ribicoff-Richardson compromise (now disavowed by Richardson) lost in an October vote, 34 to 52. A measure even closer to the administration's desires attracted no presidential support, and it lost by a similar margin.

Just as the HR 1 work requirement was detached from FAP and passed, so was the bill's provision for establishment of a national income floor for the aged, the disabled, and the blind. During the tumultuous debate over aiding young families, reform of the adult categories quietly worked its way through Congress, achieving passage in 1972 as Supplemental Security Income. Even in 1970 both houses of Congress wanted such a program. In approving the Family Assistance Plan in April 1970, the House passed a national income floor for the adult categories. And while the Senate Finance Committee blocked FAP, it reported out in 1970 an adult categories bill actually more generous to some people than the House bill. The House and Senate bills were not reconciled, and the proposals died with the Ninety-first Congress. Unlike these earlier bills, HR 1 proposed that this national income floor be administered directly by the federal government. The Senate Finance Committee agreed to this approach, dropping its previous preferences for state administration and for separating the three adult categories from one another. The Senate passed the bill by a margin of 68 to 5 in October 1972, in the midst of the presidential campaign and after hopes of passing FAP had died. The president signed the bill on October 30. Only in the closing weeks of its legislative history did the new program acquire the name by which it is now known—Supplemental Security Income (SSI).[31] This new program increased the threshold in some states at which a person qualified for benefits, and its lower reduction rate (50 percent) and relaxed means test expanded the number of beneficiaries and the level of their benefits. An addition of 2.8 million aged people alone occurred in its first year.

During the time that Congress and the administration were preoccupied with the Family Assistance Plan, the social services budget was skyrocketing out of control. The 1962 services legislation embodied in Titles IV and XVI of the Social Security Act had offered 75 percent federal cost sharing for a wide range of state services to present, past, or potential welfare recipients. Open-ended and permissively administered, the program became a gold mine by 1971 for enterprising states looking for "backdoor revenue sharing." The most successful were big states like New York, Illinois, and California. At one time California alone received two-fifths of all federal expenditures under the program. Mississippi soon proposed social services expansion requiring federal funds equal to more than half the state's budget. The federal program mushroomed from a cost of $522 million in 1970 to $1.7 billion in 1972, and the increases were continuing. Under this pressure Congress in 1972 passed a ceiling of $2.5 billion on the program. In 1974 it finally adopted legislation aimed at defining more specifically which social services the federal government should share.[32]

Interlude: 1973–1976

With the defeat of HR 1 in 1972, welfare reform efforts hit a hiatus. President Nixon and then President Gerald R. Ford did not propose new legislation, and it was not until August 1977 that President Jimmy Carter presented a bill. This lull was not for lack of efforts within HEW, however. Three major efforts there produced extensive new proposals, only to be either rejected or postponed by the White House. All these efforts were mounted by the Office of Income Security Policy in the Office of the Assistant Secretary for Planning and Evaluation (ASPE), HEW. This staff had not gotten into FAP in a big way because the ongoing analytical effort during 1969–1972 was carried on by the separate Family Assistance Planning Group also located in the Office of the Secretary. Before FAP, people in the Office of Research, Plans, Programs, and Evaluation of the Office of Economic Opportunity (located in the Executive Office of the President) had paid the most attention to negative income tax proposals. In 1972, however, ASPE was encouraged by Secretary Elliot Richardson to take a new look at welfare reform; and with the demise of HR 1, ASPE became the nerve center of the continuing struggle for a negative income tax.

In August 1972 Richardson became committed to massive rethinking and reorganization of HEW's three hundred programs. This "Mega-Proposal" would require major new integrative legislation in health, education, and social services, as well as in income security policy.[33] The income security sections of the proposal were heavily influenced by the still-continuing controversy over HR 1. This HR 1 debate over work incentives was answered in the Mega-Proposal by excluding employable people from receiving benefits and instead helping them get a job—rather like Senator Long's guaranteed job proposals. But unlike the Senate bill, the HEW proposal still allowed unemployable members of each household to receive benefits—$1800 for a four-person family (as opposed to $2700 for a family without an employable member). This family could in addition keep the first $1800 of its breadwinner's earnings; beyond that its benefits would be reduced at a rate of 50 percent, for a break-even point of $5400. This proposal was the first major HEW proposal that incorporated different guarantee levels for employable and unemployable people. Unfortunately it went too far in this respect, assuming that all employable people would have or could be given a job—a goal likely to be politically unthinkable at that time. This failing is partly attributable to the fact that the five specialists who designed the proposal had not helped design or defend the Family Assistance Plan, nor did they have any actual experience in welfare administration.[34]

In December 1972 Secretary Richardson presented the Mega-Proposal to a bemused White House meeting including John Ehrlichman and Caspar Weinberger, director of the Office of Management and Budget. Little support for the Mega-Proposal resulted, and Richardson was unable to stay behind and fight for it, for the president had already announced that Richardson was to become secretary of defense. The chances for a major proposal of this nature seemed to deteriorate further when Nixon's 1973 State of the Union message chastised Congress for making comprehensive reform impossible and proposed to concentrate on improving existing programs. Moreover Nixon replaced Richardson with Weinberger, no supporter of the Mega-Proposal and a man who as deputy director and then director of the Office of Management and Budget had been unhappy with the Family Assistance Plan. Nevertheless, Weinberger soon became a proponent of a welfare reform proposal that came closer to a pure negative income tax scheme than anything supported by any HEW secretary before or since.

When Weinberger came to HEW, he brought in two fellow Californians who were identified with Governor Ronald Reagan's approach to welfare reform. James S. Dwight, Jr., administrator of the Social and Rehabilitation Service, had been deputy director of the California Department of Finance. Robert B. Carleson, U.S. commissioner of welfare (not a standard administrative post) and special assistant to the secretary, had been commissioner of the California Department of Social Welfare. Carleson had overseen Reagan's effort to cut back the welfare case load and budget under the California Welfare Reform Act of 1971. Together, Reagan and Carleson had testified against HR 1 before the Senate Finance Committee in February 1972. While Dwight and Carleson pursued their efforts to tighten administration of the AFDC program, a new effort to produce major legislation began, spurred by a vaguely worded White House request that HEW come up with a welfare plan that could pass. Weinberger appointed a Welfare Reform Interagency Task Force, with the staff work to be done in ASPE.

After a series of briefings and debates, Weinberger became committed to the negative income tax approach.[35] He was strongly influenced by the arguments of economist Milton Friedman. The first person to design a negative income tax, Friedman had published in the 1968 *Republican Papers* an article, "The Case for the Negative Income Tax."[36] In August 1973 Weinberger's staff sent a copy of the article by diplomatic pouch to the secretary while he was on a mission to the Soviet Union. In October Friedman himself was brought to HEW headquarters to brief the secretary. Weinberger came to see the negative income tax, not just as a solution to the welfare mess, but as a way to cut down bureaucracy and protect the privacy of beneficiaries. He was particularly enthusiastic about giving the job of administration to the Treasury department, in order to integrate the federal tax and transfer efforts. Using Friedman's arguments, Weinberger was able in November 1973 to obtain Nixon's approval to write a full-blown proposal. When this presidential decision was made, Secretary of the Treasury George Schultz appointed the Task Force on the Administrative Feasibility of an Income Maintenance System. Although the Internal Revenue Service members of the Task Force were not eager to take on new welfare responsibilities, the task force concluded in its April 1974 report that it would be practical to administer a negative income tax from the Treasury.

The Watergate scandal had begun to erupt in 1973, and by 1974 the Nixon White House was entirely distracted from the welfare reform initiative. With the accession of Gerald Ford to the presidency in August, Weinberger's efforts resumed. By this time HEW had produced a detailed proposal, the Income Supplement Program (ISP). Unlike the Mega-Proposal, ISP sought to "cash out" food stamps, and it did not depend on the creation of many new public service jobs. Unlike the Family Assistance Plan, ISP would cover childless couples and unattached individuals as well as families. At the federal level it was a pure negative income tax, though this name was meticulously avoided. The basic payment was $3600 for a family of four. With a reduction rate of 50 percent the break-even point was $7200. No distinction in basic payment or reduction rate was made between employable and unemployable people. However, the states would be permitted to supplement the incomes of families that previously had received AFDC, as well as others. Also, the states would be required to implement a work registration requirement.

Secretary Weinberger formally proposed the Income Supplement Program to President Ford in November 1974.[37] While a congressman, Ford had voted for the Family Assistance Plan in both 1970 and 1971. However, he was under increasing pressure from the right wing of his party, particularly from Reagan, who was preparing to challenge Ford for the Republican nomination. In September Reagan had published a *Blueprint for National Welfare Reform*, declaring that California had cut its welfare rolls by 350,000, and that the federal government should follow the example. Thus in January 1975 Ford postponed a decision on ISP. Nelson Rockefeller, now vice-president, supported ISP within the White House. But faced with the Reagan challenge, Ford announced that he did not want Rockefeller as his vice-president in his next term. During this period some outside pressure for extension of welfare was exerted by the Subcommittee on Fiscal Policy of the Joint Economic Committee. The committee's series of studies and hearings done between 1972 and 1974 remains the definitive treatment of the existing welfare system and possible new approaches. In December 1974 Chairman Martha Griffiths (Democrat, Michigan) introduced the Subcommittee's Tax Credit and Allowances Act, with many striking similarities to the Income Supplement Program. There was speculation that Griffiths's long friendship with Ford might persuade him to support her ideas. But he continued to postpone the decision, faced with a nearly successful effort by Reagan to wrest the nomination from him. In 1976 Ford reportedly vowed that if he was reelected, he would propose ISP to Congress. Ford's defeat by Jimmy

Carter required the internal process of consensus building to begin anew.

Since 1972, Senator Long had pressed for passage of an earned income tax credit, and he finally got his way in 1975 with legislation for a refundable credit of up to $400 for each family with children. Those with no children or no earnings got nothing. The benefit rose as earnings grew to $4000 and then was reduced by a rate of 10 percent until it was phased out at an income of $8000. The benefit was paid on an annual basis and administered by the Internal Revenue Service as a part of the personal tax return. Those with income taxes less than the credit received a refund for the difference. Many liked the approach because a person could not receive benefits, a work bonus, unless he was employed. The tax credit was also advanced as a means of protecting the poor from regressive Social Security payroll taxes, although childless people were denied such relief; the tax credit did not cover them. Long had first proposed the measure in 1972, as part of the HR 1 package that his committee put in the place of the House-passed Family Assistance Plan. When that attempt failed, Long proposed the tax credit as a part of the Social Services Amendments of 1974. President Ford opposed the credit as a poorly targeted boondoggle, and the House insisted that it be dropped in conference. In 1975, however, both Long's Finance Committee and the House Ways and Means Committee linked the tax credit to a $22.8 billion emergency tax cut needed to pull the country out of recession. Although Ford again attacked the proposal, it was totally overshadowed by other issues and the breakneck speed with which both houses hurried the tax cut through. This lack of debate is remarkable, considering the huge cost of the measure ($1.4 billion in 1977).

Anticlimax: 1977–1978

In 1977 the Carter administration brought the nation, for the first time in five years, back into a debate over comprehensive welfare reform. Jimmy Carter had been the only southern governor to support the Nixon Family Assistance Plan. In August 1977 Carter proposed his own Program for Better Jobs and Income (PBJI).[38] Carter envisioned replacement of AFDC and SSI with a nationally administered system of guarantees. The Food Stamp program would be completely abolished, although Medicaid, housing subsidies, and a few other in-kind programs would remain. Under PBJI, benefits would be a combination of cash assistance from HEW and an expanded earned income tax credit from the Treasury. Like the Canadian proposals of 1973, the 1977 Carter proposals divided beneficiaries according to their employability, subjecting them to varying benefits. A family of four not expected to work would receive income "support" of $4200, while a family with an employable head would receive income "supplementation" of up to $2300. Beneficiaries in the first group would have their benefits reduced at a 50 percent rate starting with the first dollar of earnings. Those in the second group would ultimately be subject to a 50 percent reduction rate, but only after they had been allowed to keep the first $3800 in earnings. Those expected to work included all able-bodied people without children, the head of a two-parent family, and mothers with no children under fourteen. Mothers with no children under seven would be expected to work at least part-time.

According to the Carter bill, those expected to work would receive no benefits during an initial eight-week period of job search (mothers with children of ages seven to thirteen would continue to receive benefits, however). If no job were found after that period, the recipient would be eligible to be moved to the support tier, providing higher benefits. But to minimize this eventuality, Carter proposed a guarantee that if an employable person could find no job, he would be offered a specially created job. The most expensive and controversial part of the bill was this provision for 1.4 million public service jobs. To encourage a preference for normal jobs over these specially created jobs, a person could not take one of the latter until after five weeks of looking elsewhere and could not collect the earned income tax credit for earnings in public service employment.

A central feature of the Carter plan, which it shared with the Mega-Proposal, was that it provided a similar benefit structure to all groups with earned income above a certain level; that is, the same reduction rate and break-even level applied to all. This arrangement occurred because recipients of the lower benefit did not suffer any loss of benefits in their first $3800 of earnings. At that point recipients of the higher benefit would already have had it taxed down to the same level of $2300. Beyond that point, the two federal tiers were indistinguishable; a person working full time for an entire year was treated just the same in both schemes.[39] Actually, the tiers did differ somewhat because of federal policy toward efforts by states to supplement the federal payment. Federal incentives were designed to induce the states to provide more help to those not expected to work than to employable, two-parent families with children, thus assuring that the latter encountered a lower reduction rate. Thus a family of four with no member expected to work could receive a state-federal benefit of $6370 (just under the poverty line) with a reduction rate of 70 percent. The two-parent families could only receive state supplements up to $4700 (75 percent of the poverty line), but would suffer a reduction rate of no more than 52 percent.

The two-tier aspect of the Program for Better Jobs and Income was either illusory or restricted to the sphere of state supplementation. In contrast, analysts in the Department of Labor unsuccessfully proposed an explicitly two-tier plan: the supplementation tier would have a benefit of $2100 and a reduction rate of 25 percent, while the support tier would have a benefit of $4200 and a reduction rate of 50 percent. The department proposed to administer supplementation, leaving the support tier to HEW. The Labor plan offered lower reduction rates than the HEW plan at higher levels of earnings. On the other hand, the HEW plan had lower reduction rates at the initial levels of earnings. Since the recipient could keep all of his first $3800 in earnings, the reduction rate in that range was zero. Combining these work incentives with the 50 percent rate at higher ranges of earnings, the HEW plan actually had a lower average tax rate than the Labor plan.

The Carter welfare reform proposals had several features specifically beneficial to the states and localities. As in the 1969 Family Assistance Plan, each was guaranteed a saving of at least 10 percent in the first year of the program. Special incentives were provided for state supplements where, as in about forty states, the basic federal payment would be lower than existing AFDC levels. Another measure attractive to the states and localities was a proposed $600 million grant for emergency assistance; the federal government would foot part of the bill for general assistance for the first time since the 1930s.

The Carter welfare reform package called for the abolition of the Food Stamp program. But even while agonizing over comprehensive reform of the welfare system, the administration had moved quickly to suggest improvements in the Food Stamp program when it came up for renewal in 1977. Among the changes proposed were abolishing the purchase requirement and simplifying the deductions allowed before a person's income is considered in need of augmentation. Elimination of the purchase requirement had received bipartisan support in 1976 in the form of a bill jointly sponsored by senators George McGovern and Robert Dole. Food stamps were already free for families with income of less than $30 a month. By making them free for all other beneficiaries, the program would encourage more participation by those eligible. Congressional passage of the proposals reflected the familiar pattern by which rural congressmen supported food stamps in exchange for urban support for farm price supports. This coalition was especially explicit in the House where the measure passed by the lopsided margin of 317–102 on July 27, 1977.

Within days of taking office, Carter committed his administration to producing a welfare reform package by May 1, less than four months away. Though this deadline was not met, it lent a frantic quality to internal deliberations that were already plagued by the natural disorganization characteristic of a new administration. Carter assigned HEW secretary Joseph Califano to lead a three-month study of welfare reform. Although HEW was the nominal leader of the effort and was able to dominate many deliberations concerning cash welfare, officials of the Department of Labor (especially Arnold Packer, assistant secretary for policy evaluation and research) engaged in an effective guerrilla campaign that secured a massive jobs component in the president's program. As the public part of the welfare reform study, HEW conducted a massive outreach, soliciting opinions from nine thousand participants in meetings or hearings and from another five thousand who wrote or phoned.[40] The showpiece of the welfare reform study was the thirty-two-member Consulting Group on Welfare Reform chaired by Henry Aaron, the new HEW assistant secretary for planning and evaluation (ASPE). This group included representatives from the Executive Office of the President, six cabinet departments, six congressional committees, and three intergovernmental groups, as well as poverty lawyers and one AFDC recipient. Each week the group held one public meeting and one private one. Actually, the major debate was going on largely between the departments of Labor and HEW, and this conflict did not always surface in the public meetings. This faceoff meant that proposals favored by neither department but preferred by others received less attention. Aaron quickly winnowed the various proposals to three leading choices, all of which proposed to expand cash assistance to people outside AFDC. This narrowing of options ruled out other ideas that an internal paper said had received "significant attention" but actually had not been considered seriously within HEW: (1) cutting back on the existing AFDC system, (2) moving incrementally such as by a federally funded AFDC-U program nationwide, (3) devolving more welfare responsibilities to the states by a new block grant approach, (4) integrating income transfers with the tax system, and (5) expanding social insurance to include more people currently receiving public assistance. The leading choices outlined were (1) a negative income tax (supported most strongly by the ASPE staff in HEW), (2) guaranteed jobs at the living wage (supported by the Labor Department and by a welfare reform task force of the New Coalition, an umbrella group comprising five powerful intergovernmental organization), and (3) the triple track, a combination of work bonuses and unemployment compensation (supported by the AFL-CIO and by Tom Joe, a veteran of the FAP debates who was regarded favorably by the Carter White House).

On March 25 at his first briefing on welfare reform, Carter asked that the proposals be analyzed by his touted zero-cost planning technique. Analysts were to dissect existing programs and then rebuild them by increments whose value could be determined and compared. New spending would also be considered in $1 billion increments. Carter insisted that the plan presented to him require no new funds, leaving to him the decision of whether a plan requiring new funds would be preferable. While this procedure was aimed at preserving presidential prerogatives, it actually disrupted the policy process and isolated Carter from important decisions made in the following months. The disruption began at an April 11 briefing when Carter rejected the three leading choices because each would require billions of dollars in new spending. Secretary Califano, who had the unexpectedly dubious honor of presenting the alternatives to the president, argued in vain that the additional cost was necessitated by Carter's desire both to extend welfare to new groups and to protect those groups already receiving benefits. Faced with these arguments, the president rebelled: "Are you telling me that there is no way to improve the present welfare system except by spending billions of dollars? In that case, to hell with it! We're wasting our time."[41] Carter was apparently beginning to see the zero-cost constraint as not just a planning tool but as an end in itself. He sent the planners back to design proposals that really would involve no new spending.

Carter's insistence that a reformed welfare system must cost no more than existing programs made it impossible for the administration to agree on a welfare reform package in time for his May 1 deadline. In part, this delay occurred because the analysts were sidetracked in a fruitless effort to reconcile conflicting goals. But the major reason for the delay was that most policymakers outside the White House and some within the president's executive office, believed that unless the freeze on spending were lifted, no significant reform was possible. Curiously, however, this belief and the delay that it engendered did not prevent the internal debates from continuing to examine major initiatives that clearly would exceed the president's spending limit. The departments of HEW and Labor jousted over their respective proposals for consolidated cash assistance and public service jobs. Despite the deadlock over their proposals, these departments conspired to suppress the third alternative, Tom Joe's triple track, in subsequent presentations to the president. However, Joe had friends in the White House who saw that his proposals continued to receive a hearing.

On May 2, the president issued a general statement outlining the administration's goals for welfare reform.[42] The statement left the major questions about cash assistance undecided. The statement did, however, clearly commit the administration to enough public jobs to give "every family with children and a member able to work" access to employment. For months, Labor and HEW had fought over this issue. Analysts in the Labor department, which would administer job portions of the welfare reform package, had sought a public jobs program large enough to guarantee many people a job. HEW officials, who would have no jurisdiction over jobs, had questioned whether the program would work and whether Congress would buy it. Having made these arguments to the president, HEW officials were surprised to hear him make such a strong commitment to public service employment. (In fact, Carter went beyond his text, declaring that all those eligible "will have a job"; Labor secretary Marshall subsequently pointed out that the commitment was to seeing that jobs were available, not to placing everyone in a job.)

The president's commitment to a massive jobs program possessed an air of unreality because of his continuing insistence, publicly declared on May 2, that his welfare reform package would have no higher cost than the present system. It was doubtful that these goals were compatible. And even if the jobs program would not break Carter's spending freeze, it would surely soak up enough funds to effectively frustrate most of the other aspects of comprehensive welfare reform. Nevertheless, the Labor victory prompted HEW to press its case for consolidated cash assistance, and by the end of May the administration was virtually agreed on the

HEW plan. HEW and Labor coincided on the need for a work requirement, but they disagreed on what benefit structure to offer families whose heads were expected to work. Concerned that these families retain an incentive to work, the Department of Labor advanced a plan that would provide them a lower benefit and a lower reduction rate than received by those not expected to work. In contrast, the initial HEW plan sought to provide the same benefit structure to all recipients. In response to criticism from the Labor Department, HEW eventually modified its proposal to provide a lower benefit to those actually working. However, the benefit structure did not treat people differently according to whether or not they were expected to work. Thus anyone who after trying to find a job was unable to do so, would receive the same benefits, while a common benefit structure would also be shared by all those with earned incomes over $3800 a year. By the end of May the administration had adopted the modified HEW plan for federal benefits, but the matter of supplementation by the states remained to be settled.

In June and July, the Labor department won back from HEW some of the ground it had lost in May. HEW proposed to mandate the same limits on state supplementation for unemployable and employable recipients alike. However, some states were already paying recipients generous amounts of aid, and representatives of the Labor department and the Council of Economic Advisors worried that to extend such aid to employables would discourage them from working. Moreover, an increase in the basic benefit available to employables would expand the total number of people receiving benefits, a situation that could be prevented only by raising the reduction rate, an action that would itself reduce work incentives. As it was, the HEW incentives for state supplements envisioned a rather high reduction rate of 60 percent for employables and unemployables alike. DOL proposed as an alternative that no state supplementation be given to two-parent families with children.

The dispute over state supplementation was resolved by William Nordhaus of the Council of Economic Advisors, who proposed a scheme whereby state supplements would be much lower for those expected to work and would involve a reduction rate no higher than 52 percent, compared to 70 percent for unemployables. The consensus was that it might not seem fair to give lower benefits to an employable person even if no job were available, but that if this person were given high benefits and a high reduction rate, it would be difficult to dislodge him from welfare even when a job became available.

Like the commitment to a jobs program, the evolution of a cash assistance plan implied much higher spending than President Carter was willing to consider. The internal momentum of these proposals was not accompanied by a loosening of the president's interdiction of new welfare spending. At the climactic April 11 briefing, Secretary Califano had methodically shown the president that new initiatives in jobs or cash welfare would force a difficult tradeoff between protecting existing beneficiaries and providing fiscal relief to state and local governments. The momentum toward major initiatives in both cash welfare and jobs made that tradeoff particularly acute. Yet Carter remained adamant in opposing any increase in cost, and he did not change his mind until two months of pressure from outside the administration forced him to. In late May, Califano, with Marshall's approval, unsuccessfully warned Carter,

The politics of welfare reform are treacherous under any circumstances and they can be impossible at no higher initial cost because it is likely that so many people who are now receiving benefits will be hurt. The states are our natural allies in welfare reform—most members of Congress would still prefer not to deal with the subject at all—and there is virtually no relief in this proposal for governors and mayors.[43]

With Carter unsympathetic to such arguments, administration analysts sought budgetary room for his initiatives by cutting back in ways that invited just the kind of opposition that Califano and Marshall had warned of. For example, the administration planned to restrict existing benefits to teenage mothers living with their parents, and it sharply limited the amount of fiscal relief offered to states and localities. Savings were also sought by lowering the basic payment under PBJI. By early July it had dropped from $4700 (75 percent of the poverty level) to $4200 (65 percent of the poverty level).

Carter was slow to see the political drawbacks of cutting back on some people's benefits or starving state and local governments, despite the fact that the Democratic coalition included advocates of the poor and leaders of cities and states with large welfare costs. Representative of many of these pressures was Abraham Beame, mayor of New York City, a traditionally Democratic stronghold with many active organizations of welfare beneficiaries and with a special need for fiscal relief. At the April 11

White House meeting, Stuart Eizenstat, director of the domestic policy staff, had reminded Carter of his promise to Beame during the presidential campaign to reform welfare in a way that would relieve the city of many of its welfare costs. Yet the welfare package emerging in late May greatly disappointed Beame, and by July he was spearheading a coalition of the U.S. Conference of Mayors and other groups to press Carter to relax his spending limit.

As the external pressures mounted, the Carter administration began to feel pressed by its August deadline for presenting a completed plan to Congress and the public. On July 25 Califano sent a long memo to the president containing a zero-cost proposal as requested but also including a number of more expensive plans, along with strong arguments for them. The president's domestic policy staff stressed that the zero-cost proposal included fiscal relief for the states and localities only at the price of lowering benefits for 6.1 million current AFDC beneficiaries. Carter finally relaxed his cost constraint, agreeing to $2.8 billion in new spending. More fiscal relief was added, and controversial restrictions on existing benefits were dropped.

Carter unveiled his welfare reform package on August 6, 1977, in Plains, Georgia. It received a favorable initial reception from groups representing existing recipients and from states and localities. In September the National Governors Conference endorsed the proposals 31 to 4—a milestone never attained by the Nixon plan. However, in buying the support of such groups, the administration risked provoking opposition to the increased cost of the program. This danger was made worse by the inaccuracy of the administration's estimate of the real costs of the reform. The program's cost, and the estimates themselves, both became key issues in the subsequent debates.

The initial congressional enthusiasm for PBJI overshadowed some dangers that the administration had discounted in preparing the plan. Senator Long, unmollified by the emphasis on jobs, attacked the plan. He charged that "the overwhelming majority of the personnel who put the plan together in the Department of Health, Education, and Welfare were here before President Carter came on the scene and they will be there after he is gone."[44] More ominously, the chairman of the House Ways and Means Committee, Al Ullman (Democrat, Oregon), did not like the administration's bill either, despite repeated efforts to conciliate him. Whereas Wilbur Mills had been the Family Assistance Plan's most potent congressional ally, Ullman had been in the tiny minority of three that had voted against it in committee in both 1970 and 1971. (Ullman replaced Wilbur Mills as chairman in 1974.) As early as the spring of 1977 Ullman warned Califano that he was "deadset against any kind of negative income tax or guaranteed annual income" because it was "unworkable and a political disaster."[45]

Within a month after Carter formally unveiled his welfare reform package, the House began to examine the bill through a special Welfare Reform Subcommittee composed of twenty-nine members from the three standing committees with jurisdiction over parts of the bill (Agriculture, Education and Labor, and Ways and Means). Speaker Thomas P. O'Neill (Democrat, Massachusetts) had used such a committee successfully to pilot the president's energy proposals through the House during the preceding months. Chaired by Congressman James C. Corman (Democrat, California), the subcommittee held twenty-two days of hearings in Washington, D.C., and nine states, filling nine volumes. The committee aired a vast number of criticisms of the Carter plan. It devoted much initial attention to the costly and untested proposal to create 1.4 million public service jobs. Would there be enough jobs of the right kind? Would they upset the private labor market? Would states and localities be able to use the jobs for essential services? Would eligible people have incentives to take public jobs? Would they then receive enough training and incentives to move into private jobs? Could the jobs program be administered successfully?

The House subcommittee eventually passed most of the administration's job proposals intact, but in other areas it either showed ominous divisions or it introduced amendments unhelpful to the bill's progress. Three standing committees would eventually have to ratify major parts of the bill affecting food stamps, employment programs, and AFDC, and the chairman of each committee opposed key sections of the bill. For example, Thomas Foley (Democrat, Washington), chairman of the Agriculture Committee opposed the bill because it would do away with food stamps. Debates arose concerning work incentives, regional equity, and other issues. By December the program faced growing Congressional concern. Yet a majority of Corman's subcommittee remained committed to comprehensive reform, even to the extent of liberalizing the Carter bill's benefits and eligibility. A poverty advocacy group observed that the Corman changes produced a "better bill for recipients."[46] Some of these changes went against the purposes of the Carter bill. The House subcommittee amended the state supplementation provisions to allow the states to provide employable people the same 70 percent reduction rate provided to those not expected to work. The House revisions actually provided less short-term fiscal relief to states and localities than the Carter bill. Many of the House changes drove up the bill's costs. The Congressional Budget Office (CBO) estimated that the Corman bill would have a net cost to the federal government of more than $20 billion, nearly $3 billion above updated estimates of the cost of the Carter bill.[47]

From the beginning, costs were an issue for the Carter plan. In November the CBO challenged the cost estimates advanced by HEW and OMB for the administration. According to CBO reckoning, the net cost of the measure to the government would be nearly $10 billion more than the $2.8 billion estimated by HEW and OMB. Among CBO's objections was that HEW and OMB had excluded from the program's costs the nearly $3 billion transferred through the proposed change in the Earned Income Tax Credit. HEW had also offset the cost of the new program by the expected availability of revenues earmarked for poor people by the president's proposed crude oil equalization tax—which Congress was in the process of rejecting. The administration figures also offset the cost with expected savings from tightened control over fraud and abuse in welfare programs (including Medicaid, which was not to be touched by PBJI) and from cutbacks in unemployment insurance. The CBO argued that "these sources could be available with or without the welfare reform initiative" and therefore should not be treated as offsets.[48] But in some cases the Carter plan could legitimately be credited with the saving of some revenues being spent on programs that it would replace. CBO questioned HEW's contention that PBJI would replace countercyclical CETA jobs, arguing that these jobs were scheduled to end anyway in the event of economic recovery. As it turned out, Congress renewed some of these jobs in 1978.

The Carter administration's use of offsets to downplay the costs of the welfare reform package did not fool Congress and the public, although the ploy may have successfully misled the president himself about the real costs of his proposals. Although the administration should have been more straightforward, most assumptions underlying these offsets had been stated from the beginning in material released to the press when the president presented his proposals in August 1977.[49] But even aside from the question of offsets, HEW and OMB disagreed with CBO over costs.

Although HEW eventually conceded that the bill's net cost to the federal government was at least $8.8 billion, the CBO held to its higher estimate, even raising it to $17.4 billion. The continuing disagreement over cost estimates eventually helped doom Carter's proposals.

Even though the special House Welfare Reform Subcommittee passed the Corman bill in February 1978, the congressional mood was turning against the measure. In January the administration utterly missed its announced deadline for proposing a national health insurance bill. Reforming welfare before deciding the health question would create special uncertainties. Medicaid was more expensive than AFDC in some states, and the Carter bill could not solve both problems. To make matters worse for the Carter bill, bad economic news was casting doubt on the administration's optimistic assumptions on future problems and the availability of tax revenues to deal with them.[50] And, finally, 1978 was an election year. Every member of the House would be up for reelection, and none relished having to defend a vote for an expensive new program with such a limited constituency. Al Ullman had been from the beginning an irreconcilable opponent of the administration's proposals, and now other congressmen came to his side. Shortly before the February vote Ullman introduced his own modest welfare reform bill. Just before passing the Corman bill, the subcommittee only narrowly (13 to 16) defeated Ullman's bill.

By March welfare reform was "pretty much dead in the water" by the candid analysis of one White House source.[51] Into this vacuum marched Republican senators Henry Bellmon (Oklahoma) and Howard Baker (Tennessee), introducing their own bill with Senator Ribicoff as cosponsor. Like the Ullman bill, the Baker-Bellmon bill was avowedly "incremental." Net costs to the federal government would be $5 billion to $8 billion for the Ullman bill and $9.3 billion for the Baker-Bellmon bill. These bills did not propose to universalize cash welfare nor to "cash out" food stamps. AFDC was to be left in state hands, but both bills mandated national standards in benefits and required an AFDC-U program in every state. Both proposed expansion of the earned income tax credit, and both sought to create jobs (Baker-Bellmon, 375,000 under CETA, Ullman, 500,000 under WIN). The Ullman bill was distinctive in sharply limiting AFDC-U benefits to seventeen weeks and requiring recipients to pay back the government when they had worked their way off welfare ("recoupment"). By thus lowering the benefits of present and future beneficiaries, the Ullman bill's price tag was less, but it provoked the virulent opposition of organizations and congressmen aligned with beneficiaries. The Baker-Bellmon bill avoided some of these difficulties and also consciously courted the states and localities, offering them more fiscal relief than even the Corman bill, and nearly as much as the Carter bill. To make these political gestures, however, the Baker-Bellmon bill had to cost more than the Ullman bill.

In introducing their bill, Baker and Bellmon shrewdly captured some of the valuable middle ground that Ullman was monopolizing, and their bill helped impart some new momentum to welfare reform. The bill caught the imagination of editors and of state and local leaders. Considered a prospect for the 1980 Republican presidential nomination, Baker was not unaware that a constructive, moderate initiative in welfare reform could enhance his image. Curiously, Baker and Bellmon both came from states without an AFDC-U program, even though their bill proposed to require every state to have one. Nevertheless hometown news accounts characterized the proposals as "thriftier" than Carter's.[52] However, the Washington-based archconservative weekly *Human Events* castigated Baker and Bellmon for pushing a "guaranteed income plan."[53]

With the Carter and Corman bills becalmed or downright repudiated, members of the administration warmed to the Baker-Bellmon and Ullman proposals. The narrowness of the margin by which the Corman proposal passed the special subcommittee in February had convinced some ASPE analysts that common ground had to be found, and this view spread upward through the bureaucracy. Two contrasting positions taken by HEW Secretary Califano in Senate testimony illustrate the change. In February Califano said, "Chairman Ullman's plan and other incremental proposals would not, in our view, effectively come to grips with the problems of the existing system." By March he was saying "The introduction of the Ullman and Baker-Bellmon-Ribicoff proposals reflects an emerging consensus for significant reform upon which to build."[54] In April Califano began discussions with supporters of the Ullman and Baker-Bellmon measures; welfare specialists in HEW, Congress, and outside organizations churned out suggestions for compromise. These negotiations were constrained by the administration's need to avoid alienating those who still supported its comprehensive package. Corman and the majority of subcommittee members had defended the administration bill against Ullman's in February, and they still felt it had a chance on the floor. The intergovernmental groups, strongest supporters of the administration's approach, wanted to be assured that a compromise would provide enough fiscal relief. With the support and ideas of analysts in HEW and the Urban Institute, the New Coalition eventually made a breakthrough. In May the coalition invited Ullman and Moynihan to discuss the status of welfare reform, in a meeting chaired by Governor Michael S. Dukakis (Democrat, Massachusetts). In a judgment echoed by Moynihan, Ullman pronounced the Carter and Corman bills dead: "We are in May of an election year and all the options that might otherwise be possible are not available to us."[55] Ullman plugged his own bill but expressed a willingness to bargain. He urged the New Coalition to work out a compromise, estimating that it had only three weeks in which to act. Within days the coalition was pushing a new proposal, and negotiations between the administration, Ullman, and Corman began in earnest.

The New Coalition's bill included features common to both the Ullman and Baker-Bellmon bills. It did not extend cash welfare to single persons and childless couples, but it did expand the earned income tax credit for families with children. It also mandated AFDC-U for all states and established a national floor for AFDC. Like the Ullman bill, the proposal included many new public service jobs; like the Baker-Bellmon bill, it provided generous fiscal relief to states and localities.[56] The proposal had startling and not coincidental similarities to compromises suggested by internal ASPE memos as early as February and by limited-circulation working papers emanating from the Urban Institute. Bargaining is especially difficult when the issues and implications are so complex, and the progress of the negotiations, possibly even their very existence, owed much to coaching from these analysts. By June (too late, some felt), the White House joined HEW in negotiating with the rest. A major meeting on June 7 included Dukakis, Ullman, Corman, Califano, and Marshall; Stuart Eizenstat, director of the Domestic Policy Staff in the Executive Office of the President; and leaders of the House Education and Labor Committee. This assemblage agreed on broad outlines of a compromise that closely approximated the New Coalition proposal.[57] Costs were a major unknown in the negotiations, with estimates ranging from $7 billion to $13 billion. The talks soon hit a fatal snag when more detailed analysis showed that the compromise would cost at least $14 billion.[58] Despite Ullman's avowals of cooperation, he did not relent in insisting that any compromise must cost no more than a net of $10 billion. The administration had convinced Corman to cut billions from his preferred position, but no one wanted to go all the way down to Ullman's level, especially if it meant consenting to some of the restrictive methods his bill used to keep the price tag low. As it was, groups and congressmen who were aligned with welfare beneficiaries were not enthusiastic about the compromise. The Center on Social Welfare Policy and Law, an organization with allies on the Corman subcommittee, questioned whether the New Coalition compromise offered "sufficient clear gains to offset the losses, including the loss of any hope for more comprehensive reform in the near future if this bill or anything like it were to pass."[59]

On June 22 Speaker O'Neill announced that efforts to negotiate a compromise House bill had failed, and he implicated the Senate in this quiet death of welfare reform. The House negotiators had asked O'Neill "whether further attempts at compromise would be worthwhile since the Senate might not act anyhow."[60] He reported that Senate leaders felt the bill could not be considered before January. Blaming the Senate was only a convenient way for the House to excuse its own inability to deal with welfare reform (the past hostility of the Senate to welfare reform would seemingly have justified the House in refusing to consider welfare reform in the first place). The failure had deeper roots. The positions of Ullman and the others were not getting any closer. Moreover the House was becoming increasingly negative about welfare spending. Not only were elections less than five months away, but Washington was reverberating with the lopsided decision by California voters on June 6 to amend the state constitution to drastically cut property taxes. The voters were revolting not simply against government spending but specifically against welfare programs. On June 13 the House responded symbolically by voting a 2 percent cut in the appropriations for HEW and four other departments. How times had changed since the heady days less than a year before when the administration set out to sell Congress on its comprehensive proposals! O'Neill judged that even a compromise based on the New Coalition proposals would have "very rough going in the House's present budget-cutting mood."[61] Some observers feared that the attitude toward welfare reform could only worsen. But based on its dislike of the compromise, the Center on Social Welfare Policy and Law argued that it was "hard to say that any time could clearly be worse than now."[62]

A few days after O'Neill had announced that House efforts to produce a compromise bill had failed, Senator Daniel P. Moynihan declared:

Anticlimax

"Welfare reform is not dead in the 95th Congress. It is alive and well in the United States Senate." Moynihan joined two other senators, Long and the majority whip, Alan Cranston (Democrat, California), in proposing a "no-frills" bill scheduled to cost $5 billion by 1982. Though termed the State and Local Welfare Reform and Fiscal Relief Act of 1978, this bill was not welfare reform in the same way that the other bills were. The only change proposed in the structure of AFDC was to switch it from a cost-sharing to block grant basis, an idea originated by Robert Carleson. The federal contribution would be equal to the 1978 federal share plus part of the 1978 state and local share of AFDC. Although later versions of the proposal sought to meet criticism for preventing low-benefit states from increasing benefits, the block grant approach would in effect place a cap on AFDC spending. And except for a modest increase in the earned income tax credit (a step Congress was likely to take in any event), the proposal made no extensions in the basic system of cash assistance, even the modest ones suggested in the Ullman and Baker-Bellmon bills: no national AFDC benefit floor, no extension of AFDC-U, no public service jobs. Ullman immediately attacked the Moynihan-Cranston-Long bill as "permanent and sizeable relief without reform." Henry Aaron, HEW assistant secretary for planning and evaluation, called for a bill that not only "contains . . . fiscal relief but brings about some structural reforms."[63] An unmistakable reason for Long's support of the measure was that by offering five years of fiscal relief to the states and localities—$2.5 billion by 1982—it would erase the single greatest impetus for significant expansion of the country's welfare programs.

Long's desire to buy off the states and localities was transparent, but why were Moynihan and Cranston, professed supporters of expanding the welfare system, advancing a proposal that could delay major reform for years? This inconsistency stemmed from inescapable political logic. Californians had just slashed the revenues available for the state's welfare programs and were now asking Cranston urgently for funds. For Moynihan, the never-ending fiscal emergencies in his constituency were categorical imperatives. The state of New York would receive $300 million a year in new federal aid. The possibility that the bill would endanger chances for a nationwide AFDC floor or universalization of AFDC-U mattered little in New York, which already had high benefits and an AFDC-U program. This fixation on fiscal relief was not unique to New York or California. In September the executive director of the National

Association of Counties urged county officials to support the Moynihan-Cranston-Long bill as the "last chance for fiscal relief this year."[64] Opposition to the proposal proceeded on two tracks. Within the Finance Committee, Senator Ribicoff sought to block it. And outside the committee, Senator Edward M. Kennedy (Democrat, Massachusetts) proposed his own welfare reform bill and promised to offer it as an amendment. With a cost of $7.1 billion, the Kennedy bill had some features of the New Coalition compromise. At the encouragement of the White House, analysts in HEW had aided the senator in preparing his proposal. With their bill stalled, Moynihan and Long persuaded the committee to recommend $400 million in fiscal relief as part of a tax bill. Opposed by the administration, this step was defeated on the Senate floor.[65]

Moynihan's alliance with Long was ironic in view of his previous leadership in the fight for the Family Assistance Plan, and some former allies considered it a betrayal. However, this move was consistent with the senator's outspoken desire to think first of New York and with his hardening conservatism on welfare issues. In January 1978 Moynihan lectured a White House conference that his state had spearheaded New Deal policies that helped the South and West, arguing that when New York was in trouble those areas should return the favor.[66] His position on welfare reform apparently represented a feeling that New York could not always afford to stand up for underprivileged people if they lived in other regions. It also stemmed from a willingness to bargain with Long for avowedly liberal purposes. According to one report, Moynihan had not originally supported the block grant approach, preferring straight fiscal relief. Long then insisted on block grants as the price for his support of the legislation. In general, Moynihan was more willing to compromise with Long than many welfare reformers liked. When criticized, Moynihan chided the liberals for being alarmist and unrealistic. Tartly expressed in his book on the 1970 defeat of the Family Assistance Plan, this disdain had grown since the book's publication.

Moynihan's increasing discomfort with liberal views about welfare began to show in July 1977, when he gained Long's support for including one year of fiscal relief in a committee bill, HR 7200. The House had passed this minor bill in June 1977, but before passing it in November the Senate Finance Committee freighted it with controversial restrictions. When House leaders and the administration objected that the measure would damage the prospects for major reform and would be repressive,

Moynihan scoffed, "The worst of the amendments to H.R. 7200 would never have come out of conference anyway, but by raising the rhetoric, they are creating the same kind of ideological split that killed welfare reform in the past."[67] Eventually the administration compromised, agreeing to Long's and Moynihan's desire for a year of fiscal relief if it was not linked to HR 7200. Instead, the relief was added to a major Social Security bill. Signed in December by President Carter, the Social Security Amendments of 1977 included $187 million in relief of state and local welfare costs for fiscal year 1978.[68]

While the chances for major change in AFDC in 1978 were dwindling, Congress renewed and changed the Comprehensive Employment and Training Act (CETA) and the Earned Income Tax Credit program. In 1978 CETA provided 725,000 public service jobs at a cost of $11.4 billion. The 1978 legislation lowered the number of jobs to 625,000 and targeted them better on structurally unemployed people with a need for training aimed at the normal job market. Efforts to go further in this direction were resisted by local governments wishing to continue using CETA to absorb personnel costs. Less controversial was the move to expand and make permanent the earned income tax credit. Signed by the president in November as a part of the Revenue Act of 1978, the legislation increased the maximum benefit to $500 per year, payable monthly. The highest benefit was paid to someone earning $5000. The benefit began to taper off at $6000 income. At a 15 percent reduction rate, benefits stopped at $10,000. The 1978 legislation integrated the tax credit with withholding taxes. A recipient's taxes were reduced by his employer in correspondence to benefits, and if the benefit exceeded the individual's tax liability, the federal government added to his paycheck. Under the 1978 legislation the tax credit for the first time would be treated as earned income in determining eligibility for AFDC. However, the benefit continued to be payable only to families with children.[69]

In the aftermath of the failure of the Program for Better Jobs and Income, the Carter administration decided to propose to the new Congress a considerably more modest welfare reform package. In December 1978 the administration agreed on a price tag of about $6 billion in new funds for the initial year of the program. By March 1979 the outlines of the package became known, and it was formally unveiled in May 1979. Like the 1977 proposals, the new package proposed a nationwide minimum benefit amounting to 65 percent of the poverty level. However, the 1979 plan added to AFDC only intact two-parent families and did not include childless couples or unattached individuals. The earned income tax credit and food stamps would be retained, although recipients of Supplemental Security Income would have their Food Stamp benefits cashed out and thus would receive larger checks. The 1979 proposals envisioned the creation of 618,000 public jobs, less than one half as many as the 1977 proposals. Only two-parent families would be guaranteed a job, and only after an eight-week job search period. The $937 million in fiscal relief to the states and localities was less than half of that provided by the 1977 proposals.

5
The Canadian Social Security Review and Its Aftermath

The Orange Book proposals became the subject of the most intensive federal-provincial consultations ever attempted in Canada.[1] Between 1973 and 1976 the process included eight full-dress two-day meetings of the Federal-Provincial Conference of Ministers of Welfare, seven of them held in Ottawa on the neutral ground of the Government Conference Center. Like all formal federal-provincial meetings in Canada, these meetings were convened and chaired by the federal representative (Marc Lalonde, minister of national health and welfare). A body similar to the Conference of Ministers was the Continuing Committee on Social Security, composed of deputy ministers of welfare and chaired by the federal deputy minister, A. W. Johnson and later by his successor Bruce Rawson. The Continuing Committee met formally at least ten times and informally six times, about a third of the time in Ottawa. Both the Conference of Ministers of Welfare and the Continuing Committee were serviced by a secretariat staffed by federal civil servants and by one official each from Quebec and Ontario. Meetings were preceded by weeks or months of preparation. In addition to these federal-provincial meetings, three interprovincial conferences of ministers of welfare occurred, in Quebec City, Winnipeg, and Charlottetown. Interspersed among these top-rank meetings were dozens of formal or informal meetings at the middle levels, about a third held in Ottawa and the rest convened at one time or another in every province. The brunt of the Social Security Review was borne by working parties of provincial and federal civil servants, of which three were formed: income maintenance, social services, and employment. Overall direction of the Working Party on Income Maintenance was given to T. Russell Robinson, while similar duties with respect to the Working Party on Social Services were given to John Osborne (both men were assistant deputy ministers). The most active of these groups was the Working Party on Income Maintenance, which held more than twenty-five meetings across Canada, from St. John's to Victoria. Most of these meetings took two days, and some took three or four. In addition, Lalonde made several nationwide tours, discussing the Social Security Review with leaders individually in each capital.

The results of this massive experiment in federal-provincial policymaking were mixed. Agreements on Family Allowances and the Canada Pension Plan emerged almost immediately; other proposals lost out almost as quickly, specifically those for a massive employment strategy. The federal-provincial negotiating system dealt in earnest with two main proposals, income maintenance and social services. The federal proposals on income support and supplementation attained rough agreement but sharp disagreement on financing and jurisdiction ultimately aborted them. The social services proposals, on the other hand, sprang to life within the conference context and came close to enactment by Parliament in 1977 and 1978. The failure of the federal-provincial consultation process to foster similar agreement in income maintenance prompted the federal government in 1978 to propose a Refundable Child Tax Credit that would be entirely federally funded and run. This legislation passed in November 1978.

Progress: 1973–1974

The Orange Book proposals on support and supplementation consisted of two-tiers. The support program would include not only the usual complement of the retired and disabled but also "single-parent families, and people who are not presently employable by reason of a combination of factors such as age, lack of skills, or length of time out of the labor market." Although the amount was never fully specified, and the provinces would have some discretion over it, one figure sometimes mentioned was $4200 for a family of four. Reduction rates under this support program would offer little incentive to work—75 percent was a common figure in early discussions. But for those expected to work, a whole different program was envisioned—supplementation. It was designed for "those who are working but whose incomes are inadequate" because of low wages or family size.[2] The basic benefit in this program was considerably lower than under the support program. In most discussions it was under $1000 for a family of four. The reduction rate would be very favorable to work; most proposals had it under 40 percent.

While the most original part of the 1973 federal proposals was on support and supplementation, the first and most expensive outcome of the Social Security Review was action on federal proposals to reform Family Allowances. Hardly had the Social Security Review begun when the ministers agreed on this reform, which was then introduced in Parliament in July 1973. The allowances were to be tripled, and their distribution would be determined by the provinces, so long as the average was $20 per child and the minimum was $12 per child. The measure would have a net cost of more than $800 million, far more than the estimated $160 million cost of the FISP reform of Family Allowances debated between 1970 and 1972. However, Parliament and the provinces agreed to the 1973 measure easily, and it was so popular that for the inflationary period before it took effect in January 1974, an interim increase also passed. Unlike FISP, the 1973 reform did not cut off any existing Family Allowances. It did arrange to tax back some benefits from people with taxable incomes; but because of the increase in benefits, a family with income of even $25,000 a year would be receiving more than before.[3] A special incentive for provinces to support the measure was that they too would be able to collect taxes on Family Allowances, effectively transferring more federal funds into provincial coffers. The provision allowing discretion in the setting of benefits was of course very important to Quebec, which immediately varied them according to age and number of children. The only other provinces that vary the benefits are Alberta (by age) and Prince Edward Island (by size of family).

Other expensive reforms associated with the first year of the Social Security Review were in pensions. The Orange Book proposed to expand the range of earnings over which contributions under the Canada Pension Plan were to be assessed, index benefits more closely to the cost of living, and make other changes. The October 1973 Federal-Provincial Conference of Ministers of Welfare approved these changes, and Parliament enacted them in December. According to the original Canada Pension Plan legislation, these changes required the permission of two-thirds of the provinces with at least two-thirds of the country's population. No similar permission was required to change Old Age Security (OAS) and Guaranteed Income Supplements (GIS). Even before presentation of the Orange Book, the government had moved to increase benefits under these programs. The Speech from the Throne mentioned the proposals in January 1973, and consultations were made with the provinces prior to including the increases in the budget that was presented in February. Parliament made the changes effective in April 1973, and in October it passed another government proposal to make cost-of-living adjustments in OAS and GIS quarterly instead of annually. Together these changes amounted to more than $400 million in new social spending.

Trudeau and Lalonde had promised to make the Social Security Review a truly comprehensive one, harmonizing and possibly even combining separate programs for social assistance, social services, social insurance, demogrants, and manpower programs. Very early, however, the Social

Security Review abandoned the idea of changing the existing demogrant and social insurance programs, whether in creating a uniform new national structure or in allowing the provinces greater discretion in redesigning them. Even though demogrants are more prevalent in Canada than in the United States, the ministers did not turn to them as the "solution for the whole of the social security problem." Similarly, by February 1974 the ministers of welfare agreed that the replacement of the demogrant and social insurance programs with a single guaranteed income scheme "would not be likely to be found to be practical as an immediate goal."[4] However, in addition to rejecting these "simplistic solutions," the Social Security Review also did not pursue the devolution of federal programs long demanded by Quebec. Lalonde unsuccessfully sought the cabinet's approval to extend the Social Security Review to the independent Unemployment Insurance Commission. Representatives of that federal program had attended early meetings of the review in order to detect threats to its independence. By May 1974 they were refusing to cooperate, and in November the Social Security Review gave up any plans to touch Unemployment Insurance. When new legislation on this program was passed in 1975 and 1978, it had no connection with the review. In a similar way chances of the review's touching the basic structure of the demogrant programs quickly evaporated. The passage of piecemeal improvements in Old Age Security pensions, Guaranteed Income Supplements, and Family Allowances helped moot the case for more comprehensive change. It is possible that the Quebec representatives could have prevented this outcome, but they were handicapped because the review was not being held at the top political level. Bureaucratic boundaries were more difficult to challenge, and the review never took on the global aspect that had marked earlier constitutional discussions. This outcome was very frustrating for Quebec. The province gave the review less attention from then on, though its representatives wished to avoid blame if the review should fail.

Once the Social Security Review had drifted away from considering fundamental change in the demogrant and social insurance programs, attention focused on the proposals for support and supplementation aimed specifically at the poor. By February 1974 the Working Party on Income Maintenance was exploring these proposals as well as some for child-related forms of aid. The ministerial and other meetings very rapidly ran into trouble, however, because five provinces had objections to the federal proposals: Quebec, Ontario, Manitoba, Saskatchewan, and British Columbia. Though the federal proposals followed the two-tiered approach of the Castonguay-Nepveu report, Quebec was ambivalent. Passage of the plan would distract attention from its basic demand that the federal government give the provinces more control over programs outside the social assistance sphere. Moreover the province was adamant that the federal government have no direct role in administering the proposed new supplementation tier. This objection was especially important because the Orange Book had differed from the Castonguay-Nepveu report in not explicitly providing for consolidated administration of employable and unemployable families. Quebec preferred not to separate the two benefit schedules into different programs, deliberately leaving the boundary between the two tiers fuzzy enough to allow for administrative discretion and demographic fluidity. A strict work requirement should be avoided because, especially in Quebec, there were not enough jobs to go around. Despite these objections, Quebec was determined to take a constructive position in the Social Security Review. Ontario's reaction to the federal proposals was more negative. The province's Progressive Conservative leaders were unhappy with the very idea of expanding the social assistance rolls to new groups and did not want the welfare rolls to lose their "categorical" nature. Instead Ontario had for several years been proposing that employed people with low earnings be aided through the tax system by a refundable tax credit. This position was supported by the Ontario minister of community and social services and, perhaps more importantly, by the minister of treasury, economics, and intergovernmental affairs (TEIGA).[5]

The objections of the other three provinces to the federal proposals were more far-reaching than those of Quebec or Ontario. British Columbia, Manitoba, and Saskatchewan were all ruled by the New Democratic Party (NDP). Their representatives opposed the idea of treating employable and unemployable people differently. Able-bodied people should not be limited to benefits too low to live on, and those not expected to work should not be penalized for working by confiscatory reduction rates. Moreover the NDP provinces felt that separation of the two groups perpetuated stigma: employable people should not be subjected to a degrading work requirement, while unemployable people should not be segregated and treated as hopeless cases. In thus proposing a single scheme embracing a high guarantee and a favorable reduction rate, the

NDP provinces advocated a program much more expensive than the federal proposals. Since the federal government was slated to pay the major share of the difference, the provincial proponents of the change were not concerned about expense.

While some of the larger provinces preferred a more expensive unitary program to the two-tier federal proposals on income support and supplementation, the smallest provinces wondered whether they could afford even the federal approach. They preferred to retain the existing Canada Assistance Plan while asking the federal government to increase Family Allowances. This view did not carry much weight with the larger provinces or with the federal government, but throughout the Social Security Review it removed the smaller provinces as possible allies of the federal approach to supplementation.

Despite the ominous disagreements emerging at the ministerial level, the Working Party on Income Maintenance methodically worked to narrow and refine the options. In February 1974 the Conference of Ministers of Welfare directed the working party to examine six major proposals, three of them child-related. The first three were (1) a unitary negative income tax system, (2) separate support and supplementation tiers providing different guarantees and reduction rates through transfer payments, and (3) a system similar to the second but with the supplementation provided through refundable tax credits (Ontario's proposal). The child-related proposals were (4) income-tested child allowances, (5) refundable child tax credits, and (6) increased Family Allowances. During 1974 the Working Party on Income Maintenance produced for the review the *Background Paper on Income Support and Supplementation* (released to the public in February 1975). In November the ministers of welfare rejected the three child-related options and directed the working party to explore further the other three approaches. According to the communiqué announcing this decision, the rejected options would not cover all the poor nor promote the "optimum integration of income maintenance programs."[6] The September 1974 Interprovincial Conference of Ministers of Welfare—no federal authorities in attendance—had endorsed the idea of a guaranteed income. The communiqué called for provincial discretion in setting the level of benefits, within the bounds of certain national standards.[7]

Some provinces found it easy to endorse the notion of supplementing the incomes of working families because they were already instituting programs to do just this. The Canada Assistance Plan had never been restricted to certain categories of beneficiaries, but until the 1970s, provinces and municipalities usually discouraged employable recipients. Beginning in 1973 several provinces established programs specifically for this purpose. In October 1973 British Columbia adopted a regulation that allowed the family of an employable recipient to keep up to $100 a month in earnings; however, benefits were reduced in direct correspondence to further earnings, and the program never became very significant.[8] In October 1974 Saskatchewan began operating its Family Income Plan (FIP). The first full-scale program of its type in North America, FIP provided a basic payment of $1800 for a family of four whose income did not exceed $6647 (1977). Earnings caused benefits to be reduced by 50 percent up to a break-even point of $10,247.[9] In addition to these initiatives by British Columbia and Saskatchewan, Ontario experimented with a related Low-Income Supplementation of Earnings program.

With the increasing provincial efforts to loosen the restrictions on beneficiaries of social assistance, benefits threatened to surge ahead of those that would be provided under the support and supplementation proposals then being discussed in the Social Security Review. This problem was arising in the exemption of assets as well as of earnings. The disparity threatened to create opposition to the new federal proposals from recipients or their advocates. To head off this problem, federal officials circulated to the provinces some proposed ceilings that were later adopted at the April 1975 meeting of welfare ministers. These guidelines specified that, in addition to work expenses, a province could exempt each month up to $100 in earnings for a family or an amount equal to one-quarter of the benefits. The guidelines also put an upper limit on the assets exempted: $3100 for a family of four. The guidelines did not restrict nonliquid assets such as a home or a car. Even so, some provinces, especially British Columbia and Nova Scotia, already exceeded these ceilings. Thus the guidelines stated: "The Canada Assistance Plan will continue to recognize already approved provincial regulations that, in some particularities, may provide for higher asset exemption levels." A final effect of the 1975 guidelines was to give formal recognition to this already accepted principle: "Assistance under the terms of the Canada Assistance Plan may be made available to low income members of the labour force on the same basis as it is provided to those on social assistance."[10]

The Orange Book gave top priority to the proposal for an employment strategy: "The first strategy in providing income security to Canadians must be to provide people with jobs—with income through employment—rather than income through social assistance."[11] To achieve these ends, government should provide services helping the chronically unemployed enter the job market and should where necessary sponsor the creation of jobs through a community employment program. The proposal came from the health and welfare department, but the power to adopt or veto it lay with the manpower department. The Department of Manpower and Immigration did not support the Social Security Review, even though it chaired the Working Party on Employment Strategy. Eventually the review had to drop the employment strategy as an element of welfare reform.

In October 1973 the Continuing Committee on Social Security directed the Working Party on Employment Strategy to prepare four reports: an analysis of those with "particular and continuing difficulty" in finding steady work, an analysis of the existing disincentives to work, an exploration of possible new approaches for policy in this area, and a description of the "nature, objectives, and clientele" of a new employment strategy. The working party had less than four months to complete this task, and although it postponed its efforts on the second report, it was able to produce reports on the other subjects by February 1974.

The report of the Working Party on Employment Strategy contributed very little to progress in this area. The report identified the target population as "employable welfare recipients," as well as a range of other problem groups, such as natives, the aged, and others. A wide range of remedies was discussed, including training and support services to enhance a person's employability, as well as job creation through public service employment and incentives to private enterprise. The working party rigidly restrained itself from drawing any policy inferences that would be more appropriately made by political leaders. A disclaimer in the main report emphasized:

It does *not*, itself, develop the substance of such a strategy. The paper does not, in other words, purport to say what should be done, but rather how one might view the problem and organize one's conception of solutions. It cannot be over-emphasized that the paper is not meant to suggest either that any specific policy approach should be adopted or that any relevant programs should take a particular form or substance.[12]

The writers need not have worried, because very few specific policy options are even mentioned in their report, much less recommended. The report restrained itself so well from pronouncing on policy questions that it substantially failed to present meaningful alternatives and their implications. Even the provincial submissions are vague, except for the Quebec report which makes concrete proposals and estimates their cost.

A primary reason for the vagueness of discussions on employment seems to have been profound disagreement over program goals. The provinces disagreed among themselves about how large the program should be, who its clients should be, and what balance of training and job creation it should have. Officials at both levels were fearful of antagonizing businessmen by damaging the private labor market. Moreover the provinces disagreed with the federal government over which level should administer the program.[13] Two previously successful manpower programs, Opportunities for Youth and the Local Initiatives Program, had involved federal subsidies made directly to local governments or other units, and the provincial governments now wanted a hand in any such program. Moreover federal manpower authorities did not want to give any control of their programs to Health and Welfare Canada, and similar struggles were doubtless going on at the provincial level. With disagreements this profound, the best way to avoid a deadlock was to keep discussion at the most general and inoffensive level.

With the report of the Working Party on Employment Strategy in hand, the Conference of Ministers of Welfare endorsed a community employment strategy including the wide range of approaches already mentioned. Obviously the program remained to be articulated into programs and priorities. When specific proposals began to emerge in November 1974, it was clear that the manpower authorities envisioned no major increase in the federal role. Twenty pilot projects were to be negotiated with the provinces.[14] This small upshot of the year of debate prompted cynics to see the employment "strategy" as an excuse for not having a program. It was not until two years later, after the Social Security Review was completed, that the minister of manpower and immigration, in October 1976, finally outlined concrete nationwide efforts at job creation. As far as the Social Security Review was concerned, questions of work training and job creation simply could not be discussed.[15]

In July 1974 a federal election produced a solid majority in Ottawa for the Liberal government, which picked up thirty-two seats. The Liberal platform had endorsed a guaranteed income for those who could not work and supplementation for those who could. This election produced far less an impression of a welfare backlash than the 1972 election had. Since 1972, the government had been waging a well-publicized crackdown on unemployment insurance "rip-offs." If the pressures for cutting back welfare were reduced, so were those for expanding it dramatically. The electoral result left the Liberals under less pressure from the Left to carry out their promises on income security. The sharpest criticism of the government occurred at the June 1974 Canadian Conference on Social Welfare when delegates aligned with the National Anti-Poverty Organization led a revolt against the Orange Book proposals. Without specifically mentioning the government's two-tier plan, the conference endorsed the idea of a guaranteed income and opposed any program that required a "degrading process for establishing eligibility."[16]

A major issue in the 1974 election was Canada's faltering economy. Inflation raged and unemployment reached recession levels. After a long period of debate Trudeau imposed wage and price controls in October 1975. This changing environment was not friendly to expensive new social programs, especially as the bills for the 1973 increases in Family Allowances, OAS, and GIS began to come due. This austere mood soon threatened to derail the Social Security Review, producing several federal decisions in 1975 that enraged the provinces. Most significant was the cabinet's rejection in February of Lalonde's request for an immediate commitment of funds for the new support and supplementation system ($2 billion including existing CAP expenditures). Instead the cabinet would agree only to the full amount as of 1978—three years away. Lalonde's request faced opposition from John Turner, minister of finance, and his allies on the Treasury Board.[17] Prime Minister Trudeau did not intervene. This reverse came at the very time when federal initiative was most essential if the Social Security Review was to succeed. Instead Lalonde was forced to tell the provinces that the federal side was not ready to cooperate.

Crisis: 1975

During 1974 the Social Security Review had moved smoothly, if slowly. But in 1975 it encountered shocks that sank the income security proposals while boosting other proposals regarding social services. Of the three guaranteed income proposals singled out by the Social Security Review in November 1974, the one closest to the federal government's initial proposals had the least support. The NDP provinces supported a unitary scheme, while Ontario preferred the alternative containing a tax credit approach. Nevertheless Lalonde at the February 1975 Conference of Welfare Ministers announced that the federal government would agree to fund only the two-tier support-supplementation transfer approach. Having initiated a widely heralded consultative process, the federal side had ignored criticisms and held to its original proposals. However, provinical irritation at this surprise was eclipsed by horror at the details Lalonde was now filling in about the federal position. Supplementation benefits would be administered by whatever level of government was already dealing with the beneficiary.[18] While this approach reserved a role for the provincial social assistance offices, it also assured a role for the Unemployment Insurance Commission, a national agency in the classic mold. As if this proposal was not enough to alienate the provinces, Lalonde compounded the rift with the news that the federal government would have to delay funding of the proposed package. To sweeten the sour news, Lalonde offered to raise the federal share of the supplementation tier to above half, though he was unable to specify how far. In any case the damage was done. The communiqué emerging from the February 1975 conference reports general agreement on the two-tier approach, but on other matters it is quite silent. Actually, behind the scenes, the provinces were very restive, and the tensions exploded at the next federal-provincial meeting in April 1975.

At the April meeting Lalonde attempted to conciliate the provinces by formalizing the federal government's offer to increase its eventual share of spending. According to the federal timetable, the support program would be introduced in 1976 at a cost of $350 million beyond the current cost of CAP. In the first year the federal government would finance only half the support program. However, it would finance two-thirds of the $650 million new supplementation program, and once that program was in place, it would also pick up a greater fraction of provincial support costs, amounting to between 55 percent and 65 percent.[19] The maximum supplementation benefit would be $2500 for a family of four, with a reduction rate of 33 percent; the reduction rate for support payments would be 75 percent.[20] Estimates were that the proposals would cost $1 billion in new funds and that the federal government would eventually pay 70 percent of this cost. However generous these proposals were in the long run, they did nothing to meet the short-run needs of the provinces. As the provinces justly pointed out, the financial stringency that prompted the federal government to delay its contribution did not stop it from asking them to pay out much of their share immediately. Moreover the poorer provinces objected to paying any share of the supplementation scheme.[21]

In addition to these disagreements over federal cost sharing, the April 1975 meeting was wracked by conflict over which level of government should administer the supplementation tier. In his opening remarks Lalonde proposed "that we attempt to remove from contention, at least for the time being, the question as to which government should deliver the income supplements." He further recommended that the federal and provincial sides jointly commission an independent study that would be "a rather more objective evaluation than perhaps our respective bureaucracies might provide us with. . . ."[22] The provinces exploded at this proposal. The NDP provinces still preferred a unitary benefit schedule, and two had left the February meeting feeling that this was still a possibility.[23] Nearly all the provinces, and particularly Quebec, objected even to considering federal jurisdiction over the supplementation tier. Claude Forget, Quebec's minister of social affairs, remarked: "Does the federal side seriously expect financial participation by Quebec in a program administered by Ottawa?"[24] Not only did the federal proposal seek to administer separately what many provinces felt should fall under the same program, but it also envisioned possible federal jurisdiction over the more popular clientele, much as it had done with Guaranteed Income Supplements for the aged poor. The federal government might take over the responsibility for aiding people who worked, leaving the provinces the dubious privilege of helping the rest. Neither side was unaware of the political stakes involved in this question.

With the internal politics of the Social Security Review now foundering, outside groups were concerned but could do little to restore the momentum. The leading lobby, the Canadian Council on Social Development (CCSD), had always been ambivalent about the federal proposals, which were not as generous as proposals that CCSD leaders had been advocating since the late 1960s. When Lalonde announced the 1975 delay in funding of the supplementation proposals, CCSD's Reuben Baetz sharply criticized the action. Baetz also complained that the government proposals were still not specific enough, and he criticized the government in other ways.²⁵ (Baetz' rhetoric should perhaps be read along with his later joining the cabinet of the Progressive Conservative government in Ontario.)

After the April 1975 rupture a June meeting was canceled and a September meeting postponed. The welfare ministers did not again discuss welfare issues until February 1976. Federal-provincial relations worsened still further as 1975 wore on. In presenting the federal budget in June, Finance Minister John Turner proposed new restrictions on unemployment insurance and announced a federal ceiling on federal payments for provincially administered national health insurance. The provinces received advance warning of neither announcement. The changes tightening up unemployment insurance would save the federal government money but would shunt some beneficiaries onto provincial social assistance rolls. If the federal government piqued the provinces on unemployment insurance, it terrified them on health insurance. Health consumes a large share of provincial budgets, and now without warning they faced a limit on what was previously an open-ended federal cost-sharing arrangement. And Lalonde had given them no advance warning, even though his department administers the program. In August an interprovincial meeting of health ministers, including many of the same people from the Social Security Review, unanimously condemned the federal action.²⁶

With federal-provincial relations at a low point in 1975, federal authorities wanted to get something done. Social services became the beneficiary of this effort. The Orange Book had made some desultory proposals for improving and extending social services, and a federal-provincial Working Party on Social Services had examined the subject in 1974.²⁷ The Working party was severely constrained by the paucity of data on provincial social services. Only the Castonguay-Nepveu report surveyed the whole range of services available or needed in a province. Thus the working party's initial report "took a very broad—perhaps overly philosophical—approach to social service questions."²⁸ The report asked the continuing committee for more guidance on which options to reconsider, but the continuing committee directed the working party not to meet again until further notice, which never came. By 1975 the social services strategy seemed likely to fade into the same oblivion that had swallowed the employment strategy. But in early 1975 Deputy Minister Johnson worked out with John Osborne a proposal for legislation allowing cost-sharing for universal as well as means-tested services. Partly in response to provincial desires expressed at the December 1974 interprovincial conference in Winnipeg, the federal proposal placed special emphasis on providing rehabilitation in the home instead of in institutions.[29]

Marc Lalonde presented the federal social services proposals to the April 1975 federal-provincial meeting, and they emerged as the only element of agreement from that tumultuous gathering. The communiqué expressed the hope that the new legislation embodying this "sweeping change" could be worked out and put into force as early as 1976.[30] Discussions proceeded during the ten-month hiatus of formal meetings of the Social Security Review. In June 1975 Johnson left the department to become head of the Canadian Broadcasting Corporation, and in August he was replaced as deputy minister by Bruce Rawson, a former deputy minister of welfare in Alberta. Rawson worked well with his provincial counterparts as well as with federal program specialists. At the next Conference of Welfare Ministers in February 1976, tentative agreement was reached on draft specifications for the social services legislation. Added to the shareable services were residential services for adults not already covered by existing health insurance schemes (a provision that was later removed).[31] The legislation was introduced in the House of Commons in June 1977, though because of later events it was never voted on.

Death and Transfiguration: 1976–1978

The internal crisis of the Social Security Review came at a time when the external supports for guaranteed income proposals were declining. In 1975 the welfare backlash grew in the provinces. Ontario and others took some well-publicized steps to cut spending. In a 1975 election the Progressive Conservative government in Alberta was returned with an increased majority. In contrast, the NDP government in Saskatchewan was returned to office with a reduced majority, and the NDP government was ousted in British Columbia, where the victorious Social Credit party under William Bennett, Jr., had made a big issue of welfare waste and abuse. And while the welfare backlash grew throughout Canada, opposition to extending the welfare system also grew. The National Anti-Poverty Organization (NAPO) had consistently advocated guaranteed income proposals, but not until early 1976 did it produce formal proposals. NAPO called for a unitary benefit structure with a basic payment of $7000 (excluding Family Allowances), and a break-even point of $13,500.[32] The proposals could not have come at a more unpromising time. NAPO leaders quickly perceived that the very notion of guaranteed income was becoming unpopular in Canada, and they began searching for a different name, eventually hitting on the term *Canadian dividend*.

In preparing for the February 1976 meeting of the Federal-Provincial Conference of Ministers of Welfare, the first since April 1975, Lalonde and Rawson realized that the provinces would not agree to separately administered support and supplementation programs, particularly if the federal government insisted on administering aid to working families. The federal side regrouped and made concessions in cost sharing and particularly in jurisdiction. It promised to pay two-thirds of the cost of supplementation, allowing a total supplement of $960 for a family of four, with a reduction rate of 35 percent. In the support tier the federal government would pay two-thirds of benefits up to a point and half the remainder. Support benefits could vary from province to province, but they would always be subject to a reduction rate of 70 percent. To limit costs, the federal proposals would open the supplementation tier only to families with children and to persons over fifty-five years of age.

The major concession in the February 1976 proposals was to offer the provinces exclusive jurisdiction over supplementation, within federal guidelines on eligibility. According to a later communiqué, a major factor leading to this proposal was "recognition that provinces could deliver this particular program more efficiently by utilizing existing administrative capacities.[33] An easier explanation is that the provinces would settle for nothing less. The discretion that this proposal gave them was very great. The $960 was simply a maximum that the federal government would help fund; provinces would be free to provide supplements less than that or add to it from their own funds. The National Council of Welfare warned that as a result, "there would not be a single supplementation plan for the whole of Canada, as suggested in the Orange Paper, but rather ten separate provincial plans."[34] Moreover the federal proposal explicitly provided that the provinces could administer the two tiers under a single administration, a concession they had sought unsuccessfully for nearly three years. It would be possible to turn the "two-tier" scheme into a unitary program with virtually the same guarantees and reduction rates. With this sweeping federal concession now on the table, the welfare ministers agreed to meet in June "with the objective of achieving agreement on the detailed design of a support/supplementation system and completing the Social Security Review before summer of 1976."[35] As events developed, June was indeed the last meeting of the Social Security Review, but not with the agreeable results expected. In preparation for the meeting federal officials in March polled the provincial capitals privately, but they made little effort to sell the February proposals; Lalonde and Rawson made no final tour. Perhaps, knowing the magnitude of the concessions offered, they assumed that the provinces would be overjoyed. They were not.

The eighth and final meeting of the Federal-Provincial Conference of Ministers of Welfare was held in June 1976. At this meeting seven provinces agreed "in principle" with the proposals. New Brunswick and Prince Edward Island reserved judgment, while Ontario rejected the proposals outright. The majority of seven disguised significant misgivings about the plan. One provincial minister was quoted as saying that "Agreement in principle doesn't mean a province is necessarily going to participate."[36] Actually, only Quebec and British Columbia supported the federal proposals wholeheartedly. Saskatchewan and Manitoba (still ruled by the NDP), argued that the plan should give more to the working poor and should not be limited to families. Nova Scotia and Newfoundland were as concerned as the other Atlantic provinces about the costs of the proposals. Indeed virtually all the provinces were uneasy about the costs. The economic downturn had cut back as much on provincial as on federal revenues. Welfare ministers who did not like the federal proposals willingly stepped aside and, as one remarked, "let the finance ministers kill it." To reassure governments about the financial burden, Lalonde felt it necessary to argue that the proposals, taken in conjunction with other reforms, would "not result in any increase in social security expenditures relative to the G.N.P."[37]

Ontario had been silent during most of the Social Security Review, critical mainly of extending the welfare rolls to new groups, but the province had begun to raise new questions at the February 1976 federal-provincial meeting. In April Ontario tabled a report at the Federal-Provincial Conference of Finance Ministers challenging federal estimates of the cost of the proposals. Then at the June meeting of ministers of welfare, supposedly the time for final consensus to be reached, the Ontario minister objected that the federal proposals only worsened the patchwork nature of the system. He said, "We're looking for something simple," but refused to make any specific suggestions."[38] The province knew very well that the Social Security Review had conceded since 1974 that the support and supplementation proposals would not touch existing demogrant and social insurance programs. This obstructionism earned a heartfelt condemnation by Lalonde: "I can think of no single significant proposal for reform brought to the table by the government of Ontario.... Substantive criticism of federal proposals—indeed any comment on them at all—was largely missing."[39] Ontario's change of heart is perhaps not so unaccountable considering that it was then waging a new campaign, emulating the long, lonely one mounted by Quebec, to force the federal government to vacate existing shared-cost programs and turn over to the provinces enough taxing authority to "pay the bills." Thus Ontario was opposing the new welfare proposals in order to force the federal government into fundamental concessions.

While the support and supplementation proposals slowly faded from the scene, the social services proposals smoothly emerged. When the bill was introduced in Parliament in June 1977, a press release hailed it as "one of the main achievements of the Social Security Review."[40] But federal officials were becoming disillusioned with the open-ended cost-sharing approach embodied in the bill. This sentiment had been reflected in the June 1975 federal ceiling on payments for provincial health programs. Federal proposals, agreed to by the provinces and enacted in April 1977, replaced shared-cost programs in health and higher education with a single new block grant, with few strings attached and federal participation no longer open ended.[41] Quebec had always been uneasy about the cost-sharing aspects of the 1977 social services bill, and the new regime there sought to reopen the question. Ontario, too, now agreed that the cost-sharing approach denied it flexibility and autonomy.

In September 1977, in one of his last actions before leaving Health and Welfare Canada to become minister of state for federal-provincial relations, Marc Lalonde proposed that social services, like health and higher education, be put on a lump sum rather than a cost-sharing basis. The proposal was generally well received, although it was clear that Quebec, Manitoba, and Prince Edward Island would not fare as well under block funding as under the shared-cost proposals of the June 1977 bill. These provinces have been willing to spend more dollars to qualify for federal cost-sharing in social services. In 1977–78 Prince Edward Island received more federal contributions for social services per capita ($34) than any other province, and Quebec ($32) and Manitoba ($29) were not far behind it. Quebec has a long tradition of reliance on public institutional care. The province has more beds in juvenile institutions than all the rest of Canada. Federal contributions for social services per capita in Quebec are fully twice those in Ontario, which at $16 per capita (1977–78) are the lowest in Canada.[42] Provinces doing well under the existing cost-sharing arrangements would be hurt under block grants because a ceiling would be placed on federal spending and per capita payments made to each province would eventually converge. These provinces were not the only ones that worried about the block grant approach. Though Saskatchewan would do well under block funding, the province's socialist leaders opposed the proposal on principle, because it would cut national social spending loose from strong central purposes. But after negotiation to assure some protection against inflation, most provinces supported block funding. Quebec strongly preferred it even though the province would clearly lose money compared to the shared-cost alternative. As a rule the provincial finance ministries supported the change, while departments that actually administered the services were ambivalent or opposed, because existing programs would lose the protection afforded by cost sharing.

By March 1978 tentative agreement on the new social services block funding proposals was reached, and in May, Monique Bégin, minister of national health and welfare, introduced the bill in Parliament.[43] Only then did groups representing clients and social workers object to the bill's abandonment of any federal guarantees that the money would provide certain minimum services nationwide. Technically a province could use the social services block grant to build highways or for any other purpose. The only constraint was that the federal government would review and renew the program after ten years. Once Health and Welfare Canada and the provincial authorities were behind the social services block funding legislation, client-oriented groups probably would have found it nearly impossible to block the legislation in Parliament. As it turned out, however, the bill was laid aside while the income security issue was revived in 1978. No hearings were held on the social services bill, and it was formally shelved in November 1978.

The impasse over income support and supplementation that resulted from the June 1976 meeting prompted federal authorities to consider new strategies. To accommodate the different timetables of the provinces and to get around those provinces that were simply opposed to the federal proposals, Lalonde declared the federal government willing to "accord the provinces a full degree of flexibility with respect to the timing and phase-in of implementation" and said it would be possible to proceed "on the basis of signed federal-provincial agreements under the proposed new legislation."[44] The federal government had used this strategy to get Medicare started in 1966 over Ontario's objections. It would invite constitutional questions, because a province might challenge the unilateral move morally or legally. Lalonde warned that the federal government "will take whatever steps it views as necessary" to achieve a program aiding the working poor.[45] By 1977, however, his hopes of implementing the new system piecemeal had faded, largely because so few provinces were willing to participate. In an August 1977 letter formally withdrawing the federal offer to share costs, he wrote that "only two provinces have indicated a clear commitment to implement the proposal."[46] These provinces were apparently Saskatchewan and Quebec. Quebec in November 1976 had experienced a dramatic change in government, with Bourassa's Liberals replaced by the Parti Québecois under René Lévesque. The Liberals in Ottawa were unwilling to initiate a new program that would begin under the auspices of their ideological enemies in Quebec City. Lalonde's August letter instead stated that the federal government would continue to examine proposals for supplementing incomes through the tax system.

In the months following the abortive June 1976 federal-provincial conference, the federal government began to hint that it might unilaterally initiate a program of refundable tax credits. Like the U.S. program passed in 1975, a Canadian tax credit scheme would provide benefits only to families with children. Unlike the U.S. practice, benefits would be available even to those with no income. Recipients paying no taxes would receive a cash payment, while those paying taxes would have them reduced correspondingly. Manitoba had used the tax credit approach in its cost-of-living tax credit and property tax credit programs (neither was child related). Ontario was friendly to tax credits, having long preferred them to the approach it had just rejected in the Social Security Review. During 1977 an interdepartmental group of federal officials prepared a report on "tax-transfer integration," coming up with a somewhat more pessimistic view of the feasibility of administering welfare benefits through the tax system than did their U.S. counterparts in 1974. (A public report on the subject was eventually released in November 1978.[47]) A more immediate and optimistic conclusion of the deliberations was that the tax credits could indeed be used as a limited form of income supplementation. Proposals for a tax credit were plausible because they involved no provincial spending, avoiding considerations that killed the support and supplementation proposals. The tax credit proposals reached the cabinet during the summer of 1977, but no action was taken for a year. The context was one of economic crisis, government retrenchment, and impending election. As the country neared the end of the fourth year of wage and price controls, the economy was in worse shape than ever. Inflation continued and unemployment was still high. The Canadian dollar was worth even less abroad than the moth-eaten U.S. dollar.

Reflecting the new mood, Prime Minister Trudeau promised on August 1, 1978, to cut $2 billion from the federal budget for the coming fiscal year. From a projected budget of $55 billion, that was a very significant amount. On August 24 Finance Minister Jean Chrétien announced major new federal proposals. Within four months Parliament had passed this entire program. While Chrétien proposed new advances in tax credits and aid to the aged, he also proposed to cut back on existing Family Allowance and Unemployment Insurance benefits. Family Allowances were to drop from $26 to $20 per child, producing a federal saving of $690 million. And a wide range of Unemployment Insurance regulations would be tightened up, leading to an expected drop of 10 percent in the number of beneficiaries and a federal saving of $580 million in fiscal year 1979–1980. Some of these savings would be shifted to other social spending. Guaranteed Income Supplements would be raised $20 monthly per household, providing aid to the neediest aged. And the Refundable Child Tax Credit would begin.[48]

The Canadian child tax credit is in some ways closer to a welfare program than the U.S. earned income credit, and in other ways it is less so. Both programs are limited in that they aid only families with children; they do not touch childless couples and unattached individuals, though poverty in these groups is high. Canadian benefits are related to the number of children; in the United States the benefit is the same whether the family has one child or many. Moreover benefits in the Canadian program are not contingent on having earned income. A family with no earned income receives the full benefit; in the U.S. program, a family with no earned income receives no benefits. The two programs are similar in that benefits as of 1979 were quite low: $200 per child in Canada,

$500 per family in the United States. The Canadian benefit for a family of four is less than half that in the 1976 supplementation proposals. In certain ways the U.S. program comes closer to the welfare model. Canadian benefits are paid at the end of the year through the personal tax return, while the U.S. benefits are now paid monthly and are thus available when needed. During debates leading to passage of the Canadian program, the government argued that it would be administratively inefficient to distribute benefits more frequently than once a year.[49]

The Canadian tax credit is poorly targeted on the low-income population. As amended in 1978, the U.S. program provides the highest benefits at $5000 earnings, and no one with more than $8000 in earnings receives any benefits. In contrast, the Canadian program gives benefits to families with rather high incomes, some of them in the top income quintile (table 1.4). Families with an income of up to $18,000 a year receive the full benefit, and then the benefits taper off very slowly, at a reduction rate of 5 percent. For a one-child family, benefits do not stop until income exceeds $22,000. For large families, the break-even point exceeds $40,000. Moreover, the basis for benefits is net income. Since some families are able to deduct contributions to pension and savings plans from their income, some may receive benefits at gross incomes even higher than those mentioned. Because of this extreme spread of benefits across the class structure, only $300 million of the program's initial annual cost of $810 million went to families below the Statistics Canada low-income cutoff.

That the child tax credit was not very redistributive certainly helped it to pass. Introduced in the House of Commons in October 1978, the proposal marched through without controversy and without amendment. The government's bill passed the House in late November and passed the Senate a few weeks later. Neither opposition party objected to the benefit structure. The broad popularity of the measure was in striking contrast to the resistance that toppled the Family Income Security Plan between 1970 and 1972. The benefits under FISP were not spread as widely as under the child tax credit. Moreover, FISP proposed to end Family Allowance benefits to high-income families, whereas the 1978 child tax credit legislation was financed by keeping Family Allowances as a demogrant but decreasing them for everyone (including the poor). Lest the public not notice that these proposals were not very redistributive, a fact sheet distributed by the government on behalf of the legislation emphasized that a "three-child Ontario family with $40,000 income will get only about $50 less in federal assistance for their children next year."[50] Rather than attack the child tax program for leaving too little for the poor, the New Democratic Party chose to attack the decision to reduce the level of family allowances. The more bluntly targeted a program is, the more popular it is, even to a socialist party. And no one forgot, least of all the reigning Liberals, that the initial lump sum benefit under the tax credit program would arrive in millions of households during the spring of 1979, shortly before the impending federal election. However, such measures were not enough to save the Liberals. On May 22 they were turned out of office by the Progressive Conservatives, with Joe Clark as the New Prime Minister.

6
The Rules of the Game: Deductive and Inductive Styles of Policymaking

Policy development can be compared to a process of learning, and there is more than one way to learn. In a study of scientific advising, Don K. Price has made an important distinction between the deductive pattern in Great Britain and the inductive pattern in the United States.[1] Because British government is centralized, new ideas can be imposed from above, whereas in the decentralized United States they must fight their way to the top. Canadian government is in its way no more centralized than U.S. government, but special features of Canadian decentralization, combined with some inherited British institutions, give Canada a comparatively deductive style of policymaking. Before introducing a proposal into Parliament, Canadian federal leaders take heed of preferences of the electorate, the party platform, the provinces, bureaucrats, and experts. Vigorous conflict and bargaining occur at this stage. But once a proposal emerges, it does not change much in principle; public debate adds or subtracts little. From then on, policy proceeds from the top down. In contrast, policy in the United States is often made from the bottom up. In proposing legislation, the president does his best to anticipate inductive pressures, but rarely does Congress accept his ideas unchanged. Voters, interest groups, elites, experts, and others grasp specific issues and bargain to fit them into the ultimate mosaic of policy.

This distinction between deductive and inductive styles of policymaking differs from the common distinction between incremental and comprehensive changes in policy. Although it is sometimes argued that only incremental change is possible in U.S. politics, it would be more accurate to say that a certain coalitional strategy, an inductive one, is most characteristic. What matters is not whether a proposal is incremental or comprehensive but whether it lends itself to such a coalition. Some comprehensive changes clearly fit that specification. In fact, policy development in the United States more than in other countries depends on occasions of intense innovation. Similarly, deductive policymaking does not necessarily produce comprehensive new policies. It may be that a country like Canada is the real outpost of gradualism.[2]

Deductive and inductive styles of policymaking are rooted in important differences in political structure and culture. At times the political differences between Canada and the United States are overshadowed by socioeconomic similarities. Such kinship has promoted similarities in the level of resources spent on the poor. But even when socioeconomic pressures are the same, political differences will cause them to express themselves in different ways, some not reflected in aggregate spending figures. A given political system can block or boost certain public demands.

Canadian and U.S. political decentralization are vastly different. National government in the United States is unrivaled in its authority to set social policy, but this "central" government is itself divided into competing institutions, making agreement dependent on transitory coalitions. The system gives special opportunities to interest groups and to entrepreneurship by public officials, bureaucrats, and outside experts. In Canada responsibility for social policy is shared between national and regional governments. Accommodation requires a delicate process of discussion and negotiation between top leaders that limits the influence of groups, public opinion, and even legislators. The tightness of the policymaking circle is increased by the centralization of power within federal and provincial governments. Richard Simeon has argued that this centralization helps sweep away veto points such as those found in the United States.[3]

According to the inductive style of U.S. politics, a policy passes not because it follows stark ideological, class, or other cleavages in the society but because it attracts a motley coalition drawn from a range of groups. In designing and presenting his Family Assistance Plan, President Nixon sought to draw on both liberal and conservative support. In Richard Nathan's terms, conservatives sought to build a fire under welfare recipients, while liberals sought to put a cushion under them.[4] As a result, FAP embodied such contradictions. And in campaigning for his bill, Nixon did not construct a global defense, delineating all the reasoning behind the proposal and waiting for people to approve. That was just as well; such scrutiny would have shown FAP to be built on somewhat contradictory assumptions. Rather, Nixon played up specific parts of his proposal to different constituencies, building from this specific support inductively up to a general, conclusive majority. A coalition of this nature is inherently transitory and unstable, however. That problem is not serious with some proposals, but in this case Nixon's clever strategy backfired. By appealing to conservatives, he weakened liberal support for the bill; by appealing to liberals, he alienated potential conservative support. Thus the attempt to assemble simultaneous conservative and liberal support called into being an equally varied coalition opposed to the measure, a coalition that turned out to be even stronger.

Just as Nixon sought to exploit the inductive features of U.S.

policymaking, Canadian federal officials chose a strategy that capitalized on the deductive nature of their policy process. T. R. Robinson, assistant deputy minister of policy research and long-range planning, described the approach:

The idea was to rethink the basic concepts, examine the evolving nature of social security issues, and work from basic principles—i.e., "from the top down"—in pursuit of viable reform proposals. Constraints resulting from potential costs, administrative exigencies, existing programme patterns, and finally any difficulties with respect to financial arrangements or jurisdictional issues, were to emerge as the issues (and choices) became more and more specific. They were not to encumber the first stages of the review. The evolution was to be from the "desirable" to the "practical," with as little departure from the former as possible.[5]

Of course, the review did not proceed smoothly along these lines. The issues of cost sharing and jurisdiction derailed attempts to reach a consensus. Federal policymakers depended on a deductive strategy that was not equipped to solve these immense problems piecemeal. Indeed, just when conflicts over jurisdiction and financing had become most intense in the April 1975 meeting of welfare ministers, the federal communiqué emerging from this meeting dreamily declared, "A consensus has been reached on the broad features of a new guaranteed income system," and officials have been "instructed to work out the details of an operational design for an income support and supplementation (guaranteed income) system of the kind Ministers [have] agreed on."[6] The deductive approach ignored crucial questions of practicality that desperately needed resolution. Because no effort had been made to resolve these difficult questions in the early stages of the Social Security Review, little room for compromise remained when they finally reached the agenda. Moreover the tightness of the Canadian policymaking circle ensured that outside groups were not tuned in enough to the proceedings to step in and rescue the proposals once they had been derailed.

Not all the differences in policymaking can be attributed to political factors; the sizes of the two political systems also made a difference. Canada's population is about the same as California's, and in 1976 the country's CAP case load of 1.50 million was only slightly larger than the state's AFDC case load of 1.45 million. Because of the difference in national size, Canadian policymakers did not have the data and assistance available to U.S. federal officials. The difference in scale not only lessened resources but also cut down the number and strength of interest groups, experts, and journalists vying for influence. Other things being equal, this difficulty should be somewhat compensated for in a small system by the greater access of citizens to their leaders.[7] But federal-provincial politics in Canada erects special barriers to participation by nongovernmental actors. This self-contained aspect of Canadian politics is itself promoted by the country's scale. A major reason that federal-provincial conferences work as well as they do is that only ten provinces participate. A conference of fifty states is hardly a conference at all. A final influence of scale is that it promotes the central government's fragmentation in the United States and its integration in Canada. Nearly every Canadian federal official with responsibility for welfare policy is housed in one of two adjacent buildings in Ottawa. Many of those involved in federal policymaking know each other, if only to share an elevator on their way to work. In contrast, the HEW bureaucracy is notoriously sprawled all over Washington and Baltimore. Still further dispersion is indicated by the fact that the Labor, Agriculture, Treasury, and Housing and Urban Development departments, Congress and its many subdivisions, and other organizations are also involved in U.S. welfare debates.

Inescapable Similarities

This book emphasizes political differences between Canada and the United States, but it is premised on their strong similarities in society and economy. This kinship is sometimes strong enough to overshadow differences in political structure, producing similar profiles in the size and distribution of benefits. Socioeconomic factors in common produce a politics that puts a limit on total spending and favors the aged over other poor groups in distributing that spending. Most fundamental is the limit that political economy places on total welfare spending. Industry and the public are willing to pay no more than a certain level of taxes, and government spending faces other restraints based on its effect on the private economy. Programs that promote economic growth or aid powerful constituencies absorb funds that otherwise might be spent on welfare benefits. Moreover, welfare spending faces further resistance when it threatens the labor market or social mores. These limits are so entrenched in Canadian and U.S. politics that they scarcely need be debated openly. They are most noticeable when macroeconomic changes increase or decrease the level of spending permissible. The Canadian Social Security Review was launched in the comparative prosperity of 1973, and within the year, Parliament had enacted two billion dollars worth of expansions in Family Allowances, Old Age Security pensions, and Guaranteed Income Supplements. In 1975, however, a suddenly cost-conscious cabinet sent the review reeling by imposing a delay and forcing Lalonde to scale down the federal proposal to exclude the childless. By 1976 most provinces were unwilling to join the program, despite federal offers of improved cost sharing. When the federal government on its own enacted the Refundable Child Tax Credit program in 1978, this step had to avoid committing new funds, a constraint that helped justify a cut in Family Allowances but also limited the size of the new program.

Economic constraints were equally decisive in U.S. policy debates. The initial thinking on FAP in 1968–1969 assumed that the new system should not cost more than two billion new dollars. And when the economy had troubles in 1971, the chances for welfare reform faded, because Nixon delayed the effective date of the measure. An even more dramatic demonstration of the limits that economy places on politics was the rapid demise of the 1977 Carter welfare proposals. Even as the measure was working its way out of committee, it was widely considered a dead letter. In a sour economy an expensive bill suddenly had little chance. Even more remarkable, efforts to fashion reforms costing half as much also broke up under a wave of austerity. The administration learned its lesson, proposing a modest package in 1979.

Another factor in common was government expansion of aid to the aged. Increases in Social Security benefits are an election-year tradition in the United States. Although the Nixon administration welfare reform proposals for families did not pass, Congress easily passed its proposals for providing a federally guaranteed income to the needy aged and other "adult" categories. Though Congress forced the Carter administration in 1979 to pare down many of its 1977 proposals, it was likely to welcome the 1979 proposal to cash out food stamps for SSI recipients. In Canada increases in Old Age Security pensions occurred no matter what else was on the political agenda. Though the Family Income Security Plan failed in 1970–1972, Canada went ahead with big expansions in pensions and made permanent the Guaranteed Income Supplement program. Family Allowances, another "motherhood" issue, were increased in 1973 even though the Social Security Review dragged on for several more years without producing equivalent change in the welfare system. While neither country felt a similar push to improve the benefits of younger welfare recipients, welfare reform proposals triggered some resistance to reducing existing benefits. The problems of how to achieve welfare reform without reducing benefits-in-being continually plagued the Nixon and Carter plans. Similar problems came up in Canadian debates, although federal and provincial officials headed off the problem somewhat by agreeing to the May 1975 ceilings on earnings and income exemptions.

Finally, in both Canada and the United States the poor are politically weak. The group was not well organized to participate effectively in policy debates. In 1970 not a single member of Congress queried by two reporters remembered having received a letter in support of the Family Assistance Plan from a potential beneficiary.[8] In view of the impermanence of the U.S. National Welfare Rights Organization, the continued survival of the Canadian National Anti-Poverty Organization is remarkable. NAPO's ineffectiveness should not obscure the fact that the United States has no such group. The federal subsidies going to NAPO have been criticized from both Left and Right, but government sponsorship of a poor people's lobby seems better than having no national organization for the poor.[9]

When the poor do succeed in becoming organized, what effect can they have? As John Kenneth Galbraith has argued, the efficacy of political action by the poor historically dropped as their relative proportion in society declined.[10] Frances Fox Piven and Richard Cloward have shown that in the past the dispossessed often got results by kicking up a fuss. Such a strategy was of obvious efficacy when they were in the majority. Even when the poor represented a large minority, their unrest helped move policymakers, as during the Great Depression. But now that the poor have been reduced to a definite minority, their sheer disruptive power has dropped while the resistance of the rest has risen. Thus poor people's movements face the new danger of triggering a majority backlash. The 1968 Poor People's Campaign was the biggest gathering of the poor in the United States since the depression, but it produced little except bad publicity. Calvin Trillin remarked that the marchers had "come to Washington to show that the poor in America are sick, dirty, disorganized, and powerless—and they are criticized daily for being sick, dirty, disorganized and powerless."[11] Sometimes this backlash can have concrete costs. A major strategy of state Welfare Rights Organizations was to exploit programs for special needs under AFDC. While providing temporary windfalls for some, this strategy predictably triggered the repeal of these programs in state after state.[12]

Intergovernmental Differences

The inescapability of economics, the strength of the aged, and the weakness of the poor seem to be common to both Canada and the United States. Nevertheless the countries' political structures have created very significant variations in policymaking. Although major welfare reform proposals collapsed in both countries, the collapses were entirely different. Canadian policymakers agreed on the outlines of a new policy but disagreed on questions of jurisdiction and financing. U.S. policymakers disagreed about the very aims of reform. These different outcomes had roots in each country's geographic distribution of welfare problems and of political influence. In the United States, the welfare population and the highest welfare costs were concentrated in a few large states. In 1970 California and New York together had less than 20 percent of the U.S. general population but accounted for 30 percent of all AFDC families. Many small states, particularly in the West, had proportionately fewer recipients and costs. In Canada, on the other hand, welfare problems were not distributed clearly on the basis of a province's size. Of the two largest provinces, Ontario actually had less than its quota of welfare recipients, while Quebec had more. In 1972 Ontario had 36 percent of the country's population but only 28 percent of the welfare recipients; Quebec had 28 percent of the general population but 33 percent of the welfare recipients.[13] The other provinces also differed among themselves in the weight of their welfare load. The western provinces had less than their share of welfare recipients, while the Atlantic provinces had more.

This difference in the regional distribution of welfare problems gave welfare reform a broader appeal in Canada than in the United States. In the United States many small states did not believe that welfare costs were high enough to require a broader federal role, and their leaders opposed any efforts to expand the welfare rolls. This stance by small states was especially significant in the Senate, where representation is by state rather than by population. In Canada welfare reform was not seen as a benefit only to the large provinces, and some small provinces had a clear stake in a larger federal role. Thus Canada achieved greater consensus on the need for welfare reform, even if this consensus was rendered academic by conflicts in the design of a program.

The greater Canadian consensus on the principles of welfare reform emerged because the large provinces were not the only ones that would benefit from it and also because Canadian federalism gave more influence to provinces friendly to a change. In the United States the large states wanted welfare reform, but they were outnumbered by small states that did not. In Canada small provinces supported welfare reform, but this support may not even have been necessary, because the large provinces are not as greatly outnumbered by small ones as the large states are. The clout of the large provinces stems not just from formal representation but from informal recognition of the importance of including them in any consensus. After all, the Social Security Review was initiated largely because of Quebec's unhappiness with the existing fiscal arrangements in welfare policy. This result was achieved even though Ontario, the largest province, did not feel as much need for a change. In contrast, the representatives of large states such as New York and California were easily outvoted in their efforts to achieve welfare reform. There seems little doubt that if both Quebec and Ontario had agreed strongly on a particular proposal, it would have faced little opposition and might now be law.

The strength of the large provinces is of course attributable not only to their geographical dominance but also to the fact that provincial governments have greater power in national debates than state governments, or any other actors on the political scene in either country. Quebec's objections to the 1970 proposals to transform family allowances into the Family Income Security Plan led to changes in the bill before it was presented to Parliament. The Family Allowance legislation proposed and passed in 1973 went even further toward providing the provinces important new power over the spending of federal Family Allowance dollars. And it was in response to a 1972 interprovincial conference that the federal government came up with its 1973 proposals for a new system of income supplementation. Quebec had helped motivate this proposal by its remarkable Castonguay-Nepveu report; federal authorities wanted to regain the initiative. Of course, such single-handed provincial influence can be used to block as well as to advance proposals. Ontario, with a lower proportion of poor people in its population than the national average, was able to forestall agreement on nationwide supplementation proposals.

Intergovernmental Differences

In the United States, the states did not play as crucial a role as the Canadian provinces in bringing the expansion of welfare onto the agenda. While states such as Washington and New York offered aid to intact families in their general assistance programs, they did not use negative income tax rates. No state had a counterpart to the guaranteed income initiatives tried in British Columbia, Ontario, and especially Saskatchewan. Certainly, no state advanced any proposals nearly as ambitious as those in Quebec's Castonguay-Nepveu report. Indeed the most widely noted state proposals were Reagan's, drawn from his California effort to slash the welfare rolls. In national politics the states did not have the power of the provinces; what power they had they shared with local governments and exerted not directly but by lobbying. This intergovernmental lobby was important in calling for welfare reforms that would provide fiscal relief. The states were always highly pragmatic about this demand. When Nixon and Carter were able to design proposals giving this relief, states and localities became welfare reform's best friends. Intergovernmental groups led the coalition supporting the Family Assistance Plan in 1971–1972, and they took the lead in seeking a compromise on the Carter plan in 1978. But when the prospects for these welfare reform initiatives worsened, the intergovernmental lobby easily shifted its weight to other forms of relief, such as general revenue sharing in 1972 and the Moynihan-Cranston-Long proposal in 1978.

While Canadian federalism helped smooth the way for agreement on the substantive need for welfare reform, it also erected some practical barriers not faced by such a measure in the United States. If the provinces were strong enough to force proposals onto the agenda, they were also strong enough to veto proposals. The federal proposals for income support and supplementation were less controversial than they would have been in the United States, but near unanimous agreement was essential, and it was not achieved. If the provinces were not cooperative, the federal side deserved some of the blame, because the provinces had been antagonized in 1975 by its delay in funding and by its impolitic jurisdictional preference. But the provinces were more willful in these debates than ever before. Individually, several struck nonnegotiable positions, while as a group the provinces banded together against Ottawa in ways that had previously been taboo. The behavior of federal and provincial representatives was in seeming contrast to the public spirit that Richard Simeon found in his study of federal-provincial politics from 1963 to 1971.[14]

Have the politics of accommodation broken down in Canada? This study cannot provide a definitive answer to that question, because welfare reform is not popular enough among the public or elites for them to insist that the federal-provincial process produce results. More popular changes such as increases in family allowances and aid to the aged, and even controversial changes such as block funding in social services, achieved basic agreement relatively easily within the federal-provincial forum. Moreover, unlike some other issues, income supplementation was not a question that could be resolved only within the federal-provincial forum. After the collapse of the Social Security Review, the federal government was able on its own to enact Refundable Child Tax Credits, a modest form of supplementation.

In another sense, however, the failure of the Social Security Review to produce welfare reform was a failure for the Canadian political system, because the review had been undertaken to prove that the system works. In 1972 the provinces signaled their willingness to cooperate by calling for the discussions. Trudeau and Lalonde responded by proposing the Social Security Review as a massive new experiment in cooperation. In a 1976 article I predicted (wrongly, as it turned out) that the need to prove the federal system viable would rescue the Social Security Review from the deadlock that existed at that time.[15] Although the review was seen as a test of the federal system, the participants were unable to overcome their differences. The lessons are not encouraging for future attempts at federal-provincial negotiation, whether in policymaking or in rewriting the Canadian constitution.

By 1976 economic conditions had worsened to the point that the provinces were unfriendly to virtually any extension of social spending. Here the need for unanimity in federal-provincial politics was fatal to the Social Security Review. The Atlantic provinces, natural allies of the federal proposals, were in such economic straits that they had to reject them flatly. In this situation a poor province may actually be more influential than a rich one—"strength through weakness."[16] In Canada the chain of policy consensus depends on its weakest links. U.S. policymakers cast a wide net in seeking their bare majority coalition; this "inductive" approach helped average away regional doldrums rather than intensify their effect as in Canada.

The nature of federalism in each country shaped the agenda and the universe of possible policies. In Canada the provinces were more concerned about jurisdiction than finances; for the states the reverse was true. Thus several provinces were incredulous that in 1975 the federal government wanted them even to consider a federally administered program whose costs they shared. Yet such ideas were not only imaginable in the United States; in one case they actually passed. Under the Supplemental Security Income program, federal benefits did not quite come up to the previous level in some states. Thus federal law made supplementation by many states mandatory, and federal inducements were provided to encourage states to devote funds to added optional supplementation. This federal program told states how to spend their money; it even offered incentives to let the federal government spend their money for them. As a result, proud states like California, Massachusetts, and New York now have the federal government administer these state programs. As of 1977 the U.S. government administered mandatory supplementation for thirty-nine states, and optional supplementation for twelve states.[17]

Differences in Parties and the Legislative Process

Parties affected the Canadian and U.S. debates differently. Party politics helped motivate welfare proposals in both countries but were less dependable in the United States than in Canada in the debates themselves. Competition between parties played a big role in Canada in bringing the guaranteed income to the agenda. In 1970 the Liberal government found itself under pressure from both Left and Right to make some kind of initiative in aiding the nonwelfare poor. In 1973 the Liberals had the added pressure of their need to satisfy the New Democratic Party and thus retain their support in Parliament to maintain the minority government. In 1978 party politics probably helped hurry the Liberals to enact child tax credits; the opposition, at least, knew that the first benefits would arrive shortly before the expected federal election.

In the United States President Nixon's support for expansion of the Food Stamp program was the result of pressure from Democrats in Congress, who threatened to go ahead and pass the legislation on their own. Nixon was comparatively free to decide for himself whether to propose the Family Assistance Plan, but partisanship encouraged him to do so, allowing him to appropriate a traditionally Democratic issue. Nixon's opportunity stemmed in part from the fact that Democratic presidents had long been discouraged from making similar proposals because they justly anticipated criticism from Nixon's own party when it was in the opposition. Of course, Nixon's ability to make such a dramatic switch illustrated the difficulty a party can have in controlling a president that belongs to it. Many congressional Republicans did not like FAP, as they showed repeatedly with their votes during the ensuing struggles over the issue. Faced with the prospect of antagonizing such a large segment of the party, a president usually chooses not to go against the grain. Presidents Ford and Carter were strongly influenced in what they proposed by members of their own parties. Ford felt compelled by the conservative wing of the Republican party to defer his support for the Income Supplement Program. Carter bowed to pressure from the opposite direction. Democratic urban politicians and activists quickly convinced him to drop his initial insistence that the 1977 welfare reform package should cost no more than existing programs. However, this pressure during the formulation of the proposals was not translated later into congressional support.

A special feature of Canadian politics kept guaranteed income proposals constantly on the agenda. By giving a parliamentary foothold to regionally based third parties, the Canadian system provides a special platform for their proposals. In the 1972 federal election the Créditistes under Réal Caouette fared respectably with a platform that included an expensive system of universal guaranteed income payments. Meanwhile, George McGovern's chances of beating Nixon were being eroded by criticism of his own universal proposal, which had striking similarities to Caouette's. Because McGovern was running for president, his proposal was examined in dead seriousness. Because Caouette was not a serious contender for prime minister, he was safer in advancing the idea. The New Democratic Party had similar freedom to urge such expensive ideas as a unitary negative income tax during the Social Security Review and high Family Allowances during the 1978 debate. On the basis of two decades of observation of Parliament while an official at Health and Welfare Canada, Richard Splane concludes that the NDP "has consistently affected the mood of Commons during social welfare debates."[18]

Canadian and U.S. parties operated quite differently once the proposals were on the legislative agenda. Liberal members of Parliament had to grin and bear it when their leaders proposed the unpopular step of withdrawing Family Allowances from nearly half the recipients. Although they were delighted not to have to vote on the measure prior to the 1972 election, nearly all would have felt obligated to support the government if a vote had been held. Their unhappiness did register within the government, however; the 1973 Family Allowance proposals and legislation were in substance politically less suicidal. Pressure on Parliament to ratify government proposals is intensified when the legislation is the product of laborious negotiation between federal and provincial representatives. Such momentum was clear in the 1977 and 1978 versions of the Social Services Act. Backbenchers were probably relieved that party leaders withdrew these bills, but they would have acceded obediently if ordered to.

Whereas Liberal legislators were docile toward the government's proposals, the leading opponents of Nixon's and Carter's proposals were members of their own parties. Senator John Williams was the ranking Republican on the Finance Committee when he eviscerated the Family Assistance Plan in 1970. Most of the other Republicans on the committee resisted the president throughout 1969–1972. Nixon had to rely on Democratic votes to get as far as he did. Of course a majority of the Democrats on the Finance Committee also opposed the Family Assistance Plan. Jimmy Carter was the first president in eight years whose party had a congressional majority, but it did him little good. Al Ullman, chairman of the House Ways and Means Committee, was unalterably opposed to Carter's 1977 bill and was ultimately able to veto even a brutally scaled-down version. Other key Democrats were not happy with the administration's proposals; even Senator Moynihan, usually a friend to welfare reform, displeased the administration with a series of proposals that threatened to pull the rug out from under Carter by providing fiscal relief to states and localities without significantly changing the welfare system. And Carter's proposals became stalled before they even received much attention from Democratic Senator Russell Long, the most effective opponent of welfare reform initiatives. It was not surprising that before efforts to compromise with Ullman fell through, Carter found himself in need of help from rock-ribbed Republicans like senators Henry Bellmon and Howard Baker.

Party allegiance is so ineffective in the United States that the congressional committee system has a life of its own. It makes a great deal of difference which committee a bill is referred to and who runs the committee. As a heritage of the businesslike model of the original Social Security

Act, cash welfare programs are the responsibility of the finance committees of Congress, not the committees most concerned with human needs. This arrangement has sometimes delivered the AFDC program into the hands of its enemies, but it has also reduced the scrutiny that Congress as a whole gives it, allowing significant growth to occur anyway. The most generous committee may not be the one that can convince the rest of Congress to ratify its recommendations. The Agriculture Committee kept control of the Food Stamp program in order to have bargaining chips to win support for farm price supports. Supporters of the program's expansion did not resist, and such realpolitik served the program well.

The fate of a proposal in the United States depends not only on which committee it ends up in but on who is in control of that committee. Wilbur Mills was essential to the success of FAP in the House in 1970 and 1971. When Mills was replaced as chairman of Ways and Means by Al Ullman, the story was very different for President Carter's proposals. Ullman was able to use his influence to maroon the Carter bill and force the administration to bargain with him. The importance of individual personality is even clearer in the case of Senator Long, and it illustrates how the internal structure of Congress intensifies this impact. As chairman of the Finance Committee, Long consistently used the power of delay to its fullest and most destructive effect. His efforts to bottle up the Nixon bills in his committee in 1970 and again (for more than fourteen months) in 1971–1972 were the most important steps in the bills' double demise. Of course, delay will do no good if the full Senate supports the measure, but this weapon denies the administration the crucial power to determine when a bill comes up for a vote. Long consciously delayed consideration of FAP until the bandwagon got rolling on general revenue sharing and (in both 1970 and 1972) until an election year was at hand. Long stood ready to use similar tactics against the 1977 Carter bill, but the House relieved him of this need. In the United States a bill's chances are not determined solely by the personality and position of its enemies; the president and party leaders also lack control over their own allies. Senator Harris had been friendly to FAP, so his change of heart was particularly decisive. Though Congressman Corman strongly supported the Carter welfare proposals, he supported amendments that increased the plan's cost against White House wishes, and he opposed efforts to compromise when cost clearly became the major issue. Though professedly loyal to the bill,

Senator Moynihan repeatedly clashed with the administration on questions of political strategy.

In Canada the parliamentary allies of a bill are under tighter central control than in the United States, and opponents have fewer tools for obstruction. A rare example of a bill's being blocked was the 1972 incident when Paul Hellyer sabotaged the FISP proposals in the waning hours of the parliamentary sitting. Hellyer's role depended on an unusual parliamentary situation and the even more unusual fact that he happened to be in transit from one party to another. A better analogy to Senator Long's crucial impact was Ontario's irreconcilable opposition to the federal proposals in 1976. Like Long, Ontario favored a tax credit scheme, and this approach came to seem the only one that could pass. Although no unit of Parliament had Long's arsenal of tactics to bury a bill, the Canadian Senate Special Committee on Poverty demonstrated an independent ability to focus positive discussion on guaranteed income proposals. Like its predecessor, the Special Committee on Aging, the Special Committee on Poverty helped apply pressure on the government and helped educate the public and elites about the idea. However, the committee's influence stemmed largely from its ability to gain allies for its position; unlike a congressional committee, it had no direct power to pass or kill a measure.

To attribute decisive power to Senator Long and other congressional barons is to ignore the real extent to which many congressmen agreed with them. After all, the full Senate twice rejected the Family Assistance Plan. In 1978 the Carter plan died because hardly any congressmen wanted to keep it alive. Individual congressmen are difficult to organize into a prowelfare coalition. The public is critical of welfare costs and suspicious of welfare beneficiaries, and this concern is correspondingly strong in Congress, particularly in election years. While party leaders in Canada sometimes take antiwelfare positions, party discipline restrains individual legislators from electorally induced excesses. No such restraints exist in the United States, and demagoguery often repays itself nicely. Even prowelfare legislators occasionally feel compelled to support efforts to tighten up on welfare. When not a single senator objected to Senator Talmadge's 1971 legislation that applied the Nixon plan's strong work requirement to AFDC without adopting any of its liberal features, the responsibility belonged to every senator, not just to Senator Talmadge.

Bureaucratic Differences

By most measures, bureaucrats in the United States are more independent than in a parliamentary system like Canada's. Canadian civil servants defer to their minister and to the deputy minister and assistant deputy ministers who act in his name. U.S. civil servants are freer to pursue their own policy goals within the bureaucracy and to contact legislators, groups, and the press. This difference was very evident in welfare policymaking. In Canada, bureaucrats were shy of suggesting almost any initiatives, even when their political superiors were failing to supply any substance to debates. In contrast, in a decade of U.S. debates, bureaucrats at all levels unashamedly took leading roles. Presidents may regret this politicization, yet they sometimes have no choice but to rely on it. Jimmy Carter attempted to reclaim policymaking authority by requiring the bureaucracy to submit to him a welfare reform plan costing no more than the existing system. He hoped that this requirement would reserve for the White House the final political decisions on how much should be spent, but it did nothing of the kind. Recognizing political realities, bureaucratic debates continued to consider plans costing much more than the current system; Carter only succeeded in isolating himself from these debates. His isolation made it more difficult to influence or resist the expensive proposals eventually presented to him. And Carter's desire to retain all political prerogatives in the White House deprived him of the seasoned political analysis that normally accompanies policy proposals in the U.S. bureaucracy and that would have shown him, in time to acknowledge it gracefully, why new spending would be needed.

Sometimes bureaucrats far below the cabinet level seem to have more influence on policy than presidents do. Analysts in the HEW Office of Income Security Policy refined proposals for a negative income tax and kept the idea percolating for years. One of their antagonists, Martin Anderson, has charged that "the clamor for radical welfare reform comes essentially from a small group of committed ideologues who want to institute a guaranteed income under the guise of welfare reform."[19] I believe that Anderson's constant use of the term *radical* in this context improperly polarizes the question and considerably inflates the ideological significance of the proposals. And I know that Anderson's characterization is unfaithful to the basic moderation of most who helped design and promote these HEW proposals over the years. It is not even true that the membership of the Office of Income Security Policy remained stable during the past decade. Only a few planners who had helped design FAP were in on the design of the Mega-Proposal. Of those who helped design ISP, only one had contributed to the Mega-Proposal, and none had been involved with FAP. Many who designed PBJI dated back to the ISP effort, but even this overlap was not complete. Of course, the turnover does not deny that most people in that office over the years have been sympathetic to the negative income tax, but the language of conspiracy is inappropriate.

These qualifications noted, it is true that HEW planners were a key internal lobby in convincing two presidents to adopt negative income tax proposals. The institutional longevity of such a lobby increased the chances of success. If Johnson and Ford did not choose to back the proposals, Nixon and Carter did. U.S. bureaucratic initiative goes to lengths undreamed of in Canadian government. When President Johnson refused to support a negative income tax, specialists in the Office of Economic Opportunity (OEO) convinced a sympathetic legislator to introduce a bill in Congress proposing their plan. When the Carter plan had lost momentum in Congress, planners in HEW quietly inspired major new outside efforts to achieve a compromise.

In contrast to the activist U.S. bureaucrats, Canadian policy analysts avoided outright advocacy. The internal debates leading to the 1970 and 1973 proposals conceded to the top leaders the responsibility of setting direction. While deference by policy analysts avoided backing these leaders into a corner, it also reduced the richness of ideas from which they could choose. The difficulty of balancing neutrality against creativity was also faced by the three working parties of civil servants that serviced the Social Security Review.[20] The working parties on employment strategy and social services produced reports so vague that they were virtually useless to political leaders. The employment strategy went into hibernation. The social services strategy took on life only when the deadlock over support and supplementation produced a need for momentum in other areas. The Working Party on Income Maintenance deferred to political officials to such an extent that its reports did not face some of the basic practical issues. The *Background Paper on Income Support and Supplementation* reflected the lack of concreteness that characterized political discussions in the Social Security Review. A certain amount of advocacy by civil servants might have been excusable if it encouraged political leaders to get down to business.

More than their Canadian counterparts, U.S. welfare policy analysts were armed with data. To some extent this difference can be traced to a difference in scale. Surveys, experiments, and other projects are expensive, often beyond a small country's means. Another reason for the difference in data was the historic resistance of the provinces to federal efforts to collect information. The U.S. federal government requires the states to file monthly reports on the size of their case loads and to participate in biennial surveys that sample the case loads in detail. Canada has almost no standardized reporting of any kind, and the last nationwide survey was conducted in 1970. Instead federal officials have since 1973 sought, with increasing success, to convince the provinces to place welfare case files in a nationwide computerized system allowing federal access electronically rather than by onerous reporting requirements.[21] However, this system was not fully developed during the Social Security Review.

The absence of good data in Canada is well illustrated in the major government white papers of 1970 and 1973. These reports relied on a combination of undifferentiated national data with somewhat detailed but incompatible figures compiled by several (not all) provinces. Canadian policy analysts have become inured to the paucity of data on welfare recipients and the poor. Fittingly, some social scientists who staffed the Policy Research and Long-Range Planning Branch (Welfare) were less concerned with collecting data than with constructing theories. They were suspicious of anecdotal data such as that offered by administrators and other program-oriented specialists. This attitude was unfortunate because indirect measures are often the only ones possible, particularly in Canada.[22] Cut off from practical experience and from an empirical data base, the deductive planners risked taking a stance that was sometimes (and not always unfairly) ascribed to them: "Yes, this works in practice, but does it work in *theory*?"

The Orange Book was written before the reorganization occurred that produced the Policy Research and Long-Range Planning Branch (Welfare), but the report exhibited strengths and weaknesses similar to those in the agency's subsequent analysis. As shown in chapter 7, the strength of the federal proposals was that unemployables and those expected to work should be treated differently, with each tier to have a different basic payment and reduction rate. The designers of these proposals had learned important technical and political lessons from the fight over the Family Assistance Plan and from the Castonguay-Nepveu report. Yet the federal proposals were not equally sensitive to other technical and political problems in the delivery of benefits. The Orange Book did not say whether the two tiers should be administered separately or together, and it did not say which level of government should do what. During much of the Social Security Review, federal officials insisted on keeping open the question of delivery. They never formally proposed that the federal government administer the supplementation tier, but many federal officials preferred this alternative and a number of federal moves were aimed at keeping it alive as a possibility. Their desire to retain for the federal government a foothold in social policy was understandable in view of the alarming erosion of federal powers in Canada. Canada's later passing of a federally administered supplementation mechanism, the Refundable Child Tax Credit program, suggests that such thinking could be acted on. Moreover, the Treasury was known to look more favorably on budget requests for federally administered programs than for those that simply added to the torrent of federal dollars flowing into provincial coffers. However, the officials' desire for a federal role in administering the Orange Book proposals was contradicted by two realities: the two-tier benefit structure that emerged from the Social Security Review could not effectively be divided between programs administered separately by federal and provincial levels of government, and the provinces would not agree to such a division of responsibilities anyway.

Many provincial administrators as well as program-oriented federal officials felt that separately administered support and supplementation tiers would be unworkable.[23] But the absence of adequate data and research on the provincial programs made it difficult to establish this point with the finality that is the case in the United States. Whatever the substantive arguments that could still be made for the federal position, however, Canadian federal officials had to reckon with the political fact that several of the provinces would never agree to a division of programs giving the federal government the responsibility for the supplementation tier. Yet key federal officials were slow to recognize this problem. The reorganization in Health and Welfare Canada had cut the department off from the provinces in a very concrete sense. Unlike their federal counterparts, social scientists and planners did not dominate policymaking in the provincial welfare departments. Because administrators were influential at the provincial level, the Social Security Review might have proceeded more smoothly if more use had been made of the long-standing links between these administrators and program-oriented federal officials. Of course, planners did have a voice in some provinces, particularly Ontario, Quebec, Prince Edward Island, Saskatchewan, and Manitoba, and the frequent meetings of working parties in the Social Security Review helped promote contact between them and their federal counterparts. But this communication began too late to educate certain federal planners. Many channels to provincial governments were needed, both to guide federal decisions and to persuade the provinces to go along with these decisions. Without fully exploiting these channels, the federal government was held to an untenable position. Only when the Social Security Review threatened to fall apart did the federal position finally change to allow provinces to locate the two benefit structures under the same administration.

Ontario was an exception among the provinces. It actually favored federal control of the supplementation tier, supporting the tax credit approach that was later adopted nationwide. Did welfare administrators in that province disagree with those elsewhere and believe that a two-tier benefit structure need not be administered within the same program? Probably not, because program administrators there apparently did not determine the province's position. Ontario's stance in the Social Security Review was strongly influenced by treasury and intergovernmental affairs authorities as well as by a policy secretariat within the ministry of community and social services. Thus Ontario may have had the same gap between planners and administrators that existed at the federal level.

In resisting the administrative separation of tiers, the Canadian program-oriented federal officials seemed to more than one planner to be "committed protectors of the status quo, whose objectivity was clouded by entrenched bureaucratic interests." Strictly speaking, it is difficult to accuse the administrators of selfishness. They were pressing for a proposal, the integration of a two-tier benefit structure under a single administration, that in the Canadian context could only lead to increased provincial jurisdiction and a diminution of their own authority. In a broader sense, however, perhaps the bureaucratic ties of program-oriented officials did narrow their vision. Their ties to provincial officials were strong, and they were not as open to the brave new analytical methods that sustain negative income tax proposals. Proposals as comprehensive as those in the Orange Book could not have been produced by the old guard alone. In view of the strong outside demand for a creative federal initiative in 1973, this fact suggests that the new arrivals were needed. Bureaucratic opposition to unsettling new ideas is so common that Rufus Miles has propounded a law: "Where you stand depends on where you sit."[24] Unfortunately it is not only program administrators who obey this law. Planners, too, have their own interests and world views, and the fact that they run into opposition from other bureaucrats is no guarantee that their views are correct. A program administrator may have good reasons for opposing a specific proposal. He has an obligation to explain these reasons, just as his critics have an obligation to listen to them. By discounting the veterans' arguments as self-interested obstructionism, the planners missed special insights that could have improved the federal proposals technically and politically.

It would not be true to say that all planners did not listen to the administrators. The Policy and Program Development and Coordination Branch (Welfare) was established to promote such communication, and it sometimes succeeded. For example, in his capacity as federal representative to the working party on social services, John Osborne established a departmental advisory committee drawn from federal operating departments, and he took administrators with him to meetings to act as advisors. Moreover, some individuals within the Policy Research and Long-Range Planning Branch (Welfare) either worked closely with federal administrators, or had worked in provincial programs, or did in-depth studies of those programs. But the insights gained could not influence policymaking if top officials questioned the validity of provincial experience. One participant recalls that Al Johnson came with "pre-conceived views" about the Canada Assistance Plan, and that "this led to a certain unwillingness to consider the practical experience at hand from within this program." The program managers were not always excluded from the internal debates, but "there was a tendency to ignore conflicting views or to discount their importance." Of course, this stance by top officials probably discouraged consideration of the program managers' point of view even at lower levels; planners and managers had no incentive to work out their differences. The deductive approach had already won.

Planners in the U.S. Department of Health, Education, and Welfare have been somewhat more conscious of the administrative side of welfare reform proposals than their Canadian counterparts.[25] That is curious because economists were, if anything, even more numerous on staffs in the United States than in Canada, where they clashed with program-oriented specialists. Such clashes were less common in the United States. It was not that planners and administrators got along well—they did not. But the administrators simply played a smaller part in internal U.S. debates than in Canada. The U.S. planners were firmly in control of the proposal-writing process. As a result, they had a special responsibility to educate themselves about how programs actually worked. Of course, they did not always succeed at this task. An administrator might have caught the flaws exposed by Senator Williams that the planners allowed into the original design of the Family Assistance Plan. The analysts' unfamiliarity with administration was endemic in the Department of Labor, where the policy specialists were much more sanguine about the workability of massive jobs programs than administrative experience justified. One explanation may be that the Labor analysts were new and very few; they did not have the institutional memory or the division of labor to accumulate such experience. A special reason for the HEW planners' consciousness of administrative questions was that for several years the Office of Income Security Policy had helped to fund, design, and analyze several major income maintenance experiments. Though contractors ran these experiments, the planners in HEW were deeply involved. There was a similar Canadian experiment, but it apparently did not decisively shape the attitudes of planners toward administration.

Several other factors help explain the greater U.S. agreement between planners and administrators on the way to administer a negative income tax. U.S. planners had ulterior motives for preferring that a single agency be responsible for the scheme. Most supported a simplification of filing units as a way to prevent wasteful overlap in benefits; this preference incidentally clashed with proposals that did not integrate administration of benefits into one scheme. Also many U.S. planners preferred a unitary benefit structure contrary to the two-tier structure favored in Canada.[26] In contrast, the incentives in Canada discouraged consideration of administrative questions. Despite their expressed desire to balance the deductive with the inductive approach, Johnson and Robinson favored the deductive approach. Although the Policy and Program Development and Coordination Branch (Welfare) was supposed to serve as a common ground for planners and program administrators, it did not fully succeed in doing so and was eventually disbanded.[27] The scarcity of data discouraged self-education by the Canadian federal planners, in contrast to the infinite variety of information that U.S. planners had to contend with. The proximity in which the Canadian planners worked with other bureaucrats apparently polarized the situation. In the United States planners and administrators were not located near one another. They talked infrequently, which was probably a good thing. It is not necessarily true that a small government will promote understanding across organizational lines. Interaction between ethnic groups can actually exacerbate conflict, and the same goes for different breeds of bureaucrats.

Despite the special barriers, Canadian planners might have become more conscious of administration if they had been involved in as many welfare debates as the U.S. planners. By the time that President Carter presented his 1977 welfare reform package, planners had the guidance of two major congressional debates on FAP, major internal debates on the Mega-Proposal and ISP, and the congressional hearings of the Subcommittee on Fiscal Policy of the Joint Economic Committee, not to mention the years of struggle by OEO for the negative income tax. The Canadian planners in 1973 had only the FISP debate from which to draw lessons, and it was not until the Social Security Review that they had a chance to discuss the negative income tax thoroughly. The Orange Book drew some important lessons from welfare reform debates in the United States, but administrative lessons were apparently not among them.

The difficulties of the Canadian planners with questions of administrative feasibility seem to have been limited to issues concerning the provincial social assistance programs. In exclusively federal issues, such as pension legislation and Family Allowances, the planners knew what was practical. The same was true in the preparation of the 1978 legislation for the Refundable Child Tax Credit program, a federal one involving minimal links with provincial social assistance programs. In preparing such legislation, the Canadian planners were probably more careful than their U.S. counterparts who had designed the original Family Assistance Plan. Hugh Heclo remarks that an experienced civil servant in a parliamentary system would probably have been hypersensitive to the administrative practicalities that the FAP designers neglected.[28] It was apparently only concerning the provincial sphere that the Canadian federal planners were not primed to consider such questions. Such misunderstanding of the provinces is a frequent problem in Ottawa. It is probably less common in Canada than in the United States for a federal bureaucrat to have had experience at another level of government. Actually, Health and Welfare Canada probably has more personnel with provincial experience than the average Ottawa department; the two most recent deputy ministers, Johnson and Rawson, had served in Saskatchewan and Alberta, respectively. However, such experience is not evenly distributed, and seems particularly sparse on the planning staffs. Federal-provincial exchange of personnel should be expanded in the future as a means of improving the design of policy as well as its chances of adoption.

Differences in Nongovernmental Participation

The two countries differed sharply in the extent to which outsiders had access to knowledge and power in welfare debates. U.S. experts, media, and interests participated actively in debates on welfare policy, unlike their Canadian counterparts. The National Welfare Rights Organization and other advocacy groups helped polarize debate over the Nixon welfare reform proposals, while the administration worked closely with groups sympathetic to the proposals. In 1977 outside actors easily penetrated internal administration debates before the Carter proposals were presented to Congress. Although the "outreach" process initiated in early 1977 did not have a clear influence on policy, the administration's proposals were strongly influenced by months of feedback about earlier proposals and trial balloons. White House efforts to reach a compromise with Chairman Al Ullman and other critics of the Carter plan received special help from the Urban Institute (which served as neutral ground) and from intergovernmental organizations (which sponsored a compromise).

While U.S. policymaking circles were remarkably porous to the entry of outside participants, Canadian circles seemed hermetically sealed. Canada's federal and provincial governments tend to monopolize information. Because policy debates are carried on mainly within the governmental community, there is little presumption in favor of releasing data and analysis. A special constraint at the federal level is that all official releases must be bilingual. This requirement prevented the release of many documents that would have helped inform the public and instead kept them as internal "working documents." Moreover after the decision to release a report, time was often lost in waiting for it to be translated. This was one problem causing delay in the release of the 1975 *Background Paper on Income Support and Supplementation*. For these various reasons, there are few independent experts on welfare policy in Canada; only federal and provincial personnel have full access to the data. During the welfare reform debates, the Policy Research and Long-Range Planning Branch (Welfare) made far less use of outside consultants and contractors than did its counterpart in HEW, the Office of Income Security Policy in the Office of the Assistant Secretary for Evaluation (ASPE).

Interest groups in Canada faced similar barriers to those facing independent experts. The headquarters of the Canadian Council on Social Development (CCSD) are located only a block from the offices of Health and Welfare Canada, but the organization played little meaningful role in the Social Security Review. The National Anti-Poverty Organization (NAPO), too, had little apparent impact on the progress of debate. Even when at the 1974 Canadian Conference on Social Development it used militant tactics similar to those that served the National Welfare Rights Organization so well in the United States, NAPO had little impact on policymakers. An organization more closely involved in the internal debates than CCSD or NAPO was the National Council of Welfare (NCW). An advisory body without an independent constituency, NCW was a cheering section and conscience for the review. NCW's lack of national or provincial power bases was clear in 1975–1977 when it could only watch on the sidelines as the review fizzled out. Of course, NCW would not have been invited to participate in the internal debates if it represented a well-organized constituency. In this sense groups representing the poor in Canada face a cruel choice with respect to policy debates: to have a voice but no organizational base (as at NCW) or to have a base but no voice (as at CCSD and NAPO).

The lack of participation of interest groups in Canadian welfare reform debates was not always the result of deliberate exclusion. Indeed Canadian federal officials made strenuous efforts to encourage outside discussion of the support and supplementation proposals, but the response was far less than in the United States. John Osborne's Policy and Program Development and Coordination Branch (Welfare) had a special Opinion Analysis unit that commissioned surveys of public opinion, monitored the media, and maintained liaison with interest groups. This unit helped organize for Minister Marc Lalonde a series of bull-pen sessions in 1973 and 1974 at which he met with the public in town-hall meetings, appeared on hot-line broadcast shows, and met with opinion leaders and the media. Despite all these efforts, the public paid little attention. When the Orange Book was published, few Canadian organizations took the opportunity to reply to it. Indeed the first to do so was not a welfare group but the Chamber of Commerce. At the biennial Canadian Conference on Social Welfare held in June 1974, more than a year after the release of the Orange Book, two-thirds of the delegates admitted by a show of hands that they had not read it.[29] Whenever he spoke, Lalonde implored his audience to make themselves heard to the policymakers, and as the years went by he sounded increasingly frustrated. In December 1975 Lalonde told a Toronto audience of welfare professionals that they had failed to exert any pressure on politicians to complete the Social Security Review.[30] Similarly, in June 1976 Lalonde chided the Canadian Council on Social Development for having failed to be a "visible advocate and constructive critic of proposals for social security reform."[31]

The absence of outside pressure on the Social Security Review could not be blamed on a lack of federal efforts. The provinces deserve some of the blame; most provincial governments made no effort to solicit public reactions.[32] But the biggest reason for low public participation in Canada's welfare reform debate was that outsiders were kept outside by the closed institutional environment and the inaccessible vocabulary in which the proposals were discussed. The context of federal-provincial negotiation sharply limited the number of participants in Canadian policy debates, erecting special barriers to interest groups, Members of Parliament, and other outsiders. The communiqués released after the federal-provincial meetings usually covered up rather than reported the issue choices and conflicts being discussed inside. Moreover these communiqués came after rather than during or before the meetings. While news reports caught some of the internal debate, the public and organized groups received little sense of the decisions being made, and they were accordingly passive.

Secrecy was not the only barrier to public understanding of the Social Security Review. The debate was further enshrouded by the technical language in which it was carried on. To promote consensus, the Social Security Review was deliberately insulated against the outside world, and it used studies, proposals, and vocabulary designed to promote accommodation among elites, not to enlighten the public. The public had little chance of learning what was going on, and even outside specialists had trouble. Most social services administrators in Toronto viewed the review as a "vast, complicated and highly technical process and for that and other reasons few . . . followed its progress closely."[33] If they did not understand the debate, then who could?

An illustration of the communication gap between policymakers and the outside world was the February 1975 *Background Paper on Income Support and Supplementation.*[34] Federal and provincial authorities published this report with a real hope that it would provoke public discussion, a hope that was soon disappointed. Part of the problem lay in the report itself. Written by the Working Party on Income Maintenance, it presented some quite useful data on poverty and social expenditure, but its analysis of the policy alternatives was dated and of very limited scope. The *Background Paper* was written while the child-related policy options were still being discussed, and it devoted considerable space to them. But by the time it was released, the Federal-Provincial Conference of Ministers of Welfare had already rejected these options. In analyzing policies the paper discussed very few of the important dimensions and choices involved. It estimated some costs but did not analyze the cost-effectiveness of various delivery mechanisms, income definitions, eligibility rules, and so on. Two thoughtful observers pointed out that the *Background Paper* "vastly overcomplicates the choices before the reader" whereas "the vast majority of the design decisions are left back in the hands of the 'experts,' an 'easy out' and symbolic public input only."[35] While these authors' critique of the *Background Paper* is justified, they do not recognize the reasons for the report's shortcomings. The time for translation delayed the report's release, and the report's avoidance of substantive questions was a reflection not of deception but of the fact that even the internal debates were avoiding concrete topics.

The constriction of the Canadian policymaking circle forestalled some decisions that popular pressure would have made unavoidable in the United States. In 1973 federal-provincial negotiators determined that family allowances should for the first time be taxable. Parliament might not have swallowed this idea if it had not been the product of ticklish bargaining. Whereas the public at large would not welcome this change, the provincial governments had a special incentive to seek it, as they were to reap some of the resulting revenues. And despite Canada's historic affinity for Family Allowances, the Social Security Review had by 1974 rejected that model for future steps in supplementing income. These departures from the Family Allowance model would have been more difficult if they had been made openly. That is why the wide-open United States system would have become irretrievably addicted to ever-increasing Family Allowances if the program had ever been begun there.

An even more dramatic case where secrecy shielded Canadian proposals from potential opposition was in social services. This field has a vigorous system of interest groups, but the discussions that produced both social services bills were not open to such groups. The 1978 move toward block funding came with little warning and with less accompanying documentation about how it arose and what effect it would have. Indeed the decision in favor of cost sharing was also made behind closed doors. As one critic wrote, "The merits of the original proposals for a cost-shared Social Services Act have been totally lost to sight. But were these merits ever known?"[36] In contrast to this Canadian vacuum, interest groups were intimately involved in the U.S. crisis over social services and its resolution. Such groups helped guide the states in exploiting the cavernous loopholes in existing law, and when Congress moved to close them by capping federal spending for social services, they successfully pressed for legislation requiring the states to maintain specific types of services.

Political Culture and Political Structure

This book argues that political structure made a big difference in how Canada and the United States debated the extension of cash welfare to new groups. Others have made a strong case for the importance of political culture.[37] There are very real differences in the political culture of the two countries, but these differences do not have as important an impact on policymaking as is sometimes thought. It is risky to assume that policies arise directly from public values, without taking into account the political structure within which policies are decided.[38] Explanations based on political culture often fail to be specific, and it is difficult to identify the limits of the influence they claim. In a thoughtful critique of cultural explanations, Robert Berkhofer has pointed out that "the more some conception explains, the less it explains any one event."[39] In the U.S. and Canadian cases the most important influence of political culture was probably an indirect rather than a direct translation of substantive values into policies. In particular, Canadian political culture gives elites more freedom to be positive about welfare programs.

Although it is often argued that public values determine policy, little theoretical or empirical work has been done to show that political culture is indeed that specific. Most studies of political culture stress the citizen's orientation to the government rather than his substantive views of what exactly it should do. Comparative surveys of substantive public values are surprisingly scarce.[40] As comparable polls (chapter 1) on attitudes toward welfare programs in Canada and the United States show, these opinions are more similar than is sometimes thought. Curiously, however, the equally negative attitudes toward welfare in each country coexist with rather different attitudes toward the idea of a guaranteed income. The United States in the 1960s consistently produced survey results critical of guaranteed income proposals, while no Canadian polls were taken on this subject then. Polls taken after 1970 show some differences in attitude. One 1971 Canadian survey showed 68 percent agreeing that the government should provide poor people with an annual income or supplement to their income. Polls taken in 1972 and 1974 showed 54 percent and 58 percent of Canadians, respectively, supporting an income guarantee.[41] All these polls were taken after the Senate Select Committee and the government itself had made guaranteed income proposals, and the 1974 poll was taken after release of the Orange Book, which also endorsed the guaranteed income. In the United States public support for the guaranteed income was weaker, though not as strongly opposed as it had been in the 1960s. After President Nixon proposed his Family Assistance Plan, two of three polls that asked about public support for an income guarantee were negative. A 1977 poll taken just before President Carter formally unveiled his own Program for Better Jobs and Income still showed narrow disapproval of an income guarantee—44 percent yes, 50 percent no.[42]

While these survey results suggest different Canadian and U.S. attitudes toward extending welfare, a further look shows their limited connection to the fate of concrete proposals. It has been widely remarked that U.S. citizens, although in principle conservative about a major federal role in social policy and other fields, nevertheless qualify as "operational liberals."[43] As long as a program does not explicitly embrace socialistic principles, the U.S. public is often willing to buy it. Presidents

Nixon and Carter realized that "guaranteed income" was a red flag for many people in the United States, so they carefully avoided referring to their proposals in this way—even though both could be accurately described as guaranteed income proposals and promised higher benefits than the Canadian proposals that went by that name. Similarly the U.S. Supplemental Security Income (SSI) program actually covers more groups than Canada's Guaranteed Income Supplements, yet supporters of SSI have resisted efforts to characterize it as a guaranteed income. President Nixon not only denied that his Family Assistance Plan was a guaranteed income proposal; he continually attacked the idea of an income guarantee! Clearly U.S. surveys showing a critical attitude toward income guarantees do not tell the whole story. The U.S. public was favorable toward Nixon's concrete proposals. In the year and a half after the proposals were made, only one poll showed the public closely divided on the Family Assistance Plan; all the other polls reflected overwhelming support, ranging up to 79 percent when the plan's work requirement was listed.[44]

While substantive views on what government should do are not as different in Canada and the United States as is sometimes supposed, political culture seems to affect political outcomes indirectly by determining how autonomous elites are. The U.S. public expects that its distaste for the welfare mess and its suspicion of guaranteed income proposals be slavishly represented by politicians; Canadians are not so demanding of their leaders. This deference has allowed Canadian elites to adopt attitudes considerably more favorable to welfare programs than those of U.S. elites. Of course, this difference is not simply attributable to political culture; it is also rooted in political institutions. The values of elites depend partly on how much freedom they can carve out of the political structure. As congressional elections operate, most candidates must take a public position on the welfare system, and in some states a candidate who does not make some ritual attacks faces certain electoral defeat. In contrast, the Canadian political structure frees elites to retain their protectiveness toward welfare programs.

Popular values are also influenced by political structure. After federal authorities made guaranteed income proposals in each country, the Canadian public became more supportive of the idea than the U.S. public. This was only rational. When proposals reach that stage in Canada, they are virtually certain to pass, and the public is best advised to get used to the idea. When they reach that stage in the United States, the fight has just begun. In a 1974 poll, in the midst of the Social Security Review, 57 percent of Canadians with an opinion agreed that within ten years "All Canadians will have a Guaranteed Annual Income."[45] It would be surprising if, during any of the U.S. welfare debates, the public ever saw the issue with that kind of inevitability.

The apparent difference between Canadian and U.S. public values may actually be, as Tom Truman has argued, a sign that, Canadians "are more firmly governed than are American citizens."[46] A striking example of this institutional difference and its cultural impact was the 1978 U.S. furor over California's Proposition 13. There was no evidence that the average Canadian was any less outraged over taxes than his Californian cousins, and some officials in Quebec City and Ottawa felt that Canadians, given the chance, would vote the same way. But Canada has no system of referenda that could register such specific outrage, a fact that discourages efforts to express it and might ultimately extirpate it. Of course, the proximity of the U.S. example is important in showing Canadian leaders what the Canadian public might say if it had more opportunity to express specific opinions on policy. U.S. political developments are watched carefully in Ottawa and throughout Canada. The battle over Proposition 13 was widely reported in the Canadian press. This indirect way of estimating Canadian opinion was one component in the internal debates that produced Ottawa's announcement of dramatic spending cuts in August 1978.

Institutions and Policy Outcomes

U.S. policymaking is an inductive free-for-all in which the policymaker pieces together a coalition. U.S. policy is a patchwork quilt, while Canadian policy is made from whole cloth. Large social decisions emanate from elections and party platforms, while specific applications are left to conclaves of leaders free of outside intervention. These styles of policymaking are firmly rooted in the countries' political systems; to evaluate them is not to say that they can be easily changed or that they are the product of conscious choice. The historic sources of values and institutions are more inescapable than that. At the same time each country might learn something about itself by watching the other. Moreover political leaders and others have some power over the style of policymaking, and they might profitably compare the relative advantages and disadvantages of each approach.

The U.S. policymaking circle was much larger and more open to nongovernmental participants than Canada's, but it was not more democratic. All too often, the groups with effective organization and influential analysis were privileged groups. The poor were left out of debates. Even those groups favorable to welfare reform, such as the intergovernmental lobby, favored it for their own reasons and could not always be depended on to take positions favorable to the poor. The Canadian system was more closed to nongovernmental participation, but it was internally more friendly to the needs of voiceless downtrodden groups. Only when the internal debate became deadlocked did the lack of external pressure have its drawbacks, allowing the Social Security Review to disintegrate quickly without a public fight. This exclusiveness also forestalled objections to the 1978 Refundable Child Tax Credit legislation's spreading benefits to so many Canadians that it did not provide much help to those who needed it most.

As a result of the openness of the U.S. policymaking arena to participation by outsiders, the debate was richer in ideas but often more inconclusive than Canadian debates. A good example of the intensiveness of the U.S. debate was the endless stream of independent evaluations published of the 1977 Carter proposals. Major evaluations were done not only by congressional units such as the Joint Economic Committee and the Congressional Budget Office, but also by the Urban Institute, the Institute for Research on Poverty, the American Enterprise Institute, the Hoover Institution, and so on. These studies appeared soon enough to genuinely influence debate. This profusion of analysis is a tempting alternative to the virtual vacuum of independent analysis in Canada. Still this vacuum did not prevent Canada from engaging in a debate that was in many ways more serious and productive than U.S. debates. The simple accumulation of solid analysis does not guarantee that it will be heeded. The U.S. situation allows people to pick the evaluation that fits their prejudices, and few minds are changed. The National Welfare Rights Organization got far with its insistence that employable and unemployable people should receive the same high basic benefit and the same low reduction rate. In contrast, efforts by the NDP provinces and NAPO to press the same argument were much less successful. In the federal-provincial context, the impossibly high cost of this alternative was methodically exposed, while its public appeal was irrelevant.

It is possible to know too much about an issue if the best evidence is inconclusive or subject to alternative interpretations. An important difference between the debates over the Nixon and Carter proposals was that Congress had in the meantime founded its own Congressional Budget Office to produce independent analyses of administration proposals. A grievous blow to the Carter plan was the controversy over its cost, with the administration's estimates gravely discredited by the CBO. The Nixon bills would have had even tougher going than they did if HEW's estimates had been subjected to such analysis. Cost consciousness is fine, but many worthwhile social programs might never have been adopted if Congress had known their full costs. The social policy advances of the War on Poverty were boosted by the absence of hard information about the problems to be combated or experience with similar programs.[47] In contrast, the present glut of information makes further movement particularly difficult. Laurence Lynn, Jr. has pointed out that the profusion of experts assures any proposals an intense scrutiny that perhaps no proposal can survive gracefully. The dangers of simply talking a proposal to death are very real in the United States. With more information available, more talking can be done. Albert Hirschman argues that to undertake some large and worthwhile projects, we need a "hiding hand" that disguises their future costs and problems.[48] In contrast, a German scholar has observed of the United States that "information about the poor seems sometimes a ready substitute for reform." Canada's policy of bilingualism worsened the country's shortage of public information; but the United States might well benefit from such a barrier.

Canada's deductive style of policymaking allows little room for the multitude of interests and varied coalitions that mark U.S. politics. This closed environment promotes an oddly rationalist attitude foreign to U.S. leaders schooled in improvisation. As one official told Richard Simeon in the 1960s, "There's a tendency to think that if we cannot solve our problems by logic then we're in for real trouble."[49] A policy may in effect satisfy another party's demand, but both sides insist that the decision was reached rationally rather than by force. Power politics is disguised. It is not abolished. Or is it? Canadian embrace of deductive methods may actually promote accommodation. The federal authorities who designed the deductive strategy of the Social Security Review were not blind to the likely conflicts over jurisdiction or financing. But they hoped that the process of reaching agreement on the abstract principles of desirable policy would have a favorable spin-off on the attempt to achieve consensus on practical matters. Organization theorists warn that efforts to examine basic goals are doomed and even counterproductive and that organizational change is best achieved by proceeding incrementally from existing accommodations among operational goals. But when even the operational goals expressed within an organization are a matter of sharp conflict, this counsel of pragmatism may be useless. Indeed practical questions are sometimes more difficult to resolve than theoretical ones. Canadian federal-provincial cleavages were too stark to allow a piecemeal coalition to develop. In such a case theoretical discussions were a welcome relief.

While Canada proceeded deductively on welfare reform, deferring practical questions, the United States did the reverse. Nixon's Family Assistance Plan could survive only if different parts of it had practical appeal for different people. Explicit examination of its logical foundations would have devastated the measure. One inevitable upshot of this inductive method was that the Family Assistance "Plan" was actually a *series* of proposals, shifting with the political winds. The Carter administration, too, made a number of concessions to political reality in seeking a compromise in May and June of 1978. In contrast, the Canadian proposals for income support and supplementation did not become concrete enough for such horse trading until two years into the Social Security Review. This deliberate vagueness helped buffer them against the endless wrangling over details seen in the United States. And perhaps it helped anesthetize federal and provincial antagonists to their practical stakes. Is it naive to hope that reason can change minds?

The deductive style of Canadian politics left little room for the coalition building that marked U.S. policymaking. In the absence of a continuing direct role for nongovernmental actors, the power to shape individual policies fell to federal and provincial elites. For better and for worse, debates in this forum differed from what they would have been if conducted in public. Some observers noted a lack of zest for substantive questions that might have been introduced by public debate. Al Johnson recalled that "both federal and provincial Ministers simply didn't feel it necessary to discuss the income distribution issue in their Conferences. Rather, they saw it as the public issue—as the issue to be taken to the public, to be settled in the political process."[50] At the same time the closeted face-to-face discussions made possible some decisions not practical in the U.S. environment of inductive coalitions and ideological diversity. The federal government had little need to build a complex coalition for its 1973 proposals or to placate opposition to them. Federal and provincial officials agreed rather quickly among themselves on the desirability of supplementing the incomes of the working poor. But when the questions of jurisdiction and financing had sidetracked the reform, no outside lobby or popular movement stood ready to intervene on its behalf.

In view of the disappointing results of the Social Security Review, some federal officials closely involved with it later regretted not having taken an incremental or inductive approach that tried to accommodate these practical problems piecemeal. The disappointing outcome is testimony enough to the deficiencies of the deductive approach. But it is always easy to criticize a strategy after it has failed. A glance at the pitfalls of inductive politics, as shown by the failures of the Nixon and Carter proposals, suggests that the possible merits of the deductive model should not be overlooked. The U.S. federal government had already offered to finance much of the basic guarantee, and the states were quite willing to have it administer the program. But even with the questions of financing and jurisdiction settled, the United States was unable to agree on a program of aid to the working poor. Canada at least reached agreement on such a program in the abstract, and Canada's massive experiment in federal-provincial consultation ironically paved the way for the 1978 federal tax credit legislation. Enormous effort had gone into the whole aborted Social Security Review, and officials were loathe to start anew unless they could be more optimistic about the outcome. Indeed at the mere mention of possibly resuming the process, one provincial official at a 1977 federal-provincial conference reportedly said informally, "Oh, God, no, not another one!" Such exhaustion invited the unilateral federal step of proposing Refundable Child Tax Credits in August 1978. The collapse of the Social Security Review legitimated a federal initiative that the provinces might not otherwise have tolerated.

It is difficult to blame the deductive style of federal-provincial politics for failure to solve the problems of jurisdiction and financing, for these problems raise questions of power that have no easy answer in Canada. The deductive model, however, can be faulted for discouraging the intervention of extragovernmental political pressures that might have salvaged the Social Security Review by insisting that it produce results. Most striking about the debates was the lack of such pressure at any time. Policy questions were debated and determined between federal and provincial officials. Even Members of Parliament had virtually no input in the process. There was no forum in which organized groups or the public could receive a hearing, and they were not ready when pressure might have helped. The deductive style of Canadian politics discourages such day-to-day influence, assuming that the desires of such groups have already been expressed in the selection of leaders and platforms. Were federal and provincial leaders faithful proxies for such pressures? Arguably, they were not, when the Social Security Review ran into federal-provincial conflicts that mattered little to poor people. In 1965, before he joined the cabinet, Marc Lalonde wrote,

The dispute between levels of government in Canada is essentially connected with the power politics of the various groups involved, and has very little to do with the welfare of the individual citizens of the country.[51]

Eleven years later Lalonde glossed over this federal-provincial problem in laying some blame for the failure of the federal proposals on the Canadian Council for Social Development and other supposedly prowelfare lobbies. Arguing that they had not offered support when it was needed, he warned of a Canadian counterpart to the "unholy alliance" of liberals and conservatives that helped defeat the Family Assistance Plan in the United States.[52]

Contrary to Lalonde's analogy, the stance of Canadian interest groups, whether for or against an issue, does not matter quite as much as it does in the United States. It is difficult to fault an organization for failing to support proposals on whose design it originally had little influence. If reform dies for lack of organizational and public demand, the greatest blame rests with a political system that discourages such input. Yet it is not clear that opening up Canadian debates would produce better results. The U.S. example suggests that a political system in which prowelfare groups can save welfare reform is also one in which antiwelfare forces can destroy it. Despite their differences in political structure and culture, both Canada and the United States harbor significant opposition to the expansion of welfare. If Canadian policies had been debated in an inductive context, they probably would have encountered the same public opposition that ruined the chances for welfare reform in the United States. A hint of such pressures was provided by the substance of the 1978 legislation for a program of Refundable Child Tax Credits. The benefits would be very low and poorly targeted on the poor. In providing some benefits to two-thirds of all Canadian families, the tax credit proposal was much less redistributive than the ill-fated supplementation proposals and was politically more akin to family allowances. The federal-provincial context had promoted an approach that focused well on the poor and ignored possible public backlash. In 1978, when federal authorities were no longer encumbered—and protected—by this environment, they proposed a measure much more reflective of anticipated popular pressures.

7
The Terms of Debate: Impact of Policy Design

Because welfare reform proposals failed twice both in Canada and in the United States, it is tempting to spread the blame liberally. The failure of the Family Assistance Plan in particular triggered an orgy of recrimination. Daniel Moynihan and Vincent and Vee Burke argue that liberal dalliance with the National Welfare Rights Organization played into the hands of conservatives and was most responsible for the loss. Senator Abraham Ribicoff retorts that Moynihan "left at half time" and that it was the president who killed FAP. Other writers accuse the administration of muddled thinking and ham-handedness. Jodie Allen argues that the changes embodied in HR 1 sealed FAP's fate. Richard Nathan adds that it was the moderates whose crucial support was missing. Other explanations could center on the passage of the Food Stamp program, the Talmadge amendment, and general revenue sharing, on electoral politics, and on the waning of the welfare crisis itself. Finally Lester Salamon argues against "overexplaining the result." He points out that if only a few Senate irreconcilables like Long had instead been as favorable as Mills and Byrnes, the bill could have passed.[1] Because the fight over the Carter proposals was not as close, the list of possible culprits is shorter. The economy and the impending elections would clearly be on anyone's list. So would the misleading HEW cost estimates, and so in general would Congress's new independence of the president in the late 1970s. The Corman Committee might be blamed for increasing the cost of the administration bill, and Ullman for insisting on an unrealistically low price tag.

Rich lodes of blame can also be found in the Canadian failures. For the failure of the Family Income Security Plan, the Canadian addiction to Family Allowances is most to blame, although Paul Hellyer gave the proposal a final blow when it was most vulnerable. Everyone had a hand in the death of the Orange Book proposals, even though the substance of these proposals gained much broader backing than did any U.S. proposal. Rather, the Canadian failure was in deciding questions of jurisdiction and financing. The insistence of Quebec and other provinces on full jurisdiction certainly ruled out easy answers. Federal authorities could be blamed for disguising their own jurisdictional preferences until too late. The cabinet also clearly hurt the Social Security Review by imposing the 1975 delay, and Lalonde and Trudeau might be taxed for not doing more to avert this decision. The NDP provinces deserve mention for their insistence on a unitary benefit structure, and the CCSD for its perfectionism and its failure to defend the federal proposals when they were vulnerable. Special mention goes to the economy's astringent effect on provincial beneficence after 1975 and to Ontario's unexpected, tardy opposition in 1976.

So many factors contributed to the collapse of welfare reform in Canada and the United States that who or what to blame is almost a matter of whim. Chapter 6 sought a broader perspective by showing how political institutions shaped the rules of the game within which different players contended. Political structure deserves some blame or credit for political outcomes. But there is another way in which the responsibility for the course of these debates should be traced to the context rather than to the players. Drawing lessons from the battles themselves obscures the fact that their course and outcome were heavily influenced by choices made in the design of policy. The terms of debate are shaped by the historic configuration of programs and by the substance of the proposals being debated. The cumulation of Canadian income security policy has camouflaged the more controversial parts of welfare programs among the more popular parts. In the United States, on the other hand, the configuration of policy exacerbates the image problems of welfare, exposing the programs to public backlash. This comparison suggests the political advantages of administering aid to the poor in a consolidated program (as in Canada) rather than in separate categorical programs (as in the United States).

Political debates are haunted by past policy decisions, but they are also shaped by what current policymakers propose. The technical virtuosity as well as the political appeal of a particular proposal can be decisive in stacking the decks for or against its passage. There are inherent technical and political advantages to negative income tax proposals that use a two-tier benefit structure, and this design ensured a reception for the Canadian Orange Book proposals more positive than that invited by the design of the U.S. Family Assistance Plan. Whether two-tier or unitary, a negative income tax is most easily administered through a unified agency. While federal officials in the United States readily accepted this idea, their Canadian counterparts resisted it, with unfortunate implications for the Canadian debates. In making suggestions about how analysis and planning might better have been carried on, I do not contend that the choices were clear at the time they were made. Indeed even in retrospect these choices are not obvious; some veterans of the debates disagree with conclusions drawn in this chapter. In any event, the analysis presented here is meant not as criticism but as a way to improve future policy-making.

The Configuration of Policy: Whether Motherhood Is Good Politics

Poverty programs are ignored or despised by the public because of the low status and voicelessness of the poor as well as the social pathologies that poverty breeds. But who is being helped shapes the political appeal of such programs. In comparison with Canadian policy, the U.S. configuration of policy reinforces the political marginality of welfare recipients. In particular, public attention in the United States focuses on young families. Since the 1960s the U.S. public has been greatly concerned with increases in mother-headed families and with efforts to move such families off welfare into the working world. Commenting on the California passage of Proposition 13, the mayor of San Francisco said: "This wasn't just a tax revolt. . . . It was quite as much a vote against the welfare mother."[2] Unlike their U.S. counterparts, Canadian welfare mothers have been subject to few political attacks. Illustrative of this fact is that the National Anti-Poverty Organization felt comfortable in illustrating the cover of a major report backing new welfare spending with a drawing of a poor young woman, obviously alone and obviously pregnant.[3] Welfare advocates in the United States would resist the propagation of this image. In several ways, young, single-parent welfare families in Canada are much less vulnerable than those in the United States. Their benefits are not singled out in a special welfare program like AFDC in the United States. Within the Canada Assistance Plan as administered federally and by each province, mother-headed families share the spotlight with a number of other and more popular recipients. Also Canada has a smaller proportion of ethnic minorities on the welfare rolls.

Racial conflict is clearly a part of the reason that the United States has a greater welfare backlash than Canada. AFDC recipients include many blacks and other minorities. Since the mid 1960s the number of black families on welfare has nearly equaled the number of all other families on welfare, even though blacks represent only about 11 percent of the general population. In 1975 black families accounted for 44 percent of all AFDC families.[4] Many people resort to racial stereotypes to explain this situation. A 1978 poll showed that 36 percent of all whites agreed with the statement, "Blacks want to live off the handout."[5] In Canada welfare programs do not provoke such feelings because the recipients are not disproportionately from minority groups; 96 percent of all social assistance recipients in 1970 were white. French-speaking people did give public assistance in Canada a slightly ethnic character. While 27 percent of the general population spoke French, 40 percent of welfare recipients were in this group. However, this disproportion was largely centered in Quebec, where 81 percent of the population and 91 percent of the welfare recipients were French speaking.[6] Even so, ethnic antagonism has sometimes been injected into welfare debates. William Vander Zalm, who served as British Columbia's human resources minister from 1975 to 1978, often expressed concern that his province was becoming a haven for poor immigrants from Quebec and other provinces. Vander Zalm reacted in this way to the 1976 victory of the Parti Québecois:

Perhaps the establishment of a border between them and us would help our cause and eliminate some of the problems we faced in the past. In fact if they do separate, they'll have to get a passport to travel here.[7]

There is little evidence to justify Vander Zalm's concern. Though some new arrivals to British Columbia from Quebec do apply for welfare, the 1970 survey and a more recent one show that the proportion of Francophones on welfare is actually less than in the British Columbia population.

Despite the occasional problem of Anglo-French antagonism, ethnic conflict seems a relatively unimportant aspect of the welfare backlash in Canada. Perhaps the greater ethnic slant of the U.S. welfare rolls helps explain the backlash there. But Joe Feagin has pointed out that while antiwelfare sentiment is as strong as ever, prejudice against blacks has declined precipitously. In 1978, when antiwelfare sentiment was seemingly at a historic peak in the United States, two major polls revealed greater tolerance of racial minorities by whites. The 1978 poll result, in which 36 percent of whites agreed that blacks want to live off the handout was actually the lowest level ever recorded; in 1967 more than half of the whites had felt this way.[8] Of course, even where racial animosity has not persisted, the concentration of racial groups in welfare programs does increase the visibility of the programs and promotes stereotyping.

Race is not as important an aspect of welfare politics in the United States as it used to be, and in a fascinating way, race may actually be not so much less important in Canada. Since news and stereotypes from across the border are intermingled with Canadian culture, perceptions may not fit reality in Canada. Daniel Koenig found evidence that people in Canada are nearly as afraid as people in the United States to walk outside their homes at night, even though the level of street crime is much lower in Canada. Koenig suggested that one reason for this convergence of fear in the two countries is that violent U.S. television shows are widely screened in Canada.[9] In a similar way Canadians may pick up stereotypes about the poor from the United States. Even though few poor people in Canada are members of minorities, the average Canadian may assume that they are. Rather than producing differences in welfare politics, race may actually encourage a convergence of the two countries' public attitudes toward the poor. Comparative survey research is needed to test this hypothesis. Whether or not this particular mechanism is at work, the Canadian public is nearly as critical of welfare programs and welfare recipients as is the U.S. public. This fact alone suggests that race is an insufficient explanation for the greater political vulnerability of poverty programs in the United States. In both countries the most despised "ethnic" group is the poor.

Mother headed families are not a popular addition to the welfare rolls, but aiding them is less controversial if it is associated with aiding popular "adult" groups such as the aged and the disabled. Prior to 1951 Canada offered provincially administered assistance to the aged poor. But after that time universal pensions and conditional supplements were adopted, both administered from Ottawa. In comparison, the U.S. welfare rolls long remained more bent with age. But from the passage of the Social Security Act onward, state aid to the aged was administered separately from aid to young families, and the 1973 implementation of Supplemental Security Income made this distinction even clearer by administering aid to the aged federally while leaving AFDC to the states. Removing the "adult" groups from state programs left AFDC families as the major remaining recipient group administered at the state level.

Another important difference in the configuration of Canadian and U.S. policy is that the Canadian disabled are more dependent on aid to the poor than they are in the United States. Whereas the U.S. Social Security program has long aided the disabled, Canadian Old Age Security pensions did nothing for the disabled, who have remained prime clients of social assistance. In the 1970 survey 49 percent of all welfare families were receiving assistance because of disability, much more than the 26 percent headed by mothers. In the United States most aid for the disabled has since the 1950s been channeled through the social insurance system, draining them away from public assistance.[10] A further step in separating U.S. aid to the disabled from state-administered AFDC was the federal Supplemental Security Income program. Unlike SSI, the Canadian Guaranteed Income Supplements did not cover the disabled, only the aged. This difference has further enhanced the image of Canadian social assistance as a haven for the helpless. Moreover Canadian social assistance to the disabled automatically covers their families, while in the categorical U.S. setup these families must apply for aid under AFDC. Because the disabled outnumber mother-headed welfare families, the latter group is not as conspicuous in Canada as it is in the United States.

Another reason that mother-headed families are less exposed in Canada is that it is more common for a widow to receive social assistance. In 1970 more than one-quarter of all Canadian mother-headed social assistance families were headed by widows. The proportions of widows in the general population are roughly similar in the two countries, but Canada has a much greater proportion on welfare.[11] The reason is simple enough. Just as the Old Age Security pensions made no provision for disability, neither did they provide for the survivors of a person who died before age sixty-five.[12] This concentration of widows in a program that also aids unmarried and deserted mothers is an important source of stability in Canadian family assistance policy and one the U.S. AFDC program sorely lacks. The configuration of policy in the United States assures that the more controversial families will be considered typical of welfare recipients.

It is not easy to change the historic configuration of policy that alters the politics of motherhood in Canada and the United States. But certain marginal changes can occur. As the Canada Pension Plan and the Quebec Pension Plan continue to remove widows and the disabled from the welfare rolls, provincial social assistance rolls may increasingly resemble the AFDC rolls. On the other hand, the United States in 1977 took a modest step toward reducing the exposure of AFDC families. Prior to this time the Social and Rehabilitation Service (SRS) had been the conspicuous repository of AFDC, while SSI was administered by the Social Security Administration (SSA). In March 1977 HEW Secretary Joseph Califano abolished the SRS and moved AFDC intact into the SSA. However, AFDC remained the only state-administered category, and there seems little prospect for a change in this politically poignant fact.

Unitary Negative Income Tax Proposals: Built to Self-Destruct?

The inherited configuration of policy clearly influences the political context within which proposals are debated, and policymakers must live with this influence. They can, however, shape the political context in a different way, by the specific design of proposals that they introduce onto the agenda. In proposing a negative income tax, planners in the United States initially favored a unitary design that had definite political liabilities, while their Canadian counterparts hit upon a design that invited less political conflict.

The design of a negative income tax involves difficult trade-offs between adequacy, work incentives, and total cost, and these trade-offs become excruciating if the scheme is a unitary one. These dilemmas may seem only technical, but the implications are crucial for policy debates. The dilemma inherent in a unitary design can be avoided only if the three goals are not considered equally important. The trade-off between adequacy and work incentives is necessitated by constraints on costs, but if cost is no object, the dilemma becomes academic. Similarly, costs can easily be kept in check if we are satisfied with a very low basic benefit or with very unfavorable work incentives. These three values are hardly exhaustive. Policymakers are also concerned with principles such as financing, jurisdiction, the private labor market, big government, dignity, stigma, and political one-upmanship. But insofar as they are concerned with adequacy, cost, and work incentives, those who seek a unitary design for a negative income tax are forced to make politically distasteful trade-offs and for that reason may be well advised to seek alternatives to the unitary approach.

The interaction of guarantee level, reduction rate, and "break-even point" is portrayed in figure 7.1. The reduction rate is the rate at which an individual's next dollar of earnings causes him to lose some government benefits. In the past reduction rates were usually 100 percent—benefits were reduced a dollar for each dollar earned. By comparison, a low reduction rate—say 40 percent—would allow the recipient to keep more than half of what he earns. The lower the reduction rate, the higher the break-even point, the level of private earnings at which the last dollar

Negative Income Tax Proposals

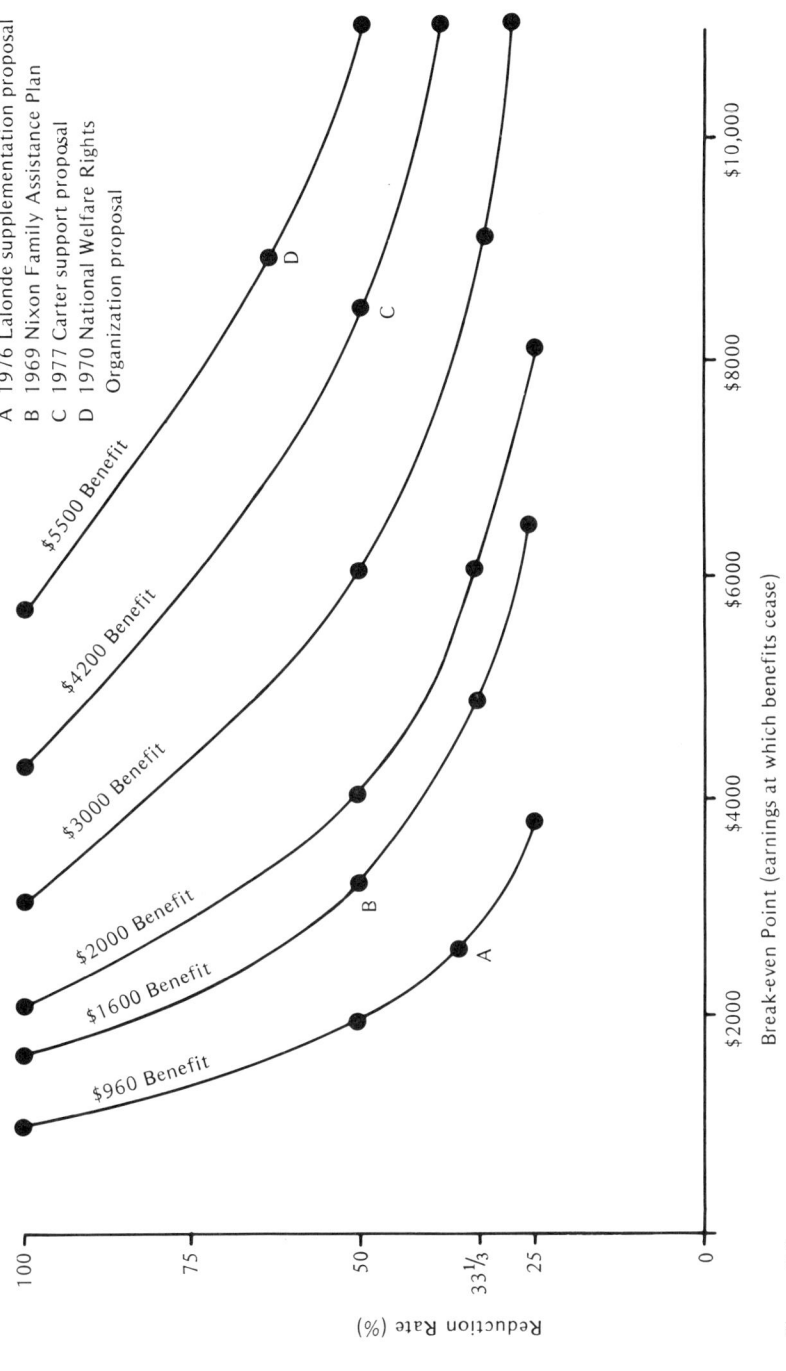

Figure 7.1
Relationship of Reduction Rate and Break-Even Point for Proposed Federal Guarantee Levels (Family of Four)

of government benefits is consumed. The relation of reduction rate and break-even point to guarantee level is best illustrated by a few examples, starting with a guarantee of $2000 and a reduction rate of 50 percent. With no earned income, the family receives the full $2000, but the head of the family can increase the family's total income by getting a job. If he (or she) earns $1000, the grant is reduced by half that amount, giving a combined income of $2500 ($1000 earned plus $1500 remaining supplement). If he earns $3000, the supplement is reduced to $500, yielding a combined income of $3500. By the time he earns $4000, the family's supplement has been reduced to zero (50 percent of $4000 = $2000 "taxed" back). A higher reduction rate wipes out the guarantee more quickly, while a lower reduction rate allows it to last into higher ranges of earnings. Thus a 75 percent reduction rate cuts the grant three dollars for every four dollars earned. By the time the recipient has earned $2667, his grant has been reduced to nothing (75 percent of $2667 = $2000). With a 33 percent reduction rate the grant drops only one dollar for every three earned. Not until the individual has earned $6000 is his grant wiped out (33 percent of $6000 = $2000).

Clearly the break-even point is highly sensitive to changes in the guarantee level. Unless the reduction rate is 100 percent, a dollar increase in the basic payment leads to more than a dollar increase in the break-even point. At a 50 percent reduction rate, the break-even point rises two dollars for every dollar that the basic payment is raised. Thus at a 50 percent reduction rate, a $960 basic payment has a $1920 break-even point, a $2000 payment has a $4000 break-even, and so on. Moreover, as the guarantee level is increased, the break-even point is more sensitive to changes in the reduction rate. Thus a decrease in the reduction rate from 50 percent to 33 percent has the following implications; for a $960 guarantee level the break-even point increases from $1920 to $2880; for a $2000 guarantee level it increases from $4000 to $6000.

These interactions have profound implications for the cost of a negative income tax program. "Improvements" such as lowering the reduction rate or increasing the basic guarantee increase the break-even point. A higher break-even point is more costly because it includes more total recipients and gives more dollars to everyone. This effect is exacerbated by the fact that more people are somewhat poor than are desperately poor. Many more families have an income between $5000 and $6000 than between $4000 and $5000. Thus even a small increase in the break-even

Negative Income Tax Proposals

point produces a geometric increase in beneficiaries. But there are sound reasons for desiring improvements in the reduction rate or the basic guarantee. For example, given a certain break-even point over $6000, even a small decline in work effort (and hence increase in benefits) produces huge cost increases because so many people are involved. U.S. experiments have revealed that work effort declines more for each increase over 50 percent in the reduction rate. But even though a 70 percent rate encourages more people to reduce their work effort and rely on the government, a program with a 50 percent rate is actually more expensive; its break-even point is higher, so it takes in many more people and pays them more dollars.[13]

Just as the reduction rate makes a big difference in the total cost of a program, so does the guarantee level. At any given reduction rate, a higher guarantee level not only causes more total benefits to be paid out per person but also increases the number of beneficiaries; a larger guarantee has a higher break-even point. In one example an increase of just 50 percent in the guarantee level increases the number of participating families by 73 percent and adds $7 billion to the cost. A doubling of the guarantee nearly triples the number of beneficiaries and increases the cost by $22 billion.[14] This problem of costs is easily overlooked in political debates. The National Welfare Rights Organization campaigned for a guarantee of $5500 with a reduction rate of 67 percent, but it was not often forced to deal with the consequence that its plan would have a net cost of $71 billion and cover half the U.S. population.[15] This problem was encountered even by people who considered their proposals moderate. Senator Ribicoff was much surprised when HEW studies revealed that his proposal for $3000 with a 60 percent reduction rate would include 40 million recipients and cost far more than the net of $13 billion he was predicting.[16]

The hidden mathematics of negative income proposals disguise the costs of irresponsible proposals and also make responsible proposals seem ungenerous. As Moynihan observed, the sliding scale under which benefits are determined in a negative income tax scheme invites mistaken opposition. Critics of his plan focused on the basic payment, even though most recipients would have other sources of income as well. Thus FAP "always appeared much less generous than it was."[17]

In debates over the Family Assistance Plan, work requirements became a sticking point. The Plan's penalty was $300 in the 1969 bill and $800 in the 1971 bill. Whether these penalties qualified as a work requirement remains an object of disagreement among experts and even among former Nixon aides. Among those who saw the provision as a genuine work requirement, liberals opposed it and conservatives hailed it. Moynihan later declared with forgivable exaggeration, "All sides of the controversy concurred in referring to any penalty as a 'work requirement,' and always for purposes of making it appear more severe than was the case."[18] At the same time the liberals and conservatives who did not see the penalty as a work requirement reversed their stances toward FAP. There was also disagreement within the administration. Moynihan later cited the fact that a family stood to lose only the parent's benefits, as proof that the plan was in fact a guaranteed income. Moynihan quotes Nixon as saying in 1969: "I don't care a damn about the work requirement. This is the price of getting the $1600." However, Richard Nathan emphasized that by 1971 Nixon "did take the 'Work' in 'Workfare' very seriously."[19]

The impossible political problems implied by a unitary negative income tax plan were well illustrated in Nixon's second try at gaining congressional approval of the Family Assistance Plan. Under pressure from states and localities clamoring for fiscal relief, the Nixon administration decided in its new 1971 bill, HR 1, to raise the basic payment 50 percent from the original $1600 to $2400. (Because this change was to be achieved by cashing out food stamps, real benefits would be no better than under the earlier version.) If HR 1 had kept the 50 percent reduction rate from the original proposals, the break-even point would have leaped from the original $3920 to $5520. That break-even point would cover 20 percent of all U.S. families and would more than triple the cost of the 1969 proposal. With so many people receiving benefits, the only way to keep costs down was to have a high reduction rate, 67 percent. While this rate was actually no higher than the effective rates found in existing legislation or in the 1969 proposals (when Food Stamp reduction rates are considered in each case), it was more visible and was particularly vulnerable to attack from conservatives concerned about allowing any disincentive to work.[20] To anticipate such criticism, the Nixon administration adopted a more severe work requirement, an action that in turn alienated many liberals. And to make matters worse for HR 1, the higher reduction rate did not fully counteract the expensive effects of the higher break-even point, and the bill still cost much more than the original FAP proposals. Its net cost to the federal government doubled to $4.6 billion.[21]

Negative Income Tax Proposals

The Family Assistance Plan suffered from the special disadvantages of unitary proposals. FAP was simultaneously criticized for its work incentives, its total cost, its work requirement, and the adequacy of its basic payment. Because the federal benefits did not distinguish between unemployable and employable poor, pressures were strong to raise the basic payment. Also one did not have to be a conservative to be concerned about work incentives for those who were employable. These political difficulties of FAP are particularly interesting because technically FAP had some features of a two-tier plan. It was unitary only in the structure of federal benefits; state supplements helped tailor benefits to the needs of particular groups. All versions of FAP envisioned that states would add to the federal benefit. These state supplements would in most cases go to families of a type traditionally aided by AFDC. The combination of federal and state payments would in effect create a support tier with high benefits and a high reduction rate, leaving it to the federal benefit structure to provide a supplementation tier to the remaining beneficiaries, with lower benefits and a lower reduction rate. While the addition of state supplements did not of course increase the work incentives over those in the federal benefit structure, it did improve the adequacy of benefits. Hidden in the outwardly unitary FAP were some features of a two-tier plan. Unfortunately, public concern about the adequacy of the federal benefit was not allayed by the proposal for state supplements. Moynihan later recalled, "It would be shown that for the welfare poor, primarily AFDC families, states would be required to supplement the amount of the negative tax at zero income. . . . Once again agreement. Once again the question, 'Yes, but how can a family of four live on $1600 a year?'"[22]

Moynihan and other FAP proponents were not successful in allaying the fears of those who saw only the unitary federal benefit structure and did not see that the state supplements helped meet the question of adequacy. Moynihan accuses FAP's opponents of ignorance or worse, yet he does not acknowledge that the proposals he helped design encouraged this kind of misunderstanding. If FAP in effect was to have a two-tier structure, then why hide this fact by making the federal benefit structure unitary? The state supplements provided FAP with the technical advantages of a two-tier system but almost completely deprived it of the political advantages that usually accompany a two-tier proposal. This political liability probably would also have plagued the 1974 Income Supplement Program (ISP) if President Ford had chosen to present it to Congress. The structure of federal benefits was again unitary, while states would be allowed to add to these benefits for some families. Only by building a two-tier plan directly into the federal benefit structure could the administration escape the contradictory pressures that tore apart the Family Assistance Plan. If FAP had included a two-tier benefit structure in the proposed federal payment, the whole painful debate would have been easier and might have ended differently. HEW planners eventually conceded some of the advantages of a two-tier plan in designing the Carter welfare reform package. And though the Carter bill failed, it did so for reasons different from the reasons why FAP failed.

The Political Appeal of Two-Tier Designs

While the unitary design of the various versions of the Family Assistance Plan helped defeat the legislation, Canada's Orange Book proposals avoided the unitary design and thus swept aside some important opposition. The Canadian proposals had two tiers, one to support those who were not expected to work, the other to supplement the earnings of those who were. Most mother-headed families would fall under the support program, with high benefits and no work requirement. Supplementation was primarily for those actually working. Whereas the Family Assistance Plan offered the same benefit structure to employable people and to those not expected to work, the Canadian proposals offered them lower benefits and better work incentives. Recipients of supplementation would have their benefits reduced by earnings at the low rate of 33 to 35 percent, much more favorable to work than the Nixon proposals. This provision could be afforded because people receiving support would be subject to the high rate of 70 to 75 percent.

The two-tier design quieted key objections. There was surprisingly little criticism in Canada of the proposed level of supplementation, even though it was far lower than that in the Nixon proposals. Minister Lalonde declared that supplementation by definition "would not provide an acceptable minimum income to people who are unable, for whatever reason, to earn an income from regular work."[23] Such people would be moved up to the support program. Work incentives never became the difficult issue in Canada that they were in the United States. The very smallness of the Canadian supplement discouraged any thought that a family could live on it or would seriously consider cutting back on its earned income.

The Canadian two-tier proposals for a negative income tax did not treat all recipients alike, but neither, in its way, would a unitary approach. Indeed a design that applies the same benefit structure to all recipients inevitably helps people differently because they have different degrees of need. Some will receive the maximum payment but little income, while others will earn significant outside income and thus receive a reduced government benefit. Those in the first group—the unemployed or unemployable—would *receive* more from the government but have less total income; the second group—the working poor—would receive less from the government but *have* more. Thus the notion of a guarantee has two very different interpretations. One sense of "guarantee" is the amount that the government pays to a family with no outside income.[24] But another sense is the higher amount a family can achieve by combining its earnings with a government supplement. For those completely dependent on the government payment its adequacy is all-important. But for workers receiving reduced benefits, the issue of adequacy is less important than the effectiveness of the reduction rate in allowing them to strive toward the break-even point and beyond.

The two-tier design for a negative income tax strikes a better balance between different notions of guarantee than does a unitary design. Those incapable of supporting themselves are guaranteed a certain level of government benefits while those capable of supporting themselves are guaranteed that their earnings will be supplemented up to a similar level. But an important objection to the two-tier approach is that supplementation will not be a meaningful guarantee if the available jobs are inadequate. It is not fair to give lower benefits to an employable person and his family if he cannot find a full-time job. Moreover, a full-time job that pays only the minimum wage will not supply enough earnings to boost a large family to the break-even point, and thus the family will not be able to take full advantage of benefits that are supposedly guaranteed. The designers of the Program for Better Jobs and Income were particularly concerned that it provide a real guarantee to employables. Thus representatives of the Department of Labor insisted that many new jobs be created to assure that an employable person could find work, and representatives of HEW insisted that if a job was not forthcoming, the recipient would move to the support tier and receive benefits similar to those received by those not expected to work.

Two-tiered negative income tax proposals have an advantage in avoiding perplexities over adequacy, work incentives, and cost; they also prevent division over work requirements. The Canadian two-tier plan had a work test, but only in the supplementation tier. A 1976 communiqué described it as follows:

> Those who do not accept appropriate employment would be ineligible for Income Supplementation and would receive support benefits at a reduced or "penalty" level consistent with the necessity to ensure that their dependents do not experience hardship.[25]

It may seem paradoxical that Canadian policymakers favored a work requirement given their historic antipathy to the idea. However, the work requirement described here is a very precisely targeted one. Unlike the FAP work requirement, it was not intended to apply to many mother-headed families. Rather it was part of a program of supplementation designed specifically for the working poor; this specialization limited its offensiveness and enhanced its appeal. The test could be seen as applying to already working volunteers rather than to unwilling victims. A work test that did not in effect exempt most mother-headed families could never have gained agreement in Canada.

The careful targeting of the Canadian work requirement made it peculiarly attractive, if not irresistible. Since those who could not or should not work were culled from the clientele for the supplementation program, the work requirement was less controversial for the rest, just as the adequacy of the basic benefit was not as great a concern. Indeed once a program (supplementation) for the employable is set up outside the program (support) for those not expected to work, the pressures are increased to exclude employables from unconditional support. Moreover, the supplementation clientele includes a larger proportion of recipients who seem employable. For this reason, the work test's administration and penalties can be fiercer. The 1971 work requirement adopted for food stamps in the United States was unique in requiring the cutoff of a family's entire benefit, not just that intended for the breadwinner. This harsh penalty was politically acceptable because recipients of food stamps include some families with an employable male head, a group that the public believes should always work. No such severe penalty has ever been allowed in the AFDC program. Even Senator Long's 1972 proposals for excluding able-bodied mothers from AFDC allowed their children to continue receiving benefits.[26] Of course, the harsher a work requirement, the less likely it is to be applied; the food stamp penalty is rarely invoked by administrators.

The harshness of the penalty in the supplementation tier of the 1976 Canadian proposals would encourage administrators to interpret the work requirement narrowly. This narrow scope was implied anyway by the provisions of the work requirement, which was known as the employment availability test. Only if jobs were actually available could an employable person be subject to it.[27] Otherwise he could continue to receive supplementation without being employed. The Castonguay-Nepveu report went a step further. Like the Program for Better Jobs and Income, it would automatically move a person from the supplementation tier to the support tier if no job were available. If the 1976 Canadian proposals had ever been implemented, it seems likely that Quebec and a few other provinces would have adapted them to this approach. The important February 1976 federal concessions effectively allowed the provinces to moderate if not eliminate the work test. Some provinces were suspicious of the very idea of a national work requirement. At best the federal government would establish standards to seek "national consistency."[28] But federal authorities would have no power to force the provinces to prosecute the requirement zealously. Since the provinces were scheduled to pay only one-third of the cost of support and supplementation, they had little incentive to restrict access to benefits. For example, national regulations would not allow a person to turn down a higher-paying job if it would reduce his need for supplementation, but no one really expected the provinces to insist on this.

Provincial independence can produce severity as well as permissiveness, and it was partly for this reason that the Social Security Review avoided calling the work requirement by that name. Despite this change in terminology, the Canadian proposals would have put in provincial hands power that could be abused. The federal government could do little if a province chose to administer the requirement in a punitive way. Admittedly the dangers are less than in the United States, where some welfare workers in Mississippi, Arizona, the Midwest, and even New York and other states may use any new restrictive powers to the fullest. But some welfare workers in British Columbia, New Brunswick, Alberta, and other areas can also be very hard on recipients if given the chance. Despite the fine targeting of the proposed Canadian work test, some families who should not be expected to work would probably have become subject to it. For those people the two-tier approach was a distinct debit, because it legitimated a stronger work requirement than would be agreed on in a unitary plan.

The arguments presented so far against unitary negative income tax schemes do not imply that the two-tier alternative is ideal; they only suggest that it has fewer liabilities. The two-tier approach has technical and political liabilities of its own, in particular, it discourages work by people in the support tier and may encourage family breakup.[29] It clearly runs afoul of the work ethic of families who are not expected to work. After all, the first adoption of work incentive reduction rates in the United States was not for work shirkers but for recipients of Aid to the Blind, who like most other poor people would prefer work to idleness. And when a 50 percent reduction rate under SSI replaced in 1974 the confiscatory rates that prevailed under state programs of aid to the aged and disabled, many recipients increased their work effort. Similarly, some mothers even of infant children are willing to work though we may not expect them to. Lee Rainwater has argued that welfare reform "should proceed on the assumption that solo mothers can work, do work, and are willing to work."[30] While it is unfortunate that such beneficiaries could not be given better work incentives under a two-tier plan, an effort to universalize favorable work incentives would probably cost more in benefits paid out than it saved by encouraging such recipients to increase their work effort.

Another troubling objection to the two-tier approach is that it preserves some of the present welfare system's incentives for a family to split up. Unlike a pure unitary negative income tax plan, the two-tier approach offers a higher basic payment to mother-headed families when the mother is not expected to work.[31] While this splitting incentive has produced criticism of two-tier plans, it is clear that the incentive is less than in the current welfare system, where intact families may be denied aid entirely. Morever, while it was common in the past to argue that only a program guaranteeing intact families the same benefits as broken families would assure family stability, recent evidence has suggested that even a unitary and universal negative income tax scheme may encourage family breakup. Increased rates of marital dissolution were found in the HEW experiments conducted in Seattle and Denver (although not in the three other experiments).[32] It is not yet known why this result occurred or even

How to Deliver Benefits

whether it is a statistical quirk. Assuming that the benefits did encourage family dissolution, however, this result is not necessarily an argument against extending aid to intact families. Troubled marriages may be forced to continue by financial desperation and perhaps should be allowed to dissolve. It would be peculiar to deny aid to poor intact families on the theory that the family that "starves together stays together."

Deciding How to Deliver the Benefits

A two-tier design for a negative income tax faces far fewer political barriers than a unitary design, and this difference contributed to the greater opposition faced by the Nixon proposals than by the 1973 Canadian proposals. But the benefit structure is not the only important consideration in the design of negative income tax proposals. Also important is how the benefits are to be administered. A two-tier benefit structure presents very special administrative problems. It entails difficult distinctions between those expected to work and those not. It is not easy to draw this line, and the employability of poor people can change abruptly, causing them to cross the line repeatedly. These difficulties are of course one reason for the attraction of a unitary negative income tax scheme, the sentimental favorite of HEW planners. But these same planners have also maintained that a two-tier benefit structure should be administered in a way that uses a common filing unit to cover families whose head belongs to either tier, thus easing the transition between tiers as if in a single program.[33] Curiously, administrative feasibility was not the leading reason that HEW planners wanted filing units to be standardized. They were more attracted by the fact that classifying beneficiaries by family or residential unit would cut a program's costs by avoiding overlap in benefits. But the end result was a preferred program structure that was also easy to administer.[34]

The preference of HEW planners for integrating the administration of support and supplementation was not rooted in fear that two tiers would be difficult to administer separately, but they were aware of the administrative advantages of their preference. Although few had direct experience with the administration of state programs, many received the equivalent of such experience in helping design and evaluate the negative income tax experiments conducted from 1967 to 1977. These experiments revealed that the employability of many families was changeable and indistinct. Similar impressions were gained from the Panel Study of Income Dynamics, conducted under OEO and HEW contract from 1967 to 1977.

Canadian federal planners did not embrace administrative integration of support and supplementation, as did their U.S. counterparts. They took this stance even though provincial experience seemed to indicate a need for integration. The experience of Saskatchewan was especially important because that province was unique on the continent in administering a two-tier negative income tax program on a large scale. Adopted in 1974, Saskatchewan's Family Income Plan (FIP) added a tier of supplemental benefits for working people to the existing welfare support provided under the Saskatchewan Assistance Plan (SAP). In many cases it was not easy to determine which of these programs an applicant belonged in. Moreover, the turnover was such that every month approximately 2 percent of each tier's case load left it for the other plan.[35] When the indeterminacy of each plan's clientele became clear, Saskatchewan authorities realized that administration should be integrated. Even before that time, some integration was achieved by requiring all SAP recipients to file an application with FIP, even if clearly ineligible. This procedure produced a central file useful for both programs. In addition, SAP files were adapted so they could be used continuously in FIP administration. The province is working toward completely integrating data processing for the two programs. A 1976 report by the Department of Social Services drew the following lessons from the Saskatchewan experience:

First, because of the overlap in the support and supplementation clientele and the movement of clients from one system to another, an interface between the support and supplementation systems is necessary.

Second, unless the support and supplementation systems are integrated, with common family unit, income definitions, and accounting periods, the interface will create numerous problems. Ideally, therefore the solution to these interface problems lies in an integrated support/supplementation program.

Third, if separate support and supplementation programs are implemented, an integrated data processing system will minimize the problems associated with the interface.[36]

Despite the experience of Saskatchewan and other provinces suggesting the need for unitary administration of a two-tier benefit structure, federal planners questioned this conclusion. Chapter 6 ventured some reasons for the federal position. Information about provincial programs was

How to Deliver Benefits

scarce in Ottawa, and the federal officials who felt closest to the provincial programs were not dominant. But another reason for Ottawa's favoring separately administered tiers was that the federal government could hope for a role in administering the supplementation tier. If a unitary scheme were adopted, the provinces would be in charge. Federal control over both tiers was politically inconceivable and was not even discussed. This political context was very different from that facing the Family Assistance Plan in the United States. FAP proposed a direct federal payment to replace many existing state-administered payments. Indeed in 1968 the National Governors' Conference called for full federal funding and increased federal control of the welfare system. In this atmosphere HEW planners routinely debated negative income tax proposals whose administration would be dominated by the federal government.

A dramatic illustration of how differences in Canadian and U.S. federalism shaped the terms of debate is the contrast of Canadian and U.S. reports compiled jointly by federal finance and welfare officials on the question of integrating transfer payments with the tax system. In November 1978 the Canadian Department of Finance released a report based on the internal discussions that had been going on since the fall of 1976 and that eventually produced the Refundable Child Tax Credit program. The report discusses only transfer programs in which the federal government pays benefits directly. Provincial social assistance programs are scarcely mentioned, even though they present the greatest problems for integration with the tax credit program and with other federal programs. In contrast, a similar joint effort of finance and welfare officials in the United States completed in April 1974 explicitly examines methods for federalizing state welfare programs as a means of integrating tax and transfer programs. This report was produced to support the Income Supplement Program then being developed within HEW, a proposal that would have absorbed many state functions.[37]

Canadian federal planners never had the luxury of assuming that the federal government could take over major responsibility for administering both support and supplementation. The provinces were unwilling to give up jurisdiction over existing social assistance cases, and most did not welcome a federal role in directly supplementing the incomes of working people, a role that the provinces preferred to keep for themselves with the help of federal dollars. In preferring a federally administered supplementation tier, federal officials were seeking what from a U.S. perspective would be a very modest role and what in Canada was perhaps needed to maintain a visible and viable central government. But this preference tied them to an administrative separation that opened their two-tier scheme to decisive technical objections. Of course, the provinces in the end won full control of the proposed system, allowing integrated administration of the two tiers. Only by legislating a tax credit administered through the federal tax system could Ottawa hope to retain a role in supplementation. This fact enhanced that alternative's desirability among federal officials after the Orange Book proposals ran aground.

As a result of the 1978 passage of Refundable Child Tax Credits, Canada now has separately administered support and supplementation programs. But this arrangement is not a full-fledged two-tier plan and is unlikely to develop into one. The tax system cannot easily be integrated with provincial welfare programs to accommodate transitions between supplementation and support that result from changes in the employability of recipients. Indeed the tax system is not well equipped to target benefits only on employable poor people, particularly because employability is difficult to determine and because this status often changes. Because targeting is difficult, the existing tax credits are paid not only to the working poor but also to the welfare poor and to many middle-income families. The universality of the supplement lessens some problems in integration of it with other programs, but at the price of spreading the funds so widely that the individual amounts available to those who need aid are very low and unlikely to rise. Moreover the tax credits are paid not monthly but yearly, reducing still further their relationship to the changing needs of beneficiaries and also reducing their work incentive effect. For these reasons, the 1978 tax credit legislation is a poor substitute for the 1973 supplementation proposals, and efforts to adapt it to these earlier proposals are likely to be frustrated.

Take-up is a special problem with administering supplementation through the same agencies that administer conventional welfare support. The stigma of welfare may discourage eligible working people from participating. Provinces offering aid to intact working families have been surprised that many do not seek such aid. The British Columbia and Ontario initiatives failed because so few people applied. In contrast, Saskatchewan was able to stimulate initial participation in its supplementation program (FIP) by making an official distinction between it and the conventional social assistance program (SAP). Though the two plans were integrated administratively, the province made special efforts to reduce the stigma of receiving supplementary FIP benefits. Application is made by mail to the central registry in Regina rather than in person to a nearby welfare office. The program began with a media campaign and a special mailing of application forms to all families in the province. Provincial authorities estimated in 1976 that about half the FIP recipients also qualified for SAP but preferred not to apply.[38] Despite this success in encouraging take-up, even FIP fell short of being universal. Participation at the outset was not complete, and it has dropped off in recent years.

Welfare programs in the United States also suffer from the problem of take-up. Though food stamps are available to virtually all poor people whatever their employment or family status, enrollment in the program has been low—38 percent of eligibles in 1974, with five states under 20 percent.[39] Although one reason is the program's purchase requirement (abolished in 1979), another is that the program aids the AFDC poor as well as working people and thus carries a stigma that many people prefer to avoid. Even the SSI program has experienced problems in take-up, because it is still perceived as welfare.

A tempting but risky solution to the problem of take-up is to separate the administration of supplements entirely from welfare programs. The tax credit programs adopted in the United States in 1975 and in Canada in 1978 were administered by federal tax authorities rather than by provincial welfare authorities. Unfortunately, this solution to the problem of take-up created new problems in administration. Support and supplementation programs are difficult to administer separately. The two countries do not have the technical or political means to integrate the management files of federal tax agencies with those of provincial and state welfare agencies. Unless and until such integration is possible, the designers of two-tier negative income tax proposals will face a difficult trade-off between success in administration and success in take-up. And this difficulty is likely to bar the expansion of a separately administered tax credit program into a full-fledged supplementation tier.

Politics and Design

The political virtues of the two-tier approach to the negative income tax were recognized by the authors of Quebec's Castonguay-Nepveu report and of the later federal Orange Book. Both reports were strongly influenced by the unfolding debate over the Family Assistance Plan, in which the drawbacks of unitary proposals were dramatically exposed. Canadians quickly learned these lessons from the Family Assistance Plan debacles, while key U.S. experts were not converted as quickly or as completely to the two-tier approach. Many U.S. writers recognized that the dilemmas in unitary negative income tax proposals had no easy answers. For example, Henry Aaron said in 1973: "The reason Congress has found it difficult to find a plan that provides universal benefits at a level regarded as reasonable, that preserves work incentives, and that is not vastly more expensive than President Nixon's proposals is that no such plan exists or can be devised: These objectives are mutually inconsistent."[40] However, during this period few people went on to draw the political lesson that a two-tier proposal was more likely to get through Congress. Robert Haveman had suggested a two-tier approach as early as 1967, and in 1971 Haveman and Robert Lampman proposed a program of supplementation for the working poor, with a basic payment of $750.[41] Another proponent of the two-tier approach was Richard Nathan, who became disenchanted with unitary proposals after he helped design and promote the Family Assistance Plan. Nathan pointed out that the conundrum of the negative income tax had been solved in practice by the rise of food stamps. In a way the United States already had two tiers, with AFDC primarily for support and food stamps for supplementation: "With multiple programs, the income supplement to the working poor (and others) can be set at a lower amount, as is currently the case with food stamps."[42]

As the Carter administration set out to design its welfare reform package, a number of insiders recognized the political liabilities of a unitary approach. For example, in a memo to the president on April 26, 1977, his domestic policy staff emphasized the attractions of the alternatives suggested by the Labor department and by Tom Joe:

> As we see it the choice is between a negative income tax, which is administratable but faces a very difficult road, at best, in the Congress, and a multiple track approach like Tom's or the Labor Department's, which faces costly administrative problems but is a more saleable program and would be equally effective.[43]

The administration went part way in adapting to these political realities by adopting a massive jobs program. With many employables pushed into public service jobs, it would be easier to argue that those expected to work were being treated differently from those not expected to work. However, the question remained how to treat those who were expected to work but did not have access to a job. Here the departments of Labor and HEW differed, and each won a partial victory. The HEW view was incorporated into the federal benefit structure, but the Labor view was observed in the provisions for state supplementation.

Planners in the Labor department fought for a two-tier plan. The supplementation tier would pay $2100 while the support tier would pay $4200; the reduction rate in the supplementation tier would be 25 percent, while the rate in the support tier would be double that. The HEW planners objected to paying less to employable people, some of whom would be unable to find jobs however strong the work incentives and however successful the jobs program. The initial HEW proposal was for a classic unitary negative income tax. However, the HEW planners soon felt compelled to meet the argument that the benefit structure should treat employable and unemployable people differently. They proposed the plan that Carter eventually adopted. HEW agreed that people with jobs should receive a lower basic payment but argued that work incentives for this group were not best served by a constant reduction rate. Instead, the reduction rate for employables should be zero for the first $3800 in earnings and rise to 50 percent thereafter. In other words, the recipient of supplementation would keep the full benefit until earnings exceeded $3800, and thereafter the benefit would be reduced at a rate of 50 percent. This 50 percent rate was of course higher than that provided in the supplementation tier of the DOL plan, but because the HEW plan's reduction rate was nil in the early ranges of earnings, its average rate was actually lower than in the DOL plan.

The genius of the HEW design for the Carter bill was that it was only nominally a two-tier plan, with the appearance that employable and unemployable people would be treated differently. The plan provided a lower benefit and a lower initial reduction rate to employable recipients, but this benefit structure applied only if a job were available; otherwise the recipient would automatically move to the support tier and be treated the same as those not expected to work. Moreover, beyond earnings of $3800 the benefit structure for employables and unemployables was identical. Thus although the Carter plan made a formal distinction between employable and unemployable groups, it managed to provide similar benefits to all families, whether or not the family head was employable. It was a victory for those who felt that a real two-tier plan would unfairly punish employable people who could not find jobs. Inside HEW, the plan came to be called the "no-compromise compromise," because the Labor Department's arguments for a two-tier program had been met without changing the unitary structure of the HEW plan.

The two-tier appearance of the Program for Better Jobs and Income was a victory for the proponents of a unitary benefit structure and unitary administration which had certain costs. By deciding not to tax back any benefits at the initial ranges of earnings, the Carter plan gave up some savings that the DOL plan achieved by having the same reduction rate at all levels. Even though the Carter plan above $3800 earnings had a reduction rate twice that of the DOL plan and thus recovered benefits at a faster rate, it could not make up for the expense of its initial generosity. As a result, the Carter plan was more expensive than the rejected DOL plan. Since cost later became a crucial objection to the Carter plan, this choice was a fateful one. The HEW effort to maintain the image of a two-tier plan without requiring the administration of differential benefit structures may have hurt the Carter welfare reform package. Although the DOL plan would have been more difficult to administer, it probably would have come closer to passage. Curiously, however, DOL planners did not stress the issue of cost in the internal debates.

The planners at HEW scarcely had time to savor their success in passing off a unitary program as a two-tier design before the Labor Department struck a blow for the two-tier approach. DOL officials preferred that those expected to work receive no state supplementation, but they settled for an arrangement in which the states were mandated to provide a low benefit and a reduction rate of no higher than 52 percent for those expected to work (whether or not they had jobs). For those not expected to work, the benefit would be much higher and the reduction rate could rise as high as 70 percent. Because only a few states would fail to provide supplements to the federal benefit, this provision effectively gave the Carter welfare plan some two-tier features. Arnold Packer, an assistant secretary of labor, argued that such a distinction was desirable not only from a policy standpoint but because it would enhance the political salability of the welfare reform package. However, these political advantages were limited by the restriction of the two-tier arrangement to state supplementation. Like ISP and FAP before it, PBJI hid its two-tier aspects in state supplementation, rather than including them in the federal benefit where they would be more visible.

The design of proposals requires analysis of the technical requirements of policy. But designers should also study the political context, because what is proposed shapes the terms of debate profoundly. The unitary approach to the negative income tax had technical advantages, but it did not grapple with the strong political demand that employable people be treated differently from those not expected to work. If the Family Assistance Plan had been explicitly two-tiered like the proposals made by the Castonguay-Nepveu report and the Orange Book, comprehensive welfare reform might not have collapsed in the United States. One indication that the U.S. political context is friendly to supplementation proposals that give a lower benefit and better work incentives to employable people is that the Food Stamp program grew so easily despite the defeat of FAP. Of course, the growth of this program occurred incrementally, a typical pattern in the United States. But even the U.S. proclivity for incremental growth does not explain the emergence of a program that aids so many employable people, including the childless and many male heads of families. Ultimately the triumph of the Food Stamp program must be attributed to its low benefits and low reduction rate. Without a fight, the two-tier approach has triumphed in the United States.

The designers of the 1977 Carter welfare reform package were apparently conscious of the political advantages of a two-tier approach, but the plan's political troubles might have been less if the designers had cleaved more faithfully to that model. For a longer time, Canadian federal officials had been convinced of the need for a two-tier plan. Unfortunately, their plan ran afoul of technical and political difficulties over the question of administration. Their hope for a federal share in the supplementation tier clashed with technical lessons from provincial programs and with provincial political resistance. Even though federal authorities did not actually propose this federal role, their desire to hold open that option probably misjudged the political context and delayed the Social Security Review until it lost momentum. The question how the supplement should be delivered was not resolved until too late. One participant recalled that Johnson and Lalonde had repeatedly insisted that the planners "stick to design questions, not delivery ones." Although this deductive approach had its political uses, ultimately the distinction was a bad one. Delivery is a crucial aspect of design. A proposal that does not consider the political context may be doomed.

8
After the Collapse: Advance and Retreat

In the past decade major welfare reform efforts dramatically collapsed in both Canada and the United States. What were the implications for the future of welfare programs? In a concrete sense this collapse did not stop the expansion of welfare benefits to new groups. Progress occurred anyway in both countries. In the long run, however, the collapse of welfare reform foreshadowed a darker future for welfare programs. No longer would national debates focus only on whether to expand welfare programs. Leaders in both countries would increasingly focus on proposals to restrict these same programs.

The collapse of welfare reform had different implications in Canada and the United States. For better and for worse, the development of welfare policy is intimately affected by the nature of a country's political institutions. In Canada, thorough debates of comprehensive policy options occur continually. Comprehensive welfare reform is much less likely to drop from the agenda in Canada than in the United States. However, debates on such proposals are not always conclusive. In fact, the less ambitious proposals debated in the United States have produced greater change in the long run, fulfilling, it may be argued, more of the goals of comprehensive welfare proposals than such proposals could politically have achieved themselves. Years of incremental change expanded benefits to new groups and increased total welfare spending. By 1977, when the Carter administration was attempting to design a welfare reform package that would cost no more than the existing system, the nation was already spending $23.5 billion on conditional income assistance. By 1979 a consensus was emerging around major elements of the compromise that nearly emerged in June 1978: a national minimum in AFDC, extension of coverage to two-parent families, and increased public jobs, among other elements. Such a welfare reform package was possible because previous incremental changes had set the stage for it. For example, the 1977 Carter welfare reform package proposed, among other things, to expand the Earned Income Tax Credit program. When the package failed to pass, Congress expanded the tax credit piecemeal. Thus subsequent reform packages were correspondingly cheaper and incremental, while actually completing the goals sought by the earlier comprehensive proposal. The year 1977 may have seen the swan song of comprehensive welfare reform, but the tragedy of that outcome was visibly diminished by subsequent piecemeal legislation.

From one perspective, the collapse of comprehensive welfare reform did not prevent progress in welfare policy, but from another perspective, the collapse was very real and now threatens existing programs. Policy does not always move in the same direction. It is wrong to see policymaking as a ratchet—always going forward, never back. In that view political systems favor more and bigger programs but discourage the dismantling of existing ones. Government expenditures worldwide seem to grow inexorably; but when one looks behind the aggregate spending figures, it is clear that reversals are also common. In both Canada and the United States the public's suspicion of welfare programs is stronger than ever, and policymakers are beginning to respond to it with unprecedented new restrictions. So far the U.S. political system has been more hospitable to the translation of the welfare backlash into restrictive policies. If Canada has been less active in expanding welfare programs, it has also been slower to entertain this backlash, although the situation may change.

Triumph of Incrementalism?

In important ways Canadian policymaking consists of high-level negotiations among competing bureaucracies and between federal and provincial authorities. Settlements emerge at this stage, and the public phase of policy debates has little impact on the decisions. In the United States such internal settlements frequently give way to the pressures of public debate centered in Congress. These contrasting styles of national choice have important implications for the course of policy development. In a 1977 article I argued that Canadian policymaking for old age security produced steadier development of programs than did U.S. policymaking.[1] Contrary to the view that the United States depends most on incremental change, the most significant change occurs there all at once during rare periods of jarring but constructive crisis. In Canada crises in federal-provincial relations are more threatening to the political order. To keep these crises only latent, policymakers work to resolve deadlocks, producing a continuous pattern of change. This contrast in policy development can be likened to the difference between the big-bang and steady-state theories of the universe. U.S. federal policy for the aged began with the tremendous innovation of Old Age Insurance, and although later legislation expanded incrementally on this scheme, the basic insurance paradigm was never overturned. Canadian old age security policy, on the other hand, never underwent a period of such dramatic change, taking instead a series of different tentative steps.

Does this difference between Canadian and U.S. policy development extend from old age security to other areas of policy? Robert Kudrle and Theodore Marmor have tested the hypothesis in unemployment insurance and income maintenance. They find that in both these fields Canadian development proceeded by a steady series of innovations while U.S. development was marked by long periods of stability punctuated by occasional episodes of rapid change. The Social Security Act of 1935 laid down the basic principles of future U.S. development, while Canadian policy was freer to experiment with new approaches. U.S. unemployment insurance has closely followed the pattern established in 1935. On the other hand, Canadian unemployment insurance since 1941 has undergone a number of changes, with major expansions undertaken in the 1950s and 1971. The 1971 legislation also rearranged the method of financing, expanding the federal role. And in 1975 and 1978 major restrictions were adopted.

A similar contrast in policy development is clear in income maintenance policy. U.S. cash welfare programs never outgrew the categorical focus laid down by the 1935 Social Security Act. Today, AFDC continues to be administered at the state level and to exclude aid to the childless and to many working families. Indeed the greatest innovation in U.S. welfare policy since the 1930s has been not in cash assistance but in in-kind programs such as Food Stamps and Medicaid. In Canada, on the other hand, cash income maintenance policy has steadily changed. The country's first major federal program was Family Allowances, a demogrant program, not a conditional one. Between 1951 and 1956 Canada adopted conditional aid to categories of the blind, the disabled, and the unemployed. Then in 1966 cash welfare was expanded to new groups, and its categorical nature was dropped. And finally, the Refundable Child Tax Credit program, a kind of negative income tax, was adopted in 1978. While all these steps were products of fundamental debate, in most cases they left the existing programs in place, merely adding a new tier of policy. Canadian policies tend to accumulate in layers. While the continuous debates produce frequent innovations, these changes do not attain the root-and-branch comprehensiveness that is occasionally possible in the United States.

These contrasting patterns of policy development shaped the major debates discussed in this book. The Nixon and Carter administrations were compelled to sell their welfare proposals as full-scale solutions to the welfare mess. In Canada, however, the federal Liberals twice presented their proposals as only the logical extension of a long-standing dialogue on the welfare system. These Canadian proposals were relatively uncontroversial, whereas the U.S. proposals never achieved that status. Because the U.S. proposals were presented as answers to the welfare crisis, they were judged by that standard and found wanting. In this respect the Canadian proposals promised less and were thus less subject to the volatile politics of welfare backlash. Political institutions shielded the proposals from extremes in the public mood. In avoiding rhetoric about the welfare mess Canadian leaders promised less than the public wanted, but in explicitly calling for a guaranteed income these leaders promised more than the public wanted. Canadian policy developed steadily with less respect for changes in the public mood. Leonard Shifrin points out the irony that the 1978 Refundable Child Tax Credit was enacted during a period of intense budgetary austerity.[2]

In one sense U.S. debates followed a continuous pattern, because each successive effort to achieve comprehensive welfare reform drew lessons from previous failures. Planners in the executive branch steadily improved their understanding of how to design a negative income tax as a result of internal and congressional debate on the OEO proposals, the successive versions of FAP, the Mega-Proposal, the Income Supplement Program, and the Program for Better Jobs and Income. The congressional hearings of the Subcommittee on Fiscal Policy of the Joint Economic Committee also contributed to this cumulative process. However, the lessons learned were of only academic value. Lessons about how to design a negative income tax were never accepted by Congress and instead were confined to the planning community. Indeed the proponents of a negative income tax were not the only ones who learned from the battles; opponents were also able to hone their arguments and to undercut the proposal with initiatives such as the Talmadge amendment and the earned income tax credit. Actual expansion of the U.S. welfare system depended not on explicitly comprehensive proposals but rather on incremental changes supported by Congress that ultimately had an implicit comprehensive effect.

Although in the past decade Canada more explicitly debated expanding its welfare system, the country actually expanded its system less than did the United States. The failure of the United States to enact explicit comprehensive changes was compensated for by decisions to expand welfare benefits incrementally. There are basically two ways for incremental expansion to proceed: liberalize existing programs, or add new programs alongside the old and unreformed ones. Both kinds of expansion occurred in the United States.

Despite the collapses of the Family Assistance Plan and the Program for Better Jobs and Income, U.S. welfare programs grew. In 1966 Frances Fox Piven and Richard Cloward argued that wild expansion and disruption of welfare programs would produce pressure for a "new federal program to distribute income." By 1971, however, they came to feel that new programs such as the Family Assistance Plan would do more harm than good, and that "the explosion of the rolls is the true relief reform." The methods they publicized helped produce this sharp rise in patronization of welfare by the poor. Such expansion could succeed only because it required no positive action by Congress. The states, not the federal government, produced it. Gilbert Steiner observed that AFDC grew easily because "the public assistance administrative apparatus was in place, readily able to move more checks to more people if so instructed."[3]

While benefits and participation in the AFDC program were growing, Congress was adding new programs, and these programs also grew quickly. At the very time when Congress rejected the Family Assistance Plan, it set the Food Stamp program on an explosive pattern of growth that eventually made it a larger drain on federal funds than AFDC. And though President Carter was unable to get his 1977 welfare reform bill through Congress, his liberalizations of food stamp benefits passed easily. Participation grew from 2 million people in 1968 to 17.8 million in January 1979, many of them father-headed families or childless people ineligible for any other program. Richard Nathan saw the coming of food stamps as the "single most important welfare change in America since the passage of the Social Security Act of 1935."[4] Similar growth occurred in the Medicaid program, which was passed in 1965 without fanfare. State-administered, the program in 1978 cost all governments nearly two-thirds more than the cost of AFDC. Other expensive and noncontroversial federal initiatives were Supplemental Security Income (1972) and the Earned Income Tax Credit (1975 and 1978). Other still less well known programs passed in recent years have added billions to the federal contribution to the poor. The Section 8 Housing Assistance program was initiated in

1974 and by 1977 it disbursed $1.1 billion annually. The Supplementary Feeding Program for Women, Infants, and Children (WIC) grew from $14 million in 1974 to $270 million in 1978. In 1972 the Joint Economic Committee's Subcommittee on Fiscal Policy counted thirty-six separate federal income transfer programs, and its list did not even include several of the recent additions mentioned here.

In view of these many recent incremental expansions of aid to the poor in the United States, did it matter that comprehensive efforts to reform the welfare system collapsed? Although explicit efforts to expand the welfare system failed, countless less dramatic decisions contributed to just such an expansion. Perhaps this expansion could only have been achieved incrementally. Barry Friedman and Leonard Hausman point out that between 1968 and 1975 federal spending on income-conditioned programs in real terms doubled, from $14.5 billion to $29 billion (in 1973 prices). "Had a particular welfare program carrying a price tag of $15 billion and phased in over seven years been debated in Congress in 1967—at the height of the Vietnam War—it surely would have been rejected."[5] In welfare debates the U.S. political system seems less friendly to explicit proposals for expansion than to policies that in a hidden or unintended way promote such expansion. Of course, there are drawbacks to achieving the goals of welfare reform only implicitly. The public may rebel against the results, feeling that it had never authorized such growth. And in terms of design, the resulting welter of separate programs is not the full functional equivalent of a carefully designed negative income tax. Overlap of programs creates special problems of cost, administrative integration, and cumulative effect on the beneficiary.

In recent decades Canada was involved more continuously than the United States in debates about the proper stance for welfare policies, yet the conclusions reached were less dramatic than those reached implicitly in the United States. Whereas the failure of the Nixon and Carter plans was allayed by the continuing growth of old programs and the quiet passage of new ones, the collapse of the Canadian proposals of 1970 and 1973 had few incremental reforms to redeem it. Of course, there were some changes. Despite the 1972 failure of the Family Income Security Plan, Parliament passed important increases in Old Age Security pensions and in Guaranteed Income Supplements. And despite the failure of the 1973 federal proposals to supplement the incomes of poor workers, several steps were taken that helped such people. Family Allowances were tripled in 1973; aid to the aged was increased in 1973, and further increases were adopted in 1978. And, finally, the very failure of the support and supplementation proposals helped pave the way for the 1978 Refundable Child Tax Credit. However, these changes did not come near to achieving the goals sought by the 1970 and 1973 welfare proposals.[6] In this respect incremental change was not as productive in Canada as it was in the United States. This conclusion is especially perplexing because the Canada Assistance Plan is actually more suitable to implicit expansion than is Aid to Families with Dependent Children. Whereas AFDC did not allow the extension of benefits to the childless or to many employed people, CAP cost-sharing could cover the latter groups. Unfortunately, the provinces were slow to take advantage of this opportunity. It was not until the mid 1970s that provincial programs began to use CAP to extend benefits to new groups, and only Saskatchewan did so in a big way.

This contrast in incrementalism suggests very different evaluations of the similar effect of incremental change in undercutting comprehensive change. In the United States Food Stamps, SSI, the Earned Income Tax Credit, and other measures steadily undermined the support for comprehensive welfare reform. In Canada, the 1973 increases in Family Allowances and old age benefits drastically reduced the pressure for comprehensive reform almost before the Social Security Review began. Though these steps helped frustrate efforts for comprehensive reform in both countries, they more closely approximated the goals of such reform in the United States than in Canada. Food Stamps eventually duplicated the benefits envisioned by the Family Assistance Plan and indeed went further than FAP by providing benefits to the childless. The Canadian increase in Family Allowances was not aimed just at the poor and was of limited size, yet it soaked up funds needed by the support and supplementation proposals. Incrementalism in both countries undermined comprehensive change, but in Canada it did not compensate for this mischief as well as it did in the United States.

During the prolonged collapse of comprehensive welfare reform efforts, Canada was not as successful as the United States at achieving similar goals incrementally. Of course, this failure was compensated for by Canada's ability in 1978 to pass a major program, Refundable Child Tax Credits. But that program did not entirely live up to previous proposals.

Benefits were less than half of those envisioned under the supplementation proposals developed during the Social Security Review. In real terms, the tax credit did not even give a family of four as many benefits as proposed under the Family Income Security Plan in 1972. Another failure of the tax credit program as comprehensive reform was that it left untouched the other income maintenance programs. Although it displaced a portion of Family Allowances and to that extent was redistributive, the tax credit was not much better targeted on the poor. Two-thirds of all Canadian families qualified for some part of the child tax credit.[7] In its demographic and political impact the program was more akin to Family Allowances than to conditional welfare programs. One defense of the tax credit program was as a "foot in the door" for the negative income tax that could be increased later and be better targeted on the poor. However, the fact that most of the beneficiaries were not below the poverty line suggests that future efforts to make the program more redistributive will be most difficult.

It is strange that after debating some very redistributive welfare reform proposals, Canada adopted a tax credit scheme whose rewards for the poor were so modest, if not minimal. Canada's comprehensive debate yielded glaringly incremental results. In contrast, the incremental development followed in the United States eventually amounted to a much more significant change, one that compared favorably with comprehensive proposals even though it was reached indirectly.

Triumph of Reaction?

Welfare debates do not always focus on attempts to expand the welfare system. The issue instead may be cutting back welfare programs. The public in both Canada and the United States is very critical of major aspects of these programs. Political leaders and institutions can moderate this pressure. Presidents Nixon and Carter answered cries about the welfare mess by presenting their proposals as the solution. Richard Van Loon has speculated that "social policy advocates must push continually for major new programs if only to keep existing ones from being dismembered."[8] Some political institutions offer special protection to welfare programs. Canada's institutions helped contain the welfare backlash and freed policymakers to consider guaranteed income proposals in explicit terms that were politically unthinkable in the United States, but Canadian leaders have been far more hesitant than U.S. leaders to curtail existing welfare programs. Political institutions are partly responsible for this difference. Leaders and institutions can moderate the welfare backlash, but they cannot ignore it. Canada, too, may eventually adopt strong policies restricting welfare programs.

Recently states have begun frankly cutting back welfare programs, but provinces have taken few such actions. While U.S. benefits have failed to keep up with inflation, Canadian benefits have in some cases risen faster than inflation. The value of maximum benefits paid by the states dropped in real terms an average of 5 percent between 1968 and 1974.[9] Nationwide Canadian figures are not available, but a rough calculation shows that between 1971 and 1975, budget standards actually rose in real terms by 18 percent in Ontario and by 29 percent in Quebec.[10] This cross-national difference may exist in part because the provinces are financially more self-sufficient than the states, but it also indicates a greater commitment to assuring adequate benefits to welfare clients. By 1976 four provinces had taken steps to index welfare benefits to the cost of living. One of these provinces was Quebec, with the largest case load in Canada. By contrast, the state with the largest AFDC case load, California, was by the early 1970s leading the nation in its efforts to cut back on welfare programs.

California's governor Ronald Reagan had been elected in 1966 partly on the strength of promises to get rid of welfare freeloaders, but the programs continued to grow for several more years. In 1971, however, Reagan obtained passage of the Welfare Reform Act, which tightened eligibility, standardized benefits, and tracked down fraud. While the courts struck down some parts of the legislation and the counties and HEW neutralized others, Reagan's program succeeded in cutting back the welfare rolls, even when the nationwide leveling off of the AFDC case load is taken into account.[11] Although Reagan left the governorship in 1974, the California backlash continued. In June 1978 the state's voters electrified the nation by overwhelmingly endorsing Proposition 13, an amendment to the California constitution that cut property taxes by 30 percent and restricted the ability of state and local governments to seek new sources of revenue. Polls showed that the voters wanted to cut welfare more than any other program.[12] The legislature obliged by slashing cost-of-living increases in AFDC benefits, and more cuts loomed when the state's budgetary surplus ran out.

Crusades against welfare spending became common by the mid 1970s, even in states with a tradition of liberalism. Faced with an acute budget crisis, Democratic governor Michael Dukakis in 1975 led the Massachusetts legislature in omitting a cost-of-living increase in AFDC benefits, as well as excluding ten thousand supposedly employable people from general relief and terminating medical relief (aid for people not qualifying for Medicaid). Despite his efforts, Dukakis was toppled in a September 1978 party primary by conservative Edward J. King, who pressed the tax issue and continually vowed to cut back on welfare programs. Advising King on welfare cutbacks during the campaign was Robert Carleson, who had worked with Reagan in California, had fought the Income Supplement Program and was now increasingly successful in promoting conservative versions of welfare reform.[13]

No provincial antiwelfare crusades have occurred in Canada on the scale of those found in Massachusetts, California, and other states. Indeed in some elections the conservative point of view fared badly at the polls. In a 1977 Ontario election the ruling Progressive Conservatives were forced to remain a minority government. And in a 1978 Saskatchewan election, the NDP government actually increased its majority. Of course, in a number of other cases the conservative side won. Liberal governments were defeated in Nova Scotia in 1978 and Prince Edward Island in 1979, leaving Ottawa the only Liberal stronghold before it too fell in 1979. Saskatchewan remained the only NDP government when the party was defeated in British Columbia in 1975 and Manitoba in 1977. The Progressive Conservatives retained their grip on Alberta in a March 1979 election. But these conservative victories did not lead to welfare cutbacks such as those pursued even by liberal politicians in the United States. It is true that various provinces have taken steps that parallel U.S. efforts to investigate welfare fraud, enforce child support obligations on absent fathers, and apply work tests, even to some mothers with children. And the popular demand for such measures is very great. But the Canadian welfare backlash has been translated into policies in only a limited way. The Canadian political system discourages the expression of pressures hostile to welfare programs. Of course, if those pressures become intense enough, then the Canadian system will respond to them, possibly in a more coordinated way than is possible in the U.S. system.

The Problem of Welfare Fraud

The Canadian and U.S. publics are both concerned with welfare fraud, yet government has done much more to track it down in the United States. Errors in distributing benefits are common in both countries. As many as 25 percent of all AFDC cases involve an error, and while reliable national figures on Canadian error rates do not exist, it would be surprising if they were strikingly different.[14] About half of U.S. errors were not the beneficiary's fault. Indeed, while money was spent unnecessarily in some cases, in others the beneficiary was shortchanged.[15] Moreover most cases of error by the client were accidental. In the United States less than 5 percent of AFDC errors were the result of deliberate fraud by clients. According to these figures, only about 1 percent of all U.S. welfare cases involve fraud. Quebec officials give a similar estimate for the level of fraud in that province, and there is no reason to think that the figure would be appreciably different in other provinces. Not all fraud is equally serious; most cases in both countries involve inconsiderable amounts of money.[16] But there are enough extraordinary cases to sustain the rumor mill and to keep newspaper editors and politicians happy.[17]

Welfare fraud is a venerable issue in U.S. state and local politics. Crusading welfare personnel founded the National Welfare Fraud Association. For the most part, however, welfare fraud has not been pursued persistently. One reason is that there simply has not been enough of it nor the tools to detect it, to make such efforts worthwhile. In the first two decades of AFDC the states had enough discretion in setting eligibility conditions that administrators could usually find many grounds for excluding people they did not like. For example, it was far more difficult to prove a case of fraud than to exclude a family simply because the mother had once borne an illegitimate child—which Louisiana routinely did under its onetime "suitable home" law.[18] As legal and administrative rulings cut back this discretion in determining eligibility, the states moved more strongly into the prosecution of fraud. Most states have routinely investigated tips from informers on possible fraud. In recent years several states, including Illinois, Washington, and Connecticut, have established "hot lines" to encourage such tips.[19] A more powerful technique has been the growing movement by states to cross-check welfare applications with nonwelfare records from the private and public sectors. In 1971 California pioneered its Earnings Clearance System to compare welfare files with earnings data from unemployment insurance records.[20] A number of states use state income tax files, public employee payrolls, motor vehicle registrations, lottery results, and even marriage licenses and death listings.[21] Private bank accounts and payrolls have also been examined in some states. In Michigan the automobile corporations and other major employers lend their payroll data to the state to comb for "welfare cheats."[22]

In the Canadian provinces the public has clearly been concerned about welfare fraud, and leaders have taken some measures to deal with it, though not as many as in the United States. It has long been the practice of private and public agencies in Toronto to compare their lists of clients at Christmas to catch anyone going to more than one place for the traditional Christmas basket. As mentioned earlier, the NDP premier of Manitoba as early as 1972 began to look into fraud, sensing the "profound, seething resentment" of voters toward welfare that helped defeat his government in 1977. Other provincial elections in 1975 and 1976 were also marked by the issue. The biggest effort to expose welfare fraud has been in British Columbia. In 1976 William Vander Zalm instituted the Ministry Inspectors Program (universally called the "fraud squad"), arguing for a possible saving of $40 million to $50 million. Although savings of that magnitude were not achieved, the program has nearly paid for itself in the amounts of recoveries agreed to, quite aside from the money saved by terminating existing benefits. Even Quebec, traditionally protective of the poor, took measures in the early 1970s to cut back on ineligibles. In March 1972 the government announced that an audit had allowed the exclusion of 7 percent of the entire case load. In 1973 the province computerized its welfare rolls, allowing a further reduction in recipients by 4 percent. Quebec routinely investigated tips by informers, as did most other provinces.

Since welfare fraud has been a state and local issue for so long in the United States, it is surprising that more national efforts have not been made to tighten up. Prior to the 1970s the main effort to do so was the 1951 Jenner amendment allowing states to disclose the names of recipients, and HEW strongly limited the effects of this law. Not until 1973 did Congress adopt meaningful requirements for quality control by states.[23] By the mid 1970s the federal government began lending its unrivaled data banks to state welfare offices. OASDI, SSI, and federal payroll records are routinely made available, and under some conditions even income tax records are used. This whole process is made easier by a 1975 requirement that all AFDC recipients be assigned social security numbers. And, with federal help, states are adopting the computer systems that make these massive matches possible. By 1977 welfare fraud had become such an obligatory issue that Secretary Califano established the Office of Inspector General to engage in investigation and prosecution of criminal activities in AFDC and other HEW programs. He declared that effective self-policing "had been sadly lacking in the Department."[24]

Welfare fraud is virtually nonexistent as a national issue in Canada. Indeed efforts such as British Columbia's have been much more controversial than their U.S. counterparts. This is true even though British Columbia's program is a mild one by U.S. standards. No hot line and no data banks are used. Only in isolated cases has a national party made an issue of welfare abuse, as the Progressive Conservatives did in 1972, focusing mainly on unemployment insurance, which unlike social assistance is a federally administered program. National politicians have been able to ignore the question of welfare fraud even though the public is concerned about it. That fraud exists as a national problem in Canada was suggested by the 1970 poll in which Canadian welfare recipients themselves felt it necessary for welfare officers to check on all beneficiaries at the time of application, "to make sure they really need it." Fully 87 percent felt that such investigations should be made regularly.[25]

The Enforcement of Child Support

Congress in 1950 ordered state welfare officials to notify local law enforcement authorities of new desertion cases, although Representative Winfield Denton was unsuccessful in convincing his colleagues to make desertion a federal crime. But concern about the problem of absent parents persisted, and Congress became restive in the 1960s when desertion and illegitimacy were more visible among minorities. In 1967 the Senate Finance Committee convinced Congress to include in the Social Security amendments a requirement that each state identify and pursue cases where a parent had failed to supply child support. Each state was required to establish an administrative unit for this purpose, with access granted to Social Security and Internal Revenue files. HEW deliberately downplayed this law, although several states established child support enforcement programs on their own. In 1970 a series of efforts began in Congress to establish meaningful national child support requirements. In the FAP legislation that passed the House in 1970, the Ways and Means Committee included provisions for the garnishment of Social Security benefits and income tax refunds. The Finance Committee convinced the Senate to pass an even more far-reaching measure making desertion a federal crime. Thus both houses of Congress had agreed to child support enforcement. But with the end of the session approaching, the two bills died because no conference was held to reconcile them. In 1971 the Ways and Means Committee hardened its approach by adding a provision for criminal penalties and the House passed it in HR 1. The Senate Finance Committee adopted a far-reaching measure, much of which the full Senate later ratified. As a condition for receiving benefits, a mother was required to assign child support rights to the government and to cooperate in locating and prosecuting the father. The bill gave responsibility for the program to the Justice Department, with wide access to government files. The bill even provided for a nationwide program of blood testing to establish paternity.[26] In the impasse that developed between the House and Senate versions of HR 1, the child support provisions passed by both houses died as they had in 1970.

In 1973–1974 the House and Senate finally got together on a major child support enforcement bill. The Finance Committee decided not to insist on its preference that the program be administered by the attorney general. Both houses passed child support proposals in 1973, although not until December did the houses coincide on legislation for the president to sign, part of the Social Services Amendments of 1974. The House-Senate conference that produced this legislation omitted the Senate bill's provision for funding blood laboratories to establish paternity. President Ford signed the bill, but with reservations about provisions that "go too far by injecting the Federal Government into domestic relations."[27] According to Senator Long's staff, Ford was influenced by HEW personnel who were strongly opposed to the congressional intent. In 1975 Ford proposed legislation modifying some features of the legislation. Although the House adopted some of these modifications, the Senate agreed to only a few changes in the 1974 approach, among them restricting access to case records and allowing a welfare mother to refuse to cooperate if pursuing the father was not in the best interests of the child.

The 1975 child support legislation required for the first time that all welfare recipients be assigned a Social Security number. It established as a condition for AFDC that all single mothers applying or benefiting must now sign away all rights to support from the absent father, making him formally a debtor in default to the state. A whole new class of criminals was created. The mother is required by law to name the absent parent and cooperate fully in tracking him down. Those who do not cooperate lose their eligibility for benefits, although their children continue to receive them. Since the absent parent owes support as a debt to the government, his Social Security benefits, income tax refunds, and all wages can be garnished. HEW is required to establish a parent locator service as a clearinghouse for information on the whereabouts of delinquent parents. Each state must assign a special agency to ascertain paternity and secure support. Federal reimbursement for these efforts was increased to 75 percent. States are subject to a penalty of 5 percent of AFDC matching funds if their program does not meet minimum federal standards. Several states, among them Washington, Massachusetts, Michigan , and California, had not waited for these inducements before establishing aggressive efforts.

Though HEW was initially ambivalent, Secretary Califano became a convert to the 1975 child support legislation, eventually citing it as a "unique tribute to the foresight of Senator Russell Long, who worked so hard to have the program passed by Congress."[28] There is little question that child support enforcement is a cost-effective way to reduce welfare spending. In 1976 and 1977 the states collected a total of $1.6 billion on the basis of a total federal-state-local administrative cost of $427 million—more than $1 billion reclaimed, with the program only in its infancy.[29] Individual states did even better. In 1977, for example, Massachusetts collected a total of $24.3 million based on a total expenditure of $3.6 million, and other states did nearly as well.[30]

Efforts to lessen welfare expenditures by strengthening child support enforcement are far less developed in Canada than in the United States. Canada's 1968 divorce act made it easier to dissolve a marriage, but made no provision for the enforcement of support orders, which are the responsibility of the provincial courts. It is estimated that 75 percent of all maintenance orders are in default. Although these harrowing figures parallel those that gave rise to the U.S. child support enforcement program, there is no analogous national effort in Canada. Even so, the provinces have taken a number of measures to reduce the burden on the welfare system of unpaid child support. Virtually all provinces require that a single mother receiving social assistance must discuss with authorities possible strategies to obtain support from the absent father, and a number of provinces explicitly provide that her assistance can be terminated if she does not cooperate. In Newfoundland a single mother can receive aid for only thirty days before authorities begin to expect some legal action to obtain support from the father, and even before then she is expected to make reasonable efforts to obtain support. In Quebec social assistance can be denied if a mother does not make some effort to obtain support from the absent father. In Nova Scotia, Manitoba, and British Columbia continued social assistance to a single mother is formally conditioned on her efforts to obtain support, although this requirement can be waived in cases of hardship. Nova Scotia and Ontario allow, and British Columbia sometimes requires, a mother to sign over to authorities her rights to support payments from the father of her children. Several provinces have demonstrated special concern about the private behavior of recipients. In Nova Scotia and Prince Edward Island a single mother can be denied benefits if authorities determine that marital separation occurred in order to qualify for assistance, and in Alberta this possibility is grounds for a special investigation. In British Columbia and Nova Scotia an unwed mother cannot receive aid if she is cohabiting with a male, even if he is not the father of her children. This regulation is more severe than in any state, because the U.S. Supreme Court has prohibited such rules.

Although the provinces have begun to tighten up in forcing welfare mothers to seek child support from absent fathers, Canada is only beginning to recognize the problem. In the United States the child support enforcement apparatus is now available not only to welfare recipients but to anyone who wishes to use it. Canadian provinces in general have not made a broad-scale effort to extract payments from absent parents.[31] There are reciprocal agreements between most provinces, by which child responsibilities can be enforced on a runaway father, but these procedures are rarely used. Such agreements have long existed in the United States as well, but the states did not utilize them extensively until the federal government forced them to. In Canada no such federal insistence has occurred. In 1976 British Columbia's minister of human resources urged a federal-provincial conference to investigate the possible savings from a more concerted national approach to child support enforcement, and the group unanimously agreed to ask the federal government to look into the question. The federal experts have faced an immensely frustrating task, because the data kept by courts on maintenance orders are very poor.

The decentralization that makes data collection on child support difficult would also present difficult barriers to the institution of a nationwide Canadian child support enforcement effort similar to that in the United States. Yet the U.S. program has been successful, and it seems likely that a Canadian program would more than pay for itself. Canadian officials remain curiously innocent of these potential returns. And perhaps they can be applauded for that: should the United States be proud that it is decades ahead in this sinister business? Still, an effective effort to enforce child support may be the proper measure to stem the hemorrhage in public support of welfare programs. The only question is whether the cure is worse than the disease.

The Spread of Work Requirements and Work Relief

Chapter 1 cited some polling data indicating that the Canadian and U.S. publics alike believe that employable welfare recipients should be subjected to a work test. Such work requirements are facts in most provinces and states. States have long had work requirements in their general assistance programs, those in which the federal government pays no share. However, before 1967 the federal government prevented the states from requiring AFDC recipients to seek work. States could refuse aid if a person had turned down a suitable job, but could not require the recipient to go out and seek work. Nevertheless some states adopted the practice of closing AFDC cases during the harvest season, based on the expectation that the recipient could easily find a job. But the principle remained that a state could close a case only when a recipient had a bona fide offer, not just because he ought to seek a job.

Beginning in 1967 work requirements emerged at the national level in the United States. The 1967 WIN amendments allowed states for the first time to apply work requirements to AFDC beneficiaries, and the 1971 Talmadge amendments made such requirements mandatory for many families, including mothers with no children under six. In 1971 Congress passed a work requirement for the Food Stamp program; if the family head refused the test, the family stood to lose all benefits, including those for dependents. Most other proposed work requirements allow children to continue receiving benefits. The pressure for ever tighter and broader work requirements has inexorably increased. A major staple of Jimmy

Carter's successful 1976 primary campaign was his criticism of the welfare mess. He repeatedly declared,

No one able to work, except mothers with pre-school children, should be continued on the welfare rolls unless job training and meaningful job were accepted. . . . If they decline the job, they should be ineligible for further benefits.[32]

The work requirements contained in Carter's 1977 Program for Better Jobs and Income were actually more far-reaching and severe than those contained in the Nixon Family Assistance Plan.[33] The irresistible march of work requirements prompted some liberal reformers to conclude that "public opinion just won't accept a system under which able-bodied adults may loaf at government expense."[34] This political fact may hold even though work requirements are often ineffective, wasteful, and basically unmanageable.

Canadian policies have increasingly reflected a concern that welfare benefits should not allow an employable person to become idle. In 1973 New Brunswick adopted a policy by which welfare benefits were limited to a certain fraction of the minimum wage, assuring that the welfare recipient could not achieve as high a standard of living as a worker. This controversial measure is a unique throwback to Elizabethan concepts of "less eligibility." While no other province applies this philosophy to all welfare benefits, most provinces pay less to a recipient considered employable than to one not expected to work. Another common way to encourage work is by a work requirement. Under the Canada Assistance Plan provinces are free to impose work requirements on recipients that the states could not touch under AFDC. All provinces require able-bodied males to seek work. When the mayor of Surrey, British Columbia (William Vander Zalm, later provincial minister of human resources), urged that welfare recipients go to work picking berries or be given shovels for other work, he was only expressing pungently what many provinces were already doing. In 1972 the Ontario Task Force on Employment Opportunities for Welfare Recipients urged that a recipient be required to accept a job, "even if he considers it demeaning."[35] Work requirements for able-bodied single males (and often for childless females) are nearly universal in Canada. Even males with children are subject. In Ontario a male head of a family may not remain on the welfare rolls without the express permission of top officials. In Manitoba a motherless family may not receive aid unless the father has a child younger than six, or the family has special needs. In most provinces some mothers are also subject to work requirements. Alberta has the most all-inclusive work requirement on the continent: in April 1978 the province adopted a regulation specifying that "a person with one child four months of age or older" is "expected to take employment or training (if required) for employment." If a mother has two children, then a child as old as twelve will exempt her from the requirement. This regulation did not apply to recipients already on the welfare rolls before the regulation was adopted.[36] Other provinces do not automatically exempt mothers from a work requirement if they have children. In Quebec mothers with no children under six may be told to get a job. In Ontario a mother receiving General Welfare Assistance may be required to work if suitable child care service is available. In Prince Edward Island a mother with school-age children can be pressured to seek work, and those with no children of elementary school age or younger are required to register for work.

While some provincial regulations are quite specific as to which mothers are subject to the work test, most provinces leave significant discretion to welfare personnel to decide whether to apply it to a particular family. An Ontario official expressed the common distrust of "a simple chronological factor" such as the age of the child, arguing for the need to "look at the social element . . . the whole family picture." Thus some provincial work requirements are very vague. A Nova Scotia regulation gives a director of assistance the power to cut off benefits "where the applicant or recipient is unwilling to accept employment and in the opinion of the Director, suitable employment is available and it is in the best interest of the family that the applicant or recipient accept employment."[37] While this regulation avoids automatically imposing a work test on some mothers that are subject to a nationwide requirement in the United States, it also gives officials power over a mother no matter how young are her children—freedom that the U.S. federal government explicitly denies the states.

While the requirement that welfare recipients seek work can be administered harshly, it is generally not; there is a shortage of jobs fitted to the skills of many recipients. In order to link welfare more closely to work, governments have increasingly gotten into the business of providing jobs to welfare recipients, which they can turn down only at the price of losing their benefits. Two quite different strategies have been tried. The 1977

Carter welfare reform package proposed to guarantee to all employable welfare applicants a public job at the minimum wage, with incentives for them to move into the private job market. A person in a public job would receive his income in the form of wages rather than welfare. In contrast, some communities force a recipient to do specified work in exchange for receiving benefits, a system called work relief or workfare. The benefits paid are not directly related to the hours worked and thus may be below the minimum wage. Rather the benefits continue to be designated as welfare, and the tasks are assigned to allow the recipient to symbolically work off his debt to society.

Federal constraints on state, provincial, or local use of federal funds for work relief were strong for many years. When nonfederal programs deal with an individual whose needs are not covered by federal cost sharing, an administrator may not hesitate to put the recipient to work. Many states long had workfare arrangements in their General Assistance programs (not federally funded), although the severity and scope of these requirements varied. In 1961 the town of Newburgh, New York, created a furor by establishing thirteen special conditions on the distribution of welfare aid. Among them was that "all able-bodied males on relief" must work off their benefits. Though state authorities quashed the Newburgh reforms, New York State at that very time required work relief for some employables.[38] The situation repeated itself in 1978, when Bordentown, New Jersey, attempted to require work relief (janitorial work in public buildings) by all able-bodied adults receiving General Assistance. The state government vetoed this plan, preferring its own requirement that the recipients accept a minimum wage job if offered.[39]

In Canadian provincial and local programs work relief was once as prevalent as in the United States. Even Saskatchewan, the most liberal area in either country, traditionally used recipients to work on roads. However, the expansion of federal cost sharing to virtually all social assistance cases reduced this practice. Federal authorities are hesitant to share the cost of welfare benefits that are provided in exchange for work. While federal welfare law in Canada allows, and in the United States requires, the use of work requirements, it does not except in very controlled circumstances allow states or provinces to require work in exchange for benefits, even if the recipient has volunteered for work relief. This federal restriction is particularly meaningful in the Canada Assistance Plan, which extends federal cost sharing to all categories of social assistance.

Federal restrictions in the United States do not apply to General Assistance programs funded entirely by the states and localities. Whereas the states can introduce work relief into these programs with impunity, the provinces are much more constrained. This difference is illustrated in the frustration of Gordon Walker, minister of corrections in the Progressive Conservative government of Ontario, who between 1975 and 1978 pressed for workfare programs. Walker proposed requiring able-bodied welfare recipients to work four hours a day in exchange for their benefits. Despite the public popularity of this proposal, the Ontario government refused to pursue it.[40] Similar proposals in the United States have long since become law in many states.

States or provinces can obtain exceptions to the federal prohibition on work relief, although only under certain conditions. For example, the Canada Assistance Plan provides for Work Activity Projects. In such projects the provinces may not deny aid to a recipient who refuses to participate, and the work must be expressly designed to prepare him for entry into the job market. Projects authorized under this provision have been relatively few, with fifty-three in 1975–1976 involving 2802 people.[41]

The historic federal restraints on state workfare projects have been as strong in the United States as in Canada, but these restraints are deteriorating quickly. States were subject to strict guidelines under Community Work and Training (1962–1968) and initially under the WIN program (begun in 1968).[42] While recipients could be placed directly in training, the provisions for employment were strict, requiring that the work be paid at the minimum wage and be designed to prepare the recipient for the job market. At various times the federal restrictions have prevented a state or locality from putting recipients to work. Ultimately it was AFDC regulations that helped New York State authorities to disallow Newburgh's proposal for work relief. In the mid 1970s the strength of the AFDC prohibition on work relief began to weaken. Utah, which had asked for a waiver of the rule in 1973, was finally granted permission in 1976 to establish a work experience and training program, although not before suffering an eighteen-month suspension of AFDC benefits for installing the program without permission. Under the program AFDC recipients with no children under six are required to work three days a week. Massachusetts established a similar program in 1978, again after lengthy negotiations with federal authorities. Related programs have been established in Oklahoma, Texas, North Carolina, and other states.[43]

HEW has faced increasing pressure from Congress to allow AFDC work relief nationwide. To Secretary Califano at a 1977 hearing Senator Long complained, "You cannot pay anybody to do a decent act with the money you administer there. I want to fix it so you can pay them to do the decent act." And fix it he did. As a part of the Social Security Amendments of 1977, Congress gave power to the secretary of HEW to authorize states to undertake projects violating the long-standing prohibition against work relief and other prohibitions in the AFDC legislation. These projects would be considered experiments, but one in each state could be implemented statewide. Also in 1977 the House voted to require food stamp recipients to work off their benefits. While this measure was dropped in conference with the Senate, the final legislation did require the establishment of fourteen pilot projects under which recipients who failed to find private jobs would be required to work off their benefits in nonpaying public jobs. It seems only a matter of time before states are given free rein in imposing workfare in exchange for AFDC and food stamps. Congressional efforts to force federal agencies to allow the states to take punitive measures against welfare recipients have usually been preludes to successful efforts to make such measures mandatory for all states. It would not be surprising if the workfare movement eventually produced such a result.[44]

How Fast the Retreat?

Canada in the past decade has not been hospitable to the curtailment of welfare programs, which is now commonplace in the United States. However, this difference between the two countries may not persist. The reason that Canadian programs are under less attack is not that the public is more supportive of these programs; antiwelfare sentiment seems equally strong in both countries. Nor are the excesses of welfare programs any less in Canada; both countries have strikingly similar problems. One reason that the backlash has been politically more effective in the United States is that welfare programs expanded all at once in the late 1960s rather than growing gradually over a longer period, as was the case in Canada. Another reason is that Canada had a historic configuration of policy that shielded unpopular recipient groups from popular indignation by camouflaging them among other more "respectable" recipients. Important, too, were the choices of policymakers in presenting proposals that invited extra political opposition in the United States and conciliated potential opponents in Canada. But perhaps the most important reason for the profound difference in welfare politics is political structure. The inductive style of U.S. policymaking allowed special footholds for the enemies of welfare reform and of welfare programs generally. Canada's deductive style of policymaking discouraged the expression of such opposition, although it also shut out supporters of reform who might have intervened when the internal debates got bogged down.

Canadian policymakers have simply not heeded the welfare backlash as faithfully as have their U.S. counterparts. The Canadian political system and the country's configuration of policy insulate welfare programs from public backlash. Canadian politics has exhibited less concern about problems of family breakup and illegitimacy, even though these problems are growing as fast in Canada as in the United States. Work requirements are spreading, but few are as far-reaching as the Talmadge amendment. Canada has no counterparts to the U.S. quality control effort, the child support enforcement program, or the workfare movement. There is no Canadian counterpart to the U.S. National Welfare Fraud Association, and no one has proposed a package of restrictions similar to those routinely debated in Congress and the state legislatures.

The unemployment insurance issue in Canada and the United States seems to challenge my view that Canada's deductive politics contained that country's welfare backlash. The Canadian Unemployment Insurance program is quite controversial, more so than social assistance. Canada's deductive style of policymaking has not prevented the passage of several recent laws, the latest in 1978, that tightened up on Unemployment Insurance. The explanation could be that the program is administered at the federal level. It is more visible nationwide; hence provincial jurisdiction does not interfere with national efforts to reform it as in the case of social assistance. Thus the argument could be that Canadian social assistance is less controversial nationwide not because political institutions buffer the programs against public feelings but because these feelings are focused away from the national level by the strong provincial control over the programs. Though U.S. public assistance programs are administered by the states, they are subject to many more federal requirements and thus invite nationwide debate.

Unemployment insurance is not a good case to cite in support of this theory that decentralization, not deductive politics, shields Canadian social assistance programs from backlash. The Canadian Unemployment Insurance program has since 1971 been as liberal as any in the world and probably would have provoked efforts to cut it back no matter which level of government administered it. Many Canadians became critical of the program, but policymakers themselves were concerned about its rising cost and its baleful effects on the labor market. Even after several cutbacks, unemployment insurance in Canada is more generous than in the United States in terms of eligibility, level and duration of benefits, and work requirement, as well as in most other ways. For example, in 1979, benefits in the United States remained at a basic rate of 50 percent of the claimant's earnings, whereas Canadian benefits were 75 percent in 1971, 67 percent in 1975; even after the 1978 cutbacks, they stood at 60 percent.[45]

Another problem with the argument that the provincial focus of social assistance programs shunts public backlash away from the federal level is that even at the provincial level there is much less political attack on the programs than in the United States. Quebec seems a prime candidate for backlash. It has the largest case load and the highest taxes in Canada. Yet the province has taken few steps to restrict access to welfare benefits. Even provinces with conservative leaders have taken little action. Sterling Lyon, who in 1977 became premier of Manitoba, had values somewhere to the right of California's Howard Jarvis, but in his first two years in office, Lyon did not press for massive welfare cutbacks. Provincial efforts to prosecute fraud and enforce child support are just beginning. British Columbia's "fraud squad" is more controversial in federal and provincial government circles than are corresponding efforts in the United States, even though that province's efforts are comparatively mild.

Clearly something more than decentralization is at work in preventing the very real disenchantment of the Canadian public with welfare programs from being expressed politically. But decentralization matters. Until very recently federal leaders felt little public pressure to question the way that the provinces spent matching funds. AFDC became a national issue in the United States because Congress rebelled when the states and localities asked for more funds. Although it never actually denied matching funds to spendthrift states, Congress engaged in a series of efforts to reduce the size of welfare rolls in the future and in general to make welfare a less attractive alternative. In contrast, when the Canadian provinces asked for more welfare money, they got it without much question.

This difference in political context is illustrated by the virtual nonexistence of national data on welfare spending and welfare beneficiaries in Canada. Whereas people in the United States can follow the size and cost of AFDC just as they follow the stock market, Canadians have no similar consciousness of national dimensions or trends in welfare programs. However, this vacuum may be the effect rather than the cause of the absence of a nationwide political movement against welfare programs. One reason for the detail of U.S. figures is that the programs have been controversial; once the Canada Assistance Plan comes under attack, perhaps better national data will be demanded.[46]

The U.S. political system gives many footholds for the critics of welfare but also raises special barriers to their success in curtailing it. A welfare opponent in the United States faces a staggering task. There are dozens of welfare programs, each with its own rationale and supporters. James Q. Wilson has argued that just as the decentralization of U.S. national government makes the passage of new programs difficult, it also makes them difficult to repeal: "A major change is, in effect, new legislation that must overcome the same hurdles as the original law, but this time with one of the hurdles—the wishes of the agency and its client—raised much higher."[47] Only an extraordinary nationwide consensus would be likely to overturn many such programs. Ironically, the most likely occasion for a negative consensus of this type occurs when the country is considering positive proposals for comprehensive welfare reform. Richard Nathan has warned that when comprehensive proposals are discussed, Congress typically discards the liberal provisions and adopts the conservative ones. He argues for a more incremental approach, summed up by the principle: "Keep your cotton-picking hands off."[48] In the United States it is particularly difficult to dismantle the welfare state piecemeal, because the repeal of each program requires a separate battle.

If large cuts in individual welfare programs are difficult to achieve directly, indirect or incremental restrictions may achieve similar goals. Reforms such as work requirements, work relief, fraud detection, and child support enforcement help constrain the growth in welfare indirectly by denying or recovering benefits and by discouraging people from applying for benefits. Because these measures do not entail a frontal attack on welfare programs, they face less organized opposition. A whole catalog of such changes was set forth in HR 7200, a bill approved by the Senate Finance Committee in 1977 but which Congress for the most part did not accept.[49] The bill proposed to increase penalties for failing to report outside earnings; provide for the deportation of aliens who could not prove that their need had arisen subsequent to their arrival in the United States; tighten the WIN work requirement by making the penalty more immediate and lengthy and by requiring that people considered employable under the Talmadge rule must not only register for work or training, but also actively search for work; increase the amount of payments that may be made not through cash but indirectly through "vendors"; and require states to issue photo identification cards to beneficiaries and to open their files to congressional investigators. Though these proposals were not enacted during the Ninety-fifth Congress, it seems only a matter of time before some become law.

If the U.S. public is not satisfied with piecemeal and indirect opportunities to chip away at welfare programs, backlash can reach such a peak that broad repeal or reorientation of the programs takes place. California voters repudiated conventional political channels in June 1978 when they endorsed Proposition 13, a constitutional amendment. After the California vote a nationwide poll showed that 57 percent of the public would support a similar measure in their state. Of all local programs, social services were most frequently mentioned as those in which too much was being spent. Another poll reported that 41 percent of the public in both California and the nation at large were "willing to cut welfare and social services a lot." During 1979 pressure grew for amending the federal constitution to require a balanced budget. A nationwide poll showed that the public supported such an amendment by the margin of 73 percent to 16 percent.[50] There were even efforts by many state legislatures to force Congress to call a new constitutional convention to write that amendment. Were the constitution amended, welfare programs could become subject to cuts more dramatic and permanent than occur in any parliamentary system. And under the threat of such an amendment, congressmen may support budgetary cuts far deeper than normal. Unless this atmosphere of crisis takes hold, however, direct cuts in U.S. welfare spending are likely to be marginal, and the major changes in the programs will focus on conditions for eligibility and on other restrictions.

In contrast to the stalemate common in the inductive U.S. system, the deductive aspects of the Canadian system make it easier for political elites to directly and dramatically curtail a welfare program once they determine that reversal is desirable. Such a change of mind began in the late 1970s. After the federal government embarked on a massive austerity program in August 1978, Minister of National Health and Welfare Monique Bégin warned that the business sector was pressing for further cuts and that social programs desperately needed defenders: "For the last two years we have not heard the voices of the poor, the old . . . just those of businessmen, small and big."[51] But businessmen have always been critical of welfare programs, while the clients of the programs have never been a strong lobby in Canada. Why then did welfare programs not come under pressure before the late 1970s? The clear answer is that Canadian political elites were friendlier to welfare programs previously. Indeed by 1976 they had agreed in principle to a new tier of welfare benefits that would supplement the income of those able to work. Fiscal limitations constrained the size and timing of this proposal and eventually helped scuttle it but did not initially threaten existing welfare programs. Criticisms of these programs emanating from the public were beside the point. The preoccupation of policymakers with proposals for extending the welfare system may actually have distracted them from public outcry for cutting it back. It would be inconceivable for a congressman to stray that far from the public mood. But in the end the Canadian leaders, too, began to heed the welfare backlash, possibly more completely than any congressman could.

Canadian leaders can turn against welfare programs either voluntarily or because the public pushes them to. The normal insulation of policymaking frees leaders to be protective of welfare programs, but it also allows them to become disenchanted with these programs. One perceptive Canadian finds that the favorite journal of many of his country's civil servants is the *Public Interest*, a neoconservative quarterly published in New York City. An intellectual movement that is still on the way up in the United States can move into Canadian government at the top. Thus if federal officials and their provincial counterparts come to believe in work requirements, child support enforcement, fraud detection, and work relief, the political barriers to these changes are actually less than in the United States.

Perhaps a more likely way to cut back Canadian welfare than for leaders to voluntarily change their minds is for the public to change these

How Fast the Retreat?

leaders' minds for them. An election, or the anticipation of one, may dramatically reverse a government's stance toward a program. With the prospect of a 1979 election, the Liberal government in August 1978 proposed deep budgetary cuts. Such proposals are as common in the United States as in Canada, but in Canada they are actually carried out. Of the $2.5 billion in proposed cuts for 1979–1980, $460 million would be in programs for housing, community grants, unemployment insurance, health, and welfare.[52] Cuts in the administrative side of government were carried out pitilessly. Health and Welfare Canada lost five hundred jobs. The Policy Research and Strategic Planning Branch lost forty-five man-years in employees, representing 40 percent of the entire staff. Budgetary cuts of this speed and severity are unheard of in the United States. In January 1979 President Carter proposed major cuts in social programs, but criticism from the affected groups and their congressional sympathizers quickly caused many of these proposals to unravel.[53] Similarities in the two countries' social and economic systems caused budgetary control to be a major national issue at just the same time, but differences in their political systems caused the budgetary debates to proceed quite differently.

The movement to formally put a lid on welfare spending is most likely to succeed in Canada. As of 1979 the Canada Assistance Plan was the country's major remaining open-ended cost-sharing program, though there were signs of a change. During 1977 and 1978 federal and provincial ministers nearly agreed to shift CAP's social services to a block grant basis, putting a lid on spending for the first time. Such a change in cash assistance as well would not be surprising. Capping CAP spending was certain to be less controversial than was the ill-fated Moynihan-Long-Cranston proposal to cap AFDC.

The United States and Canada, each in its own way, are curbing the growth in welfare programs and cutting back on existing entitlements. Which country will win this grim race? So far, the United States has implemented the welfare backlash most aggressively. However, the cutbacks have not been large or direct but rather have been in the form of indirect or incremental restrictions. Direct, dramatic reversal of welfare spending is easier in Canada, and although this has hardly begun, the country may eventually control costs more effectively than the United States. By June 1978 the Canadian Conference on Social Development, which had in two previous biennial meetings called for expansion of the welfare system, approved a resolution conceding that a big new guaranteed income program was impractical: "Current economic and fiscal conditions discourage major new expenditures aimed at reducing income inequality."[54] Few U.S. welfare lobbies have yet been willing to concede this point. Of course, Canada's greater ability to cut budgets may actually help welfare programs; if the cuts focus on nonwelfare spending, then pressures on welfare will be eased. The U.S. failure to economize anywhere invites a crisis such as the one that accompanied the passage of Proposition 13, when welfare programs were the central target of public rebellion.

The difficulty of directly controlling welfare spending in the United States might invite an acute budgetary and even constitutional crisis. However, the proliferation of incremental and indirect restrictions is making that outcome less likely. The cumulation of these restrictions helps moderate welfare costs, while also allaying public fears that welfare dollars are being wasted. The slowness with which Canada is moving toward such restrictions suggests that dramatic, direct attacks on welfare spending are more likely there. Without resort to the multifarious restrictions currently being experimented with in the United States, Canada simply will not be able to moderate welfare spending piecemeal, and the public will not feel reassured that welfare dollars are well spent. Thus welfare programs and their supporters face an unenviable choice: either risk a full-scale reversal, as may occur in Canada, or satisfy the backlash through reforms that, as in the United States, entail the risk that welfare policy will quietly lose its soul.

Public distaste for welfare programs must be filtered through political institutions, but how far welfare will retreat depends ultimately on the public's preferences. Not forever can Canadian leaders lean against the wind of welfare backlash, nor can the jungle of entrenched U.S. programs withstand the efforts of politicians to prune it back. How strongly will the welfare backlash continue? Arguably, that backlash is limited in its goals. Willing to support the truly needy, the public does not want to aid those who can support themselves and it abhors waste in administration. Seymour Lipset and others argue that the public is asking only that government spend its welfare dollars wisely.[55] However, this finding is scarcely comforting for the future of welfare programs, because the public is unlikely *ever* to be satisfied that the programs are being run well. No matter how vigorously government pursues fraud or enforces child support and work requirements, there will always be some abuses or compromises left to inspire resentment. Some level of waste may actually be optimal because the cost of wiping it out is so high. Moreover some waste cannot be eliminated at any price, or without creating new bureaucracies with their own problems of waste—an infinite regress. Even though it would be cheaper to leave people on welfare than to provide the training, jobs, and day care necessary to move them into employment, the public prefers the latter alternative.[56] Unfortunately, the cost of this alternative may become impossibly high, and job programs are notoriously difficult to administer well. And then there are the politically unhappy trade-offs in designing a benefit structure: offering a low reduction rate to all beneficiaries is too expensive, but a two-tier design does not offer good work incentives to many mother-headed families. Unfortunately and paradoxically, the public's insistence on perfect welfare programs may actually increase welfare budgets and force government to undertake new tasks that cannot be done gracefully, if at all, thus opening up the programs to redoubled criticism.

If the welfare backlash is partly rooted in public misunderstanding of the trade-offs inherent in welfare policy, then perhaps leaders and institutions matter a great deal. Government should persuade citizens that some fears are groundless. But U.S. leaders are not strong enough to make this argument, so they endlessly tighten up the programs, even while their efforts show that the diminishing returns will not satisfy the public's growing appetite for restrictions. Canadian institutions seem better suited to the task of educating the public about welfare perplexities. Such persuasion may be all that stands in the way of a massive retrenchment, because Canada has been slow to meet public demands for piecemeal restrictions. But the task of public education may never be tried. Canadian elites are themselves turning against welfare programs, possibly embarking on the restrictions that their U.S. counterparts know by experience will never satisfy the public. In coming decades each country's political situation will discourage the public's recognition that we cannot help the poor without accepting some trade-offs in policy and administration. As U.S. elites become increasingly convinced that negative reforms have limits, they will be in no institutional position to apply this lesson. And although Canadian elites are more capable of persuading the public to accept some apparent waste, they will have little desire to do so.

Notes

Sources of Quotations in Frontispiece

U.S. Divorcee: Renee Natter, "Trouble," *New York Times*, May 5, 1978. Canadian welfare recipient: Québec, *La Voix Des Hommes Sans Voix*, Annexe 22, Commission d'Enquête Sur la Santé et la Bien-être Sociale (February 1971), p. 71. Canadian Widow: Federal-Provincial Conference of Ministers of Welfare, *Welfare Recipients Speak for Themselves* (no date), pp. 6–7. Nixon: Television address to the nation, August 8, 1969; reprinted in Daniel P. Moynihan, *The Politics of a Guaranteed Income* (New York: Random House, 1973), pp. 221–22. Carter: "Text of White House Message to Congress on Proposal to Overhaul Welfare System," *New York Times*, August 7, 1977. Lalonde: Canada, *Working Paper on Social Security in Canada* (Ottawa, April 1973), p. 3.

Notes to Preface

1
Marc Bloch, "Toward a Comparative History of European Societies," in *Enterprise and Secular Change: Readings in Economic History*, ed. Frederic C. Lane, (Homewood, Ill.: Richard D. Irwin, 1953).

Notes to Chapter 1

1
Nixon speech, August 8, 1969, quoted by Daniel Patrick Moynihan, *The Politics of a Guaranteed Income* (New York: Random House, 1973), p. 222.

2
"Text of White House Message," *New York Times*, August 7, 1977; also Paul Weaver, "Do the American People Know What They Want?" *Commentary* (December 1977): "When President Carter announced his proposals for reforming welfare policy last summer in Plains, reporters were quick to take note of a peculiar feature of his statement. Not once in the course of what he had to say did he use the phrase 'welfare reform.' . . . The casual listener would have been aware, instead, of a bold presidential initiative to abolish welfare once and for all and to replace it with something completely different. . ." (p. 62).

3
Canada, Department of National Health and Welfare, *Income Security for Canadians* (Ottawa, 1970), pp. 1, 3.

4
Speech from the Throne, *Commons Debates*, January 4, 1973, p. 5.

5
Canada, Department of National Health and Welfare, *Working Paper on Social Security in Canada* (April 1973), p. 3.

6
U.S., Department of Health, Education, and Welfare, National Center for Social

Statistics, Social and Rehabilitation Service, *Trend Report: Graphic Presentation of Public Assistance and Related Data, 1971* (October 6, 1972), pp. 3, 5; Cynthia Rence and Michael Wiseman, "The California Welfare Reform Act and Participation in AFDC," *Journal of Human Resources* 13, no. 1 (Winter 1978): 55.

7
Barbara Boland, "Participation in the Aid to Families with Dependent Children," in *The Family, Poverty, and Welfare Programs: Factors Influencing Family Stability*, U.S., Congress, Joint Economic Committee, 93rd Congress, 1st Session, Studies in Public Welfare, Paper No. 12, Part 1 (November 4, 1973).

8
Canada, Statistics Canada, *Social Security: 1976*, pp. 314–315.

9
Note also that after 1966 the aged were gradually removed from the social assistance rolls by the federal Guaranteed Income Supplements, a program that had no analog in the United States until 1974. See chapters 2 and 8.

10
HEW, *Trend Report*, p. 3; Statistics Canada, *Social Security: 1978*, p. 573. The Canadian figure for 1961 is obtained by adding Old Age Assistance, Unemployment Assistance, and Allowances for Blind and Disabled Persons. The 1971 figure is obtained by adding the small remnants of these programs to the numbers under the Canada Assistance Plan.

11
Federal-Provincial Conference of Ministers of Welfare, Federal-Provincial Working Group on Costs of Welfare Programs, *Final Report* (January 1971), p. 28.

12
Statistics Canada, *Social Security: 1978*, p. 573; U.S., Department of Health, Education, and Welfare, *Public Assistance Statistics* (March 1977), p. 16; cf. Richard Van Loon, "Reforming Welfare in Canada" *Public Policy* (forthcoming).

13
Working Group on Costs of Welfare Programs, *Final Report* (January 1971), table 2. Figures are for cash assistance administered by the provinces; HEW, *Trend Report*, p. 5.

14
These figures are calculated from Alfred M. Skolnik and Sophie Dales, "Social Welfare Expenditures, Fiscal Year 1976," *Social Security Bulletin* 40, no. 1 (January 1977): 6; and Statistics Canada, *Social Security: 1978*, table I-1. The Canadian figures are obtained by adding together CAP and its predecessor programs and do not include federally administered Guaranteed Income Supplements. The U.S. figures include spending under past programs of Aid to the Aged, Disabled, and Blind, but not after 1973, when these beneficiaries moved to the Supplemental Security Income program. The U.S. figures include the federal share of Medicaid payments.

15
Skolnik and Dales, "Social Welfare Expenditures," table 3; Statistics Canada, *Social Security: 1978*, pp. 28, 29, 31.

16
Phillips Cutright and John Scanzoni, "Income Supplements and the American Family," and Phillips Cutright, "Illegitimacy and Income Supplements," both in U.S., Congress, Joint Economic Committee, Studies in Public Welfare, Paper No. 12, part 2 (December 3, 1973).

17
Canada, Statistics Canada, *Perspective Canada* (1974), table 2.12. Census families are households in which there is either a child or a married couple. U.S., Bureau of the Census, *Characteristics of the Population*, vol. 1, part 1: *United States Summary*, section 1, tables 51, 59 (1975). Families are households with children.

18
In 1974 the U.S. divorce rate was 4.62 per thousand and in Canada it was 2.00 per thousand. United Nations, Department of Economic and Social Affairs, *Demographic Yearbook: 1975*, p. 428.

19
In 1970 the illegitimacy rates were 10.7 percent in the United States and 9.6 percent in Canada (U. N., *Demographic Yearbook: 1975*, pp. 758–759). The U.S. illegitimacy rate for 1976 was reported as 14.8 percent ("Illegitimate Birth Rate Was 14.8% in '76, U.S. Says," *New York Times*, May 6, 1978). Trends in western Canada are examined in *Public Attitudes toward Illegitimacy in Alberta* (Department of Health and Social Development, 1973), chap. 3.

20
Gilbert Steiner, *The State of Welfare* (Washington, D.C.: Brookings Institution, 1971), table 2; U.S., Department of Health, Education, and Welfare, *1975 Recipient Characteristics Study*, part 1, table 22.

21
Social Planning Council of Metropolitan Toronto, *Family Income Security Issues* (Toronto, February 1976), p. 40.

22
Federal-Provincial Conference of Ministers of Welfare, *The World of the Welfare Recipient* (January 1971), p. 8.

23
Canada, Department of National Health and Welfare, *Income Security for Canadians* (1970), p. 7; Ontario Community and Social Services, *Statistical Supplement: Forty-fifth Annual Report* (1976), p. 1; Québec, Ministère des Affaires Sociales, Statistiques des Affaires Sociales, *Sécurité du Revenue* 5, no. 3 (December 1977), p. 16.

24
Similar results for the United States were obtained in a 1974 poll: 22 percent too little; 32 percent about right; and 42 percent too much. Cited in Martin Anderson, *Welfare: The Political Economy of Welfare Reform in the United States* (Stanford, Calif.: Hoover Institution, 1978), p. 61. A similar poll in 1964 showed considerably less criticism of welfare spending: 25 percent too little; 47 percent about right; 26 percent too much. George Gallup, *The Gallup Poll* (New York City: Random House, 1972), vol. 3, p. 1920. The great increase in the decade after 1964 of those willing to criticize welfare spending is itself worth careful analysis.

25
U.S. poll cited in Anderson, *Welfare,* p. 61; Canadian poll reported in Canada, Manpower and Immigration, Strategic Planning and Research, *Canadian Work Values: Findings of a Work Ethic Survey and a Job Satisfaction Survey* (1975), pp. 17, 22.

26
Josette Laframboise, *A Question of Needs* (Ottawa: Canadian Council of Social Development, 1975), p. 386.

27
Poll reported in *Current Opinion,* 4 no. 5 (May 1976), p. 50.

28
Laframboise, *A Question of Needs,* pp. 391, 394–395.

29
Harris Survey, February 1976, reported in *Current Opinion* 4 no. 7 (July 1976): 66.

30
Robert Reinhold, "Public Found Hostile to Welfare As Idea But Backs What It Does," *New York Times,* August 3, 1977.

31
Gallup, *The Gallup Poll,* vol. 3, p. 1920.

32
Joe R. Feagin, *Subordinating the Poor* (Englewood Cliffs, N.J.: Prentice-Hall, 1975), p. 103.

33
Regional Research Institute in Social Welfare, University of Southern California, *Welfare Concepts and Welfare Services: Results of an Opinion Poll of Public Attitudes.* Cited in Natalie Jaffe, *Attitudes toward Public Welfare Programs and Recipients,* Welfare Policy Project (Durham, N.C.: Duke University and the Ford Foundation, 1976), p. 4.

34
Canadian Institute of Public Opinion, "Welfare Recipient Should Take Available Work—86%," *Gallup Report,* July 17, 1976; "Big Majority Agree Man on Relief Should Take on Any Work Available," *Gallup Report,* November 7, 1962.

35
Dave Margoshes, "Alberta Policy on Mother's Jobs Toughest in Canada, Survey Shows," *Calgary Herald,* April 8, 1978. Alberta opinion seems more extreme than that found in most states. A 1972 mailed survey found that 87.1 percent felt that "a person who is able to work but unemployed should take a job if it is outside of his normal skills, and different from any job he has ever done." (In Alberta 75.8 percent of the welfare recipients also agreed with this statement.) Similarly 53.7 percent of the voters agreed that "a person who is able to work but unemployed should have to take a job if the job is in another part of the province and far from his home." (A majority of welfare recipients disagreed with this.) Indeed a follow-up survey showed that a majority of Albertans felt that a person could be expected to leave the province if a job were available elsewhere [Alberta, Department of Health and Social Development, *Survey of Public Attitudes toward Public Assistance in Alberta* (1972), pt. 1, pp. 18, 20; pt. 2, p. C-10].

36
Gallup, *The Gallup Poll,* vol. 3, pp. 1919–1920; Jaffe, "Attitudes," p. 9.

37
Feagin, *Subordinating the Poor,* p. 103.

38
Harris Survey, February 1976, reported in *Current Opinion,* 4 no. 7 (July 1976): 66.

39
Research by John Williamson cited in Feagin, *Subordinating the Poor,* p. 107.

40
Laframboise, *A Question of Needs,* p. 353.

41
Alberta, Department of Health and Social Development, *Public Assistance (1972),* pt. 2, p. C-1.

42
Quoted in John Saywell, ed., *Canadian Annual Review of Politics and Public Affairs: 1972* (Toronto: University of Toronto Press, 1974) pp. 351–352.

43
Phillips Cutright, "Political Structure, Economic Development, and Social Security Programs," *American Journal of Sociology* 70, no. 5 (March 1965); Frederick Pryor, *Public Expenditures in Communist and Capitalist Nations* (New York: Irwin, 1968); see also Koji Taira and Peter Kilby, "Differences in Social Security Development in Selected Countries," *International Social Security Journal* 20, no. 2 (1969).

44
Harold Wilensky, *The Welfare State and Equality* (Berkeley and Los Angeles: University of California Press, 1975), chap. 3. See also Wilensky, *The New Cor-*

poratism, Centralization and the Welfare State, Sage Professional Papers in Contemporary Political Sociology (Beverly Hills, Calif.: Sage, 1976).

45
Edward Tufte, *Political Control of the Economy* (Princeton, N.J.: Princeton University Press, 1978), fig. 4–2. Between 1971 and 1976 Canadian and U.S. dollars were almost exactly equal in value, a convenience that allows welfare spending and benefit levels to be compared directly with no need to consider exchange rates.

46
U.S., Department of Commerce, Bureau of the Census, *Statistical Abstract of the U.S.: 1977,* table 1513.

47
Organization for Economic Cooperation and Development, *Public Expenditure on Income Maintenance Programmes,* Studies in Resource Allocation No. 3: (July 1976), tables 1, 2, 6, 15.

48
Canada, Department of National Health and Welfare, *Working Paper on Social Security in Canada* (April 1973), p. 57; Steiner, *The State of Welfare,* p. 78.

49
It might be argued that the U.S. figures are spoiled by small states whose benefits are excessively low. An examination of the six biggest AFDC states (which in 1973 had 47 percent of all AFDC recipients) supports this argument only somewhat. The states were, in diminishing order of benefits, Michigan, New York, Pennsylvania, California, Illinois, and Ohio. The 1974 unweighted average of their normal AFDC and food stamp benefits for a family of four was $4544, higher than the nationwide averages in both the United States and Canada. But variation within this group was still more than in Canada, from $5112 in Michigan to $3576 in Ohio (see table 1.5).

The text explains why state budget standards for basic needs are not a good indication of actual benefits under AFDC. Some data on these standards are provided here for comparison with the figures used in table 1.5. The average standard of need was $3640 in July 1974. This amount was only $414 less than the average amount that states paid in both AFDC and food stamps. Since food stamp spending is high, it is clear that many states pay less in AFDC benefits than the standard of need suggests. The range in standards of need is greater even than the variation in benefits actually paid. In 1974 the lowest standard was $2208 (North Carolina) and the highest was $5472 (Wisconsin). California, the largest jurisdiction, had a standard of $4160. A list of state standards of need and a description of how each state relates the standard of need to benefits is contained in U.S., Department of Health, Education, and Welfare, *Characteristics of State Plans for Aid to Families with Dependent Children, 1974* (and later editions), tables A and B.

50
Kirsten Gronbjerg, *Mass Society and the Extension of Welfare, 1960–70* (Chicago: University of Chicago Press, 1977), pp. 157, 23, 136.

51
Alexis de Tocqueville, *Democracy in America* (Garden City, N.Y.: Doubleday Anchor, 1969), p. 705. See also Richard Titmuss, *Social Policy* (New York: Atheneum, 1974).

52
Adam Przeworski and Henry Teune, *The Logic of Comparative Social Inquiry* (New York: Wiley, 1970), p. 32. See also Henry Teune, "A Logic of Comparative Policy Analysis," in *Comparing Public Policies: New Concepts and Methods*, ed. Douglas E. Ashford, Sage Yearbooks in Politics and Public Policy (Beverly Hills, Calif.: Sage, 1978).

53
See Arend Lijphart, "Comparative Politics and the Comparative Method," *American Political Science Review* 65, no. 3 (September 1971): 688–689.

54
A nearly definitive list includes the following: By U.S. authors: Louis Hartz, *The Liberal Tradition in America* (New York: Harcourt Brace, 1964); Everett Hughes, *The Sociological Eye: Selected Papers* (New York: Aldine, 1971); Leon Epstein, "A Comparative Study of Canadian Parties," *American Political Science Review* 58, no. 1 (March 1964); Seymour Martin Lipset, "Democracy in Alberta," *Canadian Forum* (November/December 1954); Lipset, *Political Man* (Garden City, N.Y.: Anchor, 1963); Lipset, *Revolution and Counterrevolution* (Garden City, N.Y.: Anchor, 1970); and Lipset, "Radicalism in North America: A Comparative View of the Party Systems in Canada and the United States," *Transactions of the Royal Society of Canada,* Series 4, vol. 14, 1976.

By Canadian authors: Frank Underhill, *In Search of Canadian Liberalism* (Toronto: MacMillan of Canada, 1960); S.D. Clark, *The Developing Canadian Community* (Toronto: University of Toronto Press, 1968); Gad Horowitz, *Canadian Labour in Politics* (Toronto: University of Toronto Press, 1968); Joseph Wearing, "President or Prime Minister," in *Apex of Power,* ed. Thomas A. Hockin (Scarborough, Ontario: Prentice-Hall of Canada, 1971); John L. Finlay, *Canada in the North Atlantic Triangle: Two Centuries of Social Change* (Toronto: Oxford University Press, 1975); and "Special Number on Cross-National Perspectives: United States and Canada," Robert Presthus, guest editor, *International Journal of Comparative Sociology,* 18, nos. 1–2 (March-June 1977).

55
S. A. Longstaff, "John Porter's 'Vertical Mosaic': A Critique and Some Reflections on the Canadian Scene," *Berkeley Journal of Sociology* 12, (Summer 1967).

56
See Spyros Andreopoulos et al., *National Health Insurance: Can We Learn from Canada?* (New York: Wiley, 1975), Theodore R. Marmor et al., "Comparative

Politics and Health Policies: Notes on Benefits, Costs, and Limits," in *Comparing Public Policies*; U.S., Department of Housing and Urban Development, jointly with Canada, Central Mortgage and Housing Corporation and Ministry of State for Urban Affairs, *Revitalizing North American Neighborhoods: A Comparison of Canadian and U.S. Programs for Neighborhood Preservation and Housing Rehabilitation* (October 1978); and Charles W. Howe, *Comparative Analysis and Critique of the Institutional Framework for Water Resources Planning and Management: Canada, United States, and Mexico*, completion report submitted to the U.S. Department of the Interior, Office of Water Research and Technology (October 1977).

57
Sidney Verba, "Some Dilemmas in Comparative Research," *World Politics* 20 (October 1967); Alexander George, "Case Studies and Theory Development: The Method of Structured, Focussed Comparison," in *Diplomatic History: New Approaches*, ed. Paul Gordon Lauren (New York: The Free Press, 1979); and Arend Lijphart, "The Comparable-Cases Strategy in Comparative Research," *Comparative Political Studies* (July 1975).

58
Verba, "Some Dilemmas," p. 115.

59
Stein Rokkan, *Citizens, Elections, Parties* (Oslo: Universitetsforlaget, 1970), p. 71.

60
Cited in Lipset, *Revolution and Counterrevolution*, p. 72.

61
Ibid., chap. 2; Gad Horowitz, *Canadian Labour in Politics*, chap. 1; and Horowitz, "Notes on 'Conservatism, Liberalism, and Socialism in Canada,'" *Canadian Journal of Political Science* 11, no. 2 (June 1978).

62
See Lloyd Musolf, *Public Ownership and Accountability: The Canadian Experience* (Cambridge, Mass.: Harvard University Press, 1959), and William Christian and Colin Campbell, *Political Parties and Ideologies in Canada* (Toronto: McGraw Hill-Ryerson, 1974).

63
Christian and Campbell, *Political Parties and Ideologies in Canada*, p. 154.

64
Lipset, "Radicalism in North America."

65
Donald V. Smiley, *Canada in Question*, 2d ed. (Toronto: McGraw Hill–Ryerson, 1976), pp. 207–209; Daniel J. Elazar, *American Federalism: A View from the States* (New York: Crowell, 1972), pp. 158–161.

66
See Epstein, "A Comparative Study of Canadian Parties."

67
E. E. Schattschneider, *Party Government* (New York: Rinehart, 1942), p. 140.

68
F. C. Engelman and M. A. Schwartz, *Canadian Political Parties: Origin, Character, Impact* (Scarborough, Ontario: Prentice-Hall of Canada, 1975), p. 54.

69
Lipset, "Democracy in Alberta," p. 198.

70
Epstein, "A Comparative Study of Canadian Parties," p. 59.

71
Richard B. Simeon, *Federal-Provincial Diplomacy* (Toronto: University of Toronto Press, 1973), chap. 2.

72
I regret that editorial convention does not permit me in the text to use an accent as is done in French: Québec.

73
Smiley, *Canada in Question,* chaps. 1, 5.

74
Canadian Federation of Mayors and Municipalities, *Puppets on a Shoestring: The Effects on Municipal Government of Canada's System of Public Finance* (Ottawa, 1976).

75
On U.S. revenue sharing, see Richard Nathan et al., *Monitoring Revenue Sharing* (Washington, D.C.: Brookings Institution, 1975), and *Revenue Sharing: The Second Round* (Washington, D.C.: Brookings Institution, 1977); on Canadian fiscal federalism, see Advisory Commission on Intergovernmental Relations, *In Search of Balance: Canada's Intergovernmental Experience* (Washington, D.C., 1971) and Smiley, *Canada in Question,* chap. 5. In 1978 it became apparent that Ontario might for the first time qualify for an equalization payment.

76
Statistics Canada, *Social Security: 1978,* p. 576

Notes to Chapter 2

1
For a comparison of these two patterns of development as reflected in old age policy, see Christopher Leman, "Patterns of Policy Development: Social Security in the U.S. and Canada," *Public Policy* 25, no. 2 (Spring 1977).

2
Good historical sources on Canada: Donald Bellamy, "Social Welfare in Canada," in *Encyclopedia of Social Work,* 15th ed., (New York: National Association of Social Workers, 1965); Terry Copp, *The Anatomy of Poverty: The Condi-*

Notes to pp. 23–26

tion of the Working Class in Montreal, 1897–1929 (Toronto: McClelland and Stewart, 1974); and Richard B. Splane, *Social Welfare in Ontario, 1791–1893: A Study of Public Welfare Administration* (Toronto: University of Toronto Press, 1965).

On the U.S.: Josephine Brown, *Public Relief, 1929–39* (New York: Henry Holt, 1940); Blanche Coll, "Public Assistance in the United States: Colonial Times to 1860," in *Comparative Development in Social Welfare*, ed., E. W. Martin (London: George Allen and Unwin, 1972); Benjamin Klebaner, *Public Poor Relief in America: 1790–1860* (New York: Arno Press, 1976); David Rothman, *The Discovery of the Asylum: Social Order and Disorder in the New Republic* (Boston: Little, Brown, 1971); Walter Trattner, *From Poor Law to Welfare State* (Glencoe: Free Press, 1974).

3
Richard Splane, "Keynote Speech," Conference on Welfare Appeal Systems (Ottawa, November 1976), reprinted in Canada, Health and Welfare Canada, *Welfare Appeals Workshop* (April 1978).

4
Interestingly, the movement to provide differential care for the mentally ill, spearheaded by Dorothea Dix, nearly produced in the United States a national social program in the middle of the nineteenth century. A bill giving land grants to the states for the founding of mental hospitals was passed in 1854 by both houses of Congress but vetoed by President Franklin Pierce.

5
Canada, Department of Health, Division of Child Welfare, *Child Welfare Work in Canada* (1923); J. Stefan Dupré, *Intergovernmental Finance in Ontario: A Provincial-Local Perspective* (a study prepared for the Ontario Committee on Taxation); and Brown, *Public Relief*. On the minimum wage, see Sylvia Ostry and Mahmood A. Zaidi, *Labour Economics in Canada*, 2nd ed. (Toronto: Macmillan of Canada, 1973), pp. 257–263.

6
Statistics are based on Statistics Canada, *Canada Yearbook: 1975*, p. 771, and Alfred M. Skolnik and Sophie Dales, "Social Welfare Expenditures, Fiscal Year 1976," *Social Security Bulletin* 40, no. 1 (January 1977), table 1. On veterans' programs in general, see Statistics Canada, *Social Security: 1978*, chap. 3-A; Canada, Department of Veterans Affairs, *Veterans Canada: Annual Report, 1974–75*, pp. 12, 14, and passim; and Sar Levitan et al., *Old Wars Remain Unfinished* (Baltimore, Md.: Johns Hopkins University Press, 1973).

7
Statistics Canada, *Social Security: 1978*, pp. 635, 645; Levitan, *Programs in Aid of the Poor*, p. 127; Sar Levitan et al., *Indian Giving* (Baltimore, Md.: Johns Hopkins, 1975), p. 63.

8
U.S., Federal Works Agency, Work Projects Administration, *Final Statistical Report of the Federal Emergency Relief Administration*, 1942 (New York: DaCapo Press Reprint, 1972), pp. 7, 10, 17–18, 29, 78, 102–103.

9
Frances Fox Piven and Richard A. Cloward, *Regulating the Poor: The Functions of Public Welfare* (New York: Vintage, 1971), p. 98.

10
Ibid. pp. 114–115.

11
Edwin E. Witte, *The Development of the Social Security Act* (Madison, Wis.: University of Wisconsin Press, 1962), p. 164.

12
Gilbert Steiner, *Social Insecurity* (Chicago: Rand McNally, 1966), p. 21.

13
See Leman, "Patterns of Policy Development."

14
Arthur J. Altmeyer, *The Formative Years of Social Security* (Madison, Wis.: University of Wisconsin, 1968), pp. 180, 187.

15
Steiner, *Social Insecurity*, chap. 3.

16
Ibid., p. 70.

17
Vincent and Vee Burke, *Nixon's Good Deed: Welfare Reform* (New York: Columbia University Press, 1974), p. 27.

18
For an excellent account of the civil rights movement, see Frances Fox Piven and Richard Cloward, *Poor People's Movements* (New York: Pantheon, 1977), chap. 4; on the War on Poverty, see James Sundquist, *Politics and Policy* (Washington, D.C.: Brookings Institution, 1968), chap. 4, and Mark R. Arnold, "The Good War That Might Have Been," *New York Times Magazine,* September 29, 1974.

19
Timothy Matthews, "Food Stamps: Outline" (ms., 1976), p. 1. For an important study of the Food Stamp program, see Timothy Matthews, "The Microeconomics of the Food Stamp Program," B.A. thesis, Harvard College, March 1978.

20
Nick Kotz, *Let Them Eat Promises: The Politics of Hunger in America* (Garden City, N.Y.: Doubleday Anchor, 1969), p. 65.

21
See Steiner, *The State of Welfare*, p. 209; and Mark Worthington, "The Budget Process of the Food Stamp Program: An Historical Analysis" (ms., 1976), p. 6.

22
Steiner, *The State of Welfare*, p. 213; see Paul Wellstone, *How the Rural Poor Got Power* (Amherst, Mass.: University of Massachusetts Press, 1978), pp. 10–17.

23
On this and subsequent episodes in old age pension politics, see Kenneth Bryden, *Old Age Pensions and Policy-Making in Canada* (Montréal: McGill/Queens University Press, 1974).

24
On Canadian public finance during the depression, see *The Rowell/Sirois Report*, book 1, ed. Donald Smiley, Carleton Library No. 5 (Toronto: McClelland and Stewart, 1963), chap. 6; and Dupré, *Intergovernmental Finance in Ontario*, pp. 17–19.

25
This outcome is difficult to square with the view of Piven and Cloward that public assistance programs in the United States might not exist at all were they not seen as necessary to head off possible unrest and as a more restrictive means of dealing with this unrest than emergency relief (Piven and Cloward, *Regulating the Poor*, pp. 141–147). The Great Depression was at least as bad in Canada as in the United States, with equally serious riots and other disturbances; and yet no permanent federal role in public assistance emerged in Canada from the conflagration.

26
On the Bennett "New Deal" see Alvin Finkel, "Origins of the Welfare State in Canada," in *The Canadian State: Political Economy and Political Power*, ed. Leo Panitch (Toronto: University of Toronto Press, 1977), chap. 12.

27
John Morgan: "An Emerging System of Income Maintenance: Canada in Transition," in *Social Security in International Perspective*, ed. Shirley Jenkins (New York: Columbia University Press, 1969), p. 117. I owe this reference to Robert Kudrle and Theodore Marmor, "The Development of the North American Welfare State," in *The Development of Welfare States in Europe and America*, ed. Peter Flora and Arnold Heidenheimer (New Brunswick, N.J.: Transaction Press, forthcoming), chap. 3.

28
Canada, Department of National Health and Welfare, Research and Statistics Division, *Government Expenditures on Health and Social Welfare in Canada: 1927 to 1959*, Social Security Series Memorandum No. 16 (December 1961), p. 24; Advisory Commission on Intergovernmental Relations, *In Search of Balance: Canada's Intergovernmental Experience*, ACIR Report M-68 (September 1971), p. 35.

29
Canada Assistance Plan, 1966–67, c. 45, s. 1., p. 713.

30
Statement by the Prime Minister, *Commons Debates,* April 6, 1965, p. 40.

31
Rand Dyck, "The Canada Assistance Plan: The Ultimate in Cooperative Federalism," *Journal of the Institute of Public Administration in Canada* 19, no. 4 (Winter 1976): 597–598. This article provides an excellent account of the passage of CAP.

32
Canada, *Income Security and Social Services: Working Paper on the Constitution,* 1970, p. 120.

33
Text of *Memorandum of Agreement made pursuant to Part I of the Canada Assistance Plan* (Health and Welfare Canada).

34
Commons Debates, July 5, 1966 (Allen MacEachen, Minister of National Health and Welfare).

35
Claude Morin, *Québec versus Ottawa: The Struggle for Self-Government 1960–72,* (Toronto: University of Toronto Press, 1976), p. 14. Morin was Quebec's deputy minister of intergovernmental affairs when CAP was established, and later minister of intergovernmental affairs in the Parti Québecois government elected in 1976.

36
See Leman, "Patterns of Policy Development."

37
See John E. Osborne, "Canada Combats Poverty through Social Policy," *Public Welfare* 24, no. 2 (April 1966) and Dyck, "The Canada Assistance Plan," p. 590. Manpower issues during the period are discussed in J. Stefan Dupré, David Cameron, Graeme H. McKechnie, and Theodore B. Rotenberg, *Federalism and Policy Development: The Case of Adult Occupational Training in Ontario* (Toronto: University of Toronto Press, 1973).

38
Canada, Department of Health and Welfare, Policy Research and Long-Range Planning (Welfare), *The Distribution of Income in Canada: Concepts, Measures, and Issues,* Social Security Research Reports No. 4 (March 1977), fig. 7.2; Laurence Lynn, Jr., "A Decade of Policy Developments in the Income-Maintenance System" in *A Decade of Federal Antipoverty Programs,* ed. Robert Haveman (New York: Academic Press, 1977), table 3.6.

39
See Organization for Economic Cooperation and Development, *Public Expenditure on Income Maintenance Programmes,* Studies in Resource Allocation No. 3, (July 1976), pp. 64–67.

40
See Mollie Orshansky, U.S. Office of Research and Statistics, Social Security Administration, "Memorandum for Dr. Daniel P. Moynihan, Subject: History of the Poverty Line" (July 1, 1970); and Israel Putnam, "Poverty Thresholds: Their History and Future Development," both in Report of the Poverty Studies Task Force, Federal Interagency Committee on Education, The Measure of Poverty: Technical Paper 1: *Documentation of Background Information and Rationale for Current Poverty Matrix.* See also Orshansky, "Counting the Poor," *Social Security Bulletin* 28, no. 1 (January 1965).

41
Canada, Department of National Health and Welfare, Social Security Series Memorandum 19. *The Measurement of Poverty* (1970). See also "Development of a New Poverty Line," in *Poverty in Canada,* Report of the Special Senate Committee (1971), appendix.

42
See Statistics Canada, "Revision of Low Income Cut-offs" (December 17, 1973). The Canadian figure is for a family living in a city with population of 100,000–500,000, while the U.S. figure is for a nonfarm family. Canada now has five different cutoffs for locations of different size. The United States distinguishes between farm and nonfarm families and also now between male-headed and female-headed families. The U.S. lines mentioned in the text are usually nonfarm and an average of the male-headed and female-headed levels.

43
See, for example, U.S., Bureau of the Census, *Statistical Abstract of the U.S.: 1977,* tables 733, 736.

44
Lee Rainwater, "Economic Inequality and the Credit Income Tax," *Working Papers for a New Society* 1, no. 1 (Spring 1973).

45
Canadian Council for Social Development, *Income Supplements for the Working Poor,* proceedings of a conference held April 8–9, 1974 (Ottawa, 1974), p. 159; U.S., Bureau of the Census, *Statistical Abstract of the U.S.: 1977,* table 664.

46
See also Federal-Provincial Conference of Ministers of Welfare, *Background Paper on Income Support and Supplementation* (February 1975), table 7.

47
For background see U.S., Bureau of Labor Statistics, Department of Labor, "Family Budgets," in *Handbook of Methods,* chap. 12; Bureau of Labor Statistics, De-

partment of Labor, *Three Standards of Living for an Urban Family of Four Persons* (Spring 1967); and Poverty Studies Task Force, Federal Interagency Committee on Education, The Measure of Poverty, Technical Paper 4: *Bureau of Labor Statistics Family Budgets Program.*

48
Canada, Department of National Health and Welfare, Policy Research and Long-Range Planning (Welfare) *The Distribution of Income in Canada: Concepts, Measures, and Issues,* Social Security Research Reports No. 4 (March 1977), p. 21n. A description of how the different poverty lines are calculated appears in *Canadian Fact Book on Poverty,* by David Ross (Ottawa: Canadian Council on Social Development, 1975). See also Ian Adams et al., *The Real Poverty Report* (Edmonton: M.G. Hurtig, 1971), chap. 1.

49
A good summary of the U.S. debate over poverty lines appears in Henry Aaron, *Politics and the Professors* (Washington, D.C.: Brookings Institution, 1978), pp. 37–41; on Canada, see Roger Love and Gail Oja, "Low Income in Canada," in Statistics Canada, *Review of Income and Wealth,* Income and Wealth Series No. 1 (March 1977).

50
See, for example, Roger Love and Michael C. Wolfson, *Income Inequality: Statistical Methodology and Canadian Illustrations* (Statistics Canada, 1976); Health and Welfare Canada, *The Distribution of Income in Canada* (1977); and W. Irwin Gillespie, *In Search of Robin Hood: The Effect of Federal Budgetary Policies during the 1970s on the Distribution of Income in Canada* (Montréal: C. D. Howe Research Institute, 1978); and D.A. Armstrong, P.H. Friesen, and D. Miller, "The Measurement of Income Distribution in Canada: Some Problems and Some Tentative Data," *Canadian Public Policy* 3, no. 4 (Autumn 1977).

51
See Timothy M. Smeeding, "The Antipoverty Effectiveness of In-Kind Transfers," *Journal of Human Resources* 12, no. 3 (Summer 1977); Laurence Lynn, "A Decade of Policy Developments in the Income-Maintenance System," in *A Decade of Federal Anti-Poverty Programs,* pp. 92–96; U.S., Congressional Budget Office, *Poverty Status under Alternative Definitions of Income* (July 1977); Harry Schwartz, "Is Poverty Abolished?" *New York Times,* October 19, 1976, p. 39. But see Michael Harrington, "Hiding the Other America," *New Republic,* February 26, 1977.

52
See Smeeding, "The Antipoverty Effectiveness"; and Morton Paglin, "Poverty in the United States: A Reevaluation," *Policy Review* (Spring 1979). Paglin's article is drawn from his book, *Poverty and Transfers in Kind* (Stanford, Calif.: Hoover Institution Press, forthcoming).

Notes to pp. 48–49

53
Michael C. Barth, George J. Carcagno, and John L. Palmer, *Toward an Effective Income Support System* (Madison, Wis.: Institute for Research on Poverty, 1974), table 4; Social Planning Council of Metropolitan Toronto, *Family Income Security Issues* (February 1976), p. 12. As usual, the limitations of data in each country prohibit a more exact comparison.

54
Barth, Carcagno, and Palmer, *Income Support System,* table 4.

55
The available Canadian data do not allow an estimate of the proportion of nonwelfare poor who receive some benefits. See Health and Welfare Canada, Policy Research and Long-Range Planning (Welfare) Research Report No. 01, *Characteristics of the Working Poor in Canada* (September 1976), pp. 11–18.

56
See Aaron, *Politics and the Professors,* p. 37 and passim; Richard Coe, "The Poverty Line: Its Function and Limitations," *Public Welfare* 36, no. 1, (Winter 1978); Love and Oja, "Low Income in Canada."

57
U.S., Department of Health, Education, and Welfare, *The Changing Economic Status of Five Thousand American Families: Highlights from the Panel Study of Income Dynamics* (May 1974), p. 15. A Canadian study has suggested that turnover is as great in that country. Of those families with low income in either 1968 or 1969, fully 42 percent did not have a low income in the other year (Love and Oja, "Low Income in Canada," p. 44).

58
Joseph Schumpeter, *Imperialism and Social Classes* (New York: Meridian, 1971), p. 126.

59
Martin Rein and Lee Rainwater, *The Welfare Class and Welfare Reform,* Family Policy Note No. 4 (Cambridge, Mass.: Joint Center for Urban Studies, February 1977).

60
Federal-Provincial Conference of Ministers on Welfare, *The World of the Welfare Recipient* (1971), p. 113.

61
On Canada, see Love and Oja, "Low Income in Canada," pp. 44–47. On the United States see HEW, *The Changing Economic Status of Five Thousand American Families,* and Coe, "The Poverty Line." Whereas blacks accounted for 41.3 percent of poor U.S. individuals, they were 77.0 percent of persistently poor individuals (Coe, p. 35).

62
John Kenneth Galbraith, *The Affluent Society* 3rd ed. rev. (Boston: Houghton Mifflin, 1976), p. 249.

63
Newfoundland had 12.2 percent of its population on relief in 1976; seven major U.S. cities had more than 10 percent on AFDC, the highest being Baltimore at 15.6 percent. Statistics Canada, *Social Security: 1978*, p. 576; HEW, *Public Assistance Statistics*, March 1977, pp. 2–3; and Toby H. Campbell and Marc Bendick, *A Public Assistance Data Book* (Washington, D.C.: Urban Institute, 1977), pp. 13–14.

64
Michael Lipsky, *Protest in City Politics: Rent Strikes, Housing, and the Power of the Poor* (Chicago: Rand-McNally, 1970); Frances Fox Piven and Richard Cloward, *Poor People's Movements: Why They Succeed, How They Fail* (New York: Pantheon, 1977).

65
See Sidney Verba and Norman Nie, *Participation in America: Political Democracy and Social Equality* (New York: Harper and Row, 1972), p. 97. Interestingly, this quiescence is relative to each society rather than being the same cross-nationally. Thus in a 1970 survey 64 percent of Canadian welfare recipients said they had voted in the last federal election—a much higher turnout than for all voters in U.S. presidential elections. However, the Canadian poor are still at a relative disadvantage because the average turnout by all Canadians in federal elections is at least 70 percent [Federal-Provincial Conference of Ministers of Welfare, *The World of the Welfare Recipient* (1971), p. 45].

66
See Wellstone, *How the Rural Poor Got Power*; Hope Hughes Pressman, *A New Resource for Welfare Reform: The Poor Themselves* (Berkeley, Calif.: Institute of Governmental Studies, 1975); Leonard Freedman, *Public Housing: The Politics of Poverty* (New York: Holt, Rinehart, 1969).

67
For a sympathetic but critical study of NWRO by two scholars who inspired Wiley to found the organization and kept in close touch with him during its short history, see Piven and Cloward, *Poor People's Movements*, chap. 5.

Notes to Chapter 3

1
Polls listed in Hazel Erskine, "The Polls: Government Role in Welfare," *Public Opinion Quarterly* 39, no. 2 (Summer 1975).

2
Cited in Daniel P. Moynihan, *The Politics of a Guaranteed Income* (New York: Random House, 1973), p. 224.

3
See especially Leonard Hausman, "Cumulative Tax Rates in Alternative Income Maintenance Systems," in *Integrating Income Maintenance Programs*, ed. Irene Lurie (New York: Academic Press, 1975), pp. 42–43.

4
This means of constructing a low reduction rate on the basis of benefits that fall far below the standard of need allowed some states to include negative income tax rates years before the 1967 WIN amendments.

5
Robert Lampman, "Scaling Welfare Benefits to Income," *Policy Analysis* 1 (1975): 3.

6
For good discussions of these issues see U.S., Congress, Joint Economic Committee, *Welfare in the Seventies: A National Study of Benefits Available in One Hundred Local Areas*, Studies in Public Welfare, Paper No. 15, 93d Congress 2d Session (July 22, 1974); Hausman, "Cumulative Tax Rates"; Lampman, "Scaling Welfare Benefits to Income."

7
Rand Corporation, *Multiple Welfare Benefits in New York City*, cited in *HEW, 1977 Welfare Reform Study*, paper no. 4: *Critical Analysis of the Welfare System*, p. 4; Joint Economic Committee, *Welfare in the Seventies*, pp. 6–7.

8
U.S., Department of Health, Education, and Welfare, Office of Assistant Secretary for Planning and Evaluation, *Summary Report: Seattle-Denver Income Maintenance Experiment* (February 1978), table 3.

9
For criticisms of the income maintenance experiments, see Henry Aaron, "Cautionary Notes on the Experiment," in *Work Incentives and Income Guarantees: The New Jersey Negative Income Tax Experiment*, ed. Joseph A. Pechman and P. Michael Timpane (Washington, D.C.: Brookings Institution, 1975); and Martin Anderson, *Welfare: The Political Economy of Welfare Reform in the United States* (Stanford, Calif.: Hoover Institution, 1978), chap. 5.

10
U.S., Department of Health, Education, and Welfare, *Findings of the 1973 AFDC Study*, part 1, table 31; Federal-Provincial Conference of Ministers of Welfare, *The World of the Welfare Recipient* (1971), p. 13.

11
For a summary of research on WIN and other programs, see Leonard Goodwin, *The Work Incentive (WIN) Program and Related Experiences* (Department of Labor, 1977); and Maureen O'Neil and Pearl Downie, "Assessment of Employment Availability for the Support/Supplementation System" (Health and Welfare Canada, unpublished, May 1976).

12

Economic Council of Canada, *Fifth Annual Review: The Challenge of Growth and Change* (Ottawa: Queen's Printer, 1968), pp. 127, 113, 136.

13

Kenneth Bryden, *Old Age Pensions and Policy-Making in Canada* (Toronto: McGill-Queens University Press, 1974), pp. 153–154.

14

Canada, Senate, Special Committee on Poverty, *Poverty in Canada* (1971), pp. 219, xxviii, xxx.

15

Kevin Collins, "Three Decades of Social Security in Canada," *Canadian Welfare* 51, no. 1 (January/February 1976), p. 7.

16

Alan Brudner, "Guaranteed Income Project May be Accepted—But Will It Solve Welfare Problem?" *Financial Post*, May 16, 1970.

17

S. E. Gordon, "Like It or Not, Here Comes Guaranteed Income," *Financial Post*, September 8, 1973.

18

Canada, *Income Security for Canadians* (1970), pp. 2–3.

19

W. Irwin Gillespie, *In Search of Robin Hood* (Montréal: C. D. Howe Research Institute, 1978), pp. 7–8.

20

Canada, *Income Security for Canadians*, p. 38.

21

For accounts of this period, see Peter Desbarats, *René* (Toronto: McClelland and Stewart, 1977); Peter Newman, *The Distemper of Our Times* (Toronto: McClelland and Stewart, 1978); Claude Morin, *Québec versus Ottawa: The Struggle for Self-Government 1960–72* (Toronto: University of Toronto Press, 1976); Jean Provencher, *René Lévesque* (Markham, Ontario: Paperjacks, 1977); John Saywell, *The Rise of the Parti Québecois* (Toronto: University of Toronto Press, 1977); Richard Simeon, *Federal-Provincial Diplomacy* (Toronto: University of Toronto Press, 1973).

22

Canada, *Income Security and Social Services: Working Paper on the Constitution* (1970), pp. 54f.

23

Quebec, *Income Security*, report of the Commission of Inquiry on Health and Social Welfare (1971), vol. 5, pt. 3.

Notes to pp. 63–67

24
Morin, *Québec versus Ottawa,* p. 63.

25
Simeon, *Federal-Provincial Diplomacy,* p. 116.

26
Morin, *Québec versus Ottawa,* p. 64.

27
Ian Rodger, "By Winning Family Allowance Fight, Ottawa Might Undermine Bourassa," *Financial Post,* January 15, 1972; "Québec and Social Policy," in *Canadian Annual Review of Politics and Public Affairs: 1972* ed. John Saywell (Toronto: University of Toronto Press, 1974), pp. 93ff.

28
Figures are from Leonard Shifrin, "The Politics of Income Security," in *Family Income Security Issues* (Social Planning Council of Metropolitan Toronto, 1976), p. 59.

29
"Welfare and Unemployment Insurance," in *Canadian Annual Review: 1972,* p. 351.

30
Ibid., pp. 351–352.

31
"Welfare Living Is under Fire: Terms Like Sponge Reappear," *Canada Month* (July 1971): 7; *Canadian Annual Review: 1972,* pp. 351–352; John Saywell, *Canadian Annual Review of Politics and Public Affairs: 1971,* ed. John Saywell, p. 365.

32
On the 1972 election, see *Canadian Annual Review: 1972;* and John Meisel, "Howe, Hubris, and '72: An Essay on Political Elitism," in *Working Papers on Canadian Politics* (enlarged edition), ed. John Meisel, (Montreal: McGill-Queen's University Press, 1973), chap. 5.

33
Canadian Annual Review: 1972, pp. 76, 58, 352, 357, 348.

34
"Québec and Social Policy," pp. 103–104.

35
Canada, *Commons Debates,* January 4, 1973, pp. 4–5.

36
Canada, *Working Paper on Social Security in Canada* (April 1973), p. 37.

37
Ibid., p. 32.

38
Quebec, *Income Security*, pp. 259–264, 273–274.
39
Canada, *Working Paper on Social Security in Canada*, pp. 30, 32.
40
R. J. Van Loon, "Reforming Welfare in Canada: The Case of the Social Security Review," *Public Policy* (forthcoming).
41
Hugh McIntyre, "Ottawa Provides $5 Million for GAI Pilot Projects," *Financial Post*, November 20, 1971. Final Agreement on the Manitoba experiment was not reached until February 1974, and it actually began in January 1975.
42
Brudner, "Guaranteed Income Project," *Financial Post*, May 16, 1970.
43
Claude Morin argued that the federal government had used this strategy repeatedly. See Morin, *Québec versus Ottawa*, pp. 8, 24, 50, 64.
44
Quebec, *Income Security*, p. 273; T. R. Robinson, "Alternative Approaches to Income Supplementation," Paper presented to the Canadian Council on Social Development Conference on Income Supplementation (April 1973), p. 15; Van Loon, "Reforming Welfare in Canada," p. 14.
45
In 1978 the Policy Research and Long-Range Planning Branch (Welfare) was integrated with its health counterpart and was renamed the Policy Research and Strategic Planning Branch. Robinson left and was succeeded by E. M. Murphy.
46
As of October 1977 the Policy Research and Long Range Planning Branch (Welfare) had a staff of eighty-two, of whom forty had some education beyond college. Specialties were economics (twenty); mathematics, computing science, statistics (nineteen); sociology, demography (fifteen); and others.
47
Gilbert Steiner, *The State of Welfare* (Washington, D.C.: Brookings Institution, 1971) p. 119n; Bill Cavala and Aaron Wildavsky, "The Political Feasibility of Income by Right," *Public Policy* 18, no. 2 (Spring 1970).
48
See Steiner, *The State of Welfare*, p. 48.
49
Vincent and Vee Burke, *Nixon's Good Deed: Welfare Reform* (New York: Columbia University Press, 1974), pp. 35–36.

Notes to pp. 73-79

50
Nick Kotz, *Let Them Eat Promises: The Politics of Hunger in America* (Garden City, N.Y.: Doubleday Anchor Books, 1969), pp. 212ff.

51
Burke and Burke, *Nixon's Good Deed*, pp. 116ff.

52
Robert Levine, "How and Why the Experiment Came About," in *Work Incentives and Income Guarantees: The New Jersey Negative Income Tax Experiment*, ed. Joseph A. Pechman and P. Michael Timpane (Washington, D.C.: Brookings Institution, 1975), p. 21 and passim.

53
Kenneth Bowler, *The Nixon Guaranteed Income Proposal* (Cambridge, Mass.: Ballinger, 1974), pp. 44, 42. For inside accounts of this and other steps in the emergence of FAP, see "Family Assistance Program," Kennedy School of Government case program, Harvard University (two parts, 1977).

54
Ibid., p. 47; Burke and Burke, *Nixon's Good Deed*, pp. 53-63.

55
Rowland Evans, Jr., and Robert D. Novak, *Nixon in the White House: The Frustration of Power* (New York: Vintage, 1972), pp. 228-230.

56
Quoted in Burke and Burke, *Nixon's Good Deed*, p. 82.

57
Theodore Marmor and Martin Rein, "Reforming the 'Welfare Mess': The Fate of the Family Assistance Plan, 1969-72," in *Policy and Politics in America: Six Case Studies*, ed. Alan Sindler (Boston: Little, Brown, 1973), pp. 14-15; Burke and Burke, *Nixon's Good Deed*, pp. 92-93.

Notes to Chapter 4

1
Except for New York City and a few others, the cities had no responsibility for welfare programs and largely ignored the issue of welfare reform in the 1970s.

2
John Iglehart and Dom Bonafede, "Welfare Report/Nixon's Family Assistance Plan Faces Showdown on Senate Floor," *National Journal*, December 5, 1970, pp. 2636-2640.

3
Vincent and Vee Burke, *Nixon's Good Deed: Welfare Reform* (New York: Columbia University Press, 1974), p. 159.

4
See Walter Williams, "The Continuing Struggle for a Negative Income Tax: A Review Article," *Journal of Human Resources* 10, no. 4 (Fall 1975): 435–437. See also Leonard Hausman, "The Politics of a Guaranteed Income," *Journal of Human Resources* 8, no. 4 (Fall 1973): 414–417.

5
In sixteen states 15 percent of the population would receive benefits. In five it was 20 percent or more. In four states the welfare rolls would be more than quadrupled. Some of the committee's charts are reproduced in Daniel P. Moynihan, *The Politics of a Guaranteed Income* (New York: Random House, 1973) pp. 501ff.

6
Ibid., pp. 518, 525.

7
Moynihan reports that in September 1970 he and Senator Hugh Scott (Republican, Pennsylvania), the minority leader, estimated that only twenty-one of forty-three Republicans could be counted on to support it, while forty-one of fifty-seven Democrats would do so (ibid., p. 525).

8
For accounts of this episode, see ibid., p. 532; and Nick and Mary Lynn Kotz, *A Passion for Equality* (New York: Norton, 1977), pp. 269–270.

9
Moynihan, *Politics of a Guaranteed Income,* p. 533; Frances Fox Piven and Richard Cloward, *Poor People's Movements, Why They Succeed, How They Fail* (New York: Pantheon, 1977), p. 346.

10
For the details of the compromise, see Moynihan, *Politics of a Guaranteed Income,* pp. 536–538; Burke and Burke, *Nixon's Good Deed,* p. 178n.

11
John K. Iglehart, "Hunger Report/Rush-Hour Food Stamp Compromise Portends Fresh Quarrel in New Congress," *National Journal,* January 16, 1971, p. 113.

12
An excellent account of Mills' views and the Ways and Means Committee's deliberations is given by Kenneth Bowler in *The Nixon Guaranteed Income Proposal* (Cambridge, Mass.: Ballinger, 1974), pp. 71–117.

13
In April 1971 Nixon gave his bedpan speech to a Republican governors' conference, when he asserted that people should take "whatever work is available," no matter how menial.

14
See Leonard Hausman, "The Politics of a Guaranteed Income," pp. 413–414.

15
Burke and Burke, *Nixon's Good Deed,* p. 166.

16
Jodie Allen, *A Funny Thing Happened on the Way to Welfare Reform* (Washington, D.C.: Urban Institute, 1972), p. 17.

17
National Welfare Rights Organization, "$6500 Now!: The NWRO Adequate Income Plan," reprinted in Timothy Sampson, *Welfare: A Handbook for Friend or Foe* (Philadelphia: United Church Press, 1972).

18
Kotz and Kotz, *A Passion for Equality,* pp. 272–275.

19
Bowler, *Nixon Guaranteed Income Proposal,* pp. 98–99, 117–122.

20
Abraham Ribicoff, "He Left at Half Time," *New Republic* (February 17, 1973), p. 25.

21
Bowler, *Nixon Guaranteed Income Proposal,* p. 148.

22
Quoted in ibid., p. 149. A similar incident occurred in June 1972, when a benefit increase under OASDI (Old Age Insurance) was separated from HR 1 and passed separately by both houses. Indeed a number of the bill's sweeteners were gradually removed, leaving welfare reform for Congress to sour on.

23
On this period, see Dan Rather and Gary Paul Gates, *The Palace Guard* (New York: Warner Paperback, 1975), pp. 202–205. As early as January 1971 an internal White House memorandum had asked, "Can one seriously imagine those little old ladies in tennis shoes ringing doorbells in Muncie for FAP. . . ?" [quoted in William Safire, *Before the Fall* (New York: Belmont Tower Books, 1975), p. 545].

24
U.S., Senate, Committee on Finance, *Social Security Amendments of 1972,* Senate Report No. 92-1230 (report to accompany HR 1), 92nd Congress, 2d Session, September 26, 1972, chaps. 7, 9. An interview with Senator Long reflected his philosophy: "I live in the Watergate complex on the Potomac. . . . Once a day, I try to go out and take a walk. As I go along, I pick up beer cans, soft drink cans, bottles, paper cups that people are throwing on the ground. Sometimes I go around there in the evening and see some of these people sitting around there fishing or just loafing or sleeping on the grass. . . . Many of these people are drawing welfare checks. . . . Now, why can't you put some of these people who are enjoying the welfare money to work doing some of these things?" (*National Journal,* August 5, 1972, p. 1253). Other remarks by Long are conveniently col-

lected in Leonard Goodwin, "Bridging the Gap between Social Research and Public Policy: Welfare, A Case in Point," *Journal of Applied Behavioral Science* 9, no. 1 (1973), app. A.

25
Among the sixteen major organizations supporting Ribicoff were the National League of Cities, the U.S. Conference of Mayors, National Association of Counties, AFL-CIO, Common Cause, and the League of Women Voters.

26
Burke and Burke, *Nixon's Good Deed*, p. 184, Bowler, *Nixon Guaranteed Income Proposal*, p. 140; Ribicoff, "He Left at Half Time," p. 26.

27
Burke and Burke, *Nixon's Good Deed*, p. 184, Paul Leventhal, "Congressional Report/Revenue Sharing Gains in Senate as Drive for Welfare Reform Falters," *National Journal*, August 5, 1972, pp. 1250–1252.

28
Lester A. Sobel, *Welfare and the Poor* (New York: Facts on File, 1977), p. 124.

29
Leventhal, "Congressional Report," pp. 1245, 1247–1248. James Cannon, special assistant to Governor Nelson A. Rockefeller, was quoted in July 1972 as saying: "We made a decision a long time ago that revenue sharing had a better chance than welfare reform and thus shifted attention to revenue sharing" (p. 1246).

30
Sobel, *Welfare and the Poor*, p. 122.

31
U.S., Department of Health, Education, and Welfare, Social Security Administration, Report to the Commissioner of the Supplemental Security Income Study Group (January 1976), pp. 3–13.

32
Martha Derthick, "Professional Fiefdoms Appraised: The Case of Social Services," *Publius* 6, no. 2 (Spring 1976): 124, 130; Derthick, *Uncontrollable Spending for Social Services Grants* (Washington, D.C.: Brookings Institution, 1975); *Congress and the Nation*, Vol. 4, 1973–1976 (Washington, D.C.: Congressional Quarterly, 1977), pp. 414–416.

33
For background, see "Special Issue on the HEW Mega-Proposal," Laurence E. Lynn, Jr., guest editor, *Policy Analysis* 1, no. 2 (Spring 1975).

34
Frank Levy, "Observations of a Participant," *Policy Analysis* 1, no. 2 (Spring 1975): 448n.

35
On the internal HEW welfare debates in 1973, see Karen DeWitt, "Administration Task Force Develops Plans to Overhaul the Welfare System," *National Journal*, September 8, 1973; HEW, Office of the Assistant Secretary for Planning and Evaluation, *Income Supplement Program: The 1974 Welfare Replacement Proposal* (October 1976); Caspar Weinberger, "The Reform of Welfare: A National Necessity," *Journal of the Institute for Socioeconomic Studies* 1, no. 1 (Summer 1976); and "Caspar Weinberger and Welfare Reform," Kennedy School of Government case program, Harvard University (discussion draft, 1977).

36
Milton Friedman, "The Case for the Negative Income Tax," in Melvin R. Laird, ed., *Republican Papers* (Garden City, N.Y.: Doubleday Anchor, 1968).

37
On the events of 1974–1975, see John Iglehart, "HEW Wants Welfare Programs Replaced by Negative Income Tax," *National Journal*, October 19, 1974; Iglehart, "HEW's Reform Proposal Falls Victim to Economic Problems," *National Journal*, January 4, 1975; and HEW, *Income Supplement Program*. The Reagan proposals are cited and discussed in Frank Levy, "What Ronald Reagan Can Teach the U.S. about Welfare Reform," in *American Politics and Public Policy*, ed. Walter Dean Burnham and Martha Weinberg (Cambridge, Mass.: MIT Press, 1978). The proposals of the Subcommittee on Fiscal Policy are summarized in U.S., Congress, Joint Economic Committee, Subcommittee on Fiscal Policy, 93d Congress, 2d session, *Income Security for Americans: Recommendations of the Public Welfare Study* (December 5, 1974).

38
Excellent sources on the internal debates that produced the Carter proposals are "The Program for Better Jobs and Income," "The Carter Administration and Welfare Reform," and a third part not available at this writing, all in the Kennedy School of Government case program, Harvard University (discussion drafts, 1979).

39
Barry L. Friedman and Leonard J. Hausman, *Work, Welfare, and the Program for Better Jobs and Income*, A study prepared for the use of the Joint Economic Committee (October 14, 1977), p. 41.

40
U.S., Department of Health, Education, and Welfare, *Report on the 1977 Welfare Reform Study: Secretary's Report to the President* (May 3, 1977).

41
Nick Kotz, "The Politics of Welfare Reform," *New Republic*, May 14, 1977, p. 19.

42
William Chapman, "Welfare Plan Is Outlined by President," *Washington Post*, May 3, 1977.

43
David E. Rosenbaum, "Carter Reaffirms Welfare Ceiling Despite Warnings," *New York Times*, May 27, 1977.

44
"Statement of Senator Russell B. Long (Democrat, Louisiana) on Welfare Reform," (Press release; Office of Senator Russell B. Long, August 15, 1977); See also Adam Clymer, "Carter Welfare Bid Is Criticized by Long," *New York Times*, September 16, 1977.

45
Kotz, "The Politics of Welfare Reform," p. 18.

46
See Center on Social Welfare Policy and Law, "Changes in Welfare Reform Bill Made by House Welfare Reform Subcommittee," March 16, 1978. Among the major changes that the Corman bill made in the Carter bill were elimination of a limit on the benefits paid to large families, units sharing a household, families whose children have earnings, and others; and indexation of welfare benefits to the cost of living.

47
U.S., House, Welfare Reform Subcommittee of the Committees on Agriculture, on Education and Labor, and on Ways and Means, *Explanatory Material to Accompany H.R. 10950 and the Better Jobs and Income Act*, p. 55.

48
U.S., Congressional Budget Office, *The Administration's Welfare Reform Proposal: An Analysis of the Program for Better Jobs and Income* (April 1978), p. 48n.

49
For the reference to offsets in the original press briefing materials, see "Welfare Reform," *HEW News* (August 6, 1977), esp. pp. 19–20. The offsets were also explained in the text of the president's welfare message as reprinted in the *New York Times*: "Text of White House Message to Congress on Proposal to Overhaul Welfare System," *New York Times*, August 7, 1977. For a discussion of the controversy over offsets and other questions in estimating the cost of the Carter proposals, see Linda Demkovich, "The Numbers Are the Issue in the Debate over Welfare Reform," *National Journal*, April 22, 1978; and Charles Peters, "More Dollars and More Dollars and, etc.," *New York Times*, May 15, 1978.

50
See David E. Rosenbaum, "Outlook is Gloomy on Welfare Changes Proposed by Carter," *New York Times*, December 11, 1977.

51
Martin Donsky, "Compromise Talks Open in Effort to Salvage Some Welfare Reform," *Congressional Quarterly*, April 29, 1978, p. 1064.

52
Vivian Vahlberg, "Bellmon Co-Sponsoring Thriftier Bill to End Welfare Rut," *Daily Oklahoman*, March 23, 1978.

53
"Baker and Bellmon Push Guaranteed Income Plan," *Human Events*, April 1, 1978.

54
U.S., Senate, Committee on Finance, Subcommittee on Public Assistance, "Statement by Joseph A Califano, Jr., Secretary of Health, Education, and Welfare," Tuesday, February 7, 1978; the second statement, made before the Senate Human Resources Committee on March 23, is quoted in Donsky, "Compromise Talks Open," p. 1066.

55
Linda Demkovich, "State and Local Officials Rescue Welfare Reform—Too Late," *National Journal*, June 24, 1978, p. 1008; Aliceann Fritschler, "Time Short for Reform," *County News*, May 22, 1978; Fritschler, "Welfare Bill Compromise Being Eyed," *County News*, May 29, 1978.

56
National Center for Community Action, *Legislative Update* (June 1978) p. 2.

57
Aliceann Fritschler, "Welfare Reform on Move," *County News* (June 12, 1978); U.S., House, Northeast-Midwest Economic Advancement Coalition, Memorandum (undated).

58
Spencer Rich, "Major Welfare Revision Is Dead for This Congress," *Washington Post*, June 23, 1978.

59
Center on Social Welfare Policy and Law, "Welfare Reform—New Coalition Proposal," June 12, 1978.

60
Rich, "Major Welfare Revision Is Dead."

61
Ibid.

62
Center on Social Welfare Policy and Law, "Welfare Reform," p. 9.

63
The text of the bill and a statement by Moynihan are found in "State and Local Welfare Reform and Fiscal Relief Act of 1978," reprint from the *Congressional Record* distributed by the office of Senator Moynihan (September 19, 1978). The quotations of Moynihan and Ullman are from Edward C. Burke, "Senate Gets a Bill on Relief Takeover," *New York Times*, June 19, 1978. The quotation of Aaron

is from Martin Donsky, "Another Welfare Bill Proposed in Senate," *Congressional Quarterly* (July 15, 1978) p. 1775.

64
Bernard F. Hillenbrand, "Legislative Countdown," *County News*, September 11, 1978, p. 8.

65
Aliceann Fritschler, "Senate: Title XX Hike, No Fiscal Relief," *County News*, October 16, 1978.

66
A revised version of the speech was published as Daniel P. Moynihan, "The Politics and Economics of Regional Growth," *Public Interest*, no. 51 (Spring 1978).

67
David E. Rosenbaum, "Senators Fighting Carter on Welfare," *New York Times*, October 3, 1977.

68
John Snee and Mary Ross, "Social Security Amendments of 1977: Legislative History and Summary of Provisions," *Social Security Bulletin* 41, no. 3 (March 1978), p. 10: "Some Fiscal Aid in Social Security," *County News*, December 19, 1977.

69
The pages of *County News* throughout 1978 are full of stories about CETA and exhortations to county executives to lobby congressmen about the legislation. For a retrospective on the CETA battle, see "Outlook for CETA Given to NACMO," *County News* (November 13, 1978). On the earned income tax credit, see Art Pine, "Senate Unit Plans $250 Increase in Tax Exemption," *Washington Post*, September 15, 1978; "Highlights of the Tax Law Signed by President Carter," *New York Times* (November 9, 1978).

Notes to Chapter 5

1
An excellent explication of the Canadian conference system can be found in William Glaser, *Federalism in Canadian Health Services; Lessons for the United States* (New York: Center for the Social Sciences, Columbia University, 1977), pp. 7–21.

2
Canada, *Working Paper on Social Security in Canada* (April 1973), pp. 32, 30.

3
Leonard Shifrin, "The Politics of Income Security," in *Family Income Security Issues* (Social Planning Council of Metropolitan Toronto, February 1976), p. 59; National Council of Welfare, *Incomes and Opportunities* (Ottawa: November 1973), p. 26. See also Richard A. Green and David B. Perry, "The Federal Pro-

Notes to pp. 116–121

posals for Family Allowances; The Effects of Taxation," *Canadian Tax Journal* 21, no. 4 (July-August 1973).

4
A. W. Johnson, "Canada's Social Security Review 1973–75: The Central Issues," *Canadian Public Policy* 1, no. 4 (Autumn 1975): 465, 466; Federal-Provincial Conference of Ministers of Welfare, *Communiqué*, February 19 and 20, 1974 (quoted in Johnson, p. 466).

5
On TEIGA see Glaser, *Federalism in Canadian Health Services*, pp. 42–43. In 1978, TEIGA was split into separate departments concerned with intergovernmental and economic affairs.

6
Federal-Provincial Conference of Ministers of Welfare, *Communiqué*, November 20, 1974.

7
Johnson, "Canada's Social Security Review," p. 462.

8
Larry Bell, "Guaranteed Income in British Columbia," *Canadian Welfare* 48 (September-October 1973).

9
Saskatchewan, Department of Social Services, *Family Income Plan Manual* (1977); see also Graham Riches, "F.I.P. Flops," *Perception* 1, no. 5 (July/August 1978): 42.

10
Canada, Department of National Health and Welfare, Social Allowances and Services Branch, "Earnings Exemption Guideline under the Canada Assistance Plan," "Liquid Asset Exemption Guideline under the Canada Assistance Plan," and "Guideline Concerning Supplementation of Low Income Earnings under the Canada Assistance Plan" (all May 1975).

11
Canada, *Working Paper on Social Security*, pp. 22–26.

12
Federal-Provincial Conference of Ministers of Welfare, *Report of the Working Party on Employment Strategy to the Continuing Committee on Social Security* (February 1974), p. 4.

13
Shifrin, "The Politics of Income Security," p. 63.

14
Federal-Provincial Conference of Ministers of Welfare, *Communiqué*, November 30, 1974.

15
Shifrin, "The Politics of Income Security," p. 63; "Employment Strategy," speech by the Honourable Bud Cullen, Office of the Minister, Department of Manpower and Immigration (October 21, 1976).

16
On the 1974 election, see *Canadian Annual Review of Politics and Public Affairs: 1974* (Toronto: University of Toronto Press, 1976), ed. John Saywell, pp. 23–75; and Jon Pammett, Lawrence LeDuc, Jane Jenson, and Harold Clarke, *The 1974 Federal Election: A Preliminary Report,* Carleton University Occasional Papers No. 4, (Ottawa, n.d.). On the 1974 conference, see "Canadian Conference on Social Welfare," *Canadian Welfare* 49 (September/October 1974): 22.

17
Although many members of Health and Welfare Canada's Policy Research and Long-Range Planning (Welfare) Branch had once worked at the Treasury Board, they had been in the planning branch. The board's program branch tends to see the planners as ivory-tower types with no notion of fiscal limits. A discerning reader of an earlier draft of this manuscript adds that 1975 was not the first time that the minister of finance made a decision that harmed the Social Security Review: "The whole review exercise had been undermined at the outset by Finance whose 1973 Budget provided for indexation of income tax brackets and exemptions. This removed the annual tax revenue increases Johnson had been counting on to finance an expanded social security program."

18
National Council of Welfare, *Guide to the Guaranteed Income* (Ottawa: March, 1976), p. 32.

19
Ibid., pp. 33–36.

20
Leonard Shifrin, "Income Redistribution: Pipe Dreams and Pragmatism," *Perception* 1, no. 1 (September/October 1977).

21
Shifrin, "The Politics of Income Security," pp. 65–66; National Council of Welfare, *Guide to the Guaranteed Income,* pp. 33–34.

22
Canada, Department of National Health and Welfare, News Release, "Statement by the Honourable Marc Lalonde to the Conference of Federal and Provincial Ministers of Welfare," April 30 and May 1, 1975, p. 6.

23
The welfare ministers of British Columbia and Manitoba had left Ottawa before the February 1975 communiqué was released and later publicly challenged its statement that a two-tier scheme had been agreed on. However, under pressure from Lalonde they retracted their comments at the April meeting.

Notes to pp. 124–127

24
"... peut-on sérieusement s'attendre, du côté du gouvernement fédéral, a une participation financière du Québec à programme administré par Ottawa?" [quoted in *Canadian Annual Review of Politics and Public Affairs: 1975*, ed. John Saywell (Toronto: University of Toronto Press, 1977), p. 62.] Forget, a former assistant deputy minister of social affairs, had taken over as minister in November 1973 when Castonguay chose not to run for reelection to the Quebec legislature. Interestingly, Castonguay served during 1974 as a consultant to Health and Welfare Canada.

25
"Lalonde GAI Proposals . . . And A CCSD Response," *Canadian Welfare* 50 (March/April 1975): 25.

26
See Saywell, ed., *Canadian Annual Review: 1975*, pp. 57–60; Richard Van Loon, "From Shared Cost to Block Funding and Beyond: The Politics of Health Insurance in Canada," *Journal of Health Politics, Policy, and Law* 2, no. 4 (Winter 1978): 454–478.

27
See Richard Van Loon, "Reforming Welfare in Canada: The Case of the Social Security Review," *Public Policy* (forthcoming).

28
Shifrin, "The Politics of Income Security," p. 64.

29
Van Loon, "Reforming Welfare in Canada."

30
Canada, Department of National Health and Welfare, News Release, "Statement by the Honourable Marc Lalonde," pp. 7–13; Federal-Provincial Conference of Ministers of Welfare, *Communiqué*, April 30 and May 1, 1975.

31
Federal-Provincial Conference of Ministers of Welfare, *Communiqué*, February 3–4, 1976.

32
National Anti-Poverty Organization, *A New Tomorrow for Canada's Poor?* (Ottawa, 1976), pp. 10–11.

33
Federal-Provincial Conference of Ministers of Welfare, *Communiqué*, June 1–2, 1976, p. 19.

34
National Council of Welfare, *A Guide to the Guaranteed Income*, p. 38.

35
Federal-Provincial Conference of Ministers of Welfare, *Communiqué,* February 3–4, 1976, p. 5.

36
National Council of Welfare, *Guide to the Guaranteed Income,* "Addendum to the March Edition" (July 1976).

37
Federal-Provincial Conference of Ministers of Welfare, *Communiqué,* June 1–2, 1976, p. 18.

38
Ian Urquhart, "Why the Poor Are Still with Us," *Maclean's,* June 14, 1976.

39
"Canadian Conference on Social Development" (June 14–17, 1976), *Social Development* 5, no. 4 (September 1976).

40
Canada, House of Commons, Bill C-57, Social Services Act, Thirtieth Parliament, Second Session, 25–26 Elizabeth II, 1976–1977 (first reading, June 20, 1977); Department of National Health and Welfare, News Release, "New Social Services Bill Introduced in House of Commons" (June 20, 1977).

41
Federal-Provincial Conference of First Ministers, "Established Program Financing: A Proposal Regarding the Major Shared-Cost Programs in the Fields of Health and Post-Secondary Education," statement tabled by the prime minister of Canada, the Right Honourable Pierre Elliott Trudeau, June 14–15, 1976; *The Federal-Provincial Fiscal Arrangements and Established Programs Financing Act,* Revised Statutes of Canada, 1977. On the shift in federal sympathies away from shared-cost to block grant programs, see Van Loon, "From Shared Cost" and "Reforming Welfare in Canada."

42
H. Philip Hepworth, "Where Now?" *Perception* 1, no. 3 (January/February 1978): 42.

43
Canada, Department of National Health and Welfare, "Marc Lalonde Proposes New Financing Method for Federal Social Service Contributions," September 16, 1977; Bill C-55, *Social Services Act,* Canada, House of Commons, Thirtieth Parliament, Third Session, 26–27 Elizabeth II, 1977–1978 (first reading, May 12, 1978); and Department of Health and Welfare, News Release, "Monique Bégin Introduces Bill for Block Funding of Social Services" (May 12, 1978).

44
National Council of Welfare, *Guide to the Guaranteed Income,* "An Addendum to the March Edition."

Notes to pp. 131–136

45
Federal-Provincial Conference of Ministers of Welfare, *Communiqué,* June 1–2, 1976, pp. 4–5. See also Sheldon E. Gordon, "No End in Sight Yet to the Bickering," *Financial Post,* June 12, 1976.

46
George Oake, "Hopes Fading for Income Support Plans," *Edmonton Journal,* September 23, 1977.

47
Canada, Department of Finance, *Integration of Social Program Payments into the Income Tax System* (November 1978).

48
Canada, Department of Finance, "Statement by Finance Minister Jean Chrétien," August 24, 1978; "Ottawa to Reduce Baby Bonus, UIC: Major Revisions in Social Policy," *Toronto Globe and Mail,* August 25, 1978; Canada, House of Commons, Bill C-10, An Act to amend the Income Tax Act to provide for a child tax credit and to amend the Family Allowances Act.

49
Canada, *Commons Debates,* December 4, 1978, pp. 1769, 1771.

50
Canada, Department of National Health and Welfare, "Social Policy Initiatives: Fact Sheet," p. 3.

Notes to Chapter 6

1
Don K. Price, *The Scientific Estate* (Cambridge, Mass.: Harvard University Press, 1965), pp. 62–68. Hugh Heclo has compared policy development to learning [*Modern Social Politics in Britain and Sweden* (New Haven, Conn.: Yale University Press, 1974), chap. 6]. See also Christopher Leman, "Patterns of Policy Development: Social Security in the United States and Canada," *Public Policy* 25, no. 2 (Spring 1977), sect. 4. Note that the distinction drawn in the text between deductive and inductive policymaking focuses on the adoption of policies, not their implementation.

2
Leman, "Patterns of Policy Development," pp. 264–265, 280–283, 286–288. See also chapter 8, below.

3
Richard Simeon, *Federal-Provincial Diplomacy* (Toronto: University of Toronto Press, 1973), pp. 295–296.

4
Richard Nathan, "What Went Wrong with FAP: Should We Give Up?" paper presented to the National Conference on Social Welfare (Atlantic City, N.J., May 28, 1973), p. 1.

5
T. Russell Robinson, "A General Framework for the Evaluation of Social Security Policies: A Canadian Overview," background paper presented at the Research Conference on Methods of Evaluating the Effectiveness of Social Security Programmes, International Social Security Association (Vienna, 1975), p. 20.

6
Quoted in A. W. Johnson, "Canada's Social Security Review 1973–75: The Central Issues," *Canadian Public Policy* 1, no. 4 (Autumn 1975): 42.

7
Robert Dahl and Edward Tufte, *Size and Democracy* (New Haven, Conn.: Yale University Press, 1972), pp. 39, 109.

8
Vincent and Vee Burke, *Nixon's Good Deed: Welfare Reform* (New York: Columbia University Press, 1974), p. 216.

9
For a criticism that the subsidies are a means of co-opting organizations putatively dedicated to helping the underprivileged, see Martin Loney, "A Political Economy of Citizen Participation," in *The Canadian State: Political Economy and Political Power*, ed. Leo Panitch (Toronto: University of Toronto Press, 1977), chap. 15.

10
John Kenneth Galbraith, *The Affluent Society* 3rd ed. rev. (Boston: Houghton Mifflin, 1976), p. 249f. See also chapter 2 above.

11
Nick Kotz, *Let Them Eat Promises: The Politics of Hunger in America*, (Garden City, N.Y.: Doubleday Anchor, 1971), p. 158.

12
Frances Fox Piven and Richard Cloward, *Poor People's Movements: Why They Succeed, How They Fail* (New York: Pantheon, 1977), pp. 287, 305f. See also Lawrence Bailis, *Bread or Justice* (Lexington, Mass.: Lexington Books, D.C. Heath, 1974), pp. 141–143; Kirsten Gronbjerg, *Mass Society and the Extension of Welfare, 1960–1970* (Chicago, Ill.: University of Chicago Press, 1977), p. 157.

13
Sar Levitan, Martin Rein, and David Marwick, *Work and Welfare Go Together* (Baltimore, Md.: Johns Hopkins University Press, 1972), p. 17; U.S., Congress, Joint Economic Committee, *Handbook of Public Income Transfer Programs*, Studies in Public Welfare, Paper No. 2, p. 152; Canada, *Working Paper on Social Security in Canada* (1973), tables 1, 5, 7.

14
Simeon, *Federal-Provincial Diplomacy*, pp. 229ff.

15
Leman, "Patterns of Policy Development," pp. 285–286 (written in 1976).

16
See Simeon, *Federal-Provincial Diplomacy,* p. 219.

17
Donald E. Rigby, "State Supplementation under Federal SSI Program," *Social Security Bulletin* 37, no. 11 (November 1974); U.S., Senate, Committee on Finance, *The Supplemental Security Income Program,* 95th Congress, 1st Session (April 1977), p. 87.

18
Richard Splane, "Social Policy-Making in the Government of Canada: Reflections of a Reformist Bureaucrat," Chap. 11 of *Canadian Social Policy,* ed. Shankar A. Yelaja (Waterloo, Ontario: Wilfrid Laurier University Press, 1978), p. 212. See also in the same book, Max Saltsman, "Party Politics and Social Policy: The Party in Opposition," Chap. 14.

19
Martin Anderson, *Welfare: The Political Economy of Welfare Reform in the United States* (Stanford, Calif.: Hoover Institution, 1978), p. 67; see also Anderson, "Welfare Reform on 'The Same Old Rocks,' " *New York Times,* November 27, 1978.

20
The vagueness of early studies by the working parties was caused not only by deadlock over federal-provincial issues but also by disagreement within Health and Welfare Canada between economists and those oriented toward social work. See Johnson, "Canada's Social Security Review," p. 471. However, compare what Johnson says there about who was being politically realistic with my argument in the text.

21
See Christopher Leman, *Problems of Centralizing Data in Federal Systems: Welfare Programs in Canada and the United States,* Final Report of a research project funded in part by grant number 10-P-90482/101 from the Social Security Administration, U.S. Department of Health, Education, and Welfare (February 1979).

22
Ibid.; and for an excellent survey of methods that can be used to produce data indirectly when it is not available directly, see Eugene J. Webb, Donald T. Campbell, Richard D. Schwartz, and Lee Sechrest, *Unobtrusive Measures: Nonreactive Research in the Social Sciences* (Chicago: Rand McNally, 1966).

23
For a development of this point, see chapter 7.

24
Rufus E. Miles, Jr., "The Origin and Meaning of Miles' Law," *Public Administration Review* 38, no. 5 (September/October 1978): 399.

25
Compare the titles in the Staff Working Paper series of the Policy Research and

Long Range Planning Branch (Welfare) with those in the Technical Analysis Paper series of the Office of Income Security Policy, HEW.

26
See chapter 7.

27
With the merger of the Policy and Program Development and Coordination Branch (Welfare) into the Policy Research and Long-Range Planning Branch (Welfare), John Osborne, who had been Assistant Deputy Minister in charge of the former agency, became Special Adviser, Policy Development (Welfare).

28
Hugh Heclo, personal communication, January 6, 1979.

29
Leonard Shifrin, "The Politics of Income Security," in Social Planning Council of Metropolitan Toronto, *Family Income Security Issues,* proceedings of a conference (Toronto, 1976).

30
Family Income Security Issues, pp. v–vi.

31
Social Development 5, no. 4 (September 1976): 2.

32
Family Income Security Issues, p. 5. The lack of response to one such effort suggests why more were not attempted: during the Social Security Review, Quebec's Ministry of Social Affairs released a major paper aimed at informing the public of the issues at stake. It was almost totally ignored by the media.

33
Ibid., p. vi.

34
Federal-Provincial Conference of Ministers of Welfare, *Background Paper on Income Support and Supplementation* (February 1975).

35
Ted Harvey and Valorie Groskind, "A Critical Analysis of the Federal-Provincial Review *Background Paper on Income Support and Supplementation,*" in *Family Income Security Issues,* pp. 34–36.

36
H. Philip Hepworth, "Social Services Saga," *Perception* 1, no. 4 (March/April 1978): 4–5.

37
For an excellent statement of this view, see Robert Kudrle and Theodore Marmor, "The Development of the Welfare State in North America," in *The Development of Welfare States in Europe and America,* ed. Peter Flora and Arnold Heidenheimer (New Brunswick, N.J.: Transaction Press, forthcoming), chap. 3.

38
Regarding differences between the United States and Europe in social policy, compare the cultural explanation of Anthony King with the more structural explanation of Arnold Heidenheimer: King, "Ideas, Institutions, and the Policies of Governments: A Comparative Analysis," *British Journal of Political Science* 3 (July–October 1973); Heidenheimer, "The Politics of Public Education, Health, and Welfare in the USA and Western Europe: How Growth and Reform Potentials have Differed," *British Journal of Political Science* 3 (July 1973).

39
Robert Berkhofer, "Clio and the Culture Concept," *Social Science Quarterly* 53, no. 2 (September 1972).

40
The authors of the best existing comparative study of political culture emphasize: "Our study stresses orientation to political structure and process, not orientation to the substance of political demands and outputs." They point out the need for studies of the relation of cultural patterns to the substance of policy [Gabriel Almond and Sidney Verba, *The Civic Culture* (Boston: Little, Brown, 1965), pp. 28–29]. Remarkably little comparative research of the kind that they suggest has been done. For a preliminary survey of attitudes in Canada and the United States that challenges standard views of how political culture differs in the two countries, see Tom Truman, "A Scale for Measuring a Tory Streak in Canada and the United States," *Canadian Journal of Political Science* 10, no. 3 (September 1977). See also Henry Clay Lindgren and Fredrica Lindgren, "Expressed Attitudes of American and Canadian Teachers Toward Authority," *Psychological Reports* 7 (1960): p. 54. Lindgren and Lindgren argue that the publics in the two countries differ not in general values but rather in specific response to authority figures. Canadians defer to prestige-laden figures while people in the United States prefer self-made individuals who are often outside government.

41
Josette Laframboise, *A Question of Needs* (Ottawa: Canadian Council for Social Development, 1975), pp. 127–128; Canadian Institute of Public Opinion, "54% Approve—29% Oppose $3500 Minimum Income," *Gallup Report*, March 1, 1972; Canadian Institute of Public Opinion, "2-to-1 Approval Given Guaranteed Annual Income," *Gallup Report*, February 2, 1974.

42
Polls cited in Hazel Erskine, "The Polls: Government Role in Welfare," *Public Opinion Quarterly* 39, no. 2 (Summer 1975); Robert Reinhold, "Public Found Hostile to Welfare as Idea But Backs What It Does," *New York Times*, August 3, 1977, p. 1.

43
Hadley Cantril and Lloyd Free, *The Political Beliefs of Americans* (New Brunswick, N.J.: Rutgers University Press, 1967), p. 180.

44
Polls cited in Erskine, "The Polls," pp. 270–271; also Daniel P. Moynihan, *The Politics of a Guaranteed Income* (New York: Random House, 1973), pp. 268–269.

45
Canadian Institute of Public Opinion, "2-to-1 Approval Given Guaranteed Annual Income," *Gallup Report,* February 2, 1974.

46
Tom Truman, "A Critique of Seymour M. Lipset's Article, 'Value Differences, Absolute or Relative: The English-speaking Democracies,' " *Canadian Journal of Political Science* 4, no. 4 (December 1971): 513.

47
See Henry Aaron, *Politics and the Professors: The Great Society in Perspective* (Washington, D.C.: Brookings Institution, 1978).

48
Albert Hirschman, "The Principle of the Hiding Hand," in *Development Projects Observed* (Washington, D.C.: Brookings Institution, 1967). In general, see Christopher Leman, "How to Get There from Here: The Grandfather Effect and Public Policy," *Policy Analysis* (forthcoming).

49
Simeon, *Federal-Provincial Diplomacy,* p. 231.

50
Johnson, "Canada's Social Security Review," p. 470.

51
Quoted in Simeon, *Federal-Provincial Diplomacy,* p. 294.

52
Social Development 5, no. 4 (September 1976): 2.

Notes to Chapter 7

1
Abraham A. Ribicoff, "He Left at Half Time", *New Republic,* February 17, 1973; Leonard Hausman, "The Politics of a Guaranteed Income, A Review Article," *Journal of Human Resources* 8, no. 4 (Fall 1973); Tom Joe, "The Politics of a Guaranteed Income," *Social Work* 18, no. 3 (May 1973); Robert Harris, "The Politics of a Guaranteed Income," *Social Service Review* (September 1973); Jodie Allen, *A Funny Thing Happened on the Way to Welfare Reform* (Washington, D.C.: Urban Institute, 1972); Richard Nathan, "What Went Wrong with FAP: Should We Give Up?" Paper presented to the National Conference on Social Welfare (Atlantic City, New Jersey, May 28, 1973); Lester Salamon, *Toward Income Opportunity: Current Thinking on Welfare Reform,* Welfare Policy Project (Durham, N.C.: Duke University and the Ford Foundation, Spring 1977), p. 144.

Notes to pp. 174–181

2
Quoted in Mary Ellen Leary, "After Tax-Cut Fever, A Case of the Chills," *Boston Globe,* September 10, 1978, p. A3.

3
National Anti-Poverty Organization, *A New Tomorrow for Canada's Poor?* (Ottawa, 1976).

4
U.S., Department of Health, Education, and Welfare, Social Security Administration, *AFDC 1975 Recipient Characteristics Study,* part 1, table 14.

5
"A New Racial Poll," *Newsweek,* February 26, 1979, p. 48.

6
Federal-Provincial Conference of Ministers of Welfare, *The World of the Welfare Recipient* (1971), p. 6.

7
"B.C. Minister Says Separate Québec Might Cut Welfare Aid," *Globe and Mail,* November 17, 1976.

8
Joe Feagin, *Subordinating the Poor* (Englewood Cliffs, N.J.: Prentice-Hall, 1975), p. 118; George Gallup, "Integration Opposition Drops," *Boston Globe,* August 28, 1978, p. 20; and "A New Racial Poll," pp. 48–49.

9
"A Researcher in Canada Finds Exaggerated Fear of Crime in the Streets," *New York Times,* September 30, 1976, p. 2.

10
Federal-Provincial Conference of Ministers of Welfare, *The World of the Welfare Recipient* (1971), p. 1. Since 1966, the Canada Pension Plan and Quebec Pension Plan have offered disability benefits. Eventually this development will reduce the dependence of Canadian disabled on social assistance.

11
Federal-Provincial Conference of Ministers of Welfare, *The World of the Welfare Recipient* (1971), p. 1; Canada, Department of National Health and Welfare, *Income Security for Canadians* (1970), p. 7; U.S., Department of Health, Education, and Welfare, Social and Rehabilitation Service, *Findings of the 1971 AFDC Study,* part 1, table 15.

12
The survivorship features of the Canada Pension Plan and Quebec Pension Plan may eventually alter this situation.

13
U.S., Department of Health, Education, and Welfare, Office of Assistant Secretary for Planning and Evaluation, *Summary Report: Seattle-Denver Income Maintenance Experiment* (February 1978), p. 23.

14
Ibid., table 5.

15
Daniel P. Moynihan, *The Politics of a Guaranteed Income* (New York: Random House, 1973), p. 344.

16
Vincent and Vee Burke, *Nixon's Good Deed: Welfare Reform* (New York: Columbia University Press, 1974), p. 181; M. Kenneth Bowler, *The Nixon Guaranteed Income Proposal: Substance and Process in Policy Change* (Cambridge, Mass.: Ballinger, 1974), p. 130.

17
Moynihan, *Politics of a Guaranteed Income,* pp. 139–140.

18
Ibid., p. 142.

19
Ibid., pp. 219–220; Richard Nathan, "Workfare/Welfare," *New Republic,* February 24, 1973, p. 19.

20
The comparison of costs of the 1969 bill and of HR 1 if the same reduction rate were retained is found in Allen, *A Funny Thing,* p. 13. A lucid comparison of the effective reduction rates under the two bills is in Burke and Burke, *Nixon's Good Deed,* pp. 168–171.

21
Bowler, *The Nixon Guaranteed Income Proposal,* pp. 33–35, 78.

22
Moynihan, *Politics of a Guaranteed Income,* p. 140.

23
Canada, *Working Paper on Social Security in Canada* (April 1973), pp. 31–32.

24
James Tobin, "The Case for an Income Guarantee," *Public Interest* (Summer 1966).

25
Federal-Provincial Conference of Ministers of Welfare, *Communiqué,* June 2, 1976, p. 20.

26
U.S., Senate, Committee on Finance, *Social Security Amendments of 1972,* 92nd Congress, 2d session, p. 429.

27
Federal-Provincial Conference of Ministers of Welfare, *Communiqué,* November 20, 1974, p. 3; *Communiqué,* June 2, 1976, p. 20.

28
Federal-Provincial Conference of Ministers of Welfare, *Communiqué*, June 2, 1976, p. 20.

29
For a summary of arguments against alternatives to a unitary negative income tax, see Mark D. Worthington and Laurence E. Lynn, Jr., "Incremental Welfare Reform: A Strategy Whose Time Has Passed," *Public Policy* 25, no. 1 (Winter 1977).

30
Lee Rainwater, *Welfare and Working Mothers,* Family Policy Note No. 6 (Cambridge, Mass.: Joint Center for Urban Studies, 1977), p. 3.

31
For an example of such criticism as trained on two-tier aspects of the Carter plan, see U.S., Senate, Committee on Finance, *Hearings on H.R. 7200,* 95th Congress, 1st session, pp. 83–85.

32
HEW, *Summary Report;* "Moynihan Says New Studies Raise Doubts on Negative Income Tax," *New York Times,* November 16, 1978; Stephen Chapman, "Poor Laws," *New Republic* (December 2, 1978); Linda Demkovich, "Good News and Bad News for Welfare Reform" *National Journal,* December 30, 1978; and Robert Reinhold, "Test in Seattle Challenges Minimum-Income Plan," *New York Times,* February 5, 1979. Whatever the evidence and reasons that guaranteed income programs encourage family breakup, Richard Nathan has pointed out that what the public thinks about the question may be politically more important. He remarks that the popular assumption that welfare programs cause splitting produces "deep public disfavor towards welfare" (Nathan, "What Went Wrong with FAP?", p. 6).

33
In a colloquy with Richard Nathan about the latter's argument that existing programs simulate a two-tier negative income tax scheme, John Palmer emphasized the problem of people who are transitional or hard to categorize: "Under your system, which program do they belong to? How do they make the transition from one to the other as weekly hours of work increase or decrease?" [quoted in "Comprehensive Reform vs. Incrementalism," *Journal of Socioeconomic Studies* 2, no. 2 (Spring 1977): 8]. Palmer was a principal designer of the Income Supplement Program. For a discussion of the importance of filing units, see HEW, Office of the Assistant Secretary for Planning and Evaluation, *Income Supplement Program: The 1974 Welfare Replacement Proposal* (October 1976), p. 17. For a discussion of the role of the states under a system like ISP, see Mark D. Worthington, "The Role of the States in a 'Federalized' Welfare System," Technical Analysis Paper No. 12 (Washington, D.C.: Office of Income Security Policy, Office of the Assistant Secretary for Planning and Evaluation, HEW, September 1976). For an argument that a multitier benefit structure could be located within a consolidated

administration, see Worthington and Lynn, "Incremental Welfare Reform," pp. 78–79.

34

Michael C. Barth, George J. Carcagno, and John L. Palmer, *Toward an Effective Income Support System: Problems, Prospects, and Choices* (Madison, Wis.: Institute for Research on Poverty, 1974), p. 78; U.S., Congressional Budget Office, *The Administration's Welfare Reform Proposal: An Analysis of the Program for Better Jobs and Income* (April 1978), pp. 27–28.

35

Saskatchewan, Department of Social Services, *Income Support and Supplementation,* part 2, calculated from data on pp. 35–36.

36

Ibid., part 1, pp. 19–20. During the internal debates leading to the Carter welfare reform package, a task force of the U.S. Social Security Administration examined the administrative aspects of different proposals. The task force concluded that two- and three-track approaches could be administered only with the help of a "single intake point which also serves as a continuous recipient 'tracking' point." It also argued that a unitary negative income tax would create its own administrative problems, "introducing an inflexible uniformity inappropriate in the operation of an essentially needs-related program." ("The Carter Administration and Welfare Reform," Kennedy School of Government case program, Harvard University (discussion paper, 1979), pp. 54–55.

37

Canada, Department of Finance, *Integration of Social Program Payments into the Income Tax System* (November 1978); the U.S. report was never released, but it is summarized in HEW, *Income Supplement Program,* Tab K.

38

Saskatchewan, *Income Support and Supplementation,* part 1, pp. 6, 20; Graham Riches, "F.I.P. Flops," *Perception* 1, no. 4 (July/August, 1978): 42.

39

Maurice MacDonald, *Food, Stamps, and Income Maintenance* (New York: Academic Press, 1977), pp. 84–85.

40

Henry Aaron, *Why Is Welfare So Hard to Reform?* (Washington, D.C.: Brookings Institution, 1973), p. 69.

41

Robert Haveman and Robert Lampman, "Two Alternatives to FAP's Treatment of the Working Poor," discussion paper (Madison, Wis.: Institute for Research on Poverty, 1971). See also Robert F. Smith and W. Joseph Heffernan, "Work Incentives and Welfare Reform: The FAP Experience," *Mississippi Valley Journal of Business and Economics* (1971).

42
Richard Nathan, "Food Stamps and Welfare Reform," *Policy Analysis* 2, no. 1 (Winter 1976): 66. See also Nathan, "What Went Wrong with FAP," "Alternatives for Federal Income-Security Policy," in Commission on Critical Choices for Americans, *Qualities of Life* (Lexington, Mass.: D.C. Heath, Lexington Books, 1976), "The Case for Incrementalism," *Challenge* (May-June 1977), and "Comprehensive Reform vs. Incrementalism: An Exchange of Views Between Richard P. Nathan and John L. Palmer," *Journal of the Institute for Socioeconomic Studies* 2, no. 2 (Spring 1977): 3.

43
"The Carter Administration and Welfare Reform," pp. 27-28.

Notes to Chapter 8

1
Christopher Leman, "Patterns of Policy Development: Social Security in the United States and Canada," *Public Policy* 25, no. 1 (Spring 1977).

2
Leonard Shifrin, "Building the Missing Bridge," *Perception* 2, no. 1 (November/December 1978): 12.

3
Richard A. Cloward and Frances Fox Piven, "A Strategy to End Poverty," reprinted in *The Politics of Turmoil* (New York: Vintage, 1972), p. 90; See also Piven and Cloward, *Poor People's Movements: How They Succeed, Why They Fail* (New York: Pantheon, 1977), pp. 281-282; Piven and Cloward, *Regulating the Poor* (New York: Vintage, 1972), p. 348; Gilbert Steiner, "Reform Follows Reality: The Growth of Welfare," *Public Interest* 34 (Winter 1974): 65.

4
Richard Nathan, "The Case for Incrementalism," *Challenge* (May-June 1977).

5
Barry Friedman and Leonard Hausman, "Welfare in Retreat: A Dilemma for the Federal System," *Public Policy* 25, no. 1 (Winter 1977): 27.

6
For a contrary view, see Richard Van Loon, "Reforming Welfare in Canada: The Case of the Social Security Review," *Public Policy* (forthcoming).

7
Shifrin, "Building the Missing Bridge," p. 12.

8
Van Loon, "Reforming Welfare."

9
Friedman and Hausman, "Welfare in Retreat," p. 29.

10
The 1971 figure is from Canada's Department of National Health and Welfare, *Financial Aid to Persons in Their Own Homes under Provincial Social Assistance Programs* (November 1971), pp. 89, 90, 95; the 1975 figure is from John Ulmer, "Provincial Social Assistance Benefits: A Comparison," *Bulletin of Canadian Welfare Law* 4, no. 1 (Spring 1976), table I.

11
Frank Levy, "What Ronald Reagan Can Teach the U.S. about Welfare Reform," in *American Politics and Public Policy* ed. Walter Dean Burnham and Martha Weinberg (Cambridge, Mass.: MIT Press, 1978). But see Friedman and Hausman, "Welfare in Retreat," pp. 37–38.

12
Adam Clymer, "Poll Discloses Property Tax Cuts Are Widely Backed around Nation," *New York Times*, June 28, 1978; "The Big Tax Revolt," *Newsweek*, June 19, 1978; Seymour Martin Lipset and Earl Raab, "The Message of Proposition 13," *Commentary*, September 1978.

13
On Dukakis, King, and the welfare issue, see Barney Frank, "How to Succeed in Liberal Politics by Abandoning the Poor," *Real Paper*, April 8, 1978; and the following articles in the *Boston Globe*: "Reagan's Ex-Welfare Chief Counseled King," October 12, 1978; "King Vows Welfare Savings by Cutting Fraud, Ineligibles," October 21, 1978; "King's Adviser Becomes Issue," October 27, 1978; and "Those Tough Welfare Savings," November 1, 1978; "King Moves to Cut Welfare," March 8, 1979.

14
Marc Bendick et al., *The Anatomy of AFDC Errors* (Washington, D.C.: Urban Institute, 1978), p. 55; and Joe Richardson, "Fraud," in U.S., House, Committee on Government Operations, *Administration of the AFDC Program*, 95th Congress, 1st Session (April 1977), part 8, pp. 255–258.

15
Thus HEW Secretary Joseph A. Califano, Jr., reported that in the first half of 1977, $440 million was misspent in AFDC, while eligible recipients were underpaid by $45.2 million. His figures did not attempt to measure the amount denied eligible people who were wrongly excluded from the program ("$440 Million Is Said To Be Misspent in Welfare Program," *New York Times*, January 16, 1978, p. A19).

16
One of the most detailed surveys available found that the average fraud case in California in 1969 amounted to slightly over $100. See Richardson, "Fraud," p. 254.

17
For some choice examples, see "Worker is Accused of Defrauding City of $21,500 in Relief," *New York Times*, November 24, 1977; " 'Queen of Welfare'

Notes to pp. 208–212

Ordered Jailed in $239,500 Fraud," *New York Times,* December 29, 1978; "Police in Welfare Scandal," *Boston Globe,* November 29, 1978; and "15 HEW Employees Indicted on Welfare Fraud Charges," *Washington Post,* September 28, 1978.

18
Gilbert Steiner, *Social Insecurity* (Chicago, Ill.: Rand McNally, 1966), p. 165.

19
"Hot Line Helps Find Welfare Fraud," *New York Times,* September 11, 1977. After nearly three years of operation, the Washington State hot line reportedly uncovered $438,956 in fraud while it cost only $38,419 to operate ("Welfare Informers," *New York Times,* April 1, 1979).

20
See California, Health and Welfare Agency, Department of Benefit Payments, Fact Sheet No. 3, *Prevention and Detection of Welfare Fraud* (February 1977).

21
See, for example, Francis X. Clines, "About New York: Playing the Welfare Computer Hit Game," *New York Times,* February 28, 1978, p. 30.

22
"Five Concerns Join Michigan in Fighting Welfare Fraud," *New York Times,* November 21, 1977, p. 26.

23
Joe Richardson, "Quality Control Efforts," in *Administration of the AFDC Program.*

24
U.S., Department of Health, Education and Welfare, *HEW News,* April 1, 1977.

25
Federal-Provincial Conference of Ministers of Welfare, *The World of the Welfare Recipient* (October 1971), pp. 140–141.

26
U.S., Senate, Committee on Finance, *Social Security Amendments of 1972,* Report to Accompany HR 1, 92nd Congress, 2nd session (September 26, 1972), chap. 10.

27
U.S., Senate, Committee on Finance, *Child Support Data and Materials,* 95th Congress, 1st session (November 10, 1975), pp. 1–5; Office of the White House Press Secretary, "Statement by the President," January 4, 1975.

28
HEW News, January 18, 1978.

29
Spencer Rich, "Runaway Fathers Program Proves a Major Success," *Washington Post,* March 13, 1978, p. A-1.

30
HEW News, January 18, 1978; see also: HEW, Office of Child Support Enforcement, *Child Support Enforcement: Second Annual Report* (December 31, 1977).

31
See Maureen O'Neil and Shirley Ciffin, "Case Study on Divorce and Social Security in Canada," prepared for International Social Security Association Round Table Meeting, 1977.

32
Jimmy Carter, " 'A New Beginning'—Goals: Openness, Compassion, Efficiency; Presentation to the Platform Committee of the Democratic Party" (Atlanta, 1976).

33
Barry L. Friedman and Leonard J. Hausman, "Is Compulsory Work for Welfare Recipients Manageable?" paper prepared for the 1978 meetings of the Industrial Relations Research Association and the American Economics Association (Chicago, Ill., n.d.)

34
James Tobin, "Reflections on Recent History," in *Income Maintenance and Welfare Reform: Papers and Comments* (Madison, Wis.: Institute for Research on Poverty, 1974), p. 23. See also Lee Rainwater, *Welfare and Working Mothers,* Family Policy Note No. 6 (Cambridge, Mass.: Joint Center for Urban Studies, 1977), p. 4.

35
Linda Hughes, "Let Them Eat Tulip Bulbs," *MacLeans,* May 3, 1976, p. 23; *Canadian Annual Review of Politics and Public Affairs: 1975,* ed. John Saywell (Toronto: University of Toronto Press, 1977), p. 199; *Canadian Annual Review of Politics and Public Affairs: 1972,* ed. John Saywell (Toronto: University of Toronto Press, 1974), pp. 351–352.

36
Dave Margoshes, "Alberta Policy on Mothers' Jobs Toughest in Canada, Survey Shows," *Calgary Herald,* April 8, 1978.

37
Ibid.; John Ulmer, "Income Security in Canada," *Bulletin of Canadian Welfare Law* 4, no. 1 (Spring 1976): 26.

38
See Steiner, *Social Insecurity,* pp. 110–112.

39
Martin Waldron, "Bordentown's 'Workfare' Cuts Welfare to the Bone," *New York Times,* November 9, 1978; Waldron, "Workfare Order in City in Jersey Voided by Court," *New York Times,* November 22, 1978.

40
"Workfare Gathering Steam," *Toronto Globe and Mail,* December 20, 1978. See

also "Welfare a Target of London Mayor," *Toronto Globe and Mail,* December 5, 1978.

41
Canada, Department of Health and Welfare, *Canada Assistance Plan: 1975–76 Annual Report,* p. 3.

42
See Secretary Califano's statement in U.S., Senate, Committee on Finance, *Hearings on H.R. 7200,* 95th Congress, First Session. (July 1977), pp. 116–117.

43
"When States Tell People They Must Work for Welfare," *U.S. News and World Report,* July 8, 1977; reprinted in *Hearings on H.R. 7200,* p. 83.

44
For a far-sighted effort by one savvy corporation to capitalize on this trend, see "What If Workfare Replaces Welfare?" in *Annual Report: 1977* (Cambridge, Mass.: Arthur D. Little, 1978), pp. 19–21.

45
For an excellent comparative study of unemployment insurance in Canada, the United States, and other countries, see Saul J. Blaustein and Isabel Craig, *An International Review of Unemployment Insurance Schemes* (Kalamazoo, Mich.: W. E. Upjohn Institute for Employment Research, 1977).

46
See Christopher Leman, *Problems of Centralizing Data in Federal Systems: Welfare Programs in Canada and the United States,* Final report of a research project funded in part by grant number 10-P-90482/101 from the Social Security Administration, U.S. Department of Health, Education, and Welfare (February, 1979).

47
James Q. Wilson, "The Rise of the Bureaucratic State," *Public Interest* 41 (Fall 1975): 93–94.

48
Richard Nathan, "Alternatives for Federal Income-Security Policy," in Commission on Critical Choices for Americans, *Qualities of Life* (Lexington, Mass.: D.C. Heath, Lexington Books, 1976), p. 254.

49
U.S., Senate, Committee on Finance, Press Release: "Finance Committee Orders Reported H.R. 7200 Public Assistance Amendments" (September 30, 1977).

50
"The Big Tax Revolt," *Newsweek,* June 19, 1978, p. 22; Adam Clymer, "Poll Discloses Property Tax Cuts Are Widely Backed around Nation," *New York Times,* June 28, 1978; Adam Clymer, "Proposed Convention on Balancing Budget," *New York Times,* February 16, 1979.

51
Victor Malrek, "Begin Says Businesses Push for Social Aid Cuts," Toronto *Globe and Mail*, September 1, 1978.

52
Geoff Norquay, "Assessing Trudeau's Cutbacks: One Step Forward, Two Steps Back," *Perception* 2, no. 1 (November/December 1978): p. 8; Mary Trueman, "1.5 Billion in Cuts Ottawa's First Step under PM's Pledge," Toronto *Globe and Mail,* August 17, 1978.

53
"Plan to Cut Social Security Loses," *New York Times,* March 8, 1979.

54
Shifrin, "Building the Missing Bridge," p. 12.

55
See Seymour Martin Lipset and Earl Raab, "The Message of Proposition 13," *Commentary,* September 1978; and Everett Carll Ladd, Jr., "What the Voters Really Want," *Fortune,* December 18, 1978.

56
In a 1972 poll, 81 percent of the U.S. public was willing to accept the extra expense of moving people from welfare into paying jobs. (Lipset and Raab, "The Message of Proposition 13," p. 45).

Abbreviations Used in Text

AB
Aid to the Blind
AFDC
Aid to Families with Dependent Children (U = Unemployed Option)
AFL-CIO
American Federation of Labor and Congress of Industrial Organizations
APTD
Aid to the Permanently and Totally Disabled
ASPE
Assistant Secretary for Planning and Evaluation, HEW
BLS
Bureau of Labor Statistics
CAP
Canada Assistance Plan
CBO
Congressional Budget Office
CCSD
Canadian Council on Social Development
CEA
Council of Economic Advisors
CETA
Comprehensive Employment and Training Act
CFMM
Canadian Federation of Mayors and Municipalities
CPP
Canada Pension Plan
DOL
Department of Labor
FAP
Family Assistance Plan
FIP
Family Income Plan (Saskatchewan)
FISP
Family Income Security Plan
FPCMW
Federal-Provincial Conference of Ministers of Welfare
GIS
Guaranteed Income Supplement
HEW
Department of Health, Education, and Welfare
ISP
Income Supplement Program

Abbreviations Used in Text

LIP
Local Initiatives Program
NAPO
National Anti-Poverty Organization
NCSS
National Center for Social Statistics
NCW
National Council of Welfare
NDP
New Democratic Party
NWRO
National Welfare Rights Organization
OAA
Old Age Assistance
OAS
Old Age Security pensions
OASDI
Old Age, Survivors, and Disability Insurance
OEO
Office of Economic Opportunity
OFY
Opportunities for Youth
OMB
Office of Management and Budget
PBJI
Program for Better Jobs and Income
SAP
Saskatchewan Assistance Plan
SRS
Social and Rehabilitation Service
SSA
Social Security Administration
SSI
Supplemental Security Income
WIC
Supplementary Feeding Program for Women, Infants, and Children
WIN
Work Incentive Program

Index

Aaron, Henry, 109
ADC. See AFDC
Adult Occupational Training, 41
AFDC, 12, 29, 53, 56, 105, 107. See also AFDC-U
  ADC, early rationale for AFDC-U extension of, 30
  growth in benefits and participation in, 202
  growth of program for, 2
  increase in participation rate of eligible mother-headed families, 6
  incremental improvements within, 30
  major recipient group administered at state level, 176
  name change from ADC to, 31
  proportion of population receiving benefits under, 49
  redistributive feature of, 30
  U.S. trend toward standard intrastate benefits under, 39
  unmarried mothers on, 56
  and work disincentives, 31
  and work incentives, 54–55, 71
AFDC-U, 30, 31, 75, 80, 105, 107. See also AFDC
  Unemployed Father program, 72
  and work incentive legislation, 71–72
AFL-CIO, 98
Aged, aid to, 46–47, 139, 176
Aggregate studies of government spending, 12–14, 199
Agnew, Spiro T., 81
Agricultural Adjustment Act (1933), 32
Agriculture Department, purchase requirement for food stamps of, 72
Aid to Families with Dependent Children. See AFDC
Aid to the Blind, 54, 188
Aid to the Permanently and Totally Disabled, 27, 30
American Enterprise Institute, 51, 166
Anderson, Clinton, 81
Anderson, Martin, 80, 150
Appalachian aid, 32
Area redevelopment, 41
Association of Ontario Mayors and Reeves, 64

Background Paper on Income Support and Supplementation, 118, 151, 159, 161
Baetz, Reuben, 59, 124–125
Baker, Howard, 105, 106, 147
Baker-Bellmon bill, 109
  compared to Ullman bill, 105–106
Baker-Bellmon-Ribicoff bill. See Baker-Bellmon bill
Bateman Worth, 75
Beame, Abraham, 101–102
Bellmon, Henry, 105, 106, 147
Bennett, R.B., 35
Bennett, William, Jr., 126
Bilingualism policy in Canada, 167
Bloch, Marc, xiii
Block funding, 129
Block grant approach, 109, 110
  opponents of, 130
  provincial concern over, 129–130
Blueprint for National Welfare Reform, 93
Bourassa, Robert, 62, 63, 131
Breakeven point. See Negative income tax
British Columbia, 117, 119, 126
  support of Social Security Review proposals by, 128
British North America Act, 19, 36
Brookings Institution, 51
Budgetary control, 225
Bureau of Indian Affairs, 26
Bureau of Labor Statistics, cost of living estimates of, 44–45
Bureaucracy, 150–151
Burns, Arthur, 73, 74, 75, 80
Byrnes, John, 79

Califano, Joseph, 97, 98, 101, 102, 106, 177, 210
California Welfare Reform Act (1971), 92
Canada
  absence of adequate nationwide data and research in, 153
  adoption of federal program to share costs of mean-tested assistance, 36
  attitudes toward cost-sharing programs in, 19–20

Canada (cont.)
  deductive pattern of politics in, xiv-xv, xvii (see also Deductive and inductive policymaking)
  differences in politics of U.S. and, 15–22
  dominating question in politics of, 58
  effects of centralization of national government, 18
  erosion of federal powers in, 153
  federalism and guaranteed income, 58–70
  federalism in, 17
  impact of U.S. on, 15
  political boundaries and cultural division in provinces of, 19
  poverty levels in, 42–44
  scarcity of data in, 157
  war on poverty in, 41
Canada Assistance Plan (CAP), 37–38, 52, 53, 59, 61, 118, 119, 123, 155, 225
  AFDC growth compared with growth of, 2–3
  cost-sharing process in Ottawa and Quebec, 39
  elites' view of, 58
  and federal provincial politics, 41
  negative income tax rates under, 55
  proportion of population receiving benefits under, 49
  provincial administration of, 38
  Work Activity Projects of, 218
  work requirements under, 215
Canada Pension Plan/Quebec Pension Plan, 40, 62, 113, 115, 177
Canadian Association of Social Workers, 59
Canadian Conference on Social Welfare (1974), 122, 160
Canadian Council for Social Development, 51, 59, 124, 159, 160, 170, 225–226
  poverty line proposed by, 45
Canadian Guaranteed Income Supplements, 177
Caouette, Réal, 65, 146
CAP. See Canada Assistance Plan
Carleson, Robert B., 92, 207

Carter, Jimmy, 94, 141, 146, 147, 150, 151
  administration adoption of massive jobs program, 194
  administration disagreements over cost estimates of welfare reform program, 104–105
  administration proposal for more modest welfare reform package, 111–112
  benefits to states and localities of welfare reform proposals, 96
  commitment to massive jobs program, 99, 101
  cost estimates for welfare reform package, 104
  criticism of welfare mess by, 215
  Program for Better Jobs and Income of, 57–58, 78, 94–95
  relaxation of welfare spending freeze of, 102
  welfare spending freeze of, 98, 99, 101
  zero-cost planning technique of, 98–99
"Case for the Negative Income Tax," 92
Cash assistance plan, 97, 98, 101
Castonguay, Claude, 63
Castonguay-Nepveu report, 77, 125, 142, 143, 153, 187, 193, 197
  compared to Orange Book, 67–69, 117
  proposals of, 62–63
Center on Social Welfare Policy and Law, 108
CES, 27, 29
CETA, 104, 105, 111
Child support enforcement
  in Canada, 212–214
  in U.S., 210–212
Children's Bureau, 24
Chrétien, Jean, 132
Civil rights movement, 31–32
Clark, Joseph, 72, 134
Collapse of welfare reform
  definitions of, 198–199
  explanations of, 172–173
  implications of, 199–205

Comparative analysis method, xiii, 14–15
  cautionary notes on use of, xvii
  classic problem of, 10
Committee on Economic Security, 27, 29
Commodity distribution program, 33
Common Cause, 81
Community Action Programs, 32, 41
Community Work and Training, 218
Company of Young Canadians, 41
Comparison of Canada and U.S.
  aid to disabled, 176–177
  attitudes toward idea of guaranteed income, 163
  background of poverty policy, 23–26
  bureaucratic differences, 150–158
  caseloads, 4–5, 137
  common concerns, 1–10
  cost of living, 4
  data availability, 152
  effect of public debate on policymaking, 198
  family incomes, 11
  federalism, 144–145
  gross national product, 4–5
  holding socioeconomic variables constant, 10–15
  increase in total welfare spending, 3–5
  intergovernmental differences, 141–145
  legislative process, 145–149
  nongovernmental participation, 158–162
  party politics, 145–149
  policy development, 199–205
  policymaking, 136, 165–166
  political culture, 15–22
  political factors, 136–137, 219, 227
  regional distribution of welfare problems, 141–142
  relationship between planners and administrators, 151–158
  size of political systems, 137–138
  socioeconomic factors, 138–141
  tax credit, 131–132
Comprehensive Employment and Training Act. *See* CETA
Comprehensive reform, effects of incrementalism on, 204–205
Congressional Budget Office, 104, 166
Constitutional Review of 1967–1972 (Canada), 61, 63, 66
Consulting Group on Welfare Reform, 97, 98
Continuing Committee on Social Security, 113, 120
Corman, James C., 104, 148
Corman bill, 105, 106
Cost of living
  adjustments for, 115, 206, 207
  Bureau of Labor Statistics estimates of, 44–45
  Manitoba tax credit for, 131
Cost-sharing approach, 129
  for means-tested services, 126
Council of Economic Advisors, 74, 100
  1964 *Economic Report of the President*, 42
Cranston, Alan, 109
Créditistes, 146
Croll, David A., 59
Crude oil equalization tax, 104
Curtailment of welfare programs, political factors in, 219–227

Deductive and inductive policymaking, xv, 69–70, 220
  comparison of, 136, 168–171
  deductive, 167–171, 224
  deficiencies of, 169
  inductive, 165–167, 222
  relation to political context, 136–137
Demogrant program, 36, 40, 53, 60, 87
  Canadian health insurance as, 37
  critique of, 59
  and Social Security Review, 116
Denton, Winfield K., "runaway pappy" law crusade of, 30
Department of Health, Education and Welfare, 83, 155–156
  debate with Department of Labor over welfare reform proposals, 97, 98, 100
  preference for integration of administration of two-tier plan, 189–190

Department of Health, Education and Welfare (cont.)
  reorganization of three hundred programs, 91
  unitary program of, 195–196
Department of Indian and Northern Affairs, 26
Department of Labor, 156
  Children's Bureau of, 24
  debates with Department of Health, Education and Welfare over welfare reform proposals, 97, 98, 100
  and job components in President Carter's welfare reform program, 97
  standard budgets of, 44–45
  two-tier proposal of, 195–196
Department of Manpower and Immigration, 120
Department of National Health and Welfare, 24, 69
Diefenbaker, John, 37
Division of Child Welfare (Canada), 24
Divorce rate, 5
Dole, Robert, 97
Dukakis, Michael S., 107, 207
Duplessis, Maurice, 37
Dwight, J.S., Jr., 92

Earned income tax credit, 94–95, 104–105, 112, 132–133, 198. *See also* Tax credits
  in New Coalition bill, 107
  as part of Revenue Act of 1978, 111
Earnings Clearance System (California), 208–209
Economic Council of Canada, *Fifth Annual Review* of, 58–59
Economic Opportunity Act (1964), 32
Ehrlichman, John, 76, 91
  attacks on welfare reform package by, 87–88
Eizenstadt, Stuart, 102, 107
Elites
  in Canada, 16, 22, 163, 164, 224, 227
  in U.S., 164
Employment strategy, 119–121
English Poor Law, 23
Errors in distributing benefits, 208

Established Programs (Interim Arrangements) Act, 27
European countries
  comparison of Canadian and U.S. socioeconomic factors with, 10–11
  national policies for care of poor in, 23

Fair Labor Standards Act, 25
Family Allowance programs, 5, 12, 36, 48, 53, 113–116, 118, 122, 139
  cuts in, 132
Family and Youth Allowances, 60
Family Assistance Plan, 57, 151, 153. *See also* HR 1
  abandonment by intergovernmental groups of, 88–89
  as answer to general revenue sharing, 79
  coalition of nongovernmental groups favorable to, 84
  compared with Canada's Family Income Security Plan, 60–61
  effect of unitary negative income tax proposals on, 183
  influence on Quebec report of debate on, 68–69
  Nixon and, 70–77, 88–89, 136–137
  notches in, 79–80
  opposition to, 147
  two-tier features of, 183–184
  work requirements debates, 181–182
Family Assistance Planning Group, 90
Family Health Insurance Plan, 80
Family Income Plan (Saskatchewan), 119, 190
Family Income Security Plan, 60–61
Federal Emergency Relief Administration, 26–27
Federal grants
  cost-sharing in Canada and U.S., 36
  matching of funds by federal government, 38–39
  Quebec's desire for formal detachment from, 37
Federal-Provincial Conference of Ministers of Welfare, 113, 115, 127, 161

Index

Federal-provincial issues, 65, 116–117, 121, 122, 123, 143, 144, 153, 199
  Canada Assistance Plan and politics, 41
  cost-sharing and jurisdiction concessions of federal group, 127
  disagreements over federal cost-sharing, 123–124
  exchange of personnel, 158
  results of policymaking, 113–114
  two-tier program, 68, 70, 190–191
  work requirements, 187
Federal-provincial relations, 65
  as dominating question in Canadian politics, 58
  Federal Income Security Plan and crisis in, 61
  worsening of, 125
Federal spending in U.S., 203
Federalism
  in Canada, 16–17, 19–22, 141–145
  comparison of Canada and U.S., 16–22, 191
  effect of degree of diversity on shaping issues in, 21–22
  in U.S., 17, 19–22
Female-headed families, 5
FERA, 26–27
Finch, Robert, 73, 74, 79–80
Fiscal relief for states and localities, 96, 102, 106, 109, 111
FISP. *See* Family Income Security Plan
Foley, Thomas, 103
Food Stamp program, 32, 56, 72, 96–97, 182
  Carter welfare reform package and abolition of, 96
  cost of, 202
  Department of Agriculture requirements for, 82
  extension of, 33
  Food stamps, 12–13, 45, 48, 53, 55, 112
  growth in, 5, 197, 202
  impact on poverty of, 32–33
  lowering of requirements for purchase of, 72
  and shift from serving agriculture to social goals, 33
  work requirement for 82, 186–188, 214
Ford, Gerald R., 90, 93, 94, 146, 151
Forget, Claude, 124
Fraud, 208–210
Friedman, Milton, 92

Galbraith, John Kenneth, 49, 140
Gini index of poverty, 45
Gore, Albert, 81
Government spending, local, federal, and state/provincial proportion of, 20–21
Gradualism, 136
Great Depression
  in Canada, 34–35
  in U.S., 26–27
Green Books, 35
Griffiths, Martha, 93
Guaranteed income, 122, 178–184
  ambiguity of term, 53, 185
  Canadian federalism and, 58–70
  Comparison of Canada and U.S. on proposals for, 76–77
  Interprovincial Conference of Ministers of Welfare endorsement of, 118
  practical and philosophical arguments for, 52
  preludes to, 41
  public attitude toward, xiv, 52, 53, 163
  two-tier approach to, 68
Guaranteed Income Supplement program, 40, 54, 59, 60, 116, 122, 132, 139, 164
  for aged poor, 124

Haldeman, H.R., 86
  attacks on welfare reform package by, 87
Hardin, Clifford, 73
Harris, Fred, 81
Hartling, Marjorie, 51
Haveman, Robert, 194
Health and Welfare Canada, 46, 70, 121, 129, 130, 153
Health care distribution, 45–46

Health policy in Canada, 36–37
Heclo, Hugh, 157
Hellyer, Paul, 64, 148
Hodgson, James, 87
Hoover Institution, 166
House Agricultural Committee, 33, 103
House Education and Labor Committee, 107
House Ways and Means Committee of WIN program, 71–72, 78, 79, 83
House Welfare Reform Subcommittee, 105
 criticisms of Carter's welfare reform package by, 103
Housing assistance, 45, 55
 experiments with, 57
HR 1, 82–90, 182, 211
 aftermath of defeat of, 90
 as alternative to general revenue sharing, 84
 changes in Family Assistance Plan proposal made by, 83–84
 cost of, 84
 effect of Talmadge amendment on, 86
 provisions of, 82–84
 reasons for National Welfare Rights Organization opposition to, 83
HR 7200, 110, 111
Humphrey, Hubert H., 87

Illegitimacy rates, 5
Income maintenance
 in Canada, 33–34, 41
 criticism of experiments in, 57
 expenditures on, 11–12
 framework for debate on, 29
 in U.S., 33–34
 results of U.S. experiments in, 57
Income Supplement Program, 157, 201
 as pure negative income tax, 93
 work registration requirement of, 93
Incremental reform, xvi, 105, 136, 199–205
 contrast of Canada and U.S. on, 198, 199–205
 two methods of, 202
Indians, social programs for, 26

Inductive policymaking. See Deductive and inductive policymaking
In-kind benefits, 23, 45, 202
 comparison of Canada and U.S., 55
 and work incentives, 55
Institute for Research on Poverty, 51, 166
Intact families, current welfare system as unfair to, 56
Interest groups, 170
 in Canada, 159
 in U.S., 158
Intergovernmental lobby, 84, 107
 demand for fiscal relief by, 17, 22, 79, 101, 109–110
Interprovincial Conference of Ministers of Welfare, 118, 125
 endorsement of community employment strategy by, 121
 and social services legislation, 126

Jarvis, Howard, 221
Jenner amendment, 30–31, 209
Job Corps, 32
Joe, Tom, 98, 99
Johnson, A.W. (A1), 66, 69, 70, 113, 125–126, 155, 156, 168
Johnson, Lyndon B., 151
 negative income tax and administration of, 74
 passage of 1964 Food Stamp Act under, 32–33
Joint Economic Committee, 93, 166
Judicial Committee of the Privy Council, 35

Kennedy, Edward M., 110
Kennedy, John F., 32
Kennedy, Robert F., 72
Kerr-Mills bill, 27
King, Edward J., 207
King, Martin Luther, 72
King, W.L. MacKenzie, 34, 35

Labour (Standards) Code, Canada, 25
Lalonde, Marc, 66, 68, 113, 122, 139, 144, 159, 160, 170, 184
 major proposals of, 1
 and Social Security Review, 115, 116

Lampman, Robert, 74, 194
Lesage, Jean, 37, 61
Lévesque, René, 61, 131
Lewis, David, 65
Liberal government white paper, *Income Security for Canadians*, 60
Liberal Party of Canada, 121–122, 145
  endorsement of guaranteed income and supplementation by, 122
  loss of 1979 election, 134
Local Incentives Program, 41, 121
Long, Russell, 72, 80, 86, 88, 94, 102, 109, 147, 148, 186
Lorenz curves, 45
Low-Income Supplementation of Earnings program (Ontario), 119
Lyday, James, 74, 75
Lyon, Sterling, 221

Manitoba, 117, 129
  property tax credit programs in, 131
Manitoba Basic Income Experiment, 57, 68
Manpower programs, 121
Marginal tax rate, 54
Marshall, Ray, 99, 101
McCarthy, Eugene, 81
McGovern, George, 72, 97, 146
  food stamp bill of, 73
  welfare proposal similarity to demogrant proposal, 87
Means and needs-tested assistance, 5, 11–12
Medicaid, 32, 80
  cost of, 202
  growth of, 5, 202
  in U.S., 45–46, 55
Medicare, 37, 41, 131
Mega-Proposal, 91, 95, 151, 157, 201
Mills, Wilbur, 79, 82, 84, 102–103, 148
Minimum wage
  adoption of laws governing, 24–25
  in Canada, 43–44
  in U.S., 43–44
Ministry Inspectors Program, 209
Mississippi, work incentives in, 55
Model Cities, 32
Morin, Claude, 63

Most similar systems design in comparison of Canada and U.S. policy, 14
Mother-headed families, 46–48, 174
  and Canada Assistance Plan, 37, 38
  comparison of Canada and U.S. on aid to, 176–178
  public opinion on spending for, 7
Mother's aid movement, 24
Mother's allowances (Canada), 24
Moynihan, Daniel, 69, 75, 86, 107, 108–109, 147, 149, 181, 182, 183
  effect of consideration of New York's needs on welfare stance of, 110–111
Moynihan-Cranston-Long bill, 109, 143
  opposition to, 110
Munro, John, 1, 60

Nathan, Richard P., 74, 75, 194
National Anti-Poverty Organization, 51, 59, 140, 159, 166
  advocacy of guaranteed income proposals by, 126–127
  revolt against Orange Book proposals by, 122
National Association of Counties, 79, 84, 110
National Council of State Public Welfare Administrators, 79
National Council of Welfare, 51, 59, 127, 159
National Governors Conference, 79
  endorsement of Carter welfare reform package by, 102
National health insurance, 35, 125
National Welfare Fraud Association, 208, 220
National Welfare Rights Organization, 51, 79, 80, 84, 140, 158, 159, 166, 181
NDP. *See* New Democratic Party
Negative income tax, xvii
  breakeven point, 133, 178–179
  in Canadian provinces, 55
  costs of program, 180–182
  defeat of HR 1 and proposals for, 90
  definition of, 54
  definition of reduction rates, 178

Negative income tax (cont.)
  family dissolution incentives in designs of, 188–189
  first use of, 54
  Milton Friedman and, 74
  Johnson administration compared to Nixon administration on, 74–75
  political liabilities of unitary approach to, 193–194
  reduction rates, 114, 178
  relationship of guarantee level, breakeven point, and reduction rate, 178–179
  unitary design of, 178, 182
  in U.S., 70–76
  work effort decline possibility with, 56–57
Negative income tax, two-tier design, 114, 117
  Canadian preference for separation of administration of, 190–191
  Canadian proposals for, 185–189
  Family Assistance Plan and, 183–184
  objection to, 185–186
  political appeal of, 184–189, 193–194
  problems raised by, 188
  Saskatchewan experience with, 190–191
  U.S. preference for administrative integration of, 189–190
New Brunswick, 128
New Coalition, 107, 108
New Coalition bill, 107, 110
New Deal era, job-creation programs of, 28
New Democratic Party, 16, 18, 64, 68, 117, 134, 145, 146
New Democratic Party provinces, 123, 124, 166
  proposals of, 117–118
Newfoundland, 128
New Jersey Graduated Work Incentive Experiment, 74
Nixon, Richard, 141, 151
  and Family Assistance Plan, 1, 53, 70–71, 78, 136–137, 145
  and Food Stamp program, 73, 82, 145
  pressures for welfare reform exerted on, 73–74
  proposal for guaranteed income, 52
  support for nationwide AFDC guarantees, 75
  welfare reform package of, xiv-xv, 41
Nongovernmental participation, 158–162
  constraint of bilingual federal releases in Canada, 158–159
Nonwelfare poor, See Working poor
Nordhaus, William, 100
Notches
  definition of, 55
  in Family Assistance Plan, 79–80
  worst cause in U.S. of, 55–56
Nova Scotia, 119
  concern over costs of Social Security Review proposals, 128
  work incentives in, 55

October Crisis, 62
OEO. See Office of Economic Opportunity
Office of Economic Opportunity, 32, 74, 151, 157
Office of Income Security Policy, 90, 150, 151, 156, 159
Office of Inspector General, 210
Office of Research, Plans, Programs, and Evaluation, 90
Offsets, 104
Old age assistance, adoption of, 34–35
Old Age Insurance system, 12
Old Age Security demogrants, 40
Old Age Security pension (Canada), 5, 12, 35, 53, 60, 115, 116, 139
  public opinion on spending for, 7
Old Age, Survivors, and Dependents Insurance system, 29
O'Neill, Thomas J., 108
Ontario, 123, 129, 131
  Low-Income Supplementation of Earnings program, 119
  reaction to expansion of social assistance rolls in, 117
  rejection of Social Security Review proposals by, 128
  work incentives in, 55

Ontario Task Force on Employment
 Opportunities for Welfare Recipients, 215
Opportunities for Families, 83
Opportunities for Youth, 41, 121
Orange Book, 70, 152, 153, 160, 193, 197
 avoidance of unitary design in, 184–185
 changes proposed in, 66–67
 compared to Castonguay-Nepveu report, 117
 employment strategy proposal in, 119–121
 federal-provincial meetings on proposals of, 113–114
 proposals for social services in, 125
 revolt of National Anti-Poverty Organization against proposals of, 122
 similarities between Castonguay-Nepveu report and, 67–68
 two-tier design in proposals in, 114, 184–185
 use of U.S. welfare reform debates, 157
Orange Paper, 127
Osborne, John E., 69, 113, 125–126, 155, 159
Ottawa, 131
 division of power between Quebec City and, 58

Packer, Arnold, 97, 196
Panel Study of Income Dynamics, 190
Parti Québécois, 61, 131, 175
Party politics, 145–149
Policy analysts, 151, 152
Policy and Program Development and Coordination Branch (Welfare), 155, 156–157
 Opinion Analysis unit of, 159
Policy design
 conflict between planners and administrators, 154–157
 drawbacks of data, 164
 importance of, 173
 importance of data in, 152, 222
 need for political judgment in, 193
 need for practical experience in, 153–154
 role in analysts in, 76, 107, 150
 zero-cost planning in, 98–99, 101, 102
Policy development, 135. See also Deductive and inductive policymaking
 continuous versus episodic change, 199–205
Policy Research and Long-Range Planning Branch (Welfare), 69, 70, 152, 155, 159
 reorganized and renamed Policy Research and Strategic Planning Branch, 248
Policymaking
 comparison of Canada and U.S. on, 12–14, 165–167
 difference in scale and, 15
 poor left out of, xiv
Political culture
 differences between Canada and U.S., xiii, 15–16, 162–165
 effect on policy of, 16
 indirect effect on political outcomes of, 164
 overemphasis on differences between Canada and U.S., 162–165
Political economy, 10–12, 138
Political structure, effect on popular values of, 164–165
 importance to policy debates, 16–22, 165–171, 205–206, 219–227
Politics, differences in Canada and U.S., 15–22
Politics of a Guaranteed Income, 69
Poor Law Act (United Kingdom), 24
Poor People's Campaign, 72, 140
Poverty. See also Poverty line
 advocacy for the poor, 51
 attitudes toward the poor, xiv, 8, 50, 176
 characteristics of the poor, 46–47, 49
 comparison of Canada and U.S. on levels of, 42–44
 definitions of, 42–46
 federal role in programs for the poor, 26–33, 33–41
 hunger as political issue in U.S., 72

Poverty (cont.)
  market basket approach to, 42
  nonwelfare poor, 56
  persistently poor, 48–50
  political powerlessness of the poor, 49–51, 140, 166, 174
  problems of organizing the poor, 50–51
  proposals for measurement of, 42, 43, 46
  public opinion on welfare spending, 6–10
  transitory poor, 48–50
  unevenness of policy toward the poor, 46–49
  working poor, arguments for extension of some welfare benefits to, 56
Poverty line
  Canadian benefits as percentage of, 43
  Canadian Council on Social Development proposal for definition of, 45
  criticisms of definitions of, 45
  European measures of, 45
  public definition of, 43
  U.S. benefits as percentage of, 43
Poverty policy, xiii–xiv
  background in Canada, 33–41
  background in U.S., 23–33
  explanation of differences in, 12–15
Prince Edward Island, 128, 129
Program for Better Jobs and Income, 57–58, 78, 111, 151, 185, 187, 201
  consideration by Congress of, 102
  controversy over costs, 104–112
  decision of Carter administration to propose the, 97–102
  design of, 94, 194–196
  proposed cutbacks in, 101
  requirements of, 94–95
  two-tier design of, 95–96
  work requirements in, 215
Progressive Conservatives, 59, 64, 65, 68
  in Alberta, 126
Progressive era, U.S. social policy in, 24

Proposition 13, 108–109, 165, 174, 206, 223, 226
Public assistance as U.S. term for aid to the poor, xvii
Public housing, 41
Public opinion, 6–10, 163, 165, 223, 226
Public policy, incremental changes in, 29
Public service jobs, 95, 99, 111, 194
  issues raised by, 103
Public Welfare Amendments of 1962, 31

Quebec, 124, 129, 131
  ambivalence toward two-tiered approach, 117
  division of power between Ottawa and, 58
  influence on federal government of guaranteed income plan of, 68
  opposition to shared-cost programs by, 62
  public institutional care in, 130
  Schooling Allowances in, 61
  and Social Security Review, 116, 128
  varying of Family Income Security Plan benefits by, 115
Quebec Commission of Inquiry on Health and Social Welfare, 62
Quebec Pension Plan, 40, 177
Quebec Working Paper on the Constitution, 62

Race, 49, 174–176
Ralliement des Créditistes, 18, 65
Rawson, Bruce, 113, 126–127
Reagan, Ronald, 92, 93, 143, 206
Reduction rates. *See* Negative income tax
Refundable Child Tax Credit, 114, 117, 139, 153, 157, 169, 204–205
  compared with U.S. earned income credit, 132–133
  popularity of, 133
Republican Papers, 92
Research, Planning, and Evaluation Branch (Welfare), 69
Retirement insurance, 27

Revenue sharing
  backdoor, 90
  comparison of Canada and U.S. on, 20–21
Revenue sharing, general
  HR 1 as alternative to, 84
  intergovernmental lobby shift to support of, 88
Ribicoff, Abraham, 81, 85, 87, 105, 110, 181
  proposed welfare bill of, 87
Ribicoff-Richardson compromise, 89
Richardson, Elliot, 80, 81, 86, 90–91
Robinson, T. Russell, 69, 113, 137, 156
Rockefeller, Nelson A., 85, 93
Roosevelt, Franklin D., 29
  establishment of Committee on Economic Security by, 27
Ryan, William Fitts, 74

Saskatchewan, 117, 131
  and Social Security Review proposals, 128
  experience with negative income tax, 190–191
  Family Income Plan, 119
  New Democratic Party government in, 126
  two-tier program adopted in, 70
  work incentives in, 55
Saskatchewan Assistance Plan, 190
Saskatchewan New Democratic Party, 66
Schulz, George, 75, 92
Schumpeter, Joseph, 48
Section 8 Housing Assistance program, 202–203
Select Committee on Nutrition and Human Needs, 72
Senate Finance Committee, 72, 79, 80, 82, 89, 110
  guaranteed jobs bill of, 87
Senate Special Committee on Poverty (Canada), 59, 149
  proposed definition of poverty, 41
Shared-cost programs, 129
Shriver, Sargent, 74
Simeon, Richard, 143
Social and Rehabilitation Service, 177

Social assistance as Canadian term for aid to poor, xvii
Social Credit party, 126
Social insurance program
  consumption of GNP by, 5
  and Social Security Review, 116
Social Security Act of 1935, 26–30
  amendments to (1977), 111, 219
  effects of, 26–30, 200
  Title IV of, 28–29, 90
  Title XVI of, 90
Social Security Administration, 177
  market basket approach to poverty of, 42
Social Security Review (1973–77), 70, 113, 138–139, 151
  absence of outside pressure on, 160
  barriers to public understanding of, 160–162
  and demogrant program, 116
  effect of deductive approach on, 169–170
  failure of, 144
  federal proposed earnings ceilings under, 119
  outcome of, 114
  pensions in, 115
  work requirement terminology in, 187
Social services, Orange Book proposals for, 125
Social Services Amendments (1974), 94
Socioeconomic variables, 10–11, 138–141
Special Committee on Aging (Canada), 59, 149
Stanfield, Robert, 59, 65
State and Local Welfare Reform and Fiscal Relief Act of 1978, 109
State supplementation, 100–101, 104, 196–197
Statistics Canada, 132
  guideline for definition of poverty of, 42–43
  low-income cutoff of, 45
Subcommittee on Fiscal Policy, 93, 157, 201
Sullivan, Leonor, 33

Supplemental Security Income, 54, 89, 112, 145, 164, 176, 177
Supplementary Feeding Program for Women, Infants, and Children, 203
Supplementation, 122, 123, 124, 127, 184. See also Negative income tax
  impasse over, 130–131
  take-up as special problem in administration of, 192–193
  two-tier design, administration of, 153, 154
Support, 123. See also Negative income tax, two-tier design
  administration of, 153, 154
  impasse over, 130–131
Supreme Court reversal of decisions blocking social legislation, 35

Take-up, 192–193
Talmadge, Herman, 80, 85
Talmadge amendment, 201, 214
  effect on HR 1 of, 86
  work incentive amendment of, 85
Task Force on the Administrative Feasibility of an Income Maintenance System, 92
Tax Credit and Allowances Act, 93
Tax credits, 123
  in Canada, 131–133, 204–205
  comparison of Canada and U.S. on, 131–132
  in U.S., 94, 111–112
  proposals for approach to, 131–132
Tobin, James, 74
Transitional Task Force on Public Welfare, 74
Treasury Department as administrator of negative income tax, 92
Trudeau, Pierre, 59, 64, 65, 132, 144
  imposition of wage and price controls by, 122
  1973 proposal for reorganization of welfare system by, 1
  opposition to special status for Quebec by, 62
  and Social Security Review, 115
Truman administration, 30
Turner, John, 122, 125

Two-tier design, 67, 122, 123, 127. See also Negative income tax
  benefit structure of, 153
  guaranteed income plan and, 68
  of Programs for Better Jobs and Income, 95–96
  proposals for administration of, 70

Ullman, Al, 105, 107, 108, 147, 148, 158
  opposition to Carter's Program for Better Jobs and Income proposal by, 102–103
  welfare reform bill of, 105, 109
Unemployment Assistance (Canada), 38
  AFDC growth compared with growth of, 2
Unemployment insurance (Canada), 220
  public suspicion of fraud in, 9–10
  tightening in regulations of, 132
Unemployment Insurance Act (Canada)
  cuts in, 132
  as political issue, 61
Unemployment Insurance Commission, 116
Union of Manitoba Municipalities, 64
Unitary design. See Negative income tax
United States Conference of Mayors, 102
United States politics
  difference between Canadian and, 15–22
  effects of division and dispersion of power within federal government, 17–18
  inductive pattern of, xv, xvi-xvii
Universal family allowance, 36, 44
Unmarried mothers, increase on welfare rolls of, 5, 6
Urban Institute, 51, 107, 158, 166

Vander Zalm, William, 175, 209, 215
Van Loon, Richard, 67
Vendor payments, 30
Veneman, John, 75

Index

Veterans' benefits, 48
  comparison of Canada and U.S. on, 25–26
  means-tested allowances for, 25
  veterans' lobby and, 25
Veterans' programs, consumption of GNP by, 5
VISTA, 32
Voting Rights Act (1965), 32

Walker, Gordon, 218
War on Poverty, 41, 58
Watergate, 92
Weinberger, Caspar, 91–92
Welfare
  aid for the aged, xiii-xiv
  aid to mother-headed families, xiii-xiv
  attitudes affecting poor in taking advantage of, 13–14
  difficulty in comparison of programs, 3
  educational level of recipients, 57
  extension of, 56, 70–71, 163–164
  payments range of, 12
  philosophical and practical grounds for broadening, 52
  as political issue in U.S., 71
  public opinion on spending for, 6–10
  public suspicion of recipients of, 8, 9
  rising costs of, 3–4
Welfare backlash, xv, 6–10, 64, 140, 199, 205–206, 219–227
  in California, 206
  in Canada, 10, 64, 65, 126, 175, 207, 220–221
  comparison of effects of, in Canada and U.S., 219–220
  decentralization and effects of, 221
  differences responsible for greater degree in U.S. of, 15–16
  effect of provincial focus of social assistance on, 221–222
  in Massachusetts, 207
  political variables in, 10
  racial issues in, 174–176
  in U.S., 174–175
Welfare mess
  central features of, 54
  as political issue in U.S., 53

Welfare policy
  differences in configuration in Canada and U.S., 176–177
  reasons for Canadian paucity of independent experts on, 158–159
  U.S. "big bang" versus Canadian "steady state" in development of, 23
Welfare programs
  comparison of growth of Canadian and U.S., 2–3
  differences in Canadian and U.S. curtailment of, 206, 222–225
Welfare reform
  attacks by Ehrlichman and Haldeman on, 87
  Canadian deductive reasoning on, 167–171
  Canadian public participation in debate on, 160
  circumstances reducing urgency of, 85
  common Canadian and U.S. problems in, 2–6
  comparison of Canadian and U.S. attitudes toward, 52–53
  conservative version of, 207
  cost estimates on Carter's package for, 104
  delivery of benefits, 189–193
  difference in treatment of employable and unemployable groups, 195–196, 197
  difficulty in targeting, 192
  drawbacks to implicit achievement of goals of, 203
  expansion of programs in U.S., 202–203
  factors contributing to collapse of, 173–175
  fiscal relief for states and counties, 78–79
  growth of income transfer programs, 202–203
  issues for designers of, 196–197
Welfare Reform Act (California), 206
Welfare Reform Interagency Task Force, 92
Welfare Rights Organization, 140–141
Welfare rolls, xv, 5–6, 30–31

Wiley, George, 51, 84
Williams, John J., 79, 147, 156
WIN. *See* Work Incentive program
Work disincentives, 31
Work Incentive program, 71, 85, 105
  amendments to, 214
  provisions for automatic exemptions under, 85
  strict guideline for workfare under, 218
Work incentives, 54, 100, 103, 188
  in Canada, 40
  inequity caused by improvement of, 55
  and in-kind benefits, 55
  proposals for, in Orange Book, 67
  in U.S., 41, 71–72
Work relief
  in Canada, 217–218
  differences in Canadian and U.S. federal restrictions on workfare, 217–218
  federal restraints on state workfare projects, 218
  in U.S. 216–219
Work requirements, 8, 78, 85
  in Canada, 9, 64, 117, 186, 215–216
  difficulty in designing, 57
  Family Assistance Plan and, 53
  limitations on job supply and training slots, 57
  public attitude toward, 8
  in U.S., 8, 9, 181–182, 186–187, 214–215
Workfare, 182
Working Paper on Social Security in Canada. See Orange Book
Working Party on Employment Strategy, 120–121
Working Party on Income Maintenance, 113, 116
  examination of six major proposals of, 118
Working Party on Social Services, 113, 125
Working poor, 48
Works Progress Administration, 27
WPA, 27

Zero-cost planning technique, 98–99, 102

LIBRARY OF DAVIDSON COLLEGE

Books on regular loan
 presented at the